MICROECONOMICS

Arjun Y. Pangannavar

ATLANTIC
PUBLISHERS & DISTRIBUTORS (P) LTD

Published by

ATLANTIC

PUBLISHERS & DISTRIBUTORS (P) LTD

7/22, Ansari Road, Darya Ganj,
New Delhi-110002
Phones : +91-11-40775252, 23273880, 23275880, 23280451
Fax : +91-11-23285873
Web : www.atlanticbooks.com
E-mail : orders@atlanticbooks.com

Branch Office
5, Nallathambi Street, Wallajah Road,
Chennai-600002
Phones : +91-44-64611085, 32413319
E-mail : chennai@atlanticbooks.com

Printed in India at Glorious Printers, A-13, D.S.I.D.C., Jhilmil Industrial Area, Delhi-11009

Dedicated to

My elder brother
Late Shri Sattyappa Y. Pangannavar
and
His wife Late Smt Gangavva

Preface

It gives me immense pleasure to bring out this book on microeconomics to fufil the needs of students of economics pursuing graduation under semester system. It is designed as per the syllabi of Karnatak University, Dharwad and Rani Chennamma University, Belgaum prescribed for BA First and Second Semester courses. It is hoped that the book will also be helpful to the students of economics in other universities. It is also useful to those who are preparing for competitive examinations.

The book consists of ten chapters. First chapter covers the meaning, definitions, subject matter and scope of economics and approaches to economics like microeconomics and macroeconomics and static and dynamic economics. Second chapter covers utility analysis in detail, including the laws of consumption. Third chapter deals with consumer behaviour, demand analysis and elasticity of demand. Fourth chapter throws light on the concept of supply, law of supply and elasticity of supply. Fifth chapter explains in detail, the indifference curve analysis. Sixth chapter covers the production, cost and revenue analysis. Seventh chapter describes perfect competition, monopoly and price discrimination. Eighth chapter deals with monopolistic competitive market. Ninth chapter throws light on theory of distribution, marginal productivity theory, rent, wages and their theories. Tenth chapter explains in detail, interest, profit and their respective theories. A new approach has been used to make the learning of economics easy. It is a student-friendly and teacher-friendly book.

I am grateful to able teachers and other experts on the subject who extended their helpful suggestions during the completion of this book, enriching its contents.

I am also thankful to Atlantic Publishers and Distributors (P) Ltd. for the interest evinced in publishing this book. Suggestion for further improvement of the book in its subsequent editions are welcome.

Arjun Y. Pangannavar

Contents

1

Introduction to Microeconomics

1.1 MEANING AND NATURE OF ECONOMICS

The term economics is derived from the two Greek words 'Oikos' means household and 'Nemein' means management. In other words 'Oikonemein' means household management. Household management means satisfying the family wants as much as possible by economizing or wise allocation of the limited resources or income of the family.

Economics is both a social science and a human science. It studies about human activities which are economic in nature, e.g. tilling of land, working in office, selling activities, buying activities, etc. It studies about economic welfare of the community so it is a most useful social science. Hence, A.C. Pigou says "Economics is not only light bearing but also fruit bearing science."

Economics is the study of economic problems of man in the society. An economic problem is a problem of satisfying maximum number of wants with minimum resources. The question to be answered is 'Why do economic problems arise?' Economic problems arise on account of two reasons (a) wants are unlimited and (b) resources are limited.

Thus, man has been facing the problem of choice. Since wants are unlimited and want-satisfying resources are limited, man has the problem of choice between wants and between uses of resources.

Thus, in brief, economics is a study of economic activities of man. In other words, economics is concerned with production, consumption, exchange, distribution of income, development and growth activities of man. The production activities result in money earning process and consumption activities result in money spending.

1.2 DEFINITIONS OF ECONOMICS

It is very difficult to give precise definition of economics. Regarding definitions of economics, economists are categorized into two groups as (i) definitionists and (ii) non-definitionists.

Those economists who advocated that definitions are necessary, they may be called definitionists.

Those economists who advocated that definitions are not necessary, they may be called non-definitionists.

J.M. Keynes, Jacob Viner, Richard Jones, Comte, Pareto, Myrdal, and Hutchinson constitute the group of non-definitionists. According to J.M. Keynes "Political economy is said to have strangled itself with definitions." Jacob Viner says "Economics is what economists do." Richard Jones and Comte desired to do away with definitions. Thus the above referred economists were of the opinion that it is needless to waste words in defining economics and it will be a futile exercise.

Robbins and Macfie and many others come in the group of definitionists. According to these economists definitions are essential. Robbins argued that an attempt to define economics is never a waste of time. Similarly Macfie said "lack of clear definition can prove harmful". Thus they said that discussion of definition is very essential in getting a clear understanding of the subject. Hence definitions are to be studied.

However, there is need for a precise definition of economics. There are many definitions of economics which are to be studied in order to understand the nature and scope of economics.

Since there are several definitions of economics, all of them cannot be studied independently. Therefore, for the sake of convenience and clear understanding, they are grouped into four categories on the basis of the aspect on which the emphasis is placed by the various definitions. The four categories of definitions are as follows:

1.2.1 Wealth Definition or Classical Definition: The first systematic definition of economics was given by Adam Smith who is universally regarded as the father of economics. He published a book in 1776, titled *An Enquiry into the Nature and Causes of Wealth of Nations*. This book is briefly called "Wealth of Nations". In his book, he defined economics as "Economics is science of wealth". It studies production and consumption of wealth. Thus according to Adam Smith man's main aim in life is to acquire and accumulate wealth. Man is a selfish animal. Therefore he is always guided by profit motive. Thus economics deals with how wealth is produced, distributed, exchanged and consumed for the satisfaction of human wants.

The classical economists like J.B. Say, J.S. Mill, F.A. Walker, Senior and others were the followers of Adam Smith. These economists also defined economics as a science of wealth. J.B. Say says "Economics is a science which treats wealth." J.S. Mill defined Economics as "the practical science of production and distribution of wealth". F.A. Walker stated as "Economics is that body of knowledge which relates to wealth". Prof. N.W. Senior states "The subject matter of political economics is not happiness but wealth."

Definitions given by Adam Smith, J.B. Say, J.S. Mill, F.A. Walker and Senior are called wealth definitions, because they have emphasized more upon wealth. They have paid so much attention to wealth as if wealth was everything to man. No attention was given to man for whom the wealth was produced. Since these economists belonged to classical school of thought, they are considered as classical economists so their definitions are also called Classical definitions.

Main points of wealth definition:

(i) Acquisition and accumulation of wealth is the main objective of man.

(ii) Economics is study of how wealth is produced, distributed and exchanged for consumption.

(iii) The term wealth is not used in ordinary sense, meaning money or riches.

(iv) By "wealth they meant all economic goods that would satisfy human wants".

Criticisms

The wealth definition was criticised by literary men and social reformers. Thomas Carlyle, John Ruskin, Matthew Arnold and Dickens were the critics of wealth definition. Their criticisms are as follows:

(i) **Undue Importance is given to Wealth:** The greatest drawback of wealth definition is that it has given an undue importance to wealth. It has ignored the man and his welfare. Wealth is only a means and not an end in itself. The man is primary and wealth is secondary. They failed to realize this aspect.

(ii) **It is a Dismal Science:** Since religious sentiments were very strong in those days, the philosophers criticized the very idea of accumulation of wealth. They were of the opinion that economics which concentrates only on the study of the wealth is a selfish and mundane science, science of bread and butter and it is a science of filth and not of wealth.

(iii) **Economics has Many other Motives:** Classical economists felt that acquiring of wealth is the only motive of human beings. This is not true statement because in reality human beings are guided by many other motives such as charity, philanthropy, etc.

In brief, the classical economists defined economics as a science of wealth. It teaches only how to acquire wealth and how to consume it. So it is criticized. It ignored man and his welfare. Wealth is only a means and not an end in itself. The end is human welfare.

1.2.2 Welfare Definition or Neo-Classical Definition: Wealth definition was criticized by literary men and social reformers because it had various shortcomings. The neo-classical economists like Alfred Marshall and his followers like Pigou, Cannan, Ely,

Beveridge and others filled the shortcomings of the wealth definition and re-defined economics which is called neo-classical definition.

Alfred Marshall had published a book in 1890, titled *Principles of Economics* wherein he defined economics as "Political economy or economics is a study of mankind in the ordinary business of life, it examines that part of individual and social action which is most closely connected with the attainment and with the use of material requisites of well-being." Adam Smith had emphasized only on wealth but Marshall emphasized on both mankind and wealth. Hence Marshall further said, "Economics is on one side a study of wealth and on the other and a more important side a part of the study of man."

Edwin Cannan defined economics as "The aim of political economy is the explanation of the general causes on which material welfare of human beings depends." According to Prof. Pigou "Economics is a study of economic welfare, economic welfare being defined as that part of social welfare that can be brought directly or indirectly into relation with the measuring rod of money." In the words of Beveridge, "It is a study of general methods by which men co-operate to meet their material needs." Ely defined it as "Economics is the science which treats those social phenomena that are due to wealth getting and wealth utilizing activities of man."

In brief, according to neo-classicals, economics studies both wealth and welfare of man. Since it gives importance to human welfare it is called welfare definition.

Main points of welfare definition:

(i) Economics studies about mankind in the ordinary business of life.

(ii) It throws lights on economic aspects of the life of human beings.

(iii) It takes into account both man and wealth.

(iv) It studies about attainment of economic welfare by individual and society through material things.

(v) Economic welfare can be measured by money.

(vi) It classified human activities into economic-activities and non-economic activities.

Superiority of Welfare Definition: Welfare definition is superior to wealth definition on account of following reasons:

(i) **It considered both wealth and man:** Wealth definition laid its emphasis on the acquisition of wealth but welfare definition laid emphasis on the utilization of wealth for man's welfare.

(ii) **It gives primary importance to human welfare:** Welfare definition has a reference to man and his welfare.

(iii) **It considered economic welfare as a part of social welfare:** Welfare definition has given economics a status of social science.

(iv) **Welfare can be measured in terms of money:** Material welfare can be directly or indirectly measured by money.

Criticisms: Though Marshall's definition is much wider in scope than that of Adam Smith's definition, it is not free from criticisms. It has been severely criticized by Prof. Lionel Robbins and others as:

(i) **Wrong Classification:** It is wrong to classify human activities into material activities leading to welfare and non-material activities not leading to material welfare. It is because even non-material activities such as services of Doctors, Lawyers, and Teachers, etc. also promote human welfare. Therefore, economics is concerned with both material and non-material activities.

(ii) **Relation between Economics and Welfare:** The link between Economics and Welfare is also a matter of concern. There are certain activities which do not promote human welfare but still we have to study them. For example, the production consumption of alcoholic drinks is economic activities but they do not promote human welfare.

(iii) **Welfare is a Subjective Concept:** It is very difficult to define the concept of welfare. Welfare cannot be measured. Welfare is a state of mind. It refers the human happiness. It depends upon man's feelings. It certainly differs from person to person, from time to time and place to place.

(iv) **It Ignores Scarcity of resources:** Marshall's definition ignores scarcity of resources and multiplicity of wants. All our economic problems arise on account of these aspects.

(v) **Lack of Clear Distinction:** The distinction made in this definition between ordinary business of life and non-ordinary business of life is not explained clearly.

1.2.3 Scarcity Definition or Modern Definition: Prof. Robbins challenged the traditional view of the nature of economic science. He called the earlier definitions of economics as classificatory and unscientific. The word "material" unnecessarily imposes limitation. The welfare concept of Alfred Marshall lacks universality and scientific precision. Hence he gave his own definition of economics. This is the third important definition of economics. It is given by Prof. Lionel Robbins of London school of economics. In 1932 he published the book, *An Essay on the Nature and Significance of Economic Science*, wherein he gave a new definition of economics.

According to Prof. Lionel Robbins, "Economics is a science which studies human behaviour as a relationship between ends and scarce means which have alternative uses."

Main Points

Following are some of the important points of the above definition:

(i) **Wants are Unlimited:** Man experiences various kinds of wants. He has bundle of desires. For example, want for food, clothing, shelter, education, entertainment, travel, etc. If one want is satisfied another want occupies its place for satisfaction. Thus there is no limit to human wants. Some of these wants are extremely necessary for human existence such as want for food, clothing and shelter. However, most other wants arise due to the conditions of life in a civilized society. Thus wants are endless.

(ii) **Resources are Limited:** It is true that human wants are unlimited but as Robbins pointed out they alone cannot create an economic problem. The economic problem arises because the resources are limited. The resources in men, material and time available to us are unfortunately limited. Thus multiplicity of wants and scarcity of resources together give rise to economic problems. If wants were limited like those of resources or if resources were unlimited like those of wants, there would have been no problem. But the reality is that wants are unlimited and resources are limited.

(iii) **Limited Resources having Alternative Uses:** The limited resources are having alternative uses. It means a particular kind of resource can be used for different purposes. Thus there is possibility of using a particular resource only for that purpose from which the consumer is likely to maximize his satisfaction. For Ex: A plot of land can be used for different purposes, it may be used either for cultivation or for construction of a house or a factory building or for a playground which can give maximum satisfaction. Thus we have to face the problem of choice. The problem of choosing between various alternative uses. The choice implies that if we choose one thing we have to forgo others. Therefore there is necessity of economizing the use of limited resources. A man has limited income with which he has to satisfy his unlimited wants. He cannot satisfy all his wants. Therefore the question of arranging them in the order of preference arises.

(iv) **Preference of Human Wants:** Although human wants are unlimited and they can be arranged in the order of preference on the basis of the urgency or nature, wants can be arranged as (a) most urgent wants, (b) urgent wants, (c) less urgent wants, and (d) least urgent wants. The most urgent wants can be given first preference and then secondary preference to other wants. Whether a particular want is most urgent or less urgent or least urgent depends upon the person concerned. The scarcity definition given by Prof. Lionel Robbins is supported by George Stigler, Cassel, J.R. Hicks, Eric Roll, and A.P. Lerner and others. Some of them can be referred here. In the words of George Stigler "Economics is the study of principles governing the allocation of scarce means among the competing ends when the objective of allocation is to maximize the attainment of ends." According to Cassel, "Economics is the Science of Scarcity." J.R. Hicks puts it in this way "Economics is the logic of choice." The definition is described as scarcity definition because it gave importance to scarcity of resources. It is also called as modern definition because Prof. Robbins and his supporters are considered as modern economists.

Superiority of Scarcity Definition:

(i) Welfare definition is classificatory but scarcity definition is more descriptive and analytical.

(ii) Robbins has widened the scope of economics. He made economics a human science rather than a social science.

(iii) Robbins definition deals with all economic activities of human beings, i.e. material and non-material activities.

(iv) Robbins considered economics as a pure science. Thus he has increased the scientific character of economics.

(v) Robbins definition acts as basis for economic planning and analysis.

Criticisms: The scarcity definition of Robbins is also not free from criticisms. Durban, Fraser, Wootten and Beveridge are the main critics of scarcity definition. Criticisms leveled against the scarcity definition are as follows:

(i) **It Lacks Human Touch:** Robbins' idea of economics is colourless, impersonal and neutral regarding ends. It lacks human touch. Economics is concerned not only with individual problems but also with economic problems of entire society.

(ii) **It Restricted the Scope of Economics:** Robbins' definition has restricted the scope of economics. It makes merely a valuation theory. Economics is more than a value theory or resource allocation, it is an also study of human welfare.

(iii) **Theory of Economic Growth is Ignored:** Robbins' definition does not consider the theory of economic growth, which is an important branch of economics.

(iv) **It Failed to Explain some Important Economic Problems:** Some important economic problems such as poverty, unemployment, inequality of income and wealth are not explained by scarcity definition. In order to attain maximum welfare those problems need be attended.

(v) **It is not a Concrete Approach:** Robbins has made economics more abstract and complex. It has no realistic and concrete approach which is essential for the study of economics.

(vi) **Scarcity of Resources is not only the Background of Economic Problems:** Economic problems do not always arise from scarcity. They may also arise on account of abundance. For example, if there is a problem of unemployment, it is a case of not scarcity but of abundance of manpower.

(vii) **It is Based on Wrong Assumption:** It assumes that the world is static but it is wrong because the world is dynamic in nature. Ends and means are always subject to change. It ignores the process of growth and development of the economy.

1.2.4 Growth-oriented Definition or Recent Definition: According to some of the critics, economics is not scarcity centred but now it is growth centred. Moreover, the economic thinking has undergone certain changes during the last several years. Today economics is much more than a theory of resource allocation. Hence, a new thinking of definition on economics is growth definition.

Lord Keynes defines economics as, "Economics studies how the levels of income and employment in a community are determined." It studies the causes of economic fluctuations to see how economic stability could be maintained.

Prof. Benham defines it as "Economics is a study of factors affecting the size, distribution and stability of county's national income." In recent years the theory of economic growth has come to occupy an important place in the study of economics. It studies how the national income grows over years. A study of economic growth and economic stability form an integral part of the study of economics.

Prof. K.G. Seth defines economics as "Economics studies human behaviour and is concerned with changes and growth in means in relation to ends." According to P.A. Samuelson "Economics is the study of how men and society choose with are without the use of money, to employ scarce productive resources which could have alternative uses, to produce various commodities over time and distribute them for consumption now and in the future among various people and groups of society."

Main points are as follows:

(i) **It has Similarity:** There is similarity between Robbins and Samuelson in one respect. Samuelson has also stressed the problem of scarcity of means in relation to unlimited wants.

(ii) **It is a Dynamic Definition:** Prof. Samuelson made the definition more dynamic by including the element of time. The uses of words such as now and in future in respect of distribution of goods, highlight the dynamic nature of his definition.

(iii) **It is Wider in Scope:** Prof. Samuelson has widened the scope of economics because it applies not only to a money economy but also to a barter economy.

(iv) **Problem of Choice is Referred to Future Also:** Problem of choice relates not only to the present but also to the future. Human wants do not remain static. They change with the change of time. Therefore there is a need of bringing about a corresponding change in resources. Means are not be taken as given but they are to be treated as growing.

(e) **Growth of the Economy:** According to Robbins allocation of scarce resources is the central problem of economics. But it is true that the 'ordered growth of economy' is the central problem.

Superiority of Growth Definition: The growth definition is considered as superior to Robbins' definition on the following grounds:

(i) Growth definition considers not only the scarce resources but also the problems of change and growth. Briefly Robbins' definition is static whereas the growth definition is dynamic.

(ii) Growth definition considers not only the resource allocation but also employment, output and national income. Thus it is more comprehensive.

(iii) Growth definition is suited for the present growth-oriented economy.

However, to sum-up, 'Economics' is a growing science. Hence, no single definition can serve the purpose of understanding economics. To define it as a science of wealth is too narrow. To define it as a study of material welfare is also narrow. To define it as a study of scarcity is too wide. Thus every time we face with a dilemma. Therefore one may agree with Prof. Jacob Viner when he says "Economics is what economists do." Economists study resource allocation . They also study size, distribution and stability of national income. Recently the concept economic growth has also creped into the study of economics. A proper definition must cover wider fields to indicate 'what economics is'. The correct definition of 'Economics' should cover the aspects like (a) Wealth, (b) human Welfare, (c) resource allocation, and (d) national income, employment planning.

By taking all the facts discussed above into consideration Prof M.L. Jhingan defined economics in precise way as "Economics is a social science concerned with the proper uses and allocation of resources for the achievement and maintenance of growth with stability."

1.3 SCOPE OF ECONOMICS

Scope means the area or field of study. Scope of economics means the area of study of economics. In other words, it refers to boundaries within which the subject matter of economics is studied. In short, it means what we study and what we do not study in economics. The scope of economics is very wide. It includes the following.

1.3.1 Subject Matter of Economics: Economics has its own subject matter. Subject matter means what exactly we study in the subject. Every subject has its own subject matter. For example, political science studies the activities of man in relation to state and government sociology studies the society. Ethics studies the moral behaviours of man. Similarly economics studies the economic activities of man in the society. Economic activities of man relate to production and consumption of wealth to satisfy his wants. The existence of human wants is the starting point of all economic activities. Satisfaction of wants is the end of all economic activities.

If man is to live, he has to satisfy his wants. For this he needs goods and services. All goods and services which he requires for the satisfaction of his wants are not available to him freely. In other words he has to pay the price for them. For doing so, he needs money. It means he has to earn money with the help of which he can satisfy his wants. In order to earn money, he has to make efforts. When efforts are made, money is earned. Thus the money earned through efforts is used to purchase various goods and services required for the satisfaction of wants. When wants are satisfied, he finally gets satisfaction. Thus wants, efforts and satisfaction constitute the subject matter of economics. It is shown in the following circles of economic activities.

They form circle of economic activities as explained above. In a primitive society the relation between wants, efforts and satisfaction was close and direct because man was self-sufficient. But in a modern society the relation between wants, efforts and satisfaction is indirect and distant, because man is now dependent on other persons. Here in this society man produces what he does not consume and consumes what he does not produce.

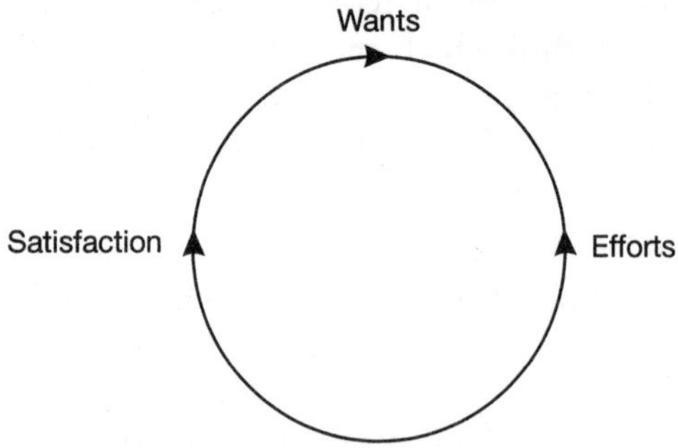

Circle of Economic Activities

Thus goods are produced by some and consumed by several people. For ex: A farmer grows crops like rice, wheat, jowar, etc. but does not consume all that he produces. He sells major portion of his crops to others for money. He, then, purchases the things he has needed to satisfy his wants. This process of selling what you do not want and buying what you want is called exchange. Today the process of exchange comes in between wants, efforts and satisfaction.

Hence the classical economists used traditional approach to study subject matter of economics. They classified economic activities into various branches as production, consumption, exchange, distribution, public finance, economic planning and growth. But modern economists used micro and macroeconomics analysis.

1.3.2 Economics is a Social Science: There are two types of sciences namely (i) Natural Sciences and (ii) Social Sciences.

Economics deals with the economic aspects of human behaviour. Therefore it is a social science. In other words, economics is a study of economic activities of man. But it is not concerned with the economic activities of an isolated individual like Robinson Crusoe. It is concerned with the economic activities of an individual as a member of group or society. In other words it studies the economic activities of man as a member of the society, influencing the members of the society and being influenced by others. Briefly economics is concerned not only with individual economic behaviour but also with group economic behaviour. Since economics is concerned with group behaviour it is regarded as a social Science. G.L. Thirkettele defines it as "Economics is a social science dealing with economic choice." It is most important social science, because it deals with many aspects of human life such as business administration and international relations, etc. It is the most logical social science. It is a dynamic science helping human being in solving different economic problems. In fact economics is considered as the "queen of social sciences".

1.3.3 Economics is both a Science and an Art: The word 'science' has been defined as a systematized body of knowledge concerning a particular branch of nature or society. A branch of knowledge becomes systematized when relevant facts are collected, classified and analyzed. This is to be done for two reasons: (a) to trace out the relation between causes and effects and (b) to formulate laws on the basis of such analysis. Economics is also a science, because it collects various facts and analyses the collected information in such a way that it formulates laws. The use of scientific, mathematical and statistical methods has made economics a full-fledged science.

Like in other sciences, we can also expect results from a particular cause in economics. In physics, according to the law of gravitation, any thing thrown upward comes down because of the gravitational force of the earth. In the same way, in economics the law of supply states that other things remaining constant the price of a commodity has a direct influence on the quantity supplied. Hence, the generalizations of economics are as accurate as generalizations of natural sciences.

Economics is also an art. Now the question arises, i.e. what is an art? An art is the practical application of the principles of science. An art is one which prescribes remedies to the practical problems. An art is the applied part of science. J.M. Keynes defines it as "An art is a system of rules for the attainment of given ends." It lays down certain rules and principles to achieve certain goals. According to the above definition of an art, economics is also an art. Because it provides us guidance to solve economic problems such as poverty, unemployment, low standard of living, population, etc.

In the words of Cossa "A Science teaches us to know; an art teaches us to do. Briefly we can say that Science explains and expounds, art directs and imposes precepts or proposes rules." Thus economics is both a science and an art. According to Cossa "science requires art, art requires science" each being complementary to each other. There are some economists who prefer to classify economics into pure economics and applied economics instead of classifying it into a science and an art. Alfred Marshall was the first economist to categorized economics into pure economics and applied economics. Pure economics is concerned with theoretical study; applied economics is concerned with the practical study.

1.3.4 Economics is a Positive Science and also a Normative Science: A positive science deals with the things as they are. It explains the causes and effects. It does not pass any moral judgments. Normative science deals with the things as they ought to be. It deals with the rightness and wrongness of things. It advocates and condemns. It investigates the truth and prescribes rules of conduct. Thus positive science is concerned with the actualities and normative science is concerned with ideals.

Economics is both positive science and normative science, because it deals with the things as they are and as they ought to be. For example: As a positive science, economics tells us that there is an inequality in the distribution of income and wealth. It also explains the causes and effects. As a normative science, it makes a moral judgment. It says that inequality in the distribution of income and wealth is wrong. It advocates for the equal distribution of income and wealth.

According to Prof. Lionel Robbins economics is just a positive science. He is of the opinion that economists have no right to comment upon the rightness and wrongness of an economic problem. However, a good number of economists are of the opinion that economics is not only a positive science but also a normative science. They are of the opinion that the function of an economist is not only to explore and explain but also to condemn and advocate. In other words the function of an economist is not only to explain some problems and analyze the causes for such problems, but also to comment on the rightness or wrongness of the problems and suggest remedies to solve the problems. Thus economics is both a positive and normative science.

1.4 IMPORTANCE OF ECONOMICS

Economics is the most important and useful social science. Every man needs the knowledge of economics. It is a fast developing social science. It studies the problems, which are important to all individuals. The statements of economists given below clearly indicate the importance of the study of economics. In the words of Prof. Dublin, "Economics is the intellectual religion of the day." According to Henry Clay, "The study of economics is at once a practical necessity and a moral obligation." Alfred Marshall has the opinion that "the aims of study of economics are to gain knowledge for its own sake and to obtain guidance in the practical conduct of life". To quote Prof. Pigou "Economics is both light bearing and fruit bearing."

Miss Barbara Wootten quotes the importance of economics as "You cannot be in any real sense a citizen unless you are also in some degree an economist". The importance of the study of economics can be understood with the help of the following points:

(i) **It Gives Mental Training:** The study of economics trains the minds of readers. It makes the readers to analyze the problems scientifically and logically think clearly and judge correctly. According to Prof. Robertson, "The main practical object in understanding the study of economics is the formation of judgments." In brief economics is an excellent mental discipline.

(ii) **It is Useful to Become Good Citizens:** The knowledge of economics and citizenship go hand in hand. To be a good citizen, it is essential to have the knowledge of economics.

(iii) **It is Useful to Study Man's Behaviour:** Economics makes a greater contribution towards understanding the behaviour of man when he is engaged in economic activities. It is a study of man and his welfare.

(iv) **It is Useful for Predictions:** Economics is useful for making predictions. With the knowledge of economics one can predict the future course of events.

(v) **It Helps to Know Working of Economic System:** A study economics helps us to understand how the complex economic system works automatically.

(vi) **It Shows Interdependence of Human Beings:** The study of economics enables us to know how man's life is interdependent. It also tells us that countries are interdependent.

(vii) **It Helps Consumers:** Knowledge of economics helps the consumers to utilize their limited income for getting maximum satisfaction. In other words it helps them to make maximum purchases with minimum income.

(viii) **It is Useful to Producers:** It helps the producers to take decisions such as what to produce? Where to produce? How to produce? Producers are able to get maximum profit by maximizing the output and minimizing the cost.

(ix) **It Helps Traders:** The study of economics is helpful to traders also. It helps them to know the market trend. The knowledge of money, banking, and trade policy of the Government will greatly help the traders.

(x) **It Helps Labourers:** It enables them to understand the importance of trade unions. Better wages, better facilities may be secured by them.

(xi) **It Helps Labour Leaders:** The knowledge in respect of labour laws, wage conditions, labour welfare enables the labour leaders to fight in favour of workers.

(xii) **It is Useful to Statesman:** The knowledge of economics is very useful to statesman. It is because these people who frame the destiny of the country. It helps them to understand the problems of agriculture, industry, trade, etc. and frame suitable economic policies for the economic development of the country.

(xiii) **It Promotes Harmonious Relations:** The study of economics promotes harmonious relations between the Government and its people. The Government collects taxes and spends the same in turn for public welfare. The Government can carry on its financial operations smoothly only when people's cooperation is available.

(xiv) **It Helps to Solve National and International Problems:** The study of economics helps us to solve some of the national problems like poverty, unemployment, inequality of income and wealth, inflation, etc. It also helps us to find out the solutions to international problems such as flow of foreign capital, International Trade and gap between developed and underdeveloped countries.

(xv) **It Helps to Understand the Problems of Underdeveloped Countries of the World:** Underdeveloped countries face many economic problems such as poverty, unemployment, etc. The knowledge of economics is useful to understand the causes of such problems and frame better economic policies to solve them.

(xvi) **It is Useful to Common Man:** Above all the knowledge of economics is useful to common man also. It helps him to know current problems, for ex: wage level, price level, money, banking, employment, standard of living, etc. The knowledge of economics certainly makes him an intelligent person.

1.5 APPROACHES OF ECONOMIC ANALYSIS

There are two approaches to study of the subject matter of economics. They are: (A) Traditional approach (B) Modern approach.

1.5.1 Traditional Approach: Under traditional approach the subject matter of economics consists of the following branches:

(i) **Consumption:** It is one of the important branches of the economics. Consumption means destruction of utility present in goods and services for the satisfaction of wants. It studies the origin of human wants, their characteristics and satisfaction. Further it also deals with (i) Law of Diminishing Marginal Utility, (ii) Law of Equi-marginal Utility, and (iii) Consumer surplus. It studies consumers' behaviour in the market.

(ii) **Production:** Production means making of goods. In economics, it is creation of utility and addition of value to goods and services. Goods and services consumed by the people have to be produced with the help of factors of production such as a land, labour, capital and organization. Production branch deals with production, cost of production, produce's behaviour and equilibrium.

(iii) **Distribution:** Distribution refers to the sharing of national income by various factors of production, because the production is the result of joint efforts of all the factors of production. They should be paid their respective rewards. Land gets rent, labour gets wages, capital gets interest, and organization gets profits. Distribution branch deals with Functional distribution and personal distribution of income.

(iv) **Exchange:** It is a process of selling what is surplus and buying what is required. It refers to transfer of goods and services through the medium of money and different credit instruments. It acts as a connecting link between consumption and production. It deals with money, banking trade and aid to trade.

(v) **Public Finance:** It refers to the financial operations of the government such as public revenue, public expenditure and public debt. In this branch we study the principles governing Taxation, Public expenditure and Public debt. Nowadays it has become a very important branch of economics.

(vi) **Economic Planning:** Another important branch of economics added recently is economic planning.

Economic planning refers to systematic, efficient and effective utilization of available limited resources for the maximization of public welfare.

(vii) **Economic Growth:** Another very important addition to the subject matter of economics is economic growth. It deals with the process of development and maintenance of economic stability.

1.5.2 Modern Approach: It consists of (a) Microeconomic Analysis, (b) Macroeconomic Analysis. Microeconomics deals with individual units like consumer, producer, firm, etc. Macroeconomics deals with aggregates like national income, group of firms, aggregates investment, aggregate consumption, etc.

Modern economic analysis has been classified broadly into two categories namely: (i) Microeconomics and (ii) Macroeconomics. These terms were first used by Prof. Ragner Frisch of Oslo University in 1933. He used the terms to explain the modern approach to the study of economics. Microeconomic approach is a traditional approach to the study of economics. It has been developed by economists like Ricardo, Marshall, and Pigou. Macro-approach is a modern approach to the study of economics. It is a recent development. It became popular after the publication of J.M. Keynes book in 1936 *General Theory of Employment Interest and Money*.

(A) **Macroeconomics:** The term "Macro" has been derived from a Greek word "MAKROS" which means "Large": Macroeconomics may be described as that branch of economic analysis which studies the economic behaviour not of the individual small units or components of the economy but of the economic system as a whole. It is a study of all the units taken together. Macroeconomics is a study of aggregates. Therefore it is called as "Aggregative Economics". It is concerned with the overall conditions of the economy, for example: (a) Total Consumption, (b) Total Production, (c) Total Savings, (d) Total Investments, (e) Total Employment, and (f) Total Income.

Macroeconomics is an important contribution of J.M. Keynes. He was the most influential economist of 20th century. Macroeconomics became popular only after the publication of his famous book *General Theory of Employment Interest and Money* in 1936.

(B) **Microeconomics:** The term "Micro" has been derived from the Greek word "MIKROS" which means "small". The word micro means a millionth part. Microeconomics may be described as that branch of economic analysis which studies the economic behaviour of the small individual units or components of the economy. In microeconomic approach the attention is concentrated on a very small part or the individual units. In other words it is a study of individual units of the economic system and not the whole economic system.

When we refer to micro approach what we mean is that it is some small part or component of the economy that we are analyzing. Examples given below will make the point more clear.

(a) **Consumer:** Here we study individual consumer's behaviour and not the behaviour of all consumers.

(b) **Price:** We study the price of a particular product or price of a particular factor of production and not the general price level.

(c) **Demand:** The demand of an individual is studied and not the aggregate demand.

(d) **Income:** Income of an individual is studied and not the national income.

(e) **Employment:** In respect of employment it is the employment in a firm or in an industry is studied and not the aggregate employment in economy.

Definitions of Microeconomics: Some definitions on microeconomics are:

- Prof. K.E. Boulding defines "Microeconomics as the study of particular firms, particular households, individual prices, wages, incomes, individual industries particular commodities."
- According to Prof. Mac-Cannel "Microeconomics is a study of the specific economic units and a detailed consideration of the behaviour of these individual units."

- According to Prof. Hansen "Microeconomics is that branch of economics which is concerned with individual firms, their output and costs, the production and pricing of single commodities, wages of individuals, etc."
- Prof. Ackley Gardner defined microeconomics as "Microeconomics deals with the division of total output among industries, products and firms and the allocation of resources among competing groups. It considers problems of income distribution. Its interest is in relative prices of particular goods and services."

Scope of Microeconomics: The Scope of microeconomics covers the following:

- Theories of product pricing.
- Theory of consumer demand.
- Theory of production and costs.
- Theories of factor pricing.
- Theories of rent.
- Theories of wages.
- Theories of interest.
- Theories of profits.
- Theories of economic welfare.
- Compensation principle.
- Social welfare function.

Types of Microeconomics: Microeconomics is classified into three categories namely (i) Micro statics, (ii) Comparative micro statics, and (iii) Micro dynamics.

(i) **Micro-Static:** Micro-static deals with the relationship between different micro variables at a given time under conditions of equilibrium assuming that no changes take place.

For example, equilibrium price of a commodity at any given time, assuming that the forces of demand and supply do not undergo any change.

(ii) **Comparative Micro-Static:** It compares the equilibrium positions of the relations between micro variables at different points of time. It is a comparative study of different equilibriums at different points of time.

(iii) **Micro Dynamics:** It studies the process whereby we reach from one equilibrium position to another.

Uses or Importance of Microeconomics: The microeconomics is useful for the following reasons. In other words, importance of microeconomics can be understood with the help of the following points:

(i) **Functioning of an Economy:** The study of micro-economics help us to understand the functioning of an economic system.

(ii) **Formulation of Economic Policies:** Microeconomics provide necessary tools for the formulation of economic policies.

(iii) **Economic Welfare:** Microeconomics help to examine the conditions of economic welfare. We can understand the standard of living of people, their welfare conditions, the level of satisfaction, and the factors that determine welfare.

(iv) **Allocation of Resources:** Micro economics help us in allocating the available scare resources in an efficient manner. It is essential that the resources are to be utilized in the best possible manner.

(v) **Analysis of Taxation:** Microeconomics is useful in understanding the implications of taxation. It is very essential for the formulation of taxation policies.

(vi) **Useful to Businessmen:** Microeconomics helps businessmen to attain maximum output with minimum costs. It enables them to know about the consumers and to assess the cost of production.

(vii) **Important for International Trade:** Knowledge of price theory is essential to know the problems of trade. For example, benefits of international trade, balance of trade, determination of foreign exchange rate, etc.

(viii) **Simple Models:** Microeconomics is useful to construct simple models. These models help us to understand economic problems.

Limitations of Microeconomics: Microeconomic analysis suffers from certain limitations. They are as follows:

(i) **Partial Picture of Economy:** Microeconomic analysis does not provide a correct and complete picture of the economy, because it concentrates only on small individual units of the economy.

(ii) **Wrong Assumptions:** Microeconomic approach is based on wrong assumptions like:

- Assumption of full employment.
- Perfect competition.
- Laisseze-faire policy. According to Keynes to assume full employment economy is to assume all our difficulties away.

(iii) **What does Apply to an Individual may not Apply to the Whole Economy:** What is true in case of an individual may not be always true in case of aggregates. Examples given below make the point clear.

- Saving by an individual is desirable but saving by the community as a whole is undesirable because if entire community starts saving, effective demand falls and employment opportunities also fall.
- Wage-cut in a particular firm or industry may result in the expansion of employment opportunities. But general wage-cut results in reduction of aggregate demand and employment.

(iv) **Inadequate Approach:** Microeconomics is not capable of studying and analyzing certain important economic problems relating to the following:

- Public finance.
- Monetary policy.
- Fiscal policy.

(v) **No Proper Guidance to Government:** The microeconomics fails to offer proper guidance to the Government to formulate appropriate economic policies.

1.5.3 Distinctions between Micro and Macroeconomics: The distinctions between these two approaches are given as under:

Microeconomics	Macroeconomics
• It deals with individual economic units. For example, firm, industry, individual consumer. Prof. Boulding says microeconomics follow the method of slicing. • Prof. Ackley Gardner says it studies the trees in the forest. It is like a plough designed to solve small problems. • It uses partial equilibrium technique (studies price output determination of goods or services in any given market situation. • Deals with the distribution of national income among factors of production. • Price theory is the central part of microeconomics. • Deals with relative price as variable. • It moves from particulars to general	• It deals with the aggregates. For example, total output of employment and income. • Macroeconomics follow the method of lumping. It studies the character of the forest. It is like a bulldozer designed to solve big problems. • It uses general equilibrium technique (studies the determination of the aggregate price output levels and fluctuations in these aggregates). • Deals with income formation, fluctuation and propagation in terms of savings and investment. • Income theory is the central part of macroeconomics. • Deals with general price level. • It moves from general to particular.

1.5.4 Interdependence of Micro and Macroeconomics: Neither approach is complete without the other. No approach serves as an alternative. It means that both approaches are equally essential to study economics. They supplement each other. Prof. P.A. Samuelson quotes "There is really no opposition between micro and macroeconomics. Both are absolutely vital. You are less than half educated if you understand the one while being ignorant of the other." The interdependence of these two approaches may be explained with the help of examples given below:

(i) **Microeconomics Requires Macroeconomics:** Every micro economic problem involves macroeconomic analysis. It can be explained with the help of an example. How much wages should be paid by a firm to its workers? This is a problem of microeconomics as it is related to a single firm. This can be solved with help of macroeconomic analysis. The wages paid by a firm depends upon wages paid by other firms in the locality. In fact wages to be paid by a firm depends not only on its demand for labour but also demand for labour in the entire industry.

(ii) **Macroeconomic Analysis Requires Microeconomics:** To understand the working of the entire economy we must get an idea of the working of individuals, households, firms and industry. The total output of the economy can be found out only by adding the output of all the firms in economy. Similarly the total income, i.e. national income can be ascertained only by adding the incomes of all individuals.

However, there is no clear cut line of demarcation between micro and macroeconomics. What is macroeconomics at one time may become microeconomics at some other time. The distinction is based on the method of study rather than its subject-matter. The study of national income in a particular country is a study of macroeconomics. But when we consider the income of the whole world the study of national income of a country becomes a study of microeconomics. Hence, the classification of economic studies into these parts is not a watertight compartment. Therefore, there is no meaning to waste time in asking a question, that is, which is superior and which is inferior. Therefore, obviously, we come nearer to the topic of interdependence of both approaches.

1.6 Static and Dynamic Economics

Static and Dynamic are the two methods to study the functioning of the economy. They are discussed as under:

1.6.1 Economic Static: The term 'Static' means a position or rest or absence of movement or unchanged. But in economics 'Static' means a state in which there is a continuous, regular, smooth and certain movement without change and there are no jerks and shocks.

According to Adam Smith economic static is a tool of analysis thus it is associated with the assumption of 'stationary state' where everything repeats itself from year to years.

A.C. Pigou defines economic static as "Just as the drops of water that from a stream are always changing but its form remains the same, so do, in a static state, the factors change but they are not of any consequence."

Characteristics or Features: The features of economic statics may be drawn on the basis of the above definitions as:

(i) **Absence of Changes:** According to Prof. Clark it is characterized by absence of five changes namely (a) size of population, (b) supply of capital, (c) methods of production (d) forms of business organization, and (e) wants of people.

(ii) **State of Rest:** Prof. Harrod says it is concerned with a state of rest, it does not mean idleness but the economy repeats itself overtime due to lack of significant investment.

(iii) **Point of Time:** According to Frisch it deals with economic phenomena that are the establishment of relation between economic values or quantities like demand, supply, price, etc. and the same point of time. It assumes that the economic values or variables in question are not influenced by past or future decisions or external factors.

Illustration: The static economics can be illustrated with the help of price mechanism in the following diagram.

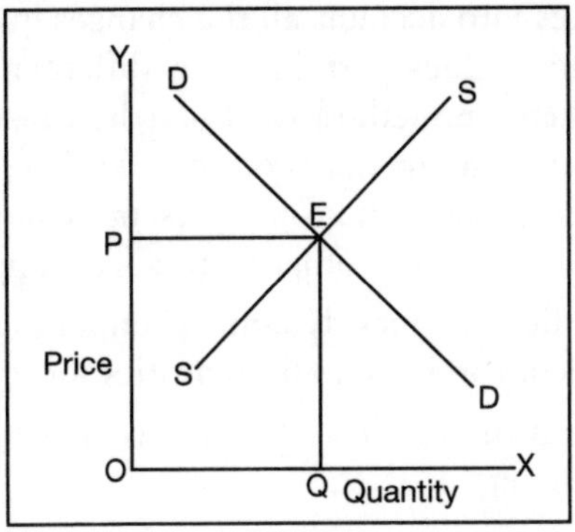

Diagram 1.1: Price Determination

DD is demand curve. SS is supply curve. At a particular point of time both the curves intersected each other at point E, equilibrium point, and determined the price P. At this state the demand and supply conditions remain unchanged. Though the individual constituent change, but the economic system does not change.

Importance: Economic static has the following significance:

(i) It is simplest method to study the complex economic system. Its heroic assumption *ceteris peribus* helps to study the relation between the economic quantities.

(ii) It is important part of traditional economics. For example, theory of rent, theory of value, etc. are its examples.

Limitations: Static economics has certain limitations which are discussed as under:

(a) It is based on unrealistic assumptions like *ceteris peribus* etc. So it fails to study the reality of the economy.

(b) It has narrow scope. It studies only stationary state of the economy so it fails to study dynamism of the economy.

(c) It takes into account only the point of time but ignored the period of time in which many changes take place.

1.6.2 Economic Dynamics: Economic dynamics is the method of economic analysis which is exactly opposite of economic statistics. It takes into account all the changes in the economy. It studies economic values pertaining to different points of time. It is a comprehensive method to study the cause and effects of all possible variations in the economy. For ex: The price of a commodity depends upon not only present demand but also past and future demands as well other factors like supply, income, etc.

Prof. J.R. Hicks defines dynamic economics as "to that part of economic theory in which all quantities must be dated".

Prof. Harrod defines it as "economy in which the rates of output are changing".

Thus dynamic economics concerned with the period of time and the study of movements and changes in the economic system.

Characteristics or Features: On the basis of above definitions the features of dynamic economics can be studied as under:

- **It has not taken into account any assumption.** It takes the real world as is it.
- **It takes into account the period of time.** It connects all economic quantities to different period of time.
- **It considers all movements and changes.** It takes into account of all the factors and their changes that influence on the variable in question, for ex: It considers the influence of all the determinants of demand like taste, income, etc. on demand at a time along with price. So it is a comprehensive method.

Illustration: Dynamic economics is illustrated in the diagram 1.2.

Dynamic economics explains how the economy moves from one equilibrium E to new equilibrium E1 when aggregate demand increased from AD to AD1. The changes in income and employment during the period of time are shown as Y1, Y2, Y3 and Y4.

Importance: It is useful in many ways as under:

- It helps remove unrealistic assumptions to study the reality of economic system.
- It is more elastic analysis to study all possible related to the particular economic problem.

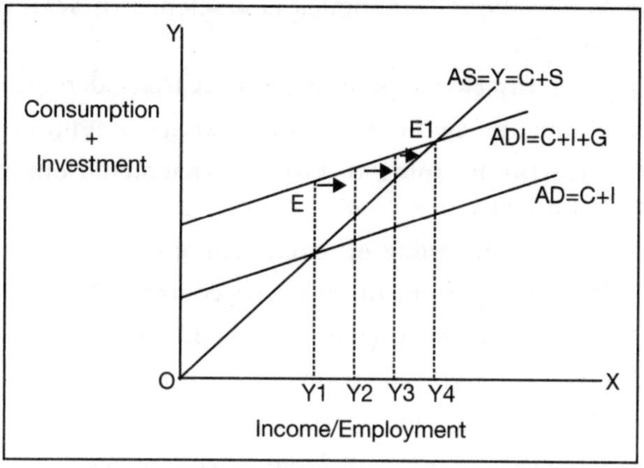

Diagram 1.2: Income and Employment Generation

Thus it is best suited to the study of the economy.

Limitations: Though it is a comprehensive method to study economic problems, it too suffers from certain limitations.

- It needs a good deal of mathematical treatment. The dynamic economic analysis gave up the assumptions and took into account the period of time which made the study more complex and complicated which needs mathematical tools to study the economic problems.
- Stonier and Hague says about it as "...that complexity would be beyond the capacity of any human brain".
- It is not yet fully developed method. So it is not possible to use it at this stage of development.

1.7 MODEL QUESTIONS

2 Marks Questions

(a) What is Economics?

(b) What is economic activity?

(c) Write about 'Economics is science of wealth'.

(d) Name any two defects of wealth definition.

(e) What does welfare definition state?

(f) Name any two superiorities of welfare definition.

(g) Write any two criticisms of welfare definition.

(h) Write about 'economics is a science of scarcity and choice'.

(i) Give any two superiorities of 'Scarcity definition'.

(j) Name any two criticisms of scarcity definition.

(k) Give the meaning of Growth-Oriented Definition of Economics.

(l) Give the meaning of macroeconomics.

(m) What do you mean by microeconomics?

(n) Name any two uses of microeconomics.

(o) Give any two limitations of microeconomics.

(p) What is economic statistics?

(q) Give the meaning of dynamic economics.

(r) Name any two features of economic statistics.

(s) Write any two features of economic dynamics.

5 Marks Questions

1. Write a short-note on wealth definition.
2. Write a short-note on growth-oriented definition.
3. Give a brief account of macroeconomics.
4. Write a short-note on economic statistics.
5. Discuss in brief dynamic economics.

10. Marks Questions

1. Explain wealth definition in detail.
2. Discuss the welfare definition.
3. Critically examine scarcity definition.
4. Define microeconomics; explain its uses and limitations.
5. Explain economic statistics and dynamics with their importance and limitations.

2

Utility Analysis

2.1 UTILITY

This chapter deals with meaning, definition and laws of utility.

2.1.1 Meaning and Definitions of Utility:

Meaning: Utility means want satisfying power of a commodity or service. It can also be described as an ability or capacity of a commodity to satisfy human want.

Definitions: The following are important definitions of utility:

- Prof. Wicksteed defines utility as "Utility as an economic concept means only desire."
- Prof. Taussig defines utility as "In economics utility is that satisfaction or advantage which is received by a man by the use of property or wealth."

In brief, the want satisfying power is called utility.

2.1.2 Features of Utility or Characteristics of Utility: The following are the important features or characteristics of utility:

(i) **Utility is different from usefulness:** In the ordinary language utility may mean usefulness. But in economics utility is not usefulness. In economics anything that satisfies human want is utility. It may be beneficial or harmful to the consumer, for ex: Alcohol, cigarette, opium, etc. are not useful to man. All goods have utility but not usefulness.

(ii) **Utility has no moral significance:** The concept of utility has no moral or ethical significance. A particular thing may be good or bad, but it possesses utility. For ex: Alcohol, cigarette, opium, etc.

(iii) **Utility is different from pleasure:** A thing may possess utility, but it may not give any pleasure to consumer at the time of consumption, for example, injections, bitter medicines, etc. Therefore, utility and pleasure are different from each other.

(iv) **Utility differs from person to person:** Utility of a good is not same for all persons. It differs from person to person. For example, a glass of water gives more satisfaction to a thirsty man than the others.

(v) **Utility differs from place to place:** A commodity may possess different utility at different places. For example, woolen goods have greater utility in place like Shimla and less utility in Chennai.

(vi) **Utility differs from time to time:** Utility also differs from time to time. For example, umbrella has greater utility in rainy season and no utility in winter. Arms and ammunitions have greater utility during war but lesser or no utility at other times.

(vii) **Utility is subjective or psychological phenomena:** Utility is subjective factor. It is experience of one's own mind. For example, the person who eats sugar alone feels its satisfaction.

(viii) **Utility is not the same thing as satisfaction:** Utility does not mean satisfaction. The following are the main differences between utility and satisfaction.

Utility	Satisfaction
(1) It is want satisfying power.	(1) It derives from consumption of a commodity.
(2) It is the expected satisfaction.	(2) It is realized satisfaction.
(3) Utility is the cause of satisfaction.	(3) Satisfaction is the effect of utility.

2.1.3 Forms of Utility: Utility can be created in many ways. In other words there are different forms of utility. They are:

(i) Form utility, (ii) Place utility, (iii) Time utility, and (iv) Service utility.

(i) **Form Utility:** Form utility refers to the addition or creation of utility by changing the form of a commodity, for example, changing wood into furniture.

(ii) **Place Utility:** Place utility refers to the creation or addition of utility to a thing by moving or transferring it from one place to other place, for example, movement of coal from a coal mine to iron and steel factory.

(iii) **Time Utility:** Time utility refers to the addition of utility to a due to change of time. For example, woolen cloth gets utility when winter arrives.

(iv) **Service Utility:** Services also possess utility. Service utility refers to the creation of utility through rendering services to satisfy human wants. For example, services of doctors, Services of lawyers.

2.1.4 Concepts of Utility: There are two important concepts of utility. They are: (i) Marginal utility (MU) and (ii) Total Utility (TU).

(i) **Marginal Utility:** Marginal utility refers to the utility derived from the consumption of last unit of a commodity. It is the addition made to the total utility by consuming one more unit of a commodity. It is also described as the rate of change of total utility caused by change in consumption. Thus Marginal Utility can be defined as:

- Marginal Utility is the utility derived from the marginal unit or the last unit consumed.
- Marginal Utility is the addition to the Total Utility. It derives from the consumption of one additional unit. Or Marginal Utility is the change in Total Utility resulting from the change in the consumption.

The Marginal Utility can be measured by using any one of the following methods or formula or measures:

Marginal Utility = Total Utility of present units of consumption – Total Utility of previous units of consumption

$$\therefore \quad MU = TU_n - TU_{n-1}$$

where, MU = Marginal Utility

TU = Total Utility

n = Present units of consumption

n – 1 = Previous units of consumption

For Example: When Arjun consumed 10 mangoes, he got Total Utility 100 utils and now he consumed 11 mangoes that gave him Total Utility 110 utils. With the help of above method Marginal Utility is measured as:

$$MU = TU_{11} - TU_{10}$$
$$= 110 - 100 = 10$$

Marginal Utility = Change in Total Utility ÷ Change in Consumption

$$\therefore MU = \Delta TU \div \Delta C$$
$$= \frac{\Delta TU}{\Delta C}$$

where, MU = Marginal utility

ΔTU = Change in total utility

ΔC = Change in consumption

(ii) **Total Utility (TU):** Total utility refers to the total amount of utility derived from the consumption of various units of a commodity at the disposal of the consumer. Total utility with reference to a single commodity may be defined as the sum of the utility derived from the consumption of all the units of the commodity.

For example: If a consumer consumes 5 units of mango and derives U_1, U_2, U_3, U_4, U_5 utils, then

$$TU = U_1+U_2+U_3+U_4+U_5$$

where, TU = Total Utility, $U_1U_2U_3U_4U_5$ utils (or amount of utility). If he consumes 'n' units of mango, then

$$TU_n = U_1+U_2+U_3+U_4+U_5+\ldots U_n$$
$$\therefore TU = \Sigma U_n$$

When the consumer consumes more and more units of a particular commodity the Marginal Utility of it declines but the

Total Utility increases up to a certain point. If the consumer continues to consume more units of a commodity the Marginal Utility becomes zero and after certain stage it becomes negative, commodity instead of giving utility it gives disutility to the consumer.

It can be seen in Table 2.1 given below.

Table 2.1: Marginal Utility and Total Utility Schedule

Units of a commodity	Marginal utility (utils)	Total Utility (utils)
1	4	4
2	3	7
3	2	9
4	1	10
5	0	10
6	–1	9

The Total Utility and Marginal Utility explained in the above table 2.1 are illustrated in the following diagram:

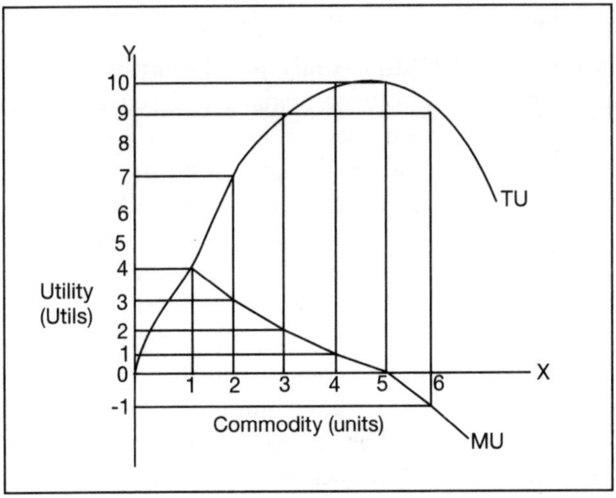

Diagram 2.1: Total Utility and Marginal Utility

The unit of a commodity is measured along 'OX' axis and total and marginal utility along 'OY' axis. TU is the total utility curve and MU is the marginal utility curve.

When the consumer consumes one unit of a commodity, the Marginal Utility is the same as Total Utility i.e. 4 utils.[1] When he consumes more and more units of a commodity, the Marginal Utility declines up to 4th unit where it becomes 1 util. The Marginal Utility of 5th unit is zero and the total utility reaches the maximum i.e. 10 utils. When he consumes the 6th unit, the Marginal Utility becomes negative (-1) and the Total Utility declines to 9 utils.

2.2 MEASUREMENT OF UTILITY

The term utility is a psychological phenomenon. In other words it is a subjective concept. It refers to a feeling of satisfaction. Since utility is a subjective factor, it is difficult to measure utility. However, some efforts have been made to measure utility. There are two different analyses to measure utility namely (i) Cardinal Utility Analysis, (ii) Ordinal Utility Analysis.

The classical and neoclassical economists advocate the Cardinal Utility Analysis. The Ordinal Utility Analysis is advocated by the modern economists. Ordinal Utility Analysis is popularly known as Indifference Curve Analysis.

2.2.1 Cardinal Utility Analysis: The terms cardinal[2] and ordinal[3] are borrowed from mathematics. The concept of cardinal utility function has been used by neo-classical economists like Marshall. The Marshallian demand analysis is based on the concept of cardinal utility. It assumes that the utility is measurable and additive. It gives numerical expression to utility. The units of measurement are imaginary. They are called utils. The term utils means "units of utility" for cardinal counting of utility. It was coined by Walras. With the help of cardinal utility function it is possible to measure and compare utility. For example, when a consumer ate first apple it gave him utility of 10 units, second apple 8 units and so on. The quantification of utility is based on consumer's previous experience and it is imaginary.

2.2.2 Ordinal Utility Analysis: The ordinal utility function is reverse of cardinal utility. It does not carry the assumption of measurability. Economists who believe in ordinal utility concept are of the opinion that quantities of utilities are immeasurable. Ordinal utility means that the consumer is assumed to order or rank the subjective utilities of goods. There is no need to assume that consumer knows the quantities of utilities.

It means that utilities derived from different goods can be arranged in a serial order such as 1st, 2nd, 3rd, 4th, etc. These numbers 1st, 2nd, 3rd, 4th, etc. are ordinal numbers. The ordinal numbers are ordered or ranked.

The ordinal utility is not a quantity. It is only an expression of the consumer's preference for one commodity over another. The concept of ordinal utility is based on the following axioms:

(a) It may not be possible for a consumer to express his utility in quantitative terms. It is possible for him to tell which of any two goods he prefers. He can tell that he prefers 'X' commodity to 'Y' and 'Z' commodities.

(b) If once he is able to give the preference, he can order for all commodities in the order of preference.

Prof. J.R. Hicks and R.G.D. Allen have supported the ordinal utility function. According to them, the theory of consumer behaviour can be explained without the use of the concept of measurability of utility. The ordinal utility analysis is the base for indifference curve analysis.

2.3 CONCEPT OF MARGIN

The concept of margin occupies an important place in modern economic theory. Modern economic analysis is said to be the marginal analysis.

Meaning: The term 'margin' means the last unit. For example, it may be a last apple consumed, last worker employed in a factory and so on. Therefore the term margin can be discussed with reference to the aspects like (a) consumption, (b) production, (c) distribution, and (d) theory of value.

2.3.1 Margin and Consumption: When the consumer goes on consuming more and more units of a commodity the utility derived from successive units goes on diminishing. Total satisfaction increases at a diminishing rate. Finally he reaches a stage where he stops the consumption. The last unit consumed by him gives him the least satisfaction. That last unit is called the marginal unit. The utility derived from that unit is called the marginal utility. It is explained in the following table 2.2.

Table 2.2: Marginal Utility Schedule

Number of apples consumed	Marginal Utility
1st apple	16 Units
2nd apple	12 Units
3rd apple	8 Units
4th apple	4 Units
5th apple	0 Unit
6th apple	- 4 Units

The consumer consumes only four apples. The 4th apple is the marginal apple. The marginal utility of that apple is 4 units. He does not consume the 5th apple because he does not get any satisfaction from it. The 6th apple gives him negative satisfaction.

2.4 LAW OF DIMINISHING MARGINAL UTILITY

The law of diminishing marginal utility is one of the most fundamental laws of consumption. Prof. Gossen first explained the original idea of this law. Prof. Alfred Marshall has further developed and popularized it. However it is considered as one of the important contributions of Prof. Alfred Marshall to theories of consumer behaviour.

The law is based upon an important feature of human wants, i.e. a particular human want is satiable at a given point of time. The law is based on the general psychology of consumers, "the more of anything a consumer gets the utility derived from that commodity decreases". It is a generalization of common psychological experience of consumers. This law is a foundation for the theory of demand.

2.4.1 Statement: According to Alfred Marshall "the additional benefit a person derives from a given increase of his stock of anything diminishes with the growth of the stock he has". As a consumer increases the consumption of any commodity, the marginal utility of that commodity diminishes. For example, a consumer's desire for apple may be very strong in the initial stage but when he goes on consuming apples, the successive units of apple will yield less and less satisfaction.

Thus the law is applicable generally to consumption or use of all goods and services. In brief, other things being equal, as the quantity of commodity consumed or acquired by the consumer increases, the marginal utility of the commodity tends to diminish.

2.4.2 Illustration: The law explains the general experience of consumers that when a consumer gets more and more of anything, the utility derived from each additional commodity slowly diminishes. This is explained with an imaginary example of a consumer consuming apples. The consumer's marginal utility and the total utilities are shown in Table 2.3.

Table 2.3: Utility Schedule

Units of Apple	Marginal Utility (Units)	Total Utility (Units)
1	50	50
2	40	90
3	30	120
4	20	140
5	10	150
6	00	150
7	–5	145

Table 2.3 explains that the first apple gives the consumer, marginal utility worth 50 units and the successive apples will yield him less satisfaction. The 6th apple gives him zero

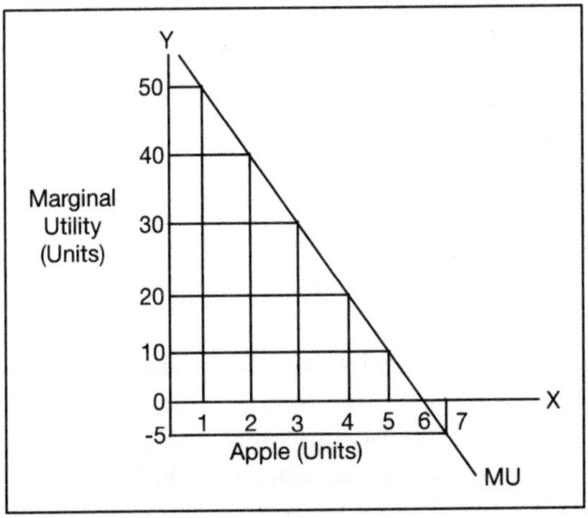

Diagram 2.2: Marginal Utility Curve

satisfaction. It is a point of satiety i.e. maximum pleasure or total utility. Any further unit of consumption provides negative marginal utility i.e. it is a point of dissatisfaction. This idea is represented in the diagram 2.2.

Consumption of units of apple are measured along X axis and marginal utility is measured along Y-axis. MU is the marginal utility curve. It has a negative slope.[4] It shows inverse relationship between consumption of units and its marginal utility. MU curve slopes downwards from left to the right. MU curve explains that as consumer eats more and more units of apple the satisfaction derived from consumption of additional unit declines.

2.4.3 Assumptions: The law is based upon following assumptions:

(i) A commodity consumed must be in suitable doses.

(ii) The units of a commodity should be homogeneous or identical in all respect.

(iii) The units must be consumed without any time gap. Consumption should be continuously.

(iv) Price of commodity, income, taste and fashions of the consumers should remain unchanged.

(v) Consumers are rational. They want maximum satisfaction from limited expenditure. So, consumers should be taken as normal.

(vi) Utility can be measured in terms of number or cardinal measurement of utility.

(vii) Constancy of marginal utility of money: It is assumed that not only the income of the consumer is given but the marginal utility of income should remain constant.

(viii) Utility of X-commodity is independent of utility of Y-commodity.

2.4.4 Exceptions and Criticisms: The law is universally applicable. Sometimes there may be some cases, where with increase in the consumption of units, marginal utility may not diminish. There are some exceptions to the law.

(a) **Rare Collections:** It is not applicable to rare collections like stamps, coins, paintings, etc. More the collection more may be the satisfaction of the collectors.

(b) **Music:** Sometimes music is treated as an exception to the law. As the person listen the music continuously, his satisfaction rises, joy enhances and he gets more pleasure.

(c) **Drunkards:** It is not applicable to drunkards. As they consume more and more doses of liquor, their satisfaction increases.

(d) **Money:** It is not applicable to money. As money-mongers get more and more money, it gives them more and more satisfaction. However, it should be also noted that more and more collection of money gives less marginal utility of money and less and less money means more marginal utility. Therefore, the value of money may be less to rich but it is more to the poor. For example, one hundred rupee note is important to a poor man rather than to a millionaire.

(e) **Too Small Size:** Law does not apply to the consumption of too small doses or size of commodity. For example, while drinking water in small doses, the marginal utility increases with every additional dose.

2.4.5 Importance of the Law: The law has an important place in economics. It helps the consumers, the producers and the government in arriving at better decisions. Its significances are:

(i) It is the bases for the law of demand: The consumer always compares the price and marginal utility before the purchase of any commodity. Therefore the consumer buys more when price falls. The Marshall's law of demand is based upon this law.

(ii) The law helps the producers to follow a better pricing policy for goods and services. He charges high price for the commodity that gives more satisfaction.

(iii) The finance minister takes the help of this law while imposing taxes on goods, services, income and wealth. More taxes are imposed on rich people because to them the marginal utility of money is less, and

(iv) The law helps the consumers to control the consumption expenditure.

2.5 LAW OF EQUI-MARGINAL UTILITY

The law of Equi-Marginal utility is the important contribution by Alfred Marshall to the theory of demand. This law is an extension of law of diminishing marginal utility. The law of diminishing marginal utility explains the consumer's equilibrium with only one commodity; whereas the law of equi-marginal utility explains consumer's equilibrium with the use of many commodities. It is a many commodity model. The law is also called the 'Law of Maximum Satisfaction' because every consumer wants to get maximum satisfaction by using his limited income. It is also called 'Law of Substitution' as consumer substitutes his expenditure on one commodity over that of another commodity in such a way that he gets maximum satisfaction. The law is also called 'The Proportionality Rule' as the ratios of marginal utility to prices of different commodities are equalized with the give marginal utility of money income of the consumer.

The law is based on three characteristics of human wants namely (i) wants are comparative, (ii) wants are substitutable, and (iii) wants are complimentary.

2.5.1 Conditions of the Law: The following are the required conditions for application of the law. They are: (i) The consumer has limited income. (ii) The consumer more than one want to satisfy. (iii) The consumer is rational and seeks maximum satisfaction. (iv) The Price of the commodity are given. The Law of Equi-Marginal utility can be explained under these conditions.

2.5.2 Statement: William Fellner states the law as "the rational consumer will distribute his purchase between two goods in such a way that the marginal utility of the expenditure he makes for good 'A' should be equal to the marginal utility of the expenditure he makes for good 'B'". The law concentrates on the marginal utilities of expenditure rather than marginal utility of goods. The marginal utility of expenditure of the goods consumed by the consumer can be obtained by dividing the marginal utility of the good by its price. According to the law, "the best division of expenditure is that at which weighted marginal utilities in all lines of expenditure are equal". In other words, the law states that other things being equal a consumer gets maximum total utility from spending his given income, when he allocates his expenditure to the purchase of different goods in such a way that the marginal utility is derived form the last unit of money spent to each item of expenditure tends to be equal.

2.5.3 Illustration: The law can be explained with the help of an example: A consumer's income is ₹ 5. He wants to buy two goods, say, Apple and Banana. The price of apple is ₹ 1 and the price of Banana is also ₹ 1. The marginal utility of expenditure on Apple and Banana are shown in the following Table 2.4:

Table 2.4: Law of Equi-Marginal Utility

Sl. No.	$\frac{MUa}{Pa} =$	MU of Apple	$\frac{MUb}{Pb} =$	MU of Banana
1	$\frac{15}{1}$	15	$\frac{14}{1}$	14
2	$\frac{14}{1}$	14	$\frac{13}{1}$	13
3	$\frac{13}{1}$	13	$\frac{12}{1}$	12
4	$\frac{12}{1}$	12	$\frac{11}{1}$	11
5	$\frac{11}{1}$	11	$\frac{10}{1}$	10
Total		65		60

For instance, when consumer spends the 1st ₹ on apple the marginal utility of expenditure is 15 units or if he spends it on banana the marginal utility of expenditure is 14 units. There are many possibilities of expenditure of ₹ 5 on these two goods. This is given in Table 2.5:

Table 2.5: Law of Equi-Marginal Utility

Expenditure	Marginal Utility of Expenditure			
	Apple		Banana	Total
1. All ₹ 5 on Apple	65	+	0	65
2. All ₹ 5 on Banana	0	+	60	60
3. ₹ 4 on Apple ₹ 1 on Banana	54	+	14	60
4. ₹ 3 on Apple ₹ 2 on Banana	24	+	27	69
5. ₹ 2 on Apple ₹ 3 on Banana	29	+	39	68
6. ₹ 1 on Apple ₹ 4 on Banana	15	+	50	65

The principle is explained with the help of diagram 2.3.

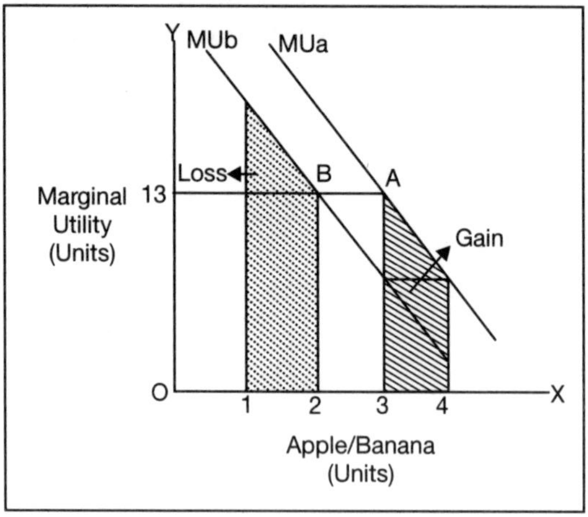

Diagram 2.3: Law of Equi-Marginal Utility

Units of banana/apple are measured along OX axis and the Marginal utility of apple and banana are shown along Y-axis. MUa curve is marginal utility of apple and MUb curve is marginal utility of banana. The consumer spends ₹ 3 on apple and ₹ 2 on banana. This gives him equal marginal utility of 13 units at points A and B. Any other possibility of expenditure, say ₹ 4 on apple and ₹ 1 on banana will give him less satisfaction and loss in utility is greater than gain in utility.

As the law said the consumer would get maximum total satisfaction when

$$\frac{\text{MU Apple}}{\text{Price of Apple}} = \frac{\text{MU Banana}}{\text{Price of Banana}} = \text{K (= Marginal Utility of Expenditure)}$$

$$\therefore \quad \frac{13}{1} = \frac{13}{1} = 13$$

The consumer out of his ₹ 5 expenditure spends ₹ 3 on 3 units of Apple and ₹ 2 on 2 units of banana. Thus he gets total utility as follows:

TU of Apple = 15 + 14 + 13 = 42

TU of Banana = 14 + 13 = 27

∴ Total Utility = TU of Apple + TU of Banana = 42 + 27 = 69

No other allocation of expenditure has the total maximum satisfaction.

2.5.4 Assumptions: The Law of Equi-Marginal Utility is based on the following assumptions:

(i) The consumer is rational and he seeks maximum total satisfaction.

(ii) Total utility is measurable in cardinal terms.

(iii) The consumer has a given scale of preference and has perfect knowledge of utility is derived.

(iv) Prices of goods remain constant.

(v) Income of the consumer is fixed.

(vi) The marginal utility of money is constant.

(vii) The wants and goods are substitutable.

2.5.5 Importance: The law is useful to consumers, producers and government and it also throws light on use of Time and Assets. It is studied as under:

(a) The consumer uses the law to get maximum satisfaction from his purchases by reallocating income.

(b) A producer tries to distribute different factors in such a way that he gets maximum profit.

(c) The government tries to spend its money in such a way that the society will be benefited maximum.

(d) The consumer's substitute different goods in such a way as to get maximum satisfaction.

(e) The law helps in making the best use of time i.e. 24 hours of a day to get maximum benefit.

(f) Likewise, assets must be distributed in different lines of investment, to get maximum profit.

2.5.6 Limitations: The law has some limitations. They are:

(a) **The assumptions are unrealistic:** The theory assumes rationality of consumers. But in real world, the consumer may be ignorant about market conditions; they may be influenced by customs and habits; they purchase host of goods where comparison becomes difficult.

(b) **The law presumes divisibility of goods:** But in real practice, some goods are indivisible and substitution will be difficult. For example, T.V.

(c) **Law is based upon measurement of utility:** But utility is subjective and it cannot be measured objectively.

(d) **The law assumes the marginal utility is constant:** But it is not so because as money is spent, the remaining units of money have greater marginal utility.

2.6 CONSUMER'S SURPLUS (CS)

A French Engineer-Economist Dupuit, in 1844, identified the concept of consumer's surplus. In economics, it was popularized by Alfred Marshall. It is based on the experience of consumers in daily life. There are certain commodities for which consumers are prepared to pay more than the actual price. The best examples are: A post card, a matchbox, a newspaper, packet of salt, etc. They are the most useful goods but they are very cheap. The excess-satisfaction that the consumers get over the actual expenditure is called consumer's surplus.

Consumer's surplus depends upon the price. Higher the price, lower will be the consumer's surplus and *vice versa*. Thus consumer's surplus is inversely related with the price. As price increases, it declines or as price declines, it increases.

2.6.1 Definition: According to Marshall Consumer's surplus is "the excess of the price which he would be willing to pay rather than go without the thing, over which he actually does pay, is the economic measure of this surplus satisfaction".

According to Taussig, Consumer's surplus is "the difference between the potential price and the actual price".

Consumer's surplus can also be explained with following formulas:

(1) Consumer's Surplus = what one is willing to pay minus what one actually prepared to pay. Or

Consumer's Surplus = Potential price—Actual price.

(2) Consumer's Surplus=Total Utility minus (Price × Quantity)

$\therefore$ CS = TU – (P × Q)

2.6.2 Explanation: The concept of consumer's surplus is explained with the help of an example: Let us assume that the market price of a commodity, say orange is ₹ 10. A consumer buys 5 oranges. His utility level is shown in Table 2.6.

Table 2.6: Consumer's Surplus

No. of Oranges	Potential Price or Marginal Utility (₹)	Actual Price	Consumer's Surplus (₹)
1	50	10	40
2	30	10	20
3	25	10	15
4	15	10	5
5	10	10	0
Total Units= 5	Total Utility =130	Total Money Spent = 50	Total Consumer's Surplus=80

Consumer buys totally 5 oranges. He pays actually ₹ 50 for 5 oranges. He gets total utility worth ₹ 130 from 5 oranges. This is potential price or what the consumer is ready to pay for oranges. Therefore, consumer's surplus is ₹ 80.

Substituting these values in formulas given above, consumer's surplus can be calculated as:

(i) Consumer's surplus = Total utility – (Price × quantity)
= ₹ 130 – (₹ 10 × 5 units)

= 130 – 50

= ₹ 80

(ii) Consumer's surplus= Potential price – Actual price

= ₹ 130 – ₹ 50

= ₹ 80

The consumer's surplus can be illustrated in the diagram 2.4.

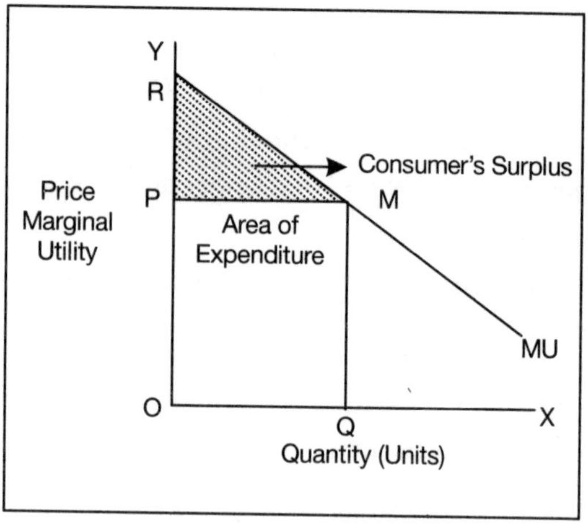

Diagram 2.4: Consumer's Surplus

The quantity of commodity purchased is measured along OX axis. The price and marginal utility are measured along OY axis. MU is the marginal utility curve. Let us assume that the price of orange = OP

Consumer buys oranges = OQ

The area of expenditure = OP × OQ

= OPQM.

The total utility he gets from oranges = ORQM.

Therefore Consumer's surplus = Area below marginal utility curve – Area of expenditure

CS = ORMQ – OPMQ

= PMR

Thus, consumer's surplus is an area below marginal utility curve and above the area of expenditure which is shown by area PMR.

2.6.3 Assumptions: The concept of consumer's surplus is based upon the following assumptions:

(a) The utility derived from the commodity can be measured.

(b) Marginal utility of money is constant.

(c) Price of the commodity remains constant.

(d) Income, fashion and taste of the consumer remain constant.

(e) It is a one-commodity model; demand for a particular commodity is assumed as independent of other commodity.

2.6.4 Importance: The concept of consumer's surplus has the practical uses as under:

(i) It is useful to the finance minister in the matter of taxation. While imposing a tax on commodity or service, care should be taken not to affect the consumer's surplus in a greater way.

(ii) It is useful to public authorities to determine the prices of some public goods or service. For example, railways, dams, roads, and postal service, etc.

(iii) It is useful to monopolist in fixing the price of the commodity. He should not fix a high price; otherwise he will take away certain amount of consumer's surplus.

(iv) It is used in the comparison of standard of living of people in different countries. More the amount of consumer's surplus, the condition of people will be better.

(v) It measures the gains from international trade. If the goods are imported at a lower price for which consumers are prepared to pay higher price, then there will be more consumer's surplus; and gains from trade will also be more.

2.6.5 Criticisms: The concept of consumer's surplus is criticized by many economists like J.R. Hicks and R.G.D. Allen. The important criticisms are:

(i) Utility is subjective factor. It cannot be measured.

(ii) Marginal utility of money cannot remain constant.

(iii) The consumer's surplus is meaningless in case of necessaries like water, petrol, food, etc. The consumers have to pay any price for such goods and the consumer's surplus will be infinite.

(iv) It is not applicable to prestige-goods.

(v) The concept is a "useless theoretical toy with no practical significance". It is imaginary with no empirical evidence.

However, the doctrine of consumer's surplus has continued to be a source of controversy for economists. Therefore Paul Samuelson remarks that "the subject of historical interest, with limited amount of appeal as a purely mathematical puzzle".

2.7 ENGEL'S LAW OF CONSUMPTION

Ernest Engel was the Head of the Prussian Statistical Bureau. He studied a good number of family budgets or standard of living and arrived at some conclusions. These conclusions are called Engel's Law of Consumption. This law was developed in Europe but it has a universal application.

2.7.1 Statement: Engel's law of consumption states:

(i) As income of the consumers increases, the percentage of expenditure on necessaries of life decreases and on contrary as income decreases the percentage of expenditure on necessaries of life increases.

(ii) Percentage of expenditure on luxuries and other recreational and cultural wants increases with an increase income and decreases when income decreases.

(iii) Percentage of expenditure in rent, fuel and light remains the same for all levels of income.

(iv) Whatever may be the income, the percentage expenditure on clothing is practically the same.

However, it should be carefully noted that it is the percentage of expenditure increase or decrease in the family budget but not the total amount of expenditure.

2.7.2 Explanation: Engel's Law can be explained with a typical family budget study. Family budget reflects standard of living. "A family budget is a statement which shows how family income is spent on various items of expenditure on necessaries, comforts, luxuries and other cultural wants."

A typical family budget of a person with monthly income of ₹ 1000 is shown in following Table 2.7.

Table 2.7: Engel's Law of Consumption

Item	Expenditure (in ₹)	Percentage
Food	750	75.0
Fuel	65	6.5
Clothing	70	7.0
House Rent	50	5.0
Lighting	15	1.5
Children's Education	10	1.0
Medical Aid	05	0.5
Traveling	04	0.4
Social Ceremonies	16	1.6
Luxuries and Entertainment	05	0.5
Miscellaneous	15	1.5
Total	1000	100

The study of above family budget, presents some conclusions. They are as follows:

(a) Small percentage of income is spent on education, social ceremonies, traveling, entertainment and luxuries.

(b) Expenditure on lighting and medical aid is negligible.

(c) Seven per cent of income is spent on dress and 6.5 per cent on fuel.

(d) The biggest item of expenditure is food, i.e. 75 per cent of income.

However, according to Engel's law of consumption it is poor man's budget is a typical one:

(i) wherein about 3/4 of income goes to food alone, and

(ii) practically negligible part of income is spent on medical aid, education or recreation.

Therefore, the studies of family budgets of rich and poor within India or outside bear the Engel's law and its conclusions. The percentage of expenditure may slightly vary but the conclusions hold well. "A very large percentage of the small incomes go to the purchase of necessaries of life whereas people with large incomes spend a small percentage of their income on these things. In case of luxuries, the case is quite opposite."

2.7.3 Importance:

(i) The Engel's Law of consumption has practical importance to the householders, economists, legislators, social reformers, etc.

(ii) The law has enabled the government agencies to study family budgets in order to formulate proper policies.

(iii) The law gives an idea to the householder to balance his expenditure over various goods to get maximum satisfaction.

(iv) It enlightens legislators and social reformers about the pattern of consumption by the people in the country; and the balancing of consumption expenditure for the welfare and better life.

(v) It guides wage policy of government and producers.

2.8 MODEL QUESTIONS

2 Marks Questions

(a) What is utility?

(b) What is marginal utility?

(c) Give the difference between Total Utility and Marginal Utility.

(d) Name any two forms of utility.

(e) Name Marshall's two laws of utility.

(f) Give the statement of Law of Diminishing Marginal Utility.

(g) Give the statement of Law of Equi-Marginal Utility.

(h) Name any two exceptions of Law of Diminishing Marginal Utility.

(i) State any two exceptions of Law of Equi-Marginal Utility.

(j) What do you mean by consumer's surplus?

(k) State Engel's Law of Consumption.

5 Marks Questions

1. Write a short note on forms of utility.
2. Write a short note on Total Utility and Marginal Utility.
3. Engel's Law of Consumption.
4. Give a brief account on Consumer's Surplus.
5. What are the limitations of Law of Diminishing Marginal Utility?
6. What are the assumptions of Law of Equi-Marginal Utility?

10 Marks Questions

1. Define Utility. Explain its forms and concepts.
2. Define Utility. Explain its features.
3. Explain the Law of Diminishing Marginal Utility
4. Explain the Law of Equi-Marginal Utility.
5. Discuss the Consumer's Surplus.
6. Discuss the Engel's Law of Consumption.

Notes

1. Util: A Unit or a yardstick to measure utility. It is used by Alfred Marshall.
2. Cardinal: Number expressing.
3. Ordinal: Ordinal number like 1st, 2nd, etc.
4. Negative slope: It refers to movement of a curve downwards from left to the right.

3

Consumption and Demand Analysis

3.1 CONSUMPTION ANALYSIS

Consumption is an important branch of economics. It is a centre point of economics.

3.1.1 Meaning and Definition of Consumption:

Meaning: The term consumption is derived from the word consummate. In the ordinary language the term consumption means destruction of utility present in a commodity. But in economics 'consumption' refers to the use of goods and services to satisfy human wants.

Definitions: The following are some of the important definitions of consumption:

- Prof. Ely defines consumption as "consumption in its broadest sense means the use of economic goods and personal services in the satisfaction of human wants".
- Prof. S.E. Thomas defines consumption as "Consumption is the exhaustion or destruction of utilities".
- J.M. Keynes defines consumption in more precise way: "It is the sole end and object of all economic activity."

3.1.2 Characteristics or Features of Consumption: The important characteristics of consumption are as follows:

(i) **It refers to use of economic goods and services:** Consumption refers only to the use of economic goods and services and not free goods because consumption always involves expenditure.

(ii) **It is destruction of utility:** Consumption is the destruction of utility present in a commodity in the process of satisfying wants. It means if the utility of any commodity is destroyed without satisfying a human want, it is not consumption.

(iii) **It changes the form of matter:** Consumption results into change in the form of the matter. It does not mean the destruction of matter. It relates only to the destruction of utility, which is found in the matter. For example, when raw jute is used for production of gunny bags, the matter is not destroyed; only the form is changed from raw jute to a gunny bag.

(iv) **It may be beneficial or harmful:** Consumption may be beneficial or harmful to human beings depending upon the type of wants satisfied. If the satisfaction of any human want is helpful to them that act of consumption is said to be beneficial. For example, the consumption of fruits, milk, fresh vegetables, food, etc. If the satisfaction of any want is harmful to health, it is case of harmful consumption. For example, consumption of alcohol, opium and other narcotic drugs.

(v) **It is a basis of all economic activities:** Consumption is the basis of all economic activities. It is beginning as well as end of all economic activities. It is a well-known fact that the existence of human wants is the starting point of all economic activities. Hence, consumption is the basis of all economic activities.

3.1.3 Types of Consumption: Consumption can be classified into three types. They are: (i) Direct consumption, (ii) Indirect consumption, and (iii) Destructive consumption.

(i) **Direct consumption:** When a commodity or a service is directly used to satisfy a human want it is called direct consumption. In brief, direct consumption is the consumption of consumer goods. For example, food, clothes, books, motorcars, pens, etc. The services of doctors, lawyers, and teachers also satisfy human wants directly. The direct consumption is also called final consumption.

(ii) **Indirect Consumption:** When commodities or services satisfy human wants indirectly it is called indirect consumption. Some articles will help for production of other articles, which will give us direct satisfaction. For ex: Machines and raw materials. If direct consumption is the consumption of consumer goods, indirect consumption is the consumption of capital goods. Capital goods help for production of consumer goods. For Ex: The printing machine will not satisfy wants directly but the books and magazines printed by it satisfy human wants directly. The indirect consumption is also called productive consumption.

(iii) **Destructive Consumption:** When goods are destroyed by fire, floods, earthquakes, etc. they are regarded as destructive consumption. In other words if the utility of any commodity is destroyed without satisfying a human want is called destructive consumption. The consumption of harmful luxuries such as alcoholic drinks, drugs, and opium is a case of destructive consumption.

3.1.4 Importance of Consumption: Consumption is the yardstick to measure the economic activities in a country. Consumption determines demand and standard of living. It is the secret of all economic progress. The importance of consumption can be discussed as:

(a) **It is an important phase of human life.** There are 'three' important phases in human life-cycle. They are: (1) Production, (2) Distribution, and (3) Consumption. Since consumption is one of the important phases of human life-cycle, it occupies an important place in economics.

(b) **It is beginning as well as end of all economic activities:** It is a beginning because consumption or satisfaction of wants gives rise to economic activities. It is an end because goods and services produced are finally consumed for the satisfaction of human wants.

(c) **It decides the pattern of production:** Consumption determines the pattern of production. In capitalist economy consumers determine what to be produced and what not to be produced. Consumer is the king in a capitalist economy. He guides the entire economic activity.

(d) **It determines the volume of production:** Consumption determines the volume of production. It decides what is to be produced and how much to be produced. Greater the amount of consumption higher will be the volume of production. It means things, which are demanded most will be produced in larger quantity.

(e) **It determines the size of income and employment:** Consumption determines the level of employment, income and standard of living of people. Consumption invites the producers to undertake investment that generates income and employment.

3.1.5 Consumer's Choice: Consumer has unlimited wants but limited resources so he cannot satisfy all his wants. He faces the problem of choice between different wants as well as between different uses of resources. He always chooses rationally. He prefers to satisfy the most urgent wants.

3.1.6 Consumer's Choice and Sovereignty: Every producer produces the things demanded by consumers. Production is complete only when things produced are sold profitably. Thus it is consumers who direct all productive activities and the distribution of economic resources between different productive activities. Therefore production is controlled and regulated by consumers. Consumers reveal their choices to producers through price mechanism that guides the producer. Hence Prof. Benham said that the consumer is the king.

3.1.7 Limitations of Consumer's Sovereignty: Consumer's sovereignty suffers from certain limitations as under:

(i) **Consumer does not behave always rationally:** It is presumed that the consumer behaves rationally. But it is not so because in reality he may be ignorant of many things. He faces problems like shortage of time, lack of ability to judge the things, lack of information, etc. Thus it may curtail his sovereignty.

(ii) **Productive ability is limited:** In a capitalist economy the sovereignty of the consumer is limited by the productive capacity of the community. The productive resources are limited in relation to the demand.

(iii) **Techniques of production influence on consumers' freedom:** The technique of production also has its effect on consumer's sovereignty. The consumers get only those goods that are made available by technology.

(iv) **Consumers have only limited income:** Income limits the consumer's sovereignty. He spends goods and services to the limit of his income.

(v) **Monopoly element in the market limits the freedom:** Under perfect competition the consumer enjoys freedom. But under monopoly he does not enjoy absolute freedom, because he has no choice. He has to accept the commodity produced by the monopolist.

(vi) **Government's Restrictions control consumer's freedom:** Consumer sovereignty is also curtailed by the restrictions of the government. For ex: Government may impose restrictions on the consumption of certain harmful drugs, opium, tobacco, etc.

(vii) **Tax policy also curtails consumer's freedom:** The direct and indirect taxes imposed by the government will also curtail the consumer's sovereignty. When taxes are imposed by the government, it reduces the purchasing power of people.

(viii) **The war period controls curtail consumers' choice:** During war period the government measures like rationing and control curtail the consumer sovereignty. Rationing and control imply the distribution of essential commodities in limited quantities to each individual or family.

3.2 MEANING OF DEMAND

In ordinary language, a demand means 'Desire' to have goods and services or something. But it is not so in economics. Demand is considered as one of the two forces of market or economy.

Alfred Marshall, in his theory of value, compared demand and supply to the two blades of a scissors. It means both play equally important role in determination of price at commodity market.

3.2.1 Definition of Demand: Mere desire for a commodity is not demand in economics. According to economists, demand means (a) a desire backed by willingness and ability to pay (b) demand is always related to price and time. Thus economists defined demand as "The quantity of a commodity will be bought per unit of price at a particular time." For example, a person demands a cup of tea at ₹ 5 per cup.

3.2.2 Demand Schedule: The tabular statement showing the different quantities of demand at different prices of a commodity during a given period of time is called demand schedule. There are two types of demand schedule: (i) Individual Demand Schedule and (ii) Market Demand Schedule.

(i) **Individual Demand Schedule:** Individual Demand Schedule is a tabular statement showing the quantities purchased by an individual consumer at various level of price in a given period of time. A hypothetical individual demand schedule is illustrated as:

Table 3.1: Individual Demand Schedule

Price of Apple (₹)	Quantity Demanded by Individual Consumer
5	10
4	20
3	30
2	40
1	50

Individual consumer demands more at low price, less at higher price.

(ii) **Market Demand Schedule:** Market Demand is a sum of individual demand of all buyers in the market. Market Demand Schedule is a tabular statement showing the quantities of a commodity demanded in aggregate by all the buyers in a market in a given period of time. It is illustrated as in Table 3.2.

Table 3.2: Market Demand Schedule

Price of Apple (₹)	Quantity Demanded by Consumer 'A'	Quantity Demanded by Consumer 'B'	Quantity of Market Demand (A+B)
5	10	15	25
4	15	20	35
3	20	25	45
2	25	30	55
1	30	35	65

Assuming that there are two consumers namely 'A' and 'B' in the market. When price per apple is ₹ 5 'A' purchased 10 and 'B' 15 apples so the market demand is 25 apples.

Market Demand = A's Demand + B's Demand

MD = IDa + IDb +... IDn

MD = Σ IDn

where, n = number of consumers in the market.

MD = 10+15= 25.

3.2.3 Demand Curve: The curve that represents the demand schedule is called 'Demand Curve'. Individual demand schedule helps to draw individual demand curve and the market demand schedule helps to draw the market demand curve. It is illustrated in the following diagram 3.1.

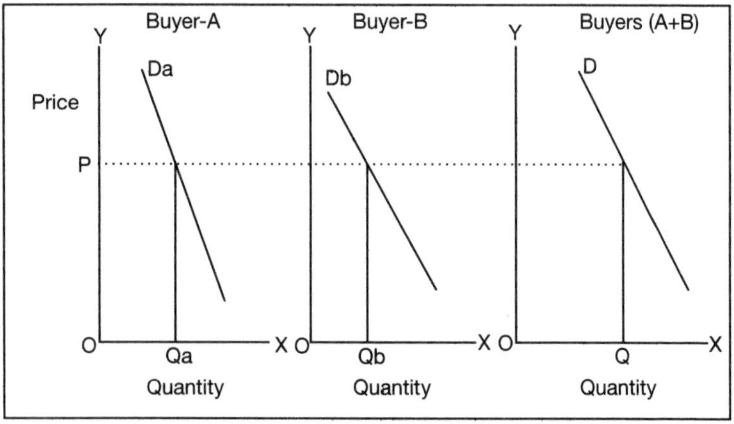

Diagram 3.1: Individual and Market Demand Curves

Price is measured along OY axis and quantity demanded along OX axis. Da is buyer-A's demand curve, Db is buyer-B's demand curve and D is the market demand curve.

Market Demand = Individual demand of buyer 'A' plus individual demand of buyer 'B'.

$$OQ = OQa + OQb$$

It means when the price of a commodity is OP buyer A's demand is OQa, buyer B's demand is OQb and the market demand is OQ.

3.3 TYPES OF DEMAND

There are various types of demand. The most important types of demand are discussed as under:

3.3.1 Joint Demand and Composite Demand: Joint demand exists in case of complementary goods. Whenever a good is jointly demanded with some other good, it is called as joint demand. For example, demand for fountain pen also means demand for ink; demand for cars gives rise to demand for petrol, etc.

Composite demand means a commodity may be demanded for many purposes. It is composed of demand for many purposes or several uses. For example, coal has composite demand because it is demanded for household use, transportation and electricity generation. So is the case with demand for steel, water and electricity, etc.

3.3.2 Direct Demand and Derived Demand: Direct demand means demand for the final product for the purpose of consumption. On the other hand derived demand is the demand for a product which is demanded to produce another product. For instance, the demand for a house is a direct demand and demand for bricks is a derived demand.

3.3.3 Consumers Demand and Producers Demand: Consumers demand means the demand for various goods and services by the consumers for consumption purpose e.g.: demand for umbrella, books, milk, biscuits, TV, etc. Producers demand is a demand by the producers for further production of other goods e.g. demands for raw materials, machineries, equipments, etc.

3.3.4 Individual Demand and Market Demand: Individual demand is the demand for goods by an individual consumer whereas market demand is the summation of individual demands in a given market.

Market demand = A's demand + B's demand + C's demand....

3.4 LAW OF DEMAND

Law of Demand is one of the important laws in economics. The law that explains the functional relation between demand and price is called 'Law of Demand'. In other words the law of demand is a general statement of the relationship between price of the commodity and its quantity demanded. It shows consumer's normal demand behaviour in relation to price variation.

3.4.1 Statement of Law: The law of demand states that "Other things being equal, people demand larger quantity of goods and services only at a lower price than at a higher price". The law explains the inverse relationship between two variables—price and quantity demanded of the commodity. When price rises demand falls and when price falls demand rises. The relation between price and quantity of demand is usually an inverse or negative relation.

3.4.2 Assumptions: The law is always stated with "other things being equal" that is *ceteris paribus* assumptions. It includes:

(i) Income of the consumer should remain constant.

(ii) Taste, fashion and habits of the consumer should remain unchanged.

(iii) Prices of related goods, i.e. substitutes and complementary goods should remain constant.

(iv) Production of substitutes should remain unchanged.

(v) There should not be prestige value for the product in question and

(vi) There is no change in government policies like taxation.

3.4.3 Illustration of the Law: Generally the law of demand is referred to market demand. The law of demand can be illustrated with the help of a demand schedule. The law of demand states the inverse relation between price and demand which is explained with the help of demand schedule as under in Table 3.3.

Table 3.3: Law of Demand

Price per unit (₹)	Quantity Demanded (Units)
5	30
4	50
3	70
2	100
1	120

The above table explains the law of demand: as price falls from ₹ 5 to 4, 3, so on the demand rises from 30 units to 50, 70, so on and in contrary demand falls with every rise in price.

With the help of Table 3.3 the law is presented graphically as below:

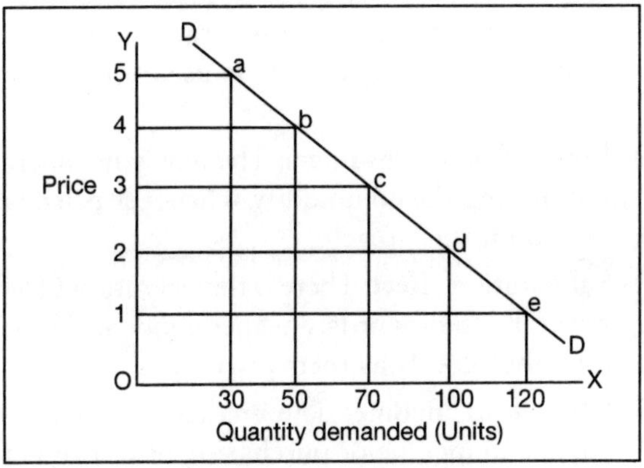

Diagram 3.2: Law of Demand

Price is measured along OY axis and quantity demanded along OX axis. When price is ₹ 1, the quantity demanded is 120 units; when the price is ₹ 5, the demand is 30 units. When corresponding points of price and quantity demanded like a, b, c, d, and e are joined, we get a demand curve like DD. Demand curve is, thus, a locus of points. In this diagram demand curve is shown as a straight-line. It can also be in the form of a curve. Demand Curve DD explains the inverse relation between demand and price, i.e. law of demand.

3.4.4 Why does Demand Curve Slope Downwards from Left to the Right: The demand curve always slopes downwards from left to the right. It has a negative slope. It shows an inverse relationship between price and quantity demanded. The reasons for why the demand curve slopes downwards from left to the right are:

(i) **Application of the law of diminishing marginal utility:** There is an inverse relationship between price and quantity demand of the commodity. Behind demand curve, there is the law of diminishing marginal utility. For example, if price falls, the consumer purchases one more unit to increase his total utility by equalizing price and marginal utility.

(ii) **Goods have several uses:** Demand curve has negative slope because whenever the price rises, the consumer will use the goods for most urgent uses; and when the price falls, the commodity is used for even less urgent uses.

(iii) **Entry of new consumers:** The new consumers will start purchasing the commodity whenever price falls. It will be within their reach.

(iv) **Substitution effect:** There is the operation of substitution effect. In other words, cheaper goods will be substituted for other goods as their price falls.

(v) **Change in income:** The change in price results into change in income or purchasing power of consumer so it effects on demand.

3.4.5 Exceptions to the Law of Demand and Criticisms: Generally consumers buy fewer goods when price rises and buy more when price falls. However, there are some exceptional cases when demand rises with rise in price and demand falls with fall in price. Following are the few exceptions:

(i) **Giffen goods:** In case of some inferior goods, even if the price falls, there will be less demand. The law of demand does not apply to such cases. Sir Robert Giffen explored this behaviour of consumers. According to him generally people prefer superior goods when the price of inferior goods falls. Such typical inferior goods are called 'Giffen goods'. This situation is called 'Giffen's Paradox.

(ii) **Prestige-goods:** There are some goods, which are status symbol goods. Rich just for show or distinction demand them e.g.: Diamonds, rare collections, paintings, etc. For such goods, higher the price higher will be the demand for them.

(iii) **Fear of shortage:** During the conditions of fear of shortage, people start stocking goods at any price.

For example, during war- time, riots and disturbances, etc. people become panicky and start buying even at higher price for future security.

(iv) **Speculation:** The law is not applicable to speculative activities. The best example for speculation is the share market. When the prices of shares show a rising tendency, traders will try to purchase more and when prices are falling they try to purchase less. There is an objective of making profits due to speculation.

In addition to the exceptions, the law of demand does not hold good where and when its assumptions are not applicable. Its assumptions are also unrealistic. So the law of demand is criticized.

3.4.6 Importance of Law of Demand:

(a) The law is helpful to the producers to fix the prices in the market. The demand schedule gives an idea about various prices and demand. He can decide the most profitable position.

(b) The law helps the finance minister to frame taxation policy. Finance minister has to calculate the effect of tax on a commodity. When tax is imposed, price rises there may be less demand and the revenue to government may be reduced. On the other hand when the tax is reduced, it may lead to rise in government revenue.

3.5 CHANGES IN DEMAND

There are two types of changes in demand. They are: (i) extension or expansion and contraction of demand, (ii) increase and decrease in demand.

The extension or contraction of demand is related to fall or rise in price which is shown on the same demand curve. The extension and contraction of demand concepts are concerned with the changes in quantity demanded.

Changes in demand referred to increase or decrease in demand due to changes in demand-determinants like price, income, etc. The increase or decrease in demand is shown by shift in demand curve to the left or right side of the existing demand curve.

3.5.1 Extension and Contraction of Demand: Extension in demand means a situation where more quantity of a commodity is demanded at a lower price. It is illustrated in the following diagram 3.3.

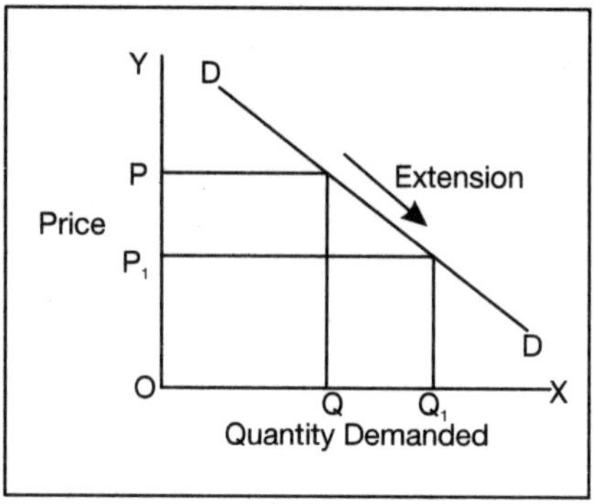

Diagram 3.3: Extension of Demand

Price is measured along with OY axis and quantity demanded along OX axis. DD is the demand curve. When the price of the commodity is OP, the demand for that commodity is OQ. When the price falls from OP to OP_1, the demand will be OQ_1. With a fall in the price of a commodity the quantity demanded is more, i.e. QQ_1. It is called the extension of demand.

Contraction of demand means a situation where lesser quantity of a commodity is demanded when price increases. It is explained in the following diagram 3.4.

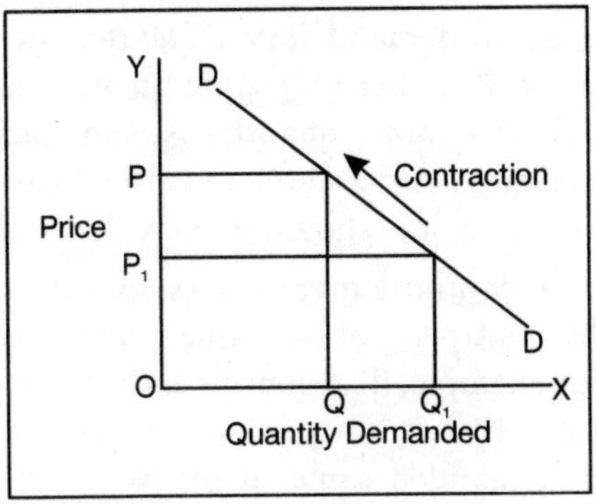

Diagram 3.4: Contraction of Demand

In the above diagram, when the price of the commodity increases from OP to OP_1, the demand declines from OQ to OQ_1. It is called contraction of demand.

3.5.2 Increase and Decrease in Demand: Increase in demand means more quantity is demanded at the same price or the same quantity is demanded at a higher price. For Example: (i) a consumer purchased more milk than before due to increase in his income or (ii) A consumer purchased same quantity of milk even at high price to meet his necessity. This is explained in the following diagram 3.5.

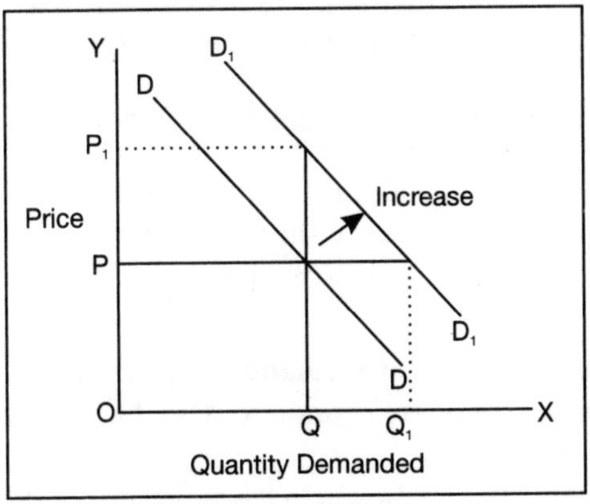

Diagram 3.5: Increase in Demand

DD is the original demand curve. The quantity demanded is OQ when price is OP. Either OQ same quantity is demanded at high price OP_1 or OQ_1 more quantity is demanded at the same price OP so the demand curve shifts upward which is right-side to the base demand curve, it is shown by new demand curve D_1D_1.

Decrease in demand means less quantity of goods is demanded at the same price or the same quantity is demanded at a lower price. For example, (i) A consumer demanded less quantity of milk than before even at low price due to change in his taste or (ii) a consumer demanded same quantity of milk even at low price because it is necessary. It is explained in the following diagram 3.6.

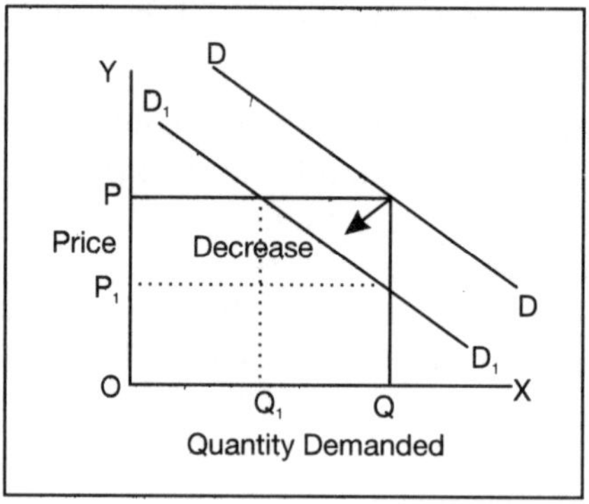

Diagram 3.6: Decrease in Demand

DD is the original demand curve. The quantity demanded is OQ when price is OP. Either OQ same quantity is demanded at low price OP_1 or OQ_1 less quantity is demanded at the same price OP so the demand curve shifts downward which is left-side to the base demand curve, it is shown by new demand curve D_1D_1.

3.5.3 Determinants of Demand: The demand is determined by many factors. They are economic, social and political factors. They are as follows:

(i) **Change in income:** The income of the consumer determines the demand for goods and services. If income increases, the demand may increase and if the income decreases the demand may also decrease.

(ii) **Prices of related goods:** The demand for a particular good depends upon the relative change in the price of related goods. The related goods may be complementary goods or substitutes. For ex: Demand for coffee depends on price of tea.

(iii) **Change in fashion:** The fashions and tastes of the consumers will determine the demand. A change in the fashion or taste may lead to fall in demand for some goods and sudden rise in demand for some other goods.

(iv) **Population:** The size of the population and its growth rate determine demand for goods. Increase or decrease in the size of population results into rise or fall in the demand for goods and services.

(v) **Change in climate:** Climatic conditions determine the demand for goods. For example: during summer season the demand for fans is more. On the other hand the demand for warm clothes will be more during the winter season.

(vi) **Taxation:** The Taxation policy of the government affects the demand for goods. If tax rate is increased on a particular commodity, the price increases and the demand may decrease; a cut in the tax rate may increase the demand for goods.

(vii) **Technical progress:** The advancement in science and technology leads to many innovations. New things will enter the market. The demand for outdated goods will decrease.

(viii) **Advertisement:** Nowaday the demand is influenced by the advertisements and propaganda. Advertisement creates fresh demand for goods. At present almost all goods and services are advertised extensively through several Medias like TV, Radio, and Press, etc.

3.5.4 Demand Function: The functional relationship between demand for a commodity and its various determinants is known as 'Demand Function'. It can be expressed mathematically as:

$$Dx = f(Px, Pr, Y, T, G, A, U)$$

where, Dx = quantity demanded for commodity 'x'

f = functional relation

Px = Price of commodity 'x'

Pr = Price of related goods like substitutes and complementary goods.

Y = Money income of the consumer

T = Taste of the consumer

G = Government budget policy

A = Effects of advertisement

U = Other unknown variables

It is multi-variables demand function.

To explain the law of demand, generally a simple demand function stated is:

$$\mathbf{Dx = f\ (Px)}$$

where, Dx = quantity demanded for commodity 'x'

f = functional relation

Px = Price of commodity 'x'

It is single variable demand function.

Demand Equation: A single variable demand function may be stated mathematically as:

$$\mathbf{D = a - b\ (P)}$$

where, D = Demand for commodity

a = Constant parameter signifying maximum quantity of demand when price is zero.

b = a parameter representing the ratio between change in demand to change in price.

P = price of commodity.

For example, when a = 200, b = 0.5, and P = 20

$\therefore$ Demand = D = 200 – (0.5 × 20)

= 200 – 10 = 190.

The nature of parameter 'b' determines the type of demand function. If 'b' is variable, the demand function will be 'Non

Linear Demand Function'. If 'b' is constant, the demand function will be Linear Demand Function.

3.6 ELASTICITY OF DEMAND

Demand is sensitive to change in its determinants so the sensitivity of demand is called 'Elasticity of Demand'. But generally the sensitivity of demand to change in price is known as 'Elasticity of Demand'. It is studied in details as under:

3.6.1 Meaning and Definitions of Elasticity of Demand: Economists Cournot and J.S. Mill evolved the concept of Elasticity of Demand. But it was Dr. Alfred Marshall who did much to develop this concept and hence it is associated with his name. Elasticity of Demand refers to the sensitiveness or responsiveness of demand to changes in price. It shows by how much the quantity demanded of a commodity changes in response to a given change in its price. In other words, Elasticity of Demand shows quantitative relationship between the two magnitudes i.e. between the price of a commodity and its quantity demanded by a consumer. It shows what percentage change in the quantity demanded of a good occurs as a result of a certain percentage change in its price. Hence Elasticity of Demand is a measure of expansion and contraction in demand in response to a given change in price.

Like the price, other factors such as taste and fashion, habits, income, expectation regarding the future, seasons, prices of related goods also influence the demand for a good. Assuming all these other factors as constant, the demand for a commodity is the function of its price. Therefore we can relate a change in quantity demanded of the commodity directly and solely to the change in the price. We see that the demand for some goods is highly sensitive to price changes, some other are less sensitive or not sensitive at all. Since the degree of sensitivity of demand to changes in price is different for different goods, we speak of highly elastic, less elastic and inelastic demand.

Economists have defined elasticity of demand in various ways. Some important definitions are:

(i) Alfred Marshall defines Elasticity of Demand as, "the elasticity (or responsiveness) of demand in a market is great or small according as the amount demanded increases much or little for a given fall in price and diminishes much or little for a given rise in price".

(ii) Stonier and Hague defines elasticity of demand as "Elasticity of Demand is, therefore, a technical term used by the economists to describe the degree of responsiveness of demand for a commodity to a fall in its price".

(iii) A.L. Meyers defines elasticity of demand as "Elasticity of Demand is a measure of the relative change in amount purchased in response to a relative change in price on a given demand curve".

All these definitions pinpoint that the degree or proportion of change in demand due to a given change in price. Thus "the term elasticity expresses the degree of correlation between demand and price".

3.6.2 Concept of Elasticity of Demand:

Elasticity of Demand can be expressed in form of following formula or equation:

$$\text{Elasticity of Demand} = \frac{\text{Proportionate Change in Quantity Demanded}}{\text{Proportionate Change in Price}}$$

$$e_d = \frac{\Delta Q/Q}{\Delta P/P} = \frac{\Delta Q}{Q} \div \frac{\Delta P}{P} = \frac{\Delta Q}{Q} \times \frac{P}{\Delta P}$$

3.7 TYPES OF ELASTICITY OF DEMAND

Economists generally distinguish four types of Elasticity of Demand. They are: (i) price elasticity of demand, (ii) income elasticity of demand, and (iii) cross elasticity of demand. They are studied as:

3.7.1 Price Elasticity of Demand: Price elasticity refers to the percentage change in the quantity demanded of a good divided by the percentage change in price. It is the ratio of a relative change in quantity demanded to a relative change in price. Price elasticity of demand establishes a functional relationship between two variables i.e. changes in price and the consequent changes in the quantity demanded. Price elasticity is the most important among different types of elasticity. Mr. Robinson defined price elasticity as, "the proportionate change in quantity demanded in response to a small change in price".

3.7.2 Concepts of Price Elasticity of Demand: Price Elasticity of Demand has five concepts or types. Alfred Marshall used the concept of Elasticity of Demand with reference to price changes and his concept of Elasticity of Demand is referred to as price elasticity. It is the measure of a relative change in quantity purchased of a good in response to a relative change in its price.

It is the measure of a relative change in quantity purchased of a good in response to a relative change in its price. Hence we can say that Elasticity of Demand is the percentage change in quantity demanded divided by the percentage change in price. The price elasticity of demand is expressed in the following formula:

$$e_p = \frac{\text{Proportionate Change in Quantity Demanded}}{\text{Proportionate Change in Price}}$$

$$e_p = \frac{\Delta Q/Q}{\Delta P/P} = \frac{\Delta Q}{Q} \div \frac{\Delta P}{P} = \frac{\Delta Q}{Q} \times \frac{P}{\Delta P}$$

e_p = Price Elasticity of Demand
Q = Quantity Demanded
P = Price
Δ = Change

Price elasticity of demand can be calculated with help of numerical example as:

Q_1 = 100 units
Q_2 = 200 units
P_1 = ₹ 4
P_2 = ₹ 2

$$\therefore e_p = \frac{\Delta Q/Q}{\Delta P/P} = \frac{\Delta Q}{Q} \div \frac{\Delta P}{P} = \frac{\Delta Q}{\Delta P} \times \frac{P}{Q} \text{ (by substituting the values)}$$

$$= \frac{Q_2 - Q_1}{Q_1} \div \frac{P_2 - P_1}{P_1} = \frac{200 - 100}{100} \div \frac{2 - 4}{2}$$

$$= \frac{\not{100}\,1}{\not{100}\,1} \times \frac{\not{2}\,1}{\not{2}} = 1$$

$$\therefore e_p = 1$$

They are five types or concepts in price elasticity of demand. They are:

(i) **Perfectly Price Elastic Demand:** The demand for a commodity said to be perfectly price elastic when demand changes in numerously or infinitely due to a little change in price of a commodity. So it is written as:

$$e_p = \infty = \text{infinity} = \left(\frac{1}{0}\right)$$

When demand is perfectly elastic the demand curve is a horizontal straight line which is parallel to 'OX' axis. The perfectly elastic demand curve is shown in the following diagram 3.7.

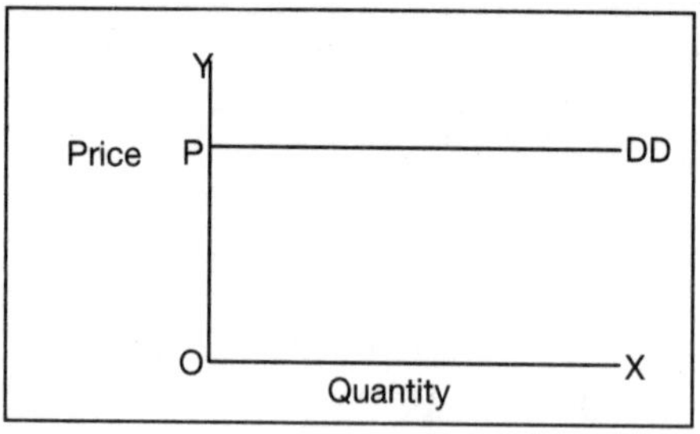

Diagram 3.7: Perfectly Elastic Demand Curve

The perfectly price elasticity of demand is shown by DD curve. It is found in perfect competitive market.

(ii) **Perfectly Price Inelastic Demand:** If demand for a commodity remains unchanged to change in price of a commodity, it is called perfectly inelastic demand or zero elastic demand. It can be written as:

$$e_p = 0\left(= \frac{1}{0}\right)$$

When demand is perfectly inelastic the demand curve is a vertical straight line. The same is shown in the following diagram 3.8.

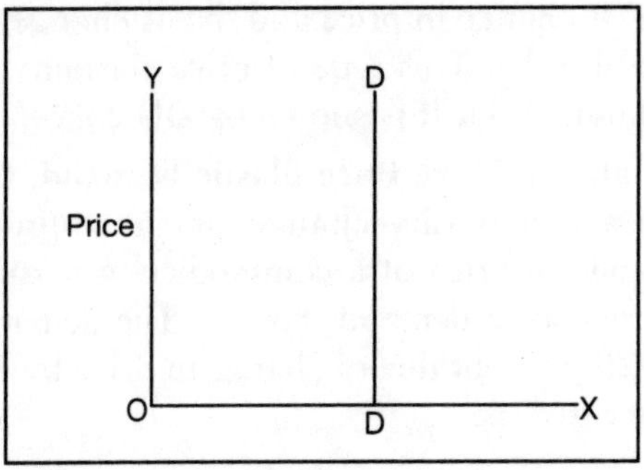

Diagram 3.8: Perfectly Inelastic Demand Curve

The demand curve DD1 is perfectly inelastic. In case of life-saving drugs or essentials of life, the price elasticity of demand is equal to zero.

(iii) **Unitary Price Elastic Demand:** If demand for a commodity changes in equal proportion to change in price, it is called unitary elastic demand. For ex: Demand changed by 10 per cent due to change in price by 10 per cent. It can be expressed as:

$$e_p = 1\left(\frac{10 \text{ per cent}}{10 \text{ per cent}}\right)$$

When elasticity of demand is equal to unity, the demand curve is straight line and diagonal. It is shown in the following diagram 3.9.

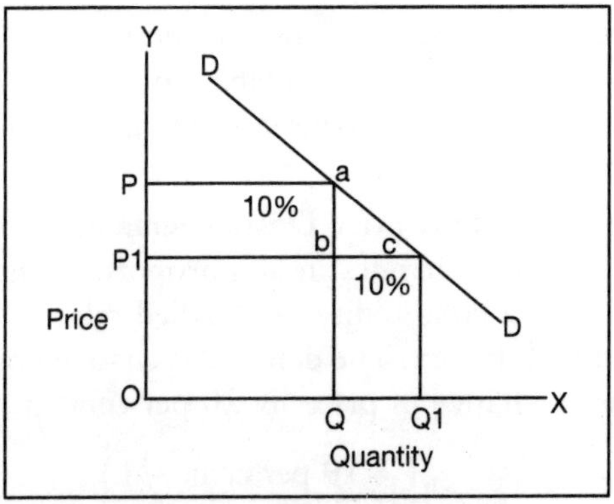

Diagram 3.9: Unitary Elastic Demand Curve

Here 'ab' is change in price and 'bc' is change in demand so bc/ab = 1 or ab = bc. This type of price elasticity of demand is found rarely in market. It is shown by DD curve.

(v) **Relatively More Price Elastic Demand:** If the demand for a commodity changes in more proportion than change in price of a commodity, it is called relatively more elastic demand. For ex: The demand is changed by 20 per cent due to change in price by 10 per cent. It is written as:

$$e_p > 1\left(= \frac{20 \text{ per cent}}{10 \text{ per cent}} = \frac{2}{1}\right)$$

The relatively more price elastic demand is shown in the following diagram 3.10.

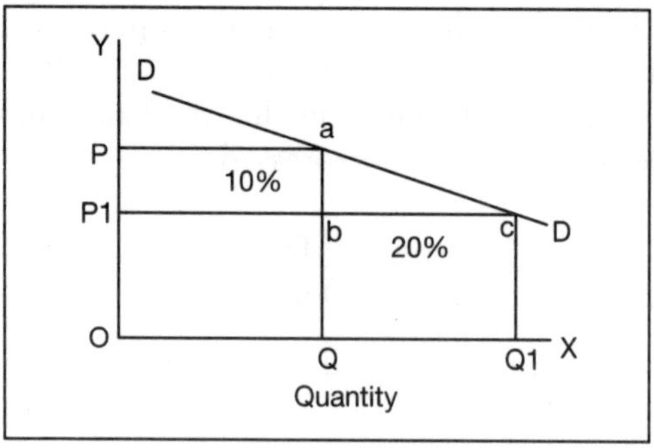

Diagram 3.10: Relatively More Price Elastic Demand

The demand is relatively more elastic which shown by DD curve. It is a flatter curve. Here bc/ab >1 or bc > ab. It is found in monopolistic competitive market and of comfort and luxurious goods and services.

(v) **Relatively Less Price Elastic Demand:** If demand for a commodity changes in less proportion than change in price of a commodity, it is called relatively less elastic demand. For ex: The demand is changed by 10 per cent due to change in price by 20 per cent. It is written as:

$$e_p < 1\left(= \frac{10 \text{ per cent}}{20 \text{ per cent}} = \frac{1}{2}\right)$$

In this case even a high percentage change in the price of a good leads to only a small percentage change in the quantity demanded. Here the demand curve is steeper. It is shown in the following diagram 3.11.

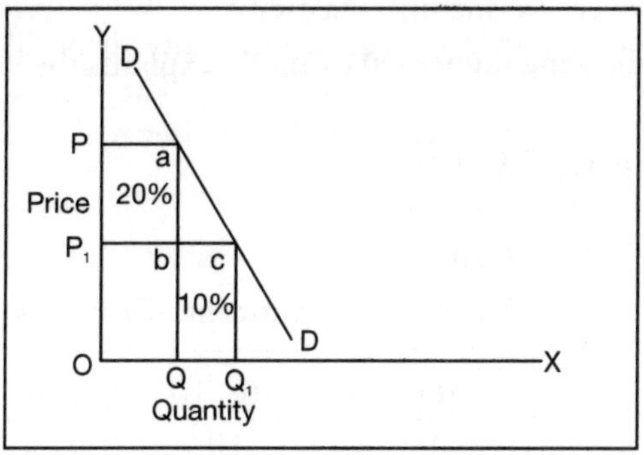

Diagram 3.11: Relatively Less Price Elastic Demand

Here the elasticity of demand is less than one i.e. bc < ab or bc/ab < 1. It is mainly found in monopoly market and of necessary goods and services.

3.7.3 Income Elasticity of Demand: Income is another determinant of demand for goods and services. Any change in income level of the consumer leads to change in the quantity of demand. Generally there is a direct relation between income and demand. Increase in income leads to increase in demand. Income elasticity of demand shows the degree of sensitiveness of quantity demanded of a commodity to a change in the income of the consumer. Income elasticity of demand for a good is the ratio of proportionate change in the purchases of a good to the proportionate change in income.

We can show income elasticity with the help of a formula:

$$\text{Income Elasticity} = e_y = \frac{\text{Proportionate change in the quantity demanded}}{\text{Proportionate change in income}}$$

$$e_y = \frac{\Delta Q/Q}{\Delta Y/Y} = \frac{\Delta Q}{Q} \div \frac{\Delta Y}{Y} = \frac{\Delta Q}{Q} \times \frac{Y}{\Delta Y}$$

where, ΔQ = Change in quantity demanded = 10 units

Q = Original quantity demanded = 50 units

ΔY = Change in income = ₹ 6

Y = Original income = ₹ 3

e_y = Income Elasticity.

The following numerical example explains the income elastic demand.

Q_1 = 10 units

Q_2 = 20 units

Y_1 = ₹ 100

Y_2 = ₹ 200 (by substituting the values)

$$\therefore \quad e_y = \frac{\Delta Q}{Q} \times \frac{Y}{\Delta Y} = \frac{20-10}{10} \times \frac{100}{200-100}$$

$$= \frac{\cancel{10}1}{\cancel{10}1} \times \frac{\cancel{100}1}{\cancel{100}1} = 1$$

So in this example income elasticity is 1.

Like price elasticity of demand, there are five types or concepts of income elasticity of demand. They are studied as under:

(i) **Zero Income Elastic Demand:** The demand for a commodity remains unchanged even if there is change in consumer's income-level, it is called zero income elastic demand. Example: purchases of salt, matchbox, etc. It can be written as: $e_y = 0$. It is shown in the following diagram 3.12.

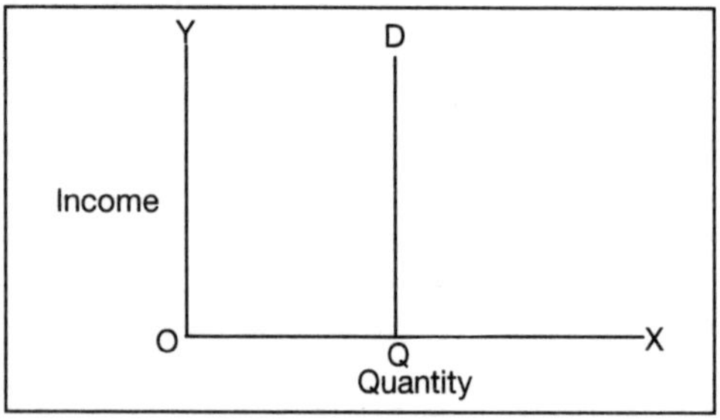

Diagram 3.12: Zero Income Elastic Demand Curve

DD is the zero income elastic demand curve.

(ii) **Negative Income Elasticity of Demand:** Generally consumers scale of preference move from inferior goods to superior goods when improves their income level. This shows a negative relation between income and demand. If increase in income leads to fall in demand, it is called negative income elastic demand. It can be written as: $e_y < 0$.

It is illustrated in the following diagram 3.13.

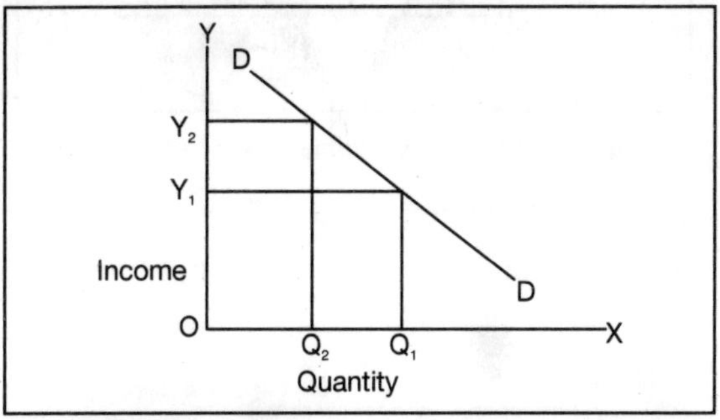

Diagram 3.13: Negative Income Elastic Demand Curve

DD is the negative income demand curve. As income increases from 'Y_1' to 'Y_2', the quantity demanded declines from 'Q_1' to 'Q_2'.

(iii) **Unitary Income Elastic Demand:** If demand changes exactly in proportion to change in income, it is called unitary income elastic demand. For ex: Demand is increased by 10 per cent due to income increased by 10 per cent. It can be expressed as: $e_y = 1$

It can also be illustrated in the following diagram.

DD is unitary income elastic demand curve. Here change in demand (10%) is equal to change in income (10%) i.e. cb = ab.

(iv) **Relatively More Income Elastic Demand:** If a proportionate change in demand is more than proportionate change in income of the consumer is called relatively more income elastic demand. For example, demand for a commodity changed by 20 per cent due to 10 per cent change in income. It is expressed as:

$$e_y > 1$$

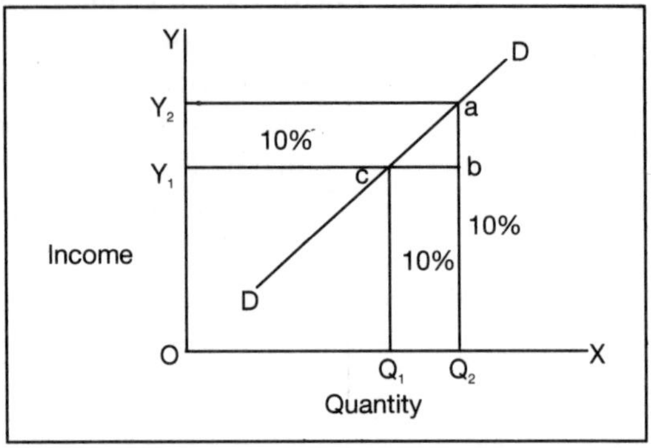

Diagram 3.14: Unitary Income Elastic Demand Curve

It can also be illustrated in the following diagram 3.15.

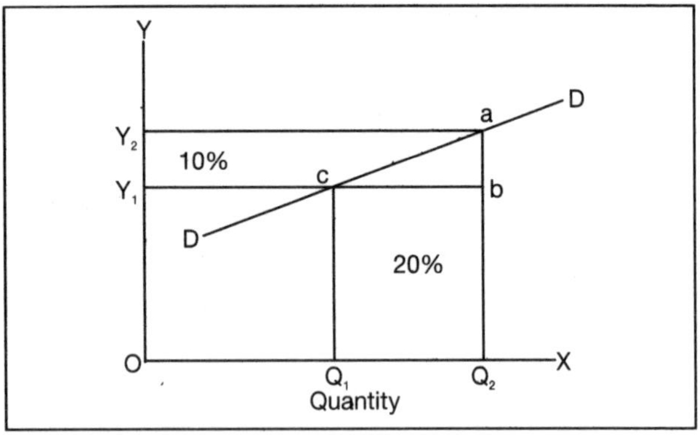

Diagram 3.15: Relatively More Income Elastic Demand Curve

DD is the relatively more income elastic demand curve. Change in demand (20%) is greater than change in income (10%) i.e. cb > ab or cb/ab > 1. Luxuries and comforts are its best examples.

(iv) **Relatively Less Income Elastic Demand:** If a proportionate change in demand for a commodity is less than a proportionate change in income of the consumer is called relatively less income elastic demand. It is written as: $e_y < 1$.

It can also be illustrated in the following diagram 3.16.

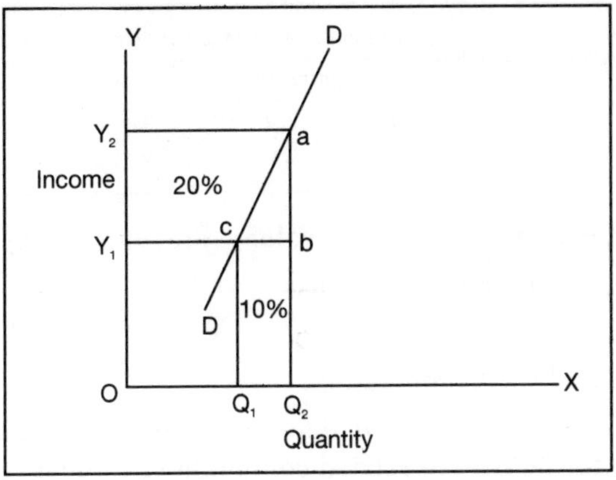

Diagram 3.16: Relatively Less Income Elastic Demand Curve

DD is the relatively less income elastic demand. Change in demand (10%) is less than change in income (20%) i.e.cb < ab. Necessary goods are its suitable examples.

To sum up, $e_y = 1$, $e_y > 1$ and $e_y < 1$ are positive income elastic demand cases. The concept of income elasticity of demand is useful to measure the incidence of taxation.

3.7.4 Cross Elasticity of Demand: The price of related goods is another important determinant of demand for a commodity. For ex: Demand for tea depends upon the price of coffee. There are two types of relations between the goods namely (i) Competitive or Substitution, for example, tea and coffee. (ii) Complementary, for example, petrol and car. There is positive relation between competitive goods and negative relation between complementary goods.

Cross Elasticity of Demand is the type of elasticity of demand. It is concerned with related goods. The proportionate change in demand for X commodity to proportionate change in price of Y commodity is called 'Cross Elasticity of Demand'. For example, demand for tea is increased by 20 per cent due to the price of coffee is declined by 10 per cent.

Cross elasticity of demand can be expressed as:

$$\text{Cross Elasticity of Demand} = \frac{\text{proportionate change in demand for X Commodity}}{\text{Proportionate Change in price of Y Commodity}}$$

$$\therefore e_y = \frac{\Delta Qx/Qx}{\Delta Py/Py} = \frac{\Delta Qx}{Qx} \div \frac{\Delta Py}{Py} = \frac{\Delta Qx}{Qx} \times \frac{Py}{\Delta py}$$

Δ = Change (= Present value – Previous value)

Q = Quantity Demanded

P = Price

x and y = Commodities.

The cross elasticity of demand should be studied with reference to the type of related commodity as under:

(i) **Substitutes or Competitive Goods:** If Tea and Coffee are substitutes, the rise in price of coffee will lead to increase in the demand for tea because the consumers will now substitute coffee for tea. It is the case of positive cross elasticity of demand. It is shown in the following diagram 3.17.

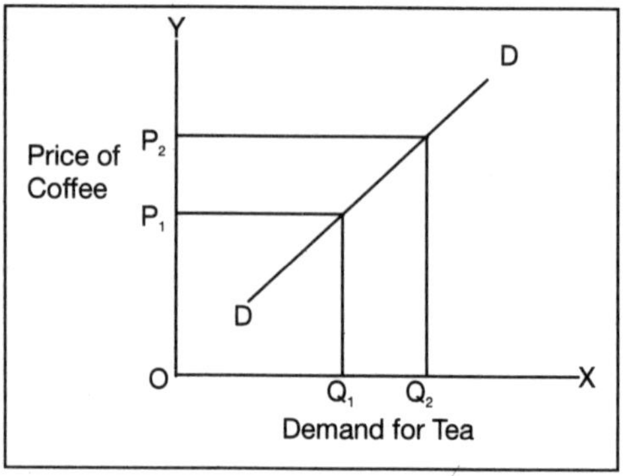

Diagram 3.17: Positive Cross Elasticity of Demand

DD is positive cross elasticity of demand curve. When price of coffee is increased from P1 to P2, the demand for tea increased Q1 to Q2

(ii) **Complementary Goods:** If the two goods are complementary, for example, petrol and car, the cross elasticity of demand (e_c) will be negative. The rise in the price of Petrol will reduce not only the demand for it but also the demand for Car, because both goods are demanded together. Here the demand curve has negative slope. It is illustrated in the following diagram 3.18.

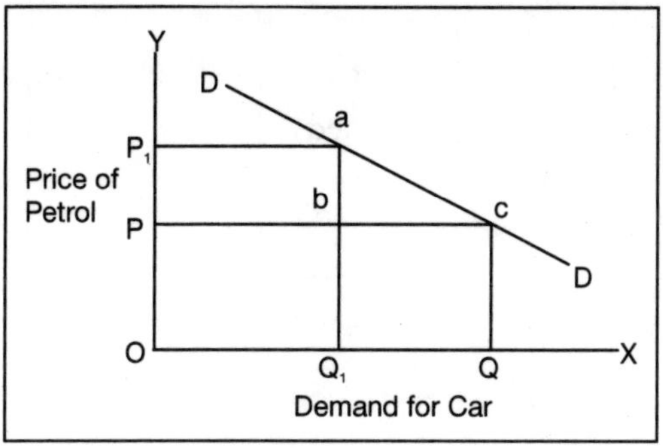

Diagram 3.18: Negative Cross Elasticity of Demand

In this case an increase in the price of Petrol from P to P_1 leads to fall in the demand for Car from Q to Q_1 i.e. $-bc/ab < 0$ and *vice versa*. DD is the negative cross elasticity demand curve.

(iii) **Perfectly Cross Elastic Demand:** If A and B two goods are perfect or close substitutes for each other, the 'e_c' will be infinite (∞). It means that the slightest change in price of A will lead to a substantial or infinite change in the quantity demanded for B. It is shown in the following diagram 3.19.

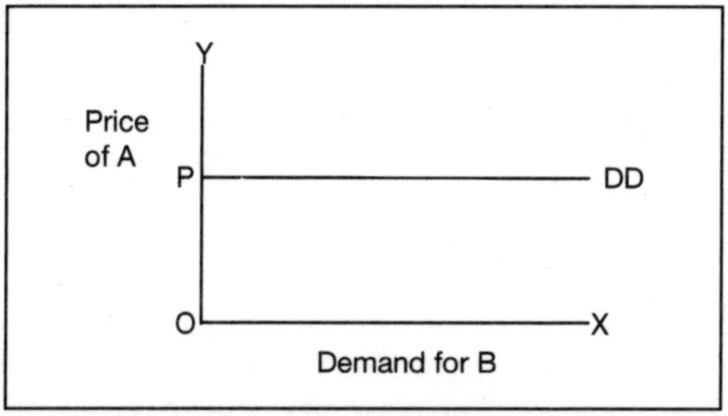

Diagram 3.19: Perfectly Cross Elastic Demand

DD is the perfectly cross elastic de mand curve.

(iv) **Zero Cross Elastic Demand:** If two goods, Salt and Sugar, are not related to each other, the 'e_c' will be zero. The demand curve will be a vertical straight-line. It is shown as in the following Diagram 3.20.

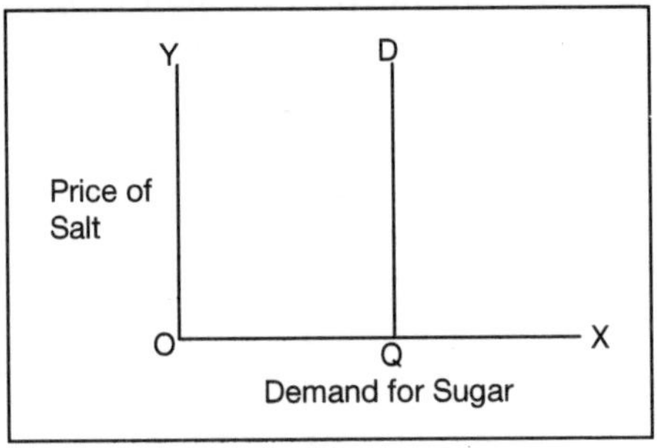

Diagram 3.20: Zero Cross Elastic Demand

To sum- up, the cross elasticity of demand depends upon the relation between the goods.

3.8 MEASUREMENT OR METHODS OF ELASTICITY OF DEMAND

Of the three types discussed above, price elasticity is the basic, most important and useful concept. Hence the different methods are devised by economists to measure price elasticity of demand.

Economists have developed three important methods for measuring elasticity of demand. They are (i) total outlay method, (ii) point method, and (iii) Arc method.

3.8.1 Total Outlay Method: This is also called expenditure method. Alfred Marshall used this method to measure elasticity of demand. Under this method the change in price and its resultant change in the outlay or expenditure on the purchase of the commodity are considered to measure the elasticity of demand. In other words, the total outlay of the consumer before and after the change in price is taken into account to measure the elasticity of demand.

There are three degrees of elasticity. They are (i) ep = 1, (ii) ep > 1, (iii) ep < 1. The elasticity of demand measured under this method is explained in the following table 3.4.

Table 3.4: Total Outlay Method

Price (₹) P	e > 1 P × Q = Total Outlay (₹)	e < 1 P × Q = Total Outlay (₹)	e = 1 P × Q = Total Outlay (₹)
Rise ↑			
10	10 x 10= 100	10 x10 = 100	10 x 10 = 100
05	05 x 30= 150	05 x 15= 75	05 x 20= 100
04	04 x 50= 200	04 x 16= 64	04 x 25= 100
Fall ↓			

P = Price (₹), Q=Quantity Demanded (Units)

The concepts of elasticity are measured as under with the help of Table 3.4:

(i) **Elasticity of demand equal to unity (e = 1):** If a given change in price does not cause any change in the total outlay or total outlay remains the same as before, i.e. ₹ 100, it is unitary elastic demand

(ii) **Elasticity greater than unity (e > 1):** If a given change in price leads to an increase in the total outlay on the good, i.e. ₹ 150 and ₹ 200, it is the case of elasticity is greater than one.

(iii) **Elasticity less than unity (e < 1):** If a given change in price leads to a decrease in the total outlay, i.e. ₹ 75 and ₹ 64, then e < 1.

Thus it may be concluded that (i) Demand is elastic when total outlay increases with a fall in price and decrease with a rise in price which is more than basic outlay. (ii) Demand is neither elastic nor inelastic when the total outlay remains the same, and (iii) Demand is inelastic when the total outlay decreases with a fall in price and increases with a rise in price but the total outlay is less than the basic outlay.

3.8.2 Point Method: Point method is also called geometrical method. Under this method, elasticity of demand is measured at any point on a demand curve. Alfred Marshall had suggested this method. Here a straight line demand curve joining the two axes is taken and the elasticity between two points on the curve is measured as:

$$\text{Elasticity} = e = \frac{\text{Lower Segment}}{\text{Upper Segment}}$$

It is illustrated in the following diagram 3.21.

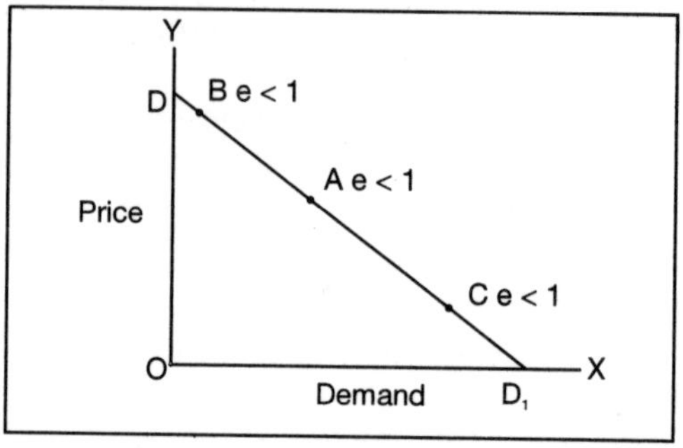

Diagram 3.21: Point Method when Demand Curve is Straight-line

DD_1 is the straight-line demand curve. A, B and C are the points on the DD_1 for which the elasticity of demand is to be measured. Elasticity of demand on any point on the DD_1 can be measured as:

(i) At point A, Lower Segment AD_1 is equal to Upper segment DA

$$\therefore e = \frac{AD_1}{DA} \text{ so } e = 1$$

(ii) At point B, Lower Segment BD_1 is greater than Upper segment DB

$$\therefore e = \frac{BD_1}{DB} \text{ so } e > 1$$

(iii) At point C, Lower Segment CD_1 is lesser than Upper segment DC

$$\therefore e = CD_1 \text{ so } e < 1$$

If the demand curve is not a straight-line but curvy and negatively sloping, the same formula will be applicable for measuring the elasticity of demand. A tangent line is drawn at the point on the demand curve whereon the elasticity is to be measured. It is illustrated in the following diagram 3.22.

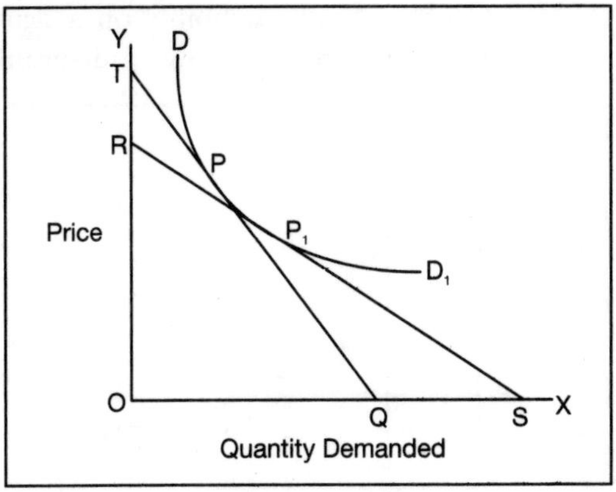

Diagram 3.22: Point Method when Demand Curve is Curvy

DD1 is a negatively sloped curve. P and P_1 are the two points on it at which elasticity is measure. TQ and RS are the two tangents drawn respectively at points P and P_1 on the DD_1. At point P, elasticity will be equal to QP/TP showing e > 1 or elasticity than greater unity. At point p1 elasticity is equal to SP_1/RP_1, showing e < 1 or elasticity less than unity.

The point method is very useful to measure price elasticity when there are very small changes in the price and the quantity demanded of the good. The point method shows that the slope of the demand curve and elasticity are not the same. Though the slope of the demand curve is uniform throughout its length, the elasticity is different at different points on the same curve.

3.8.3 Arc Method: The concept of point elasticity of demand refers to the price elasticity at a point on the demand curve. This method is used when changes in price and the resultant changes in quantity demanded are very small. But generally there are big gaps in changes in price and quantity demanded. When price and quantity changes are fairly large, elasticity will be measured over an 'arc' of the demand curve instead of at a particular point on the demand curve. That would give a correct measure of price elasticity of demand.

Prof. Boumal defines 'arc' elasticity as a measure of the average responsiveness to changes exhibited by a demand curve over some finite stretch of the curve. Any two points on a demand curve make an 'arc'. It is illustrated in the following diagram 3.23.

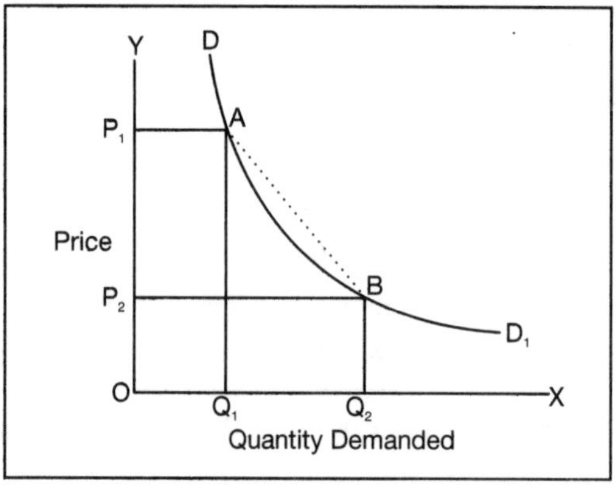

Diagram 3.23: Arc Method

If the arc elasticity is to be measured between two points, A and B, on the demand curve DD_1, the average of prices i.e. OP_1 and OP_2 and the average of quantity demanded i.e. OQ_1 and OQ_2 are to be taken. The arc elasticity formula measures the arc elasticity between AB. The closer the two points, the more accurate will be the measure of elasticity. The arc elasticity is in fact the elasticity at the midpoint between A and B on the demand curve DD_1. If there is no difference between the two points and they coincide with each other, the arc elasticity becomes point elasticity. Therefore arc elasticity formula should be used when the change in price is large.

The formula for measuring arc elasticity of demand is:

$$\text{Elasticity} = e = \frac{dq/(q1+q2)/2}{dp/(p1+p2)/2} = \frac{dq/(q1+q2)}{2} \times \frac{(p1+p2)/2}{dp}$$

$$= \frac{dq}{q1+q2} \times \frac{p1+p2}{dp} = \frac{dq(p1+p2)}{dp(q1+q2)}$$

By assigning numerical value to the above formula, the elasticity can be measured by taking the following numerical value of the demand schedule.

Table 3.5: Demand Schedule

Price (₹)	Qty. demanded (units)
15 (P1)	100 (q1)
10 (P2)	200 (q2)

With the help of Table 3.5, ₹ 15 as price and the quantity demanded as 100 units are taken as basis for measuring price elasticity with the help of point elasticity formula as under:

$$e = dq/dp \times p/q = 100/5 \times 15/100 = 3$$

If ₹ 10 as price and 200 units as quantity demanded are taken as the basis of measurement

$$e = dq/dp \times p/q = 100/5 \times 10/200 = 1$$

If arc elasticity formula is used to measure the elasticity, the result is:

$e = \dfrac{dq(p1+p2)}{dp\ (q1+q2)}$ and assign numerical value we get,

$$e = 100/5 \times (15+10)/\ (100+200) = 100/5 \times 25/300 = 1.66.$$

3.9 DETERMINANTS OF PRICE ELASTICITY OF DEMAND

The degree of elasticity of demand differs from commodity to commodity, person to person and place to place. The elasticity of demand is determined by a number of factors. They are as under:

(i) **Degree of necessity:** The intensity of demand for a good is a major factor determining elasticity. Certain goods which are absolutely essential, such as cereals, edible oil, milk, salt, drugs have high intensity of demand or have greater degree of necessity. All such goods have inelastic demand. But the demand for comforts and luxuries is elastic.

(ii) **Proportion of expenditure on the good:** It depends on the size of expenditure on good. If a good absorbs only a small proportion of total expenditure of the consumer, as for example, salt, matchbox, needle, etc., the demand is inelastic. On the other hand if a good absorbs a large proportion of total expenditure, for example, expenditure on TV's, cars, washing machines, etc, the demand is elastic.

(iii) **Existence of substitutes:** There are more competing substitutes of some goods. Demand is more elastic in case of goods which have a number of good substitutes for example, creams, tooth pastes, soaps, soft drinks, etc. On the other hand goods without substitutes like salt, have inelastic demand.

(iv) **Uses of goods:** Goods have several uses. The demand for a good having several uses is elastic for example, coal, electricity, etc. because they will be demanded more if they become cheap. They will be used only for urgent and important purposes when they become costly. The demand for such goods is always elastic.

(v) **Prices ranges:** The elasticity of demand is influenced to a very large extent by the ranges of prices. At very high price ranges or at very low prices the demand is inelastic. At moderate prices the demand is elastic.

(vi) **Time period:** Time element plays a vital role to decide the degree of elasticity. Elasticity varies with the length of time periods. The elasticity of demand is greater in the long period than in the short period. This is because the consumer has more time to make adjustments in his scheme of consumption in the long run.

(vii) **Level of income of the consumers:** The poor people with lower levels of income are more sensitive to price changes as they want to derive maximum satisfaction from their meager income. Therefore at lower level of income demand is elastic. The rich people are not so much price conscious and they continue to purchase the same quantities even though price changes. Their demand for goods is less elastic.

(viii) **Habits of consumers:** If a consumer is accustomed to use a particular good or habituated to its use, his demand for it is generally inelastic, for example, tobacco, cigarette, etc.

(ix) **Possibility of postponement of consumption:** Those goods whose consumption can be postponed without much difficulty, the demand for it is elastic, for example, building a house, buying furniture and vehicles.

3.10 IMPORTANCE OF ELASTICITY OF DEMAND

The concept of elasticity of demand is of great theoretical and practical importance. It has the following significance:

(i) **It is useful to the producers:** The concept of elasticity of demand is useful in theory of product-pricing. The producers determine price of their goods on the basis of elasticity under various market conditions. Under perfect competition, since the demand curve of an individual seller is perfectly elastic the producer should sell his output at the low price. But under monopoly or imperfect competition, the demand is less elastic and the producer is in a position to exercise some control over price. Under price-discriminating monopoly, the producer charges different prices on same commodity to different consumers on the basis of elasticity.

(ii) **It is useful to measure the degree of monopoly power:** Monopoly power means a single seller's control over the price. It represents the difference between marginal revenue and average revenue or price. This difference ultimately depends upon elasticity of demand for the product. If elasticity is less the difference between marginal revenue and price will be wider and hence monopoly power is greater. The monopoly power is low if the elasticity of demand is high. Mrs. Joan Robinson had suggested this method.

(iii) **It is useful for factor-pricing:** If the demand for a factor of production is less elastic its reward will be higher and *vice versa*. Thus the concept of elasticity of demand has great significance in the theory of distribution.

(iv) **It helps to classify goods:** The Goods can be classified as necessary goods and non-necessary goods, substitutes and complementary goods on the basis of elasticity. Less elastic demand goods are considered as necessaries and more elastic as non-necessaries. Two commodities may be considered as substitutes if cross elasticity is positive and complements when elasticity is negative.

(v) **It is useful to finance minister:** The government imposes taxes on the goods the demand for which is less elastic. If such goods are taxed, the consumers have to buy them and bear the tax burden. Therefore the government has to consider the nature of elasticity of demand for a good before imposing the tax on it.

(vi) **It plays a vital role in international transactions:** The elasticity of demand for exports and imports is of vital significance in determining the extent of gain from the international trade. Terms of trade and exchange rates are determined on the basis of each other countries' demand elasticity.

(vii) **It helps the government to formulate necessary economic policies:** The modern governments regulate output and prices in the economy on the basis of the guidance of the nature of consumer demand. The decision of the government to create "public utilities" is also based on the nature of demand elasticity. Industries supplying goods and services having inelastic demand are mostly declared as public utilities and they are being nationalized by the government.

3.11 DEMAND FORECASTING

3.11.1 Meaning of Demand Forecasting: It means forecasting or predicting or estimating the future demand for commodity or services. Following are the important objects of demand forecasting.

(1) Short-term objectives

(2) Long-term objectives

(1) Short-term Objectives: The following are the short-run objectives of demand forecasting:

(i) **Determine the size of output to be produce:** It is possible only when the producer knows probable demand for his product.

(ii) To workout cost of production.

(iii) To fix the price of product.

(iv) To fix the sales target.

(v) To know the short term financial requirements.

(2) **Long-term Objectives:** The following are the long-run objectives of demand forecasting:

(i) To decide either to expand or start a new unit of production.

(ii) To train the worker suiting to new technology.

(iii) To estimate the long-term financial requirements.

3.11.2 Methods of Demand Forecasting: The following are the methods of demand forecasting:

(1) **Survey Method:** According to survey method, the company surveys the prospective buyers in a locality. It makes the use of interview schedules or questionnaire and on that basis it works out the future demand for its product. However this is not a scientific method of demand forecasting. It is a costly method because expenses incurred to meet the prospective buyers of different places will be very high.

2. Collective Opinion Method: According to collective opinion method, the company collects information about the product from sales representatives appointed for different areas. On that basis the company works out probable demand for its product for a given period of time. One of the drawbacks of this method is that it is not suitable for product for which there is no sales representative.

3. Expert's Opinion: According to expert's opinion method company meet some of the VIP's in society and collects information about its product. On that basis it works out demand for the product in one area and multiplies it by taking all the other area where the product is sold. But it is not a scientific method of demand forecasting because difference in opinions by the experts.

4. Product Test Method: This method is useful for demand forecasting of either new product or imported old product. The company gives sample of such product to the customer by entering into the market. It takes the name and address of the customer and afterwards personally meets them to know the taste and preferences, then arrives at the conclusion about its demand in the market.

5. Trend Projection or Statistical Method of Demand Forecasting: According to trend projection company takes into account the past sales value of its product to predict its future demand.

Least Square Method is used to find the 'Best fit Line' that shows the projection trends or future sale or demand for a commodity.

Following steps are involved in the matter of forecasting demand:

(i) It works out time deviation from the mid-year.

(ii) It squares-up the Time Deviation (TD).

(iii) It takes into account the sales value of past years.

(iv) It finds out the product of TD and sales.

(v) Makes use of straight-line equation, i.e. $y = a + bx$.

(vi) Work out the sales value for next 'n' number of years.

Example 1: Suppose that the Maruti Vehicles Ltd. realized the sales value for sold-out. Maruti Cars for the last 5 years as given in the table.

Table 3.6: Sales Value for Soldout Market Cars

Years	Sales Value (₹ in Cr.)
2006	20
2007	30
2008	35
2009	45
2010	65

Working out sales value of Maruti Car for next three years is shown in Table 3.7.

Table 3.7: Working out the Values

Year	Sales(y)	TD(x) (Middle Year)	TD Square-up (x^2)	Product (xy)
2006	20	–2	4	–40
2007	30	–1	1	–30
2008	35	0	0	0
2009	45	1	1	45
2010	65	2	2	130
Total: Σn=5	Σy=195	Σx=0	Σx^2=10	Σxy=105

y = a + bx

Work out the value of 'a' and 'b'

$a = \Sigma y/\Sigma n = 195/5 = 39$

$b = \Sigma xy/\Sigma x^2 = 105/10 = 10.5$

To find out the value of sales for next 3 years, we have to substitute the value of 'a' and 'b' in the given equation.

y = a + bx   x = Value of T.D.

= 39 + 10.5 (x)

By using this equation we calculate the projection trends as:

2006= 39 + 10.5 x –2 = 18

2007= 39 + 10.5 x –1 = 29.5

2008= 39 + 10.5 x –0 = 39

2009= 39 + 10.5 x 1 = 49.5

2010 = 39 + 10.5 x 2 = 60

To know the sales value of Maruti Cars, we must take into account the next 3 years:

2011= 39 + 10.5 × 3= 70. 5 crores

2012= 39 + 10.5 × 4= 81 crores

2013= 39 + 10.5 × 5= 91.5 crores

The demand forecasting has already been in explained in the Example 2: Suppose that the HL Ltd. sold its Surf Excel product as shown in the following table 3.8.

Table 3.8: Sales Forecasting of Surf Excel Year-wise

Year	Sales (in Lakh)
2006	10
2007	20
2008	30
2009	40
2010	50

If there is relation between sales other economic indicators or Time Deviation is taken from the previous year i.e. 2005 and $\Sigma x > 0$ we have to use the following simultaneous equations to find out the values:

$\Sigma y = a\ \Sigma n + b\ \Sigma x$............ (1)

$\Sigma xy = a\ \Sigma x + b\ \Sigma x^2$........... (2)

By using above data, we can work-out the values in the following table 3.9:

Table 3.9: Working out Values

Year	Sales(y)	TD (x)(2005 Year)	Sqare-up TD (x^2)	Product (xy)
2006	10	1	1	10
2007	20	2	4	40
2008	30	3	3	90
2009	40	4	16	160
2010	50	5	25	250
Total: n=5	Σy=150	Σx=15	Σx^2=55	Σxy=550

Least Square Equation

$\Sigma y = na + b\ \Sigma x$ .... (1)

$\Sigma xy = a\Sigma x + b\ \Sigma x^2$ .... (2)

Substitute the value in the equations, it becomes

$150 = 5a + 15b$ .... (1)

$550 = 15a + 55$ .... (2)

We have to simplify equations (1) and (2) by multiplying equation 1 by 3 and subtract equation (2) from it:

$150 \times 3 = 5a \times 3 + 15b \times 3$............. (1)

$-550 \times 1 = -15 \times 1\ a - 55 \times 1b$......... (2)

$-100 = 0 - 10b$

$-100 = -10b$

$b = 100/10 = 10$

$b = 10$

Substitute the value of 'b' in equation (1):

$150 = 5a + 15 \times (10)$

or $150 = 5a + 150$

$5a = 150 - 150$

5a = 0
a = 0/5 = 0
y = a + bx
2006 y = 0 + 10 (1)=10

Now the sales value for the

2007 y = 0 + 10 (2) = 20
2008 y = 0 + 10 (3) = 30
2009 y = 0 + 10 (4) = 40
2010 y = 0 + 10 (5) = 50

3.12 MODEL QUESTIONS

2 Marks Questions

1. What is consumption?
2. What is consumer's sovereignty?
3. Define demand.
4. What do you mean by demand schedule?
5. What is demand curve?
6. State law of demand.
7. Name any two exceptions of law of demand.
8. Give the difference between extension and contraction of demand.
9. Give the difference between increase and decrease in demand.
10. Name any two determinants of demand.
11. In demand equation, a=800, b=0.7, find-out value of Q when P=5, 8 and 10.
12. Define elasticity of demand.
13. Q_0=1500, Q_1=1000, P_0=8, P_1=10. Calculate price elasticity of demand.
14. Name the types of elasticity of demand.
15. Name the methods of measurement of elasticity of demand.
16. Name any two factors determining elasticity of demand.

17. Give the meaning of demand forecasting.
18. Name any two objectives of demand forecasting.
19. Name any two methods of demand forecasting.
20. In a demand forecasting strightline equation $y = a+b(x)$, $a = 100$, $b = 5$ find out value of y when $x = 2$ and 3.

5 Marks Questions

1. Write a short-note on consumer's choice
2. Demand schedule.
3. Write a note on changes in demand.
4. Give a brief account on determinants of demand.
5. Discuss in brief cross elasticity of demand.
6. Discuss in brief income elasticity of demand.
7. Discuss in brief point method of measurement of elasticity of demand.
8. Write a note on factors determining elasticity of demand.
9. Write a note on importance of elasticity of demand.
10. Write a note on demand forecasting and its objectives.

10 Marks Questions

1. Explain consumer's choice and sovereignty.
2. Discuss the law of demand.
3. Define demand. Explain its determinants.
4. Define elasticity of demand. Explain its determinants.
5. Explain the types of elasticity of demand.
6. What is price elasticity of demand? Explain its concepts
7. Define elasticity of demand. Explain its methods of measurement.
8. Explain the demand forecasting by referring a case-study with the use of least square method.

4

Supply Analysis

4.1 SUPPLY

4.1.1 Meaning and Importance: Supply is another important force of market. Alfred Marshall called it another blade of a scissor. It plays an equally important role in theory of value. In a market economy, buyers of a product constitute the demand side and sellers of that product make the supply side of the market. Both demand for the product and the supply of the product together determine the price of the commodity. Supply means the quantity of a commodity that a producer or seller offers for sale at a given price, per unit of time. The supply of commodity is related to given price and per unit of time.

4.1.2 Distinction between Stock and Supply: Supply refers to the quantity of a commodity that a seller is willing and able to offer for sale at a particular price at a given time. Stock refers to the total quantity of a commodity available with the seller for sale.

Supply is different from stock. But it depends upon the nature of commodity. In case of durable or non-perishable goods supply differs from stock. Supply does not necessarily comprise the entire stock of any commodity in existence, but only that amount drawn into the market by the price ruling at that time. For ex: the supply of oil is not the stock of oil from all the world's oil fields, but only that amount which particular prices will bring into the market. The supply and the stock of a commodity get converted into each other according to the changes in the price of that commodity. When the price of a commodity increases, the stock becomes supply and *vice versa*.

But, in case of perishable goods it is difficult to differentiate between supply and stock, for ex: vegetable.

However, supply is different from stock because (i) supply is a part of stock (ii) supply depends upon price, and (iii) supply related to a point of time whereas stock related to the period of time.

4.1.3 Supply Schedule: A tabular statement showing different quantities of a commodity supplied at different prices by the seller is called supply schedule. It is explained in the following table 4.1.

Table 4.1: Supply Schedule

Price (₹)	Supply (Units)
1	10
2	15
3	20
4	25
5	30
6	35

The seller offered to sell 10 units of a commodity when its price is ₹ 1 and similarly he is willing and offer to sell different quantities of a commodity at different prices.

4.1.4 Supply Curve: The curve that represents the relation between price of a commodity and its supply is called 'supply curve'. The supply curve is a graphical representation of the supply schedule. It can be drawn on the basis of supply schedule. It is illustrated in the following diagram 4.1.

The quantity supplied is measured in units along 'OX' axis and price per unit is measured along 'OY' axis. 'SS' is supply curve that is obtained by plotting the data from Table 4.1. The upward slope of the supply curve indicates the rise in the supply of a commodity with the rise in its price and fall in the supply with fall in price. For Ex: at price ₹ 1 the units of a commodity supplied are 10. When the price rises to ₹ 2 and so on, the supply increases to 15 units and so on.

'SS' supply curve shows the direct relation between price and supply so the supply curve has a positive slope. The positive slope or upward movement of the supply curve shows two things:

(i) sellers' desire to make larger profit by selling more at high price and (ii) more output is supplied at high cost of production. In fact, supply curve is derived from the marginal cost curve.

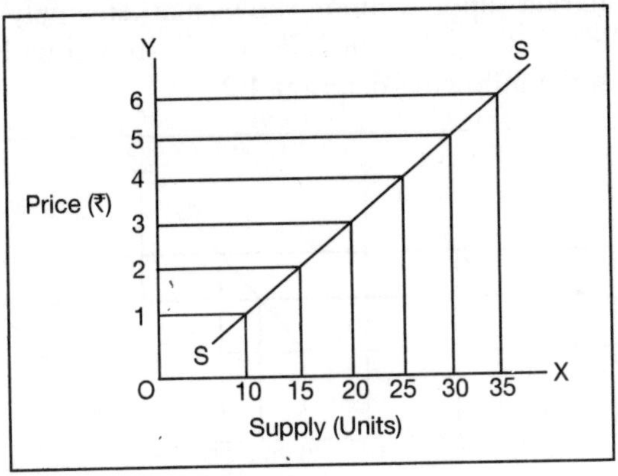

Diagram 4.1: Supply Schedule

4.1.5 Individual Supply and Market Supply: There are two types of supply schedules namely (i) Individual Supply Schedule and (ii) Market Supply Schedule.

Market consists of either one seller or more than one seller, for ex: In a mango-market there may be one or more than one seller. The quantities of a commodity offered for sale at various prices by an individual seller is called 'Individual Supply Schedule'. Similarly the quantities of a commodity offered for sale at various prices by sellers in the market is called 'Market Supply Schedule'.

Both the supply schedules are explained with example in the following table 4.2. For example, there is a mango-market in a city and there are two sellers namely Seller-A and Seller-B. The prices of mango per kilogram and supply of mangoes by individual sellers and market are given in Table 4.2.

Table 4.2: Individual and Market Supply Schedules

Price/Kg (₹)	Seller-A's Mango-supply (Kg)	Seller-B's Mango-supply (Kg)	Market Supply (Kg) (A + B)
50	100	150	250
100	150	200	350
150	200	250	450

In Table 4.2, price column shows various prices of mango per kilogram; seller-A's column shows his individual supply schedule and seller-B's column shows his individual supply schedule; market supply column shows market supply schedule. Individual market supply schedules are illustrated with the help of curves in the following diagram 4.2.

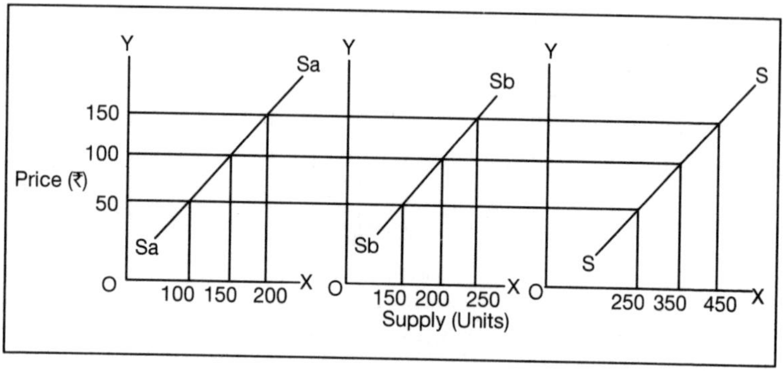

Diagram 4.2: Individual and Market Supply Curves

'OY' axis measures price per kilogram of mango; 'OX' axis measures the supply of mangoes in kilograms. 'SaSa' is the supply curve of seller-A; 'SbSb' is the supply curve of seller-B and 'SS' is the market supply curve.

Market supply is the sum total of the supply of all individual sellers so it can be calculated as:

Market Supply = Supply of seller-A + Supply of seller-B

$\therefore$ Qm = ΣQn

where, Qm = Market Supply

Σ = Total sum

Qn = Supplies of 'n' number of sellers.

In above example, when price is ₹ 50/kg, seller-A supplied 100 kg and seller-B supplied 150 kg so the market supply is as:

250 = 100 + 150

4.1.6 Supply Function: The supply function is a mathematical statement, which states the relationship between the quantity supplied of a commodity (as a dependent variable) and determinants (as independent variables). For its explanation, price is taken into account as the determinant of the quantity of supply of a commodity. The functional relation between price and supply is called 'Supply Function'. It is expressed as:

$$Qx = f\ (Px)$$

Where,

Qx = Quantity supplied of commodity X,

Px = Price of commodity X,

f = Functional Relation.

4.2 THE LAW OF SUPPLY

Law of Supply is another important contribution of Alfred Marshall to economics. It explains the relation between supply of a commodity and its price.

4.2.1 Statement of the Law of Supply: The law of supply states, "Other things being equal, the supply of a product increases with the increase in its price and decreases with decrease in its price." It implies that the supply of a commodity and its price are positively related it means supply of a commodity and its price move in same direction.

4.2.2 Assumptions of the Law of Supply: The law of supply is based on the heroic assumption "other things being equal". It covers as:

(i) Price of related goods should remain constant.

(ii) No change in technique or method of production.

(iii) There should be normal economic condition: neither inflation nor deflation.

(iv) No change in climatic conditions.

(v) There are no any natural calamities.

The law of supply operates only when the conditions assumed above are prevailed.

4.2.3 Illustration of the Law of Supply: The statement of the law of supply can be explained with the help of the example given in the Table 4.3.

Table 4.3: Law of Supply

Price of Apple/ Kg (₹)	Quantity of Apple Supplied (Kg)
50	100
60	150
70	200
80	250
90	300

The seller supplied 200 kilograms apples when the price of apple is ₹ 70 per kilogram. As the price increased to ₹ 80 and ₹ 90 the quantity supplied increased to 250 and 300 kgs. But, in contrary, when price decreased to ₹ 60 and ₹ 50 the quantity supplied declined to 150 and 100 kgs respectively. Thus the law of supply states that there is direct relation between price and the quantity of supply.

By using same example the statement of the law of supply is illustrated in the following diagram.

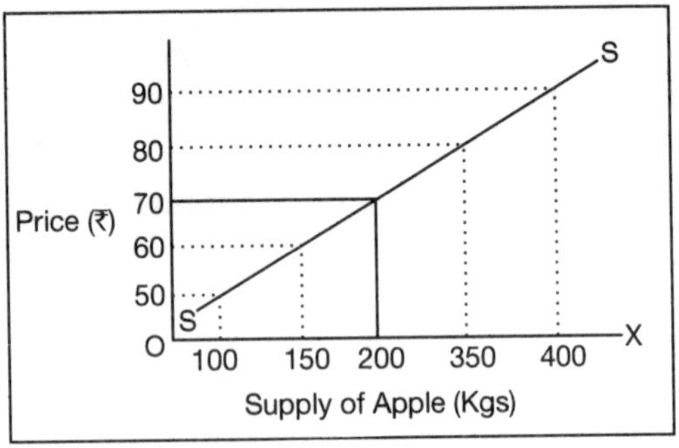

Diagram 4.3: Law of Supply

Price is measured along 'OY' axis and quantity of supply of apples in kilograms is measured along 'OX' axis. 'SS' is the supply curve that raises upwards from left to right. The supply curve has positive slope that explains the direct relation between price and supply.

When the price of apple is ₹ 100, the supply of it is 100 kgs. As its price increases ₹ 80 and ₹ 90, the supply of apples increases to 250 and 300 kgs. It is evident that, as the price increases the supply also increases. In contrary, when the price declines to ₹ 60 and ₹ 50 the quantity supplied declines to 150 and 100 kgs respectively.

This is in accordance with the law of supply. The supply curve SS clearly indicates the statement of the law.

4.2.4 Exceptions to the Law of Supply: The law of supply does not applicable to the following cases that are called exception to the law:

(i) It is not applicable to 'Auction sale'. Though the auctioneer is interested in getting higher price, the price is determined by the bidders. The auctioneer may have no scope to sell more at high price.

(ii) It is not applicable in price-falling situation: When the sellers anticipate further fall in the price of the commodity in price-falling situation they may sell more units even at a lower price and get rid of the stock of the commodity.

(iii) It is not applicable to goods that are inelastic in supply. For ex: Capital goods.

(iv) It will no bet applicable in situations like war, natural calamities, etc.

(v) It is not applicable to labour supply.

The supply of labour will increase with increase in wage up to a certain point after that any wage increase takes place, the supply of labour will not increase because labourer prefer leisure in place of work. So the supply curve of labour bends backward indicating that with the increase in wage, the supply of labour decreases. It is illustrated in the following diagram 4.4.

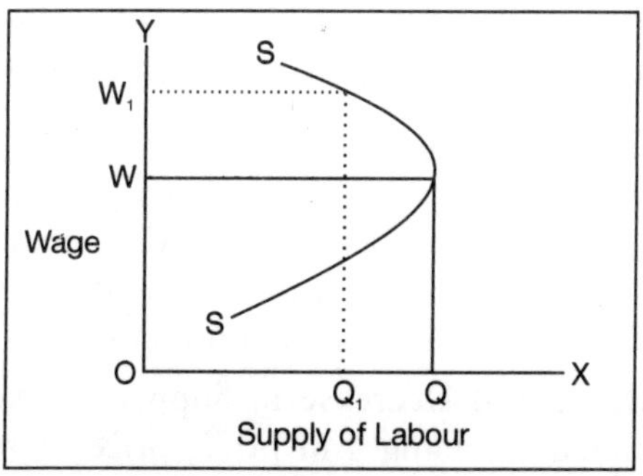

Diagram 4.4: Backward Bending Supply Curve of Labour

When the wage rate increased to 'w1', the supply of labour declined instead of rising because labourer prefers leisure in place of work. For ex: when wage increased to 'w1', the supply of labour declined to Q1. It is shown by backward bending supply curve 'SS'. It is exception to the law of supply.

For these limitations or exceptions the law of supply is criticized.

4.3 CHANGES IN SUPPLY

There are two types of changes in supply namely (i) extension and contraction of supply and (ii) increase and decrease in supply. Supply changes due to changes in the determinants of supply. The changes in supply are studied as under:

4.3.1 Extension and Contraction of Supply: These changes are related to change in price of the commodity. The expansion of supply due to rise in price is called 'extension of supply'. Similarly the decline in supply due to fall in price is called 'contraction of supply'. They are illustrated in the following diagram 4.5.

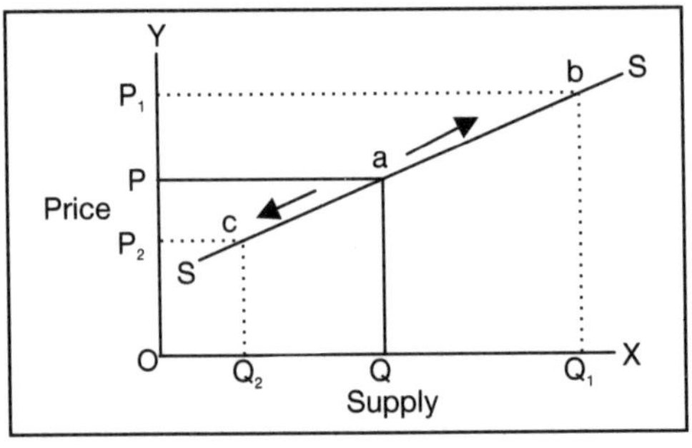

Diagram 4.5: Extension and Contraction of Supply

Price is measured along 'OY' axis and the supply along 'OX' axis. 'SS' is the supply curve. The supply expands from 'a' to 'b' or 'Q' to 'Q_1' due to rise in price from 'P' to 'P_1' that is the case of extension of supply. In contrary, the supply declines from 'a' to 'c' or 'Q' to 'Q_2' that is the case of contraction of supply.

4.3.2 Increase and Decrease in Supply: These changes in supply are related to changes in price, price of related goods like complementary goods and substitutes, cost, method of production, government policy, price of factors of production, etc. They are studied as under:

Increase in Supply: Either more quantity is supplied at same price or same quantity is supplied at low price is called 'increase in supply'. It is illustrated in the following diagram 4.6.

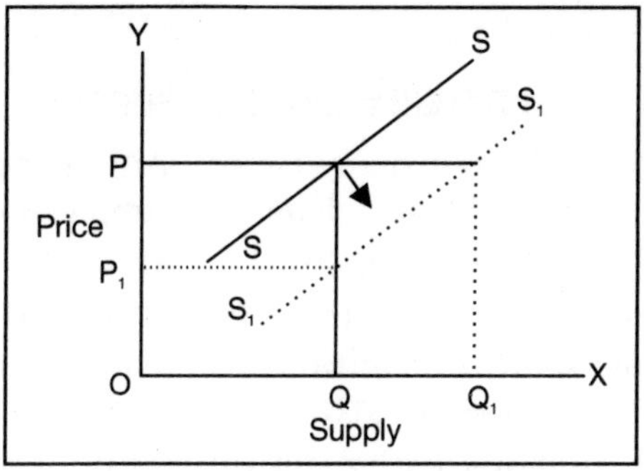

Diagram 4.6: Increase in Supply

'SS' is the original supply curve; 'P' is the base price and 'Q' is the original supply. Either at the same price 'P' the seller offered to sale more quantity i.e. Q1 or the seller offered to sale same quantity i.e. 'Q' at low price 'P1' due to decline in cost of production or increase in level of output. So new supply curve 'S1S1' shifted to the right-side of the original 'SS' curve that shows increase in supply.

Decrease in Supply: Either less quantity is supplied at same price or same quantity is supplied at high price is called 'decrease in supply'. It is illustrated in the following diagram 4.7.

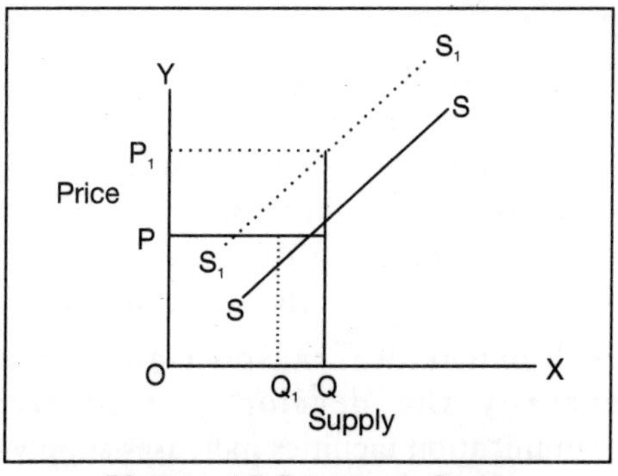

Diagram 4.7: Decrease in Supply

'SS' is the original supply curve; 'P' is the base price and 'Q' is the original supply. Either at the same price 'P' the seller offered to sale less quantity i.e. Q_1 or the seller offered to sale same quantity i.e. 'Q' at high price 'P_1' due to increase in cost of production or decrease in level of output. So new supply curve 'S_1S_1' shifted to the left-side of the original 'SS' curve that shows decrease in supply.

4.4 DETERMINANTS OF SUPPLY

Supply depends upon many factors. Any changes take place in these factors it results into changes in supply. So these factors are called 'determinants of supply'. They are discussed as follows:

(i) **Geographical Factors:** Geographical factors are geographical conditions like climate, rainfall, soil, natural calamities, etc are also influence on supply of commodities, for ex: agricultural produces.

(ii) **Cost of Production:** Cost of production controls supply of output. It depends upon price of factors of production. High cost brings low profits that discourage the producer. When prices of factors of production increase, the cost of production will go up and so the profit thus the producer produces low quantity of output and so supply will be low. In contrary, it is *vice versa*.

(iii) **Changes in the Technique of Production:** This is probably the most important factor affecting supply. The development of a new method of production or the invention of a new machine may make possible a big expansion of output at lower cost and so it increases supply.

(iv) **Effects of Taxation:** Taxation on commodities is likely to raise their prices. The imposition of a tax on a commodity is equivalent to an increase in its cost of production and reduces the size of profits so it will generally result into a decrease in supply. A reduction in taxation will have the opposite effect.

(v) **Development of Transport and Communication:** Generally the development of transport and communication facilities increases supply of goods and services in the market.

4.5 ELASTICITY OF SUPPLY

4.5.1 Meaning: This concept is parallel to the concept of elasticity of demand. It is defined as "the degree of responsiveness of Supply to a change in the price of a commodity". The supply of the commodity may increase or decrease depends upon the change in its price. Elasticity of supply can be measured by using the following formula:

$$\text{Elasticity of Supply} = \frac{\text{Proportionate change in the quantity supplied}}{\text{Proportionate change in the price}}$$

$$\therefore \qquad e_S = \frac{\Delta Qs}{Qs} \div \frac{\Delta P}{P} = \frac{\Delta Qs}{Qs} \times \frac{P}{\Delta P} = \frac{\Delta QsP}{Qs\Delta P}$$

Elasticity of Supply = Proportionate change in the quantity supplied

Where, Qs = Quantity Supplied, Δ = Change, P = Price, e_s = Elasticity of Supply.

For example $Qs_0 = 100$, $Qs_1 = 200$, $P_0 = 2$, $P_1 = 4$, calculate e_s

$$e_S = \frac{\Delta Qs}{Qs} \times \frac{P}{\Delta P} = \frac{200-100}{100} \times \frac{2}{4-2} = \frac{\cancel{100}1}{\cancel{100}1} \times \frac{\cancel{2}1}{\cancel{2}1} = 1$$

4.5.2 Concepts of Elasticity of Supply: Like elasticity of demand, supply elasticity has also five concepts or types. They are as follows:

(i) **Perfectly Elastic Supply:** A very little change in price leads to infinite change in quantity supplied is called 'perfectly elastic supply'. It can be written as: $e_s = \infty = (1/0)$. It is illustrated in the following diagram 4.8.

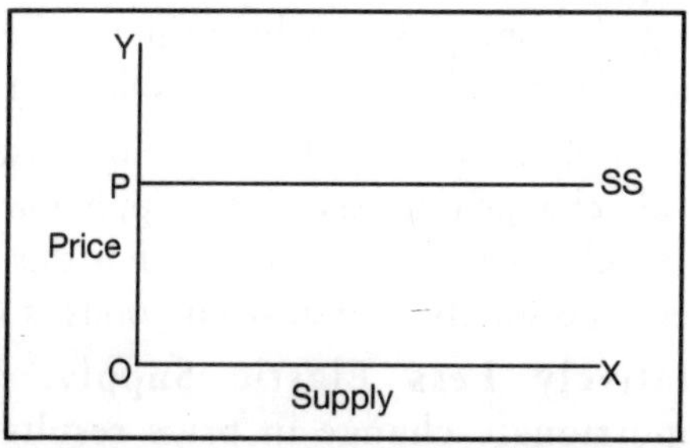

Diagram 4.8: Perfectly Elastic Supply

'SS' is the supply curve that shows supply is perfectly elastic. 'SS' curve is horizontal and parallel to 'OX' axis. Supply falls to zero when price falls a little: it increases to infinite when price rises a little. It is unrealistic and imaginary. It may also happen when new methods are invented to undertake mass production.

(ii) **Perfectly Inelastic or Zero Elastic Supply:** Any change in price does not lead to change in supply is called zero elastic supply. It can be written as: e_s = o = (1/0). It is illustrated in the following diagram 4.9.

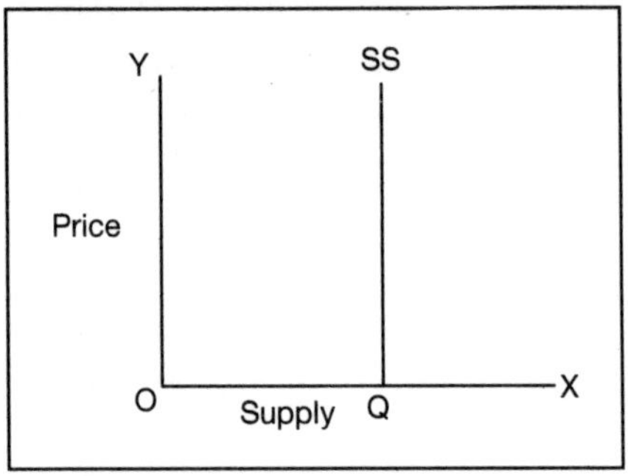

Diagram 4.9: Perfectly Inelastic Supply

'SS' is the supply curve that shows supply is perfectly inelastic. 'SS' curve is vertical and parallel to 'OY' axis. Supply remains constant at all levels of price. For ex: certain rare paintings, supply of vegetables, fish, etc.

(iii) **Relatively More Elastic Supply:** The small proportionate change in price results into a greater proportionate change in supply is called relatively more elastic supply. For example, 10 per cent change price leads to 20 per cent change in supply. It can be written as: $e_s > 1$ = (20%/ 10% = 2). It is illustrated in the following diagram 4.10.

'SS' is the supply curve, 'bc' shows change (rise) in price that resulted into 'ab' change (increase) into supply but 'ab' is greater than 'bc' (ab > bc). So $e_s > 1$ = ab/bc > 1. For this reason supply curve is flatter. The supply of industrial goods is more elastic.

(iv) **Relatively Less Elastic Supply:** The greater proportionate change in price results into a small proportionate change in supply is called relatively less

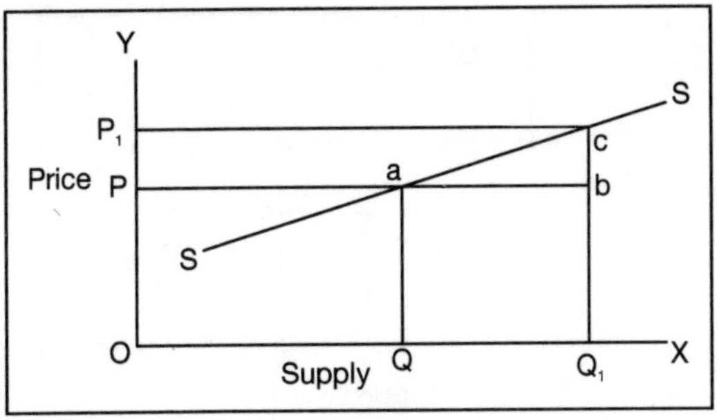

Diagram 4.10: Relatively More Elastic Supply

elastic supply. For example, 20 per cent change price leads to 10% change in supply. It can be written as: e_s < 1= (10%/20% = 1/ 2). It is illustrated in the following diagram 4.11.

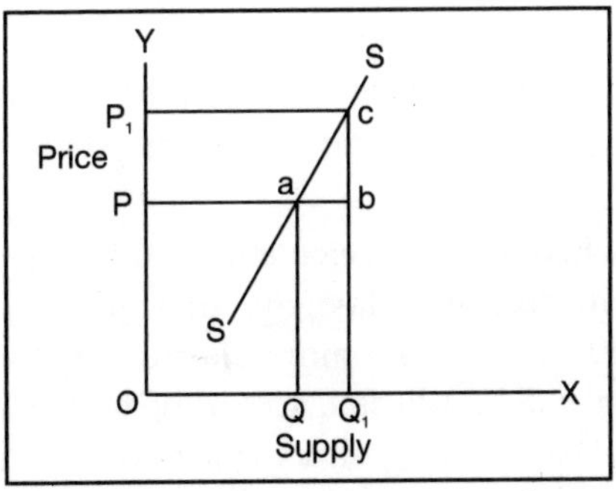

Diagram 4.11: Relatively Less Elastic Supply

'SS' is the supply curve, 'bc' shows change (rise) in price that resulted into 'ab' change (increase) into supply but 'ab' is less than 'bc' ($ab<bc$). So e_s < 1 = ab/bc < 1. For this reason supply curve is steeper. The supply of agricultural goods is less elastic.

(v) **Unitary Elastic Supply:** The proportionate change in price results into a same proportionate change in supply is called unitary elastic supply. For example, 10 per cent change price leads to 10 per cent change in supply. It can be written as: e_s = 1 = (10%/10% = 1). It is illustrated in the following diagram 4.12.

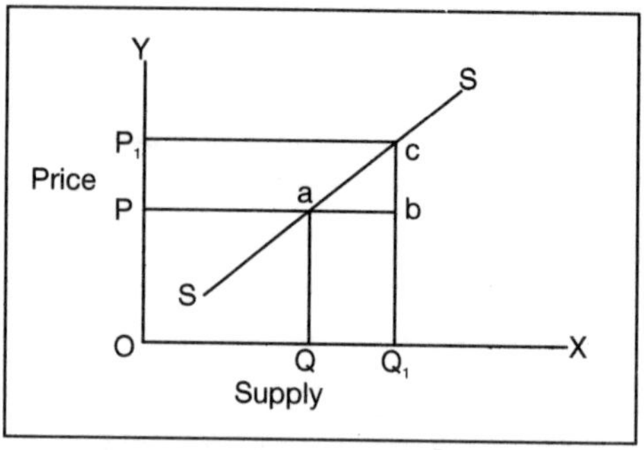

Diagram 4.12: Unitary Elastic Supply

'SS' is the supply curve, 'bc' shows change (rise) in price that resulted into 'ab' change (increase) into supply but 'ab' is equal to 'bc' (ab = bc). So $e_s = 1 = ab/bc = 1$. For this reason supply curve is straight-line or diagonal. The supply of agricultural goods is less elastic.

4.5.3 Factors Influencing Elasticity of Supply: Supply may be elastic or inelastic is depends upon the various factors. They are as follows:

(i) **Time Element:** The element of time plays an important role in deciding elasticity of supply. The longer the period of time, the more elastic is the supply because supply will be adjusted according to demand. But supply is inelastic during short-run because the size of firm and scale of operation will remain same.

(ii) **Nature of Industry:** In case of heavy industry, the supply of its output will be inelastic, because, the industry requires specialized equipment and machinery which cannot be made available in the short period. Hence, the supply of the output will become inelastic. In the contrary, the light industry requires ordinary appliances so its output can be increased quickly even during the short period hence the supply will be elastic.

(iii) **Nature of the Product:** If the commodity is agricultural good, the supply will be inelastic or if the commodity is industrial good, the supply will be elastic.

(iv) **Taxation:** Generally higher taxation imposed on the output of a commodity or on the factors required for its production may decrease the supply and lower taxation may increase the supply.

(v) **Price of the Commodity:** If the commodity has higher price, greater will be its supply. In the contrary, lower price will force the producers to reduce the production.

(vi) **Type of Market:** Elasticity of supply depends upon the type or form of market. The type of market decides the number of sellers in the market. If the number of sellers is large as in perfect competition the supply will be perfectly elastic; if sellers are more like monopolistic competition, there will be more elastic supply of the commodity and in monopoly market supply will be inelastic.

4.6 MODEL QUESTIONS

2 Marks Questions

(a) Define supply.

(b) State law of demand.

(c) What is supply-function?

(d) What is supply schedule?

(e) Name any two exceptions to law of supply.

(f) Name any two determinants of supply.

(g) What are extension and contraction of supply?

(h) Define elasticity of supply.

(i) Name any two concepts of elasticity of supply.

(j) Find-out elasticity of supply when, $Qs_0 = 100$, $Qs_1 = 250$, $P_0 = 2$, $P_1 = 3$.

(k) By giving numerical example prove $e_s < 1$.

(l) Write any one concept of elasticity of supply.

(m) Name any two determinants of elasticity of supply.

5 Marks Questions

1. Write note on Individual and Market Supply Schedules.
2. Write note on Individual and Market Supply Curves.
3. Discuss in brief the exceptions to law of supply.
4. Write note on extension and contraction of supply.
5. Write note on increase and decrease in supply.
6. Write note on determinants of elasticity of supply.

10 Marks Questions

1. Define supply. Explain supply schedule and curve.
2. Explain law of supply and its exceptions.
3. Define supply. Explain its determinants.
4. Define elasticity of supply. Explain its concepts.
5. Define elasticity of supply. Explain its determinants.

5

Indifference Curve Analysis

5.1 CONCEPT OF INDIFFERENCE CURVES

Indifference curve analysis is an alternative approach to the theory of demand. It was first evolved by Edgeworth in 1881 as an alternative to the Marshallian cardinal utility analysis of demand but he did not apply it to explain consumers demand. About a decade later, Fisher had used indifference curves to build a theory of consumer's equilibrium. Pareto adopted ordinal utility hypothesis and made indifference approach the basis of his theory of demand. Soon after Fisher, W.E. Johnson strengthened the ordinal utility approach. In 1915, Slutskey further consolidated the ordinal utility hypothesis and made it the basis of demand analysis. Two decades later, in 1934, J.R. Hicks and R.G.D. Allen published a paper on 'A Reconsideration of the Theory of Value' thereby they criticized cardinal utility theory and propounded indifference curve analysis which is based on the ordinal utility approach. A modified version of indifference curve analysis appeared in 'value and capital' written by J.R. Hicks in 1939.

5.1.1 Meaning: The specialty of indifference curve approach is that it abandoned the cardinal utility concept and adopted the concept of ordinal utility. It argues that utility is a subjective factor so it cannot be quantifiable. Hence the cardinal utility concept is unacceptable. The ordinal utility concept is quite reasonable and realistic because it argues that the consumer is capable of comparing the different levels of satisfaction obtained from consumption of two different goods or two combinations of goods. He is capable of indicating whether the satisfaction obtained from the consumption of a combination of goods is equal to or lower than or higher than another. According to the ordinalists, it is sufficient for deriving the theory of consumer behaviour when the consumer is able to rank his preferences consistently.

5.1.2 Assumptions: The indifference analysis is based on the following assumptions:

(i) **The consumer formulates his scale of preferences independently:** The consumer formulates his scale of preferences independently of the market prices of the goods keeping in view only the satisfaction which he hopes to get from various combinations of goods. In this scale of preferences, all combinations will occupy the same place i.e. the consumer will be indifferent among them. Combinations occupying a higher place in his scale of preferences will be preferred to the combinations occupying lower places in this scale. The consumer may prefer X to Y or Y to X or he may be indifferent between X and Y. This is called 'weak ordering' which recognizes the relation of preference as well as indifference. On the contrary, 'strong ordering' implies that there can be only the relation of preference, X is preferred to Y or Y is preferred to X and the possibility of consumer's indifference between X and Y is ruled out. Indifference curve analysis is based upon the weak ordering form of preference hypothesis.

(ii) **The analysis is based on ordinal approach:** It believes firmly that utility is a subjective factor so it cannot be measured in precise quantitative terms. Therefore, it asserts that utility obtained can be ranked or compared.

(iii) **The indifference curve analysis assumes that the consumer acts or behaves rationally:** It assumes that the consumer acts rationally and tries to maximize satisfaction obtainable from a given income.

(iv) **Consumer's income should remain constant:** It is assumed that there is no change in consumer's income level.

(v) **Prices of the goods should remain unchanged:** The prices of the goods that consumer prefers should remain constant.

5.1.3 Nature of Indifference Curves: Indifference curve is the basic tool of ordinal utility approach. The curve shows various combinations of two goods giving the same level of satisfaction to the consumer is called indifference curve. Since all the combinations on same indifference curve give equal satisfaction and the consumer will be indifferent between them. All combinations of the two goods lying on same indifference curve are equally desirable to or equally preferred by him. Therefore it is called indifference curve. It can be understood by constructing an indifference schedule.

5.1.4 Indifference Schedule: An Indifference Schedule is a list or schedule of various combinations of two goods that give the same level of satisfaction to the consumer. The consumer will be indifferent between combinations. The following table 5.1 shows a hypothetical schedule of a consumer:

Table 5.1: A Hypothetical Schedule of a Consumer

Combinations	Commodity Y	Commodity X	Level of Satisfaction
A	1	12	IC1
B	2	8	IC1
C	3	5	IC1
D	4	3	IC1
E	5	2	IC1

The schedule shows five combinations of the two goods, X and Y, equally preferred by the consumer. As consumer moves from combination A to E, the units of X rises and units of Y fall in the succeeding combinations. This should be the case because the consumer has to remain at the same level of satisfaction, i.e. IC1. He must get less of Y when he desires more of X. Since all the five combinations give the consumer equal satisfaction, he is indifferent whether he gets first or the last combination. The indifference schedule is illustrated in the following diagram 5.1.

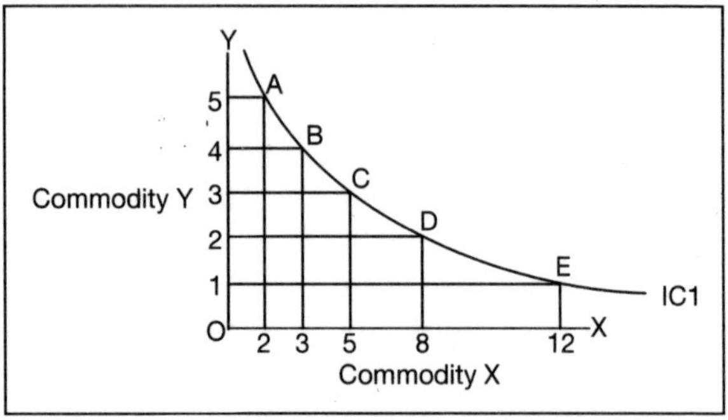

Diagram 5.1: Indifference Curve

The OX-axis measures quantities of commodity X and OY-axis commodity Y. Combinations of X and Y preferred by the consumer are shown as A, B, C, D and E. By joining these points of combinations by a continuous line we get a curve IC1 which is called 'Indifference Curve'. An IC1 may be defined as the locus of the various combinations of the two goods which give the same satisfaction to the consumer. This curve is also called 'Iso-Utility' curve as it shows equal utility at all points of combinations.

Any combination lies on IC curve gives same amount of satisfaction but the combinations lie above or below the IC curve give more or less amount of satisfaction than the combinations on IC curve.

While the consumer moving from one combination to another on the same IC, he should substitute X for Y or Y for X commodity but the marginal rate of substitution should be diminishing.

5.1.5 Indifference Map: It can be defined as the family or collection of indifference curves where each curve shows a particular level of satisfaction. For constructing an indifference map, different indifference curves are constructed and each curve shows various combinations of two goods giving the same level of satisfaction. It should be noted that more and more amounts of two goods in a combination give a higher level of satisfaction and less and less amounts give lower levels of satisfaction. The upper level indifference curves show higher level of satisfaction and lower level indifference curves show the lower levels of satisfaction. The indifference map is illustrated in the following diagram 5.2.

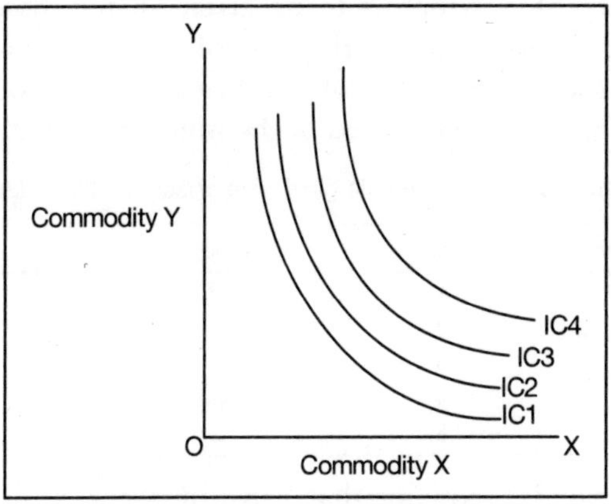

Diagram 5.2: Indifference Map

As the consumer moves from IC1 curve to IC2, IC3 and IC4, it shows that he gets higher and higher level of satisfaction. If consumer moves from IC4 to IC3, IC2 and IC1, he gets lower and lower level of satisfaction. The amount of X and Y commodities in combinations differs from IC to IC.

A consumer, subject to his income limits, prefers any combination of two goods on a higher IC to any combination on a lower IC. A higher IC represents a higher level of satisfaction than, a lower IC but 'how much' higher or 'how much' lower is not indicated. This is because in ordinal utility approach it is not possible to specify quantitative differences in various levels of satisfaction.

But the fact is that a consumer remains indifferent between different combinations of two goods on a same IC.

5.1.6 Diminishing Marginal Rate of Substitution (DMRS): The concept of Marginal Rate of Substitution (MRS) is an important tool of IC analysis of demand theory. The rate at which the consumer is prepared to exchange goods X and Y is known as MRS. In other words, MRS shows that in order to get one more X how much Y he has to sacrifice so that he continues to derive the same satisfaction as before. So the MRS of X for Y may define as the amount of Y whose loss can just be compensated by one unit addition of X. Simply MRS of X and Y represents the quantity of Y which is to be given up for the gain of an additional unit of X so that the level of satisfaction remains the same. But the marginal rate of sacrifice of Y commodity should be diminishing. It is explained in the following table 5.2.

Table 5.2: Diminishing Marginal Rate of Substitution (DMRS)

Combinations	Good X	Good Y	MRS
A	1	12	–
B	2	8	1 : 4
C	3	5	1 : 3
D	4	3	1 : 2
E	5	2	1 : 1

The table 5.2 explains that MRS of X for Y diminishes as more and more of good X is substituted for good Y. As the consumer acquires more and more of good X he is prepared to forego less and less of good Y, it is because the significance of X in terms of Y goes on diminishing with each addition to his stock of X.

For each additional unit of X, few units of Y are substituted by the consumer. The substitution of X for Y goes on diminishing as it can be seen in the last column of the Table. In the initial stages 4 units of Y are substituted for 1 unit of X. As we go on possessing additional unit of X less and less units of Y are substituted. This is referred to as the "Principle of DMRS". Generally, since an increase in the quantity of good X is always accompanied by a decrease in the quantity of good Y, the MRS is always negative. It can be written symbolically as:

$$MRSxy = dY/dX.$$

MRSxy = Marginal Rate of Substitution between commodity X and Y

d = Change.

X and Y = Commodities.

There are three important reasons for DMRS:

(i) As the stock of good X increases the desire to possess 'X' decreases because the marginal significance of good

X diminishes. On the other hand, as the stock of good Y decreases the desire to possess Y increases because the marginal significance of Y increases. Therefore, as the consumer substitutes more and more of X for Y, he is prepared to give up less and less of Y for an additional unit of X. Hence the MRS diminishes.

(ii) The Goods are imperfect substitutes of each other. If two goods, X and Y, are perfect substitutes, increase in the quantity of one and decrease in the quantity of another would not make any difference in the marginal significance of the goods. But two goods are not perfect substitutes and hence MRS of X for Y declines.

(iii) The principle of DMRS will hold good only if the increase in the quantity of one good does not increase the want satisfying power of the other. But this does not happen and hence the MRS diminishes.

The DMRS represents the slope of the IC curve. Since each increase in unit of X causes units of Y to diminish less and less, the numerical value of the slope also goes on declining. In graphic terms, the principle of DMRS means that, the slope of IC curve must always be decreasing as we move along it from left to right. It is illustrated in the following diagram 5.3.

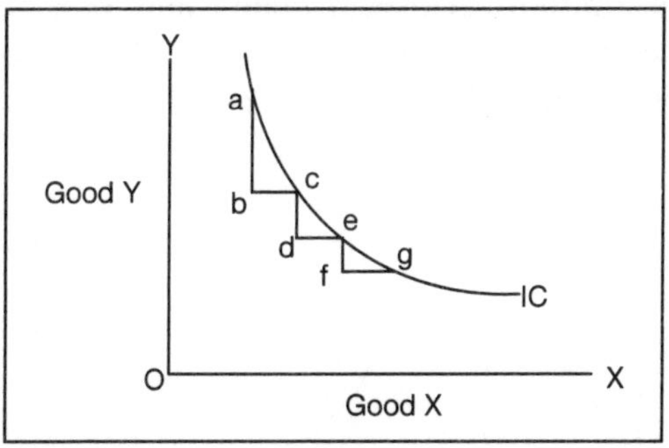

Diagram 5.3: Diminishing Marginal Rate of Substitution (DMRS)

A stair case that descends to the right is drawn along IC curve. The steps of this stair case are of equal width, i.e. bc=de=fg but of diminishing height from top to bottom i.e. ab>cd>ef. This is due to the fact that while the number of units of X continues to increase at the rate of one unit of X in the different combinations, the number of units of Y continues to decrease at a progressively diminishing rate. The curve IC thus is negatively sloped and hence represents the principle of DMRS.

In brief, MRS shows the rate at which the consumer is prepared to exchange two goods for each other. This MRS always diminishes. The IC curve is negatively sloping or convex to the origin because of the operation of the principle of DMRS. The Law of DMRS is a better and more dependable basis of the theory of consumer demand than the Marshallian Law of diminishing marginal utility.

5.2 PROPERTIES OF INDIFFERENCE CURVE

Indifference curve possesses certain properties or geometrical characteristics. They are as follows:

(i) **An Indifference curve always slopes downwards from left to the right:** The IC represents a number of alternative combinations of two goods which give the consumer the same level of satisfaction. If consumer increases the amount of one commodity in combination on same IC, he must sacrifice certain amount of another commodity in the combination for remaining on the same level of satisfaction. The marginal rate of substitution declines at diminishing rate. So IC slopes downwards from left to right. It is shown in the following diagram 5.4.

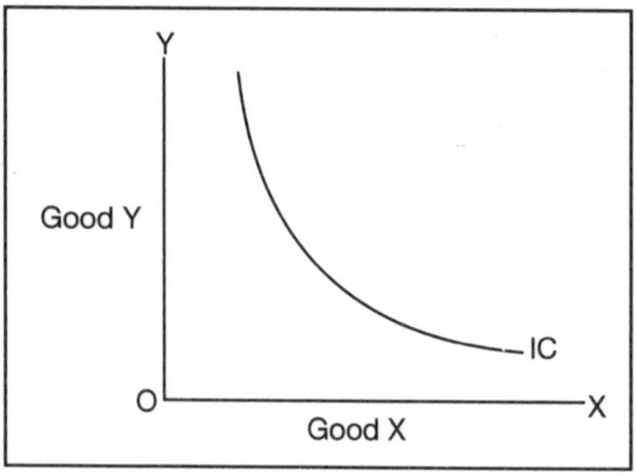

Diagram 5.4: Indifference Curve

IC is sloping downward means that when the amount of one good in the combination is increased, the amount of the other good is decreased. This is necessary because the level of satisfaction should remain same on an IC. The various combinations of two goods laying on an IC give the same satisfaction to the consumer cannot assume a slope other than downward sloping to the right. The slope of the IC at its various points will depend upon how much of good Y the consumer is willing to part with for an extra unit of good X.

If IC does not slope downward, it will be a horizontal line or a vertical line or rising upwards from left to right line or curve. But these are absurdities. They are studied as:

(a) **If IC is a horizontal straight-line:** If IC is a horizontal line, the amount of one commodity of the combinations, say good Y, will remain constant and only another commodity, say good X, will change to give same level of satisfaction. It is shown in the following diagram 5.5.

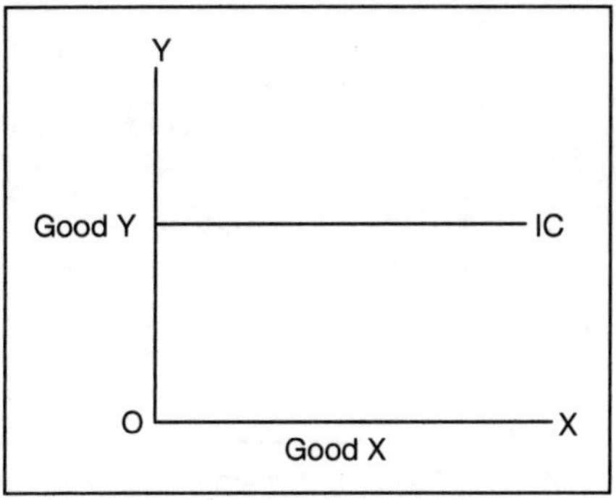

Diagram 5.5: Horizontal Straight-line IC

This is nonsensical because if, by keeping units of Y constant, an increase in the units of X will give more and more satisfaction instead giving same level of satisfaction.. So an IC cannot be a horizontal straight-line.

(b) **If IC is a vertical straight-line:** It would be similar to the case of horizontal straight-line. Here units of good X remain constant and the units of Y keep on changing in succeeding combinations. It is shown in the following diagram 5.6.

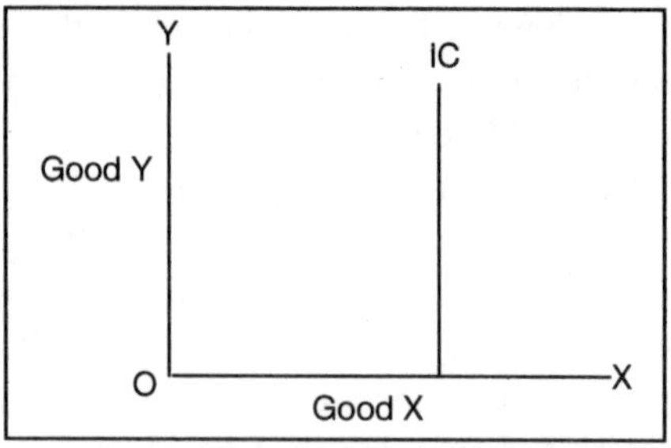

Diagram 5.6: Vertical Straight-line IC

All combinations on the curve cannot give the same satisfaction. Therefore IC cannot be a vertical straight-line.

(c) **If IC is upward sloping to the right:** It would mean that the amounts of both the goods increase as the consumer moves to the right along the curve but level of satisfaction remains same. It is shown in the following diagram 5.7.

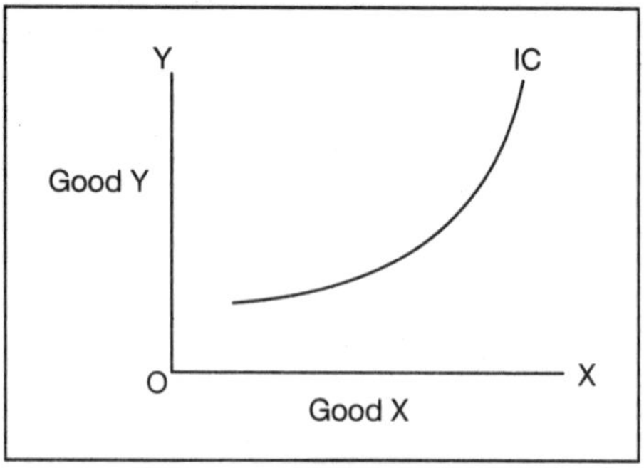

Diagram 5.7: IC Sloping Upward from Left to Right

It means that a combination, which contains more of both goods, gives the same satisfaction as the combination which contains smaller amounts of both the goods. It is clearly foolish to think so. Therefore IC cannot slope upward to the right.

In brief, so we can conclude that the IC always slopes downwards from left to the right and has a negative slope.

(ii) **IC is convex to the origin:** IC is usually convex to the origin O. It means that an IC is relatively flatter in its right hand portion and relatively steeper in its left hand portion. It is illustrated in the following diagram 5.8.

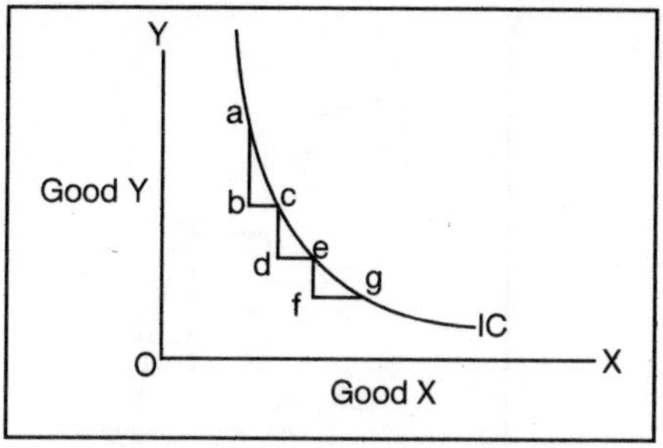

Diagram 5.8: IC is convex to the origin

This convexity is due to the operation of Principle of Diminishing Marginal Rate of Substitution between X and Y. The rate of reduction of good Y is diminishing i.e. ab>cd>ef whereas the rate of good X addition is constant i.e. bc=de=fg so MRSxy<1.

If MRSxy >1 or =1, it will also be absurdity. If IC is concave to the origin, it will imply that the MRS of X for Y increases as more and more of X is substituted for Y. This clearly violates our fundamental assumption about consumer behaviour, which states that MRSxy diminishes as consumer substitutes more and more of X for Y. Therefore if the principle of DMRS is valid, then the IC cannot be concave. Likewise IC cannot be a straight-line which implies that MRSxy remain constant as more units of X are acquired in place of Y. since MRSxy is equal to the slope of IC at a point on it and because a straight-line has the same slope throughout, the straight-line IC would mean the same MRSxy throughout. But MRSxy cannot remain constant except when goods happen to be perfect substitutes. Hence IC cannot be a straight-line as MRSxy usually falls. Both concave IC and straight-line IC cases are illustrated in the following diagrams 5.9 and 5.10.

Therefore IC is generally convex to the origin.

(iii) **ICs cannot intersect each other:** Each IC shows a particular level of satisfaction. Therefore by definition no two ICs can intersect or cut each other. Each IC is numbered on the basis of the position of ICs in the indifference map. A higher number indicates a higher level of satisfaction. Two ICs intersecting each other

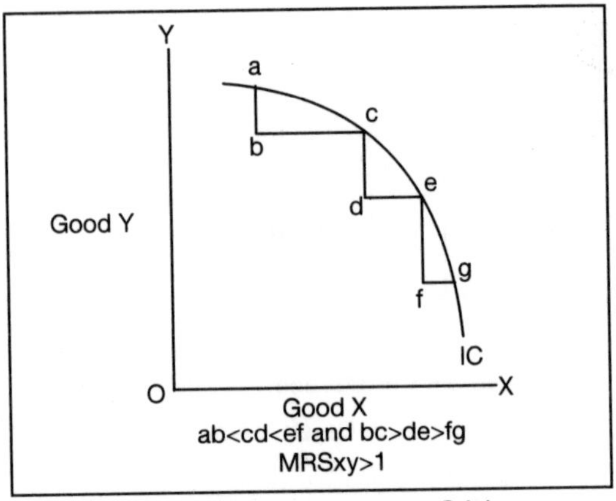

Diagram 5.9: IC Concave to Origin

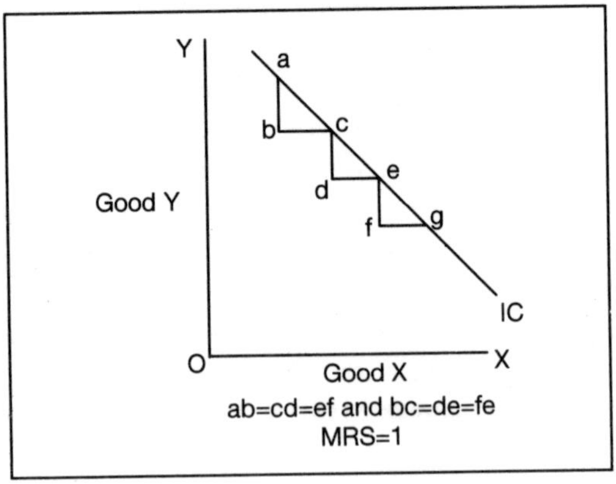

Diagram 5.10: IC Straight-line

means equating two different levels of satisfaction by force. This is untenable and illogical. Hence no two ICs cut each other. It is illustrated in the following diagram 5.11.

Two indifference curves have been shown cutting each other at point A. The IC2 shown higher level of satisfaction and IC1 represents lower level of satisfaction. At point A both IC1 and IC2 intersected each other. This means that two levels of satisfaction IC1 and IC2 should show unequal satisfaction but at point A both became equal, it is absurdity.

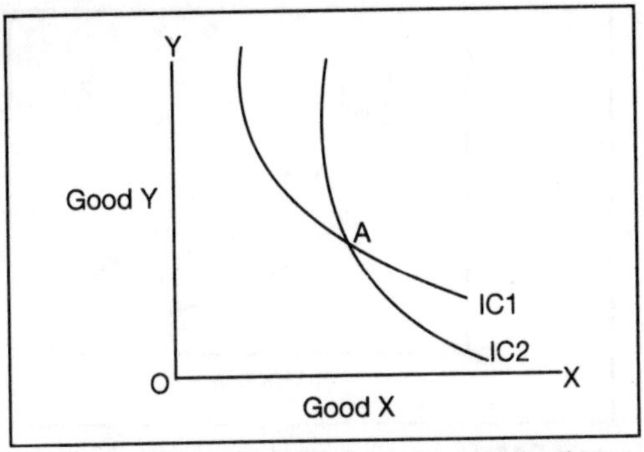

Diagram 5.11: ICs cannot Intersect each other

(iv) **ICs need not necessarily be parallel to each other:** Indifference Curves need not necessarily be parallel to each other because the rate of substitution between the two goods, X and Y need not be the same in all the indifference schedules. It is, therefore, not necessary that the ICs be parallel to each other. It is illustrated in the following diagram 5.12.

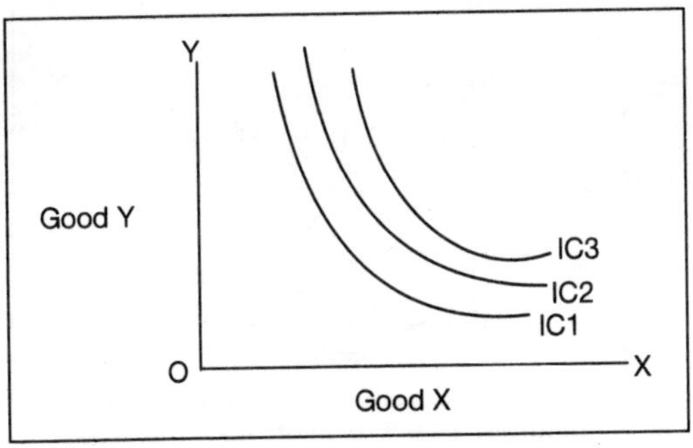

Diagram 5.12: ICs not Parallel to each other

(v) **A higher indifference curve represents a higher level of satisfaction:** In following diagram there are two indifference curves, IC1 and IC2. The combination A on the IC2 will provide the consumer more satisfaction compared to the combination B or C on IC1 as shown in diagram 5.13.

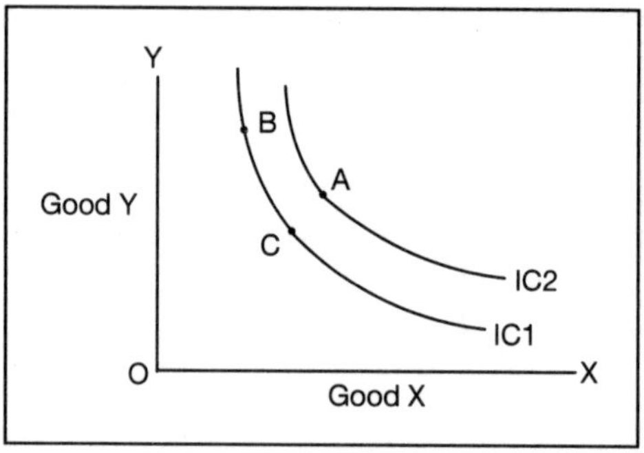

Diagram 5.13: Higher IC gives Higher Level of Satisfaction

The consumer prefers combination A to B and C. Thus an indifference curve at a higher level gives higher level of satisfaction. The ICs lie to the right of base IC give higher level of satisfaction.

(vi) **An indifference curve cannot touch either axis:** The IC touches neither OX-axis nor OY-axis. It is explained in the following diagram 5.14.

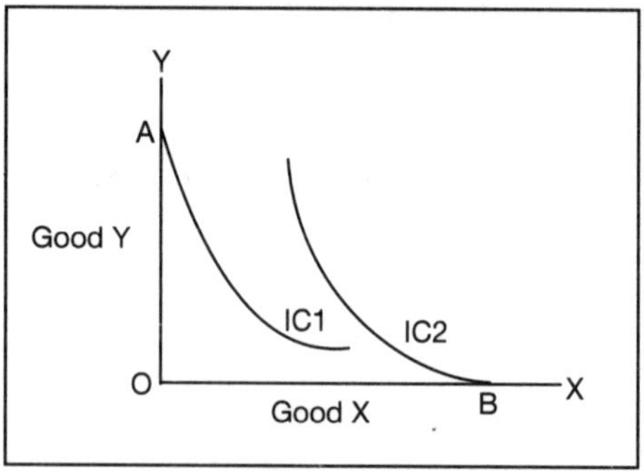

Diagram 5.14: IC cannot Touch Either Axis

If an indifference curve touches X-axis, consumer will be having OB quantity of good X and none of good Y. Similarly if an indifference curve touches the Y-axis the consumer will have OA of good Y and none of good X. But this is against the assumption of the indifference analysis i.e. the consumer should buy two goods in combination.

In brief the above discussed are the important properties of Indifference curve.

5.3 CONSUMER'S EQUILIBRIUM

The aim of the consumer is to attain the maximum level of satisfaction by spending his limited income. The equilibrium of consumer under indifference curve approach is explained by using two tools namely (i) indifference map and (ii) price-line or budget-line.

5.3.1 The Indifference Map: An indifference map consists of different indifference curves and each curve shows various combinations of two goods giving the same level of satisfaction. It exhibits consumer's scale of preferences for various combinations of two goods X and Y. It helps to explain the consumer's equilibrium under IC analysis.

5.3.2 Budget or Price Line: Price-line or budget-line exhibits the prices of two goods and consumer's money income. The consumer's ability to get preferred combination of the goods depends upon his money income and the prices of the two goods. The consumer in his attempt to maximize satisfaction will always try to reach the highest possible IC. But his attempt to do so is limited by the prices of those goods and his money income. The budget or price line shows the various combinations of the two goods that the consumer can buy at different prices with a given income level. It does not indicate which particular combination of the two goods is preferred by the consumer.

The budget line of a consumer can be explained with the help of an example: suppose the consumer has money income of ₹ 50 which he wants to spend entirely on two goods, namely X and Y, to attain maximum satisfaction. The price of X is ₹ 10 and that of Y is ₹ 5 per unit. So the consumer's budget-line is illustrated in the following diagram 5.15.

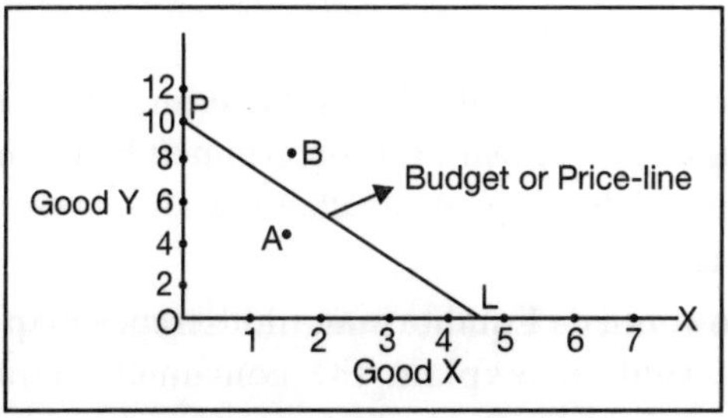

Diagram 5.15: Budget or Price-line

If consumer spends his whole income only on good X, he will get only 5 units of X or if he spends his income entirely only on good Y, he will get only 10 units of Y. The budget-line or the price-line will be drawn joining 5X and 10Y by a straight-line PL. The consumer can buy any combination that lies on the budget-line. PL line shows all those combinations of two goods, X and Y, which the consumer can buy spending his given income on the two goods at their given prices. He can have 10Y and no X, or 8Y and 1x, or 6Y and 2X, or 4Y and 3X, etc. But it should be noted that any combination of goods as B which lies above the budget-line PL will be beyond the reach of the consumer because his income will not permit him to buy that combination. Similarly combination A which lies below PL line is not desirable to him because the combination is inferior and he is capable of purchasing more with ₹ 50.

Now what happens to the budget-line if either the price of goods changes or the income of the consumer changes? If the price of one good X falls, the price of Y and income remaining constant, the budget-line will touch the X-axis at a point right to L, its other end touching the same point P as before. In other words, a fall in the price of X enables him to buy any more of X, without reducing the purchase of Y. If the price of Y falls the opposite happens.

If the income changes, prices of the two goods remaining the same, there will be a parallel shift of the budget-line. If income rises, the budget-line shifts to the right of the original budget-line PL and if income falls it shifts to the left of the original budget-line PL. The shift in budget-line indicates that the consumer's ability to purchase the two goods increases or decreases as the income rises or falls, respectively.

The slope of the budget-line is determined by the prices of the two goods but its position is determined by the income level. If prices change, the slope of its changes and if income changes, its position changes.

5.3.3 Consumer's Equilibrium: Indifference map and budget-line are the tools to explain the consumer's equilibrium. A consumer is said to be at equilibrium when he is buying such a combination of two goods as leaves him with no tendency to rearrange his purchases of goods. He is then in a position of balance in regard to the allocation of his money expenditures on combination of two goods that gives him maximum level satisfaction. The indifference map portrays consumer's scale of preferences between various possible combinations of two goods X and Y while the budget-line shows the various combinations of those two goods which he can afford to buy with his given money income at given prices of the two goods. These two tools help us show the equilibrium position of the consumer. It is illustrated in the following diagram 5.16.

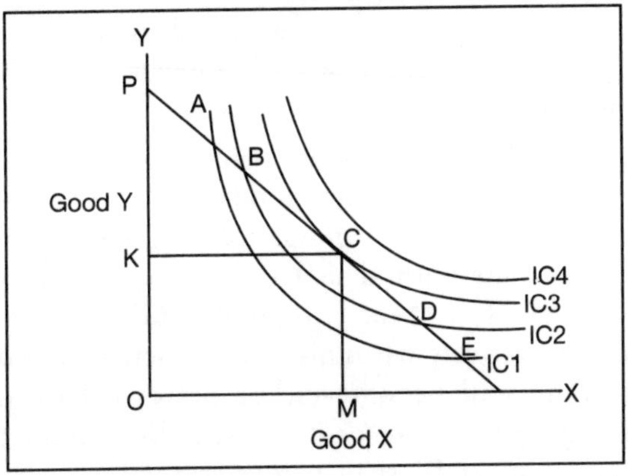

Diagram 5.16: Consumer's Equilibrium

IC1, IC2, IC3 and IC4 are the indifference curves. PL is the Budget or Price-line. A, B, C, D and E are the combinations of goods X and Y on price-line. A, B, D and E are the combinations at the points of intersection with IC1 and IC2 so their levels of satisfaction are at low. The price line tangent IC3 at C point that gives maximum or higher level satisfaction to the consumer. IC4 is above the price-line. Thus the point C is the consumer's equilibrium where he purchases OM of X and OK of Y good.

In brief, the consumer attains maximum satisfaction or equilibrium at that point where the budget-line becomes tangent to an IC.

5.4 INCOME, PRICE AND SUBSTITUTION EFFECTS

The consumer's equilibrium or level of maximum satisfaction depends upon money income of consumer and prices of commodity. Any change in income of the consumer or price of goods or both will effect on consumer's equilibrium. The income effect, the price effect and substitutions effect on consumer are discussed as under:

5.4.1 Income Effect: Assuming prices of both goods remain constant, a change in income of the consumer will effect on the consumer's equilibrium position which is called 'Income Effect'. He will be placed at higher indifference curve when his income increases, assuming prices of the two goods remaining the same; in contrary, consumer will be placed at lower indifference curve when his income declines.

The income effect shows the reaction of the consumer in regard to his purchases of the two goods X and Y when his income changes, the prices of the two goods and his preference remaining the same. It is quite natural that the consumer will be able to purchase more or less of the two goods and enjoy more or less satisfaction respectively when his income increases or decreases. Technically he will become either better-off or worse-off respectively. Every increase or decrease in his income takes him to a higher or lower IC than before respectively. The income consumption curve traces this income effect on the consumer as shown in the following diagram 5.17.

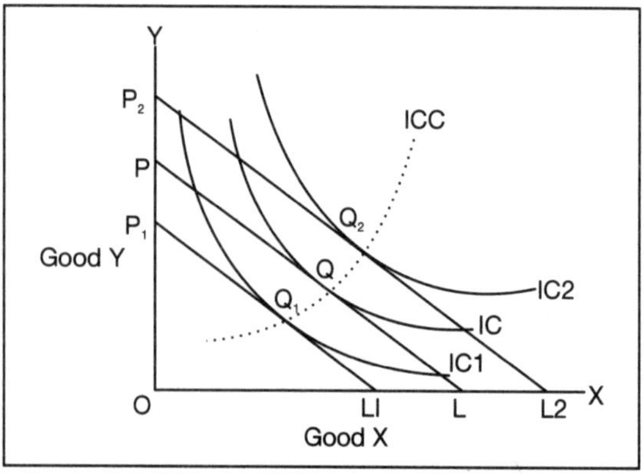

Diagram 5.17: Income Effect

PL is the original price-line and IC is the original indifference curve. The consumer is in equilibrium at Q on IC when PL is his budget-line. The budget line shifts upward to PL2 when income of the consumer will increase and he will be placed on higher indifference curve IC2 thus his new equilibrium will be Q_2. In contrary, when consumer's income declines he will be placed on lower IC1 and his new equilibrium will be at Q_1. By joining Q_1, Q and Q_2 we get 'Income Consumption Curve' (ICC) which shows the effect of income change on consumer's equilibrium.

Income effect can either be positive or negative. It is positive when the consumption of the goods increases with the increase in income. Hence the ICC will slope upwards to the right. This is the normal shape of ICC. However for some goods income effect is negative. Negative income effect implies that with the increase in income the consumer reduces his consumption. 'Inferior goods' have negative income effect. The consumer begins to substitute superior for 'inferior goods' when his income increases. For example those people who consume cheap food grains such as Maize, Ragi, Bajra, Jowar, etc. switch over to consume rice and wheat when their income increases. In such a case the ICC will either slope backward to the left or downward to the right depending upon the inferiority of the two goods consumed. Therefore the ICC can have various possible slopes.

In brief, the income effect shows the effect of changes in the income of the consumer on his purchases of the two goods. It is generally positive but there are also cases of negative income effect.

5.4.2 Substitution Effect: A 'Substitution Effect' occurs when the relative prices of goods change in such a way that the consumer concerned is neither better-off nor worse-off as a result of it. It happens because the fall in prices of some goods is neutralized by rise in prices of other goods which keeps the consumer on the same level of satisfaction or IC. While explaining substitution effect certain assumptions are made as: (i) the price of one good rises and the price of other good falls, (ii) the costlier good is compensated by the cheaper good so the consumer remains on same indifference curve (IC), and (iii) money income of the consumer remains same but real income or purchasing power of the consumer will be changed due to change in prices of the goods. The substitution effect is illustrated in the following diagram 5.18.

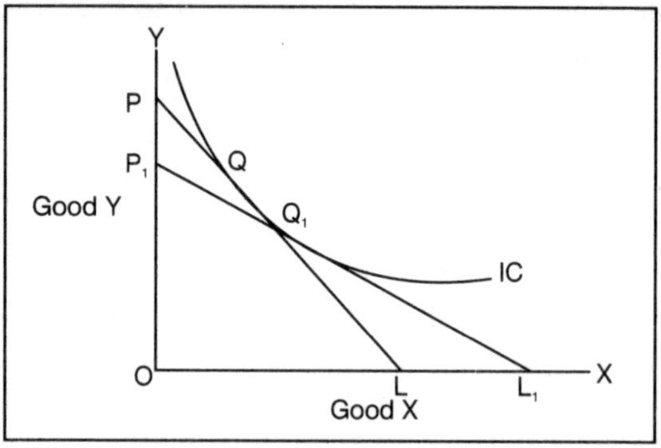

Diagram 5.18: Substitution Effect

PL is the original budget or price-line; IC is the original indifference curve of the consumer and his equilibrium is at Q. Now the price of good Y rises and the price of good X falls so his new budget or price-line is P1L1. The consumer compensated the loss of rise in price of good Y by the gain of fall in price of good X so he makes readjustment in purchase of a new combination of both good i.e. Q_1 which is also on same IC means level of satisfaction. The consumer is neither better-off nor worse-off than before. The movement from Q to Q_1 on the same IC is called 'Substitution Effect'.

In Hicks and Allen Substitution Effect, price change is accompanied by so much change in neither money income that the consumer is made neither better-off nor worse-off than before. It takes place on the same IC. The amount by which the money income of the consumer is changed, so that he remains neutral or indifferent is called "compensating variation in income". In other words compensating variation in income is a change in the income of the consumer which is just sufficient to compensate him for a change in the price of a good.

5.4.3 Price Effect: The effect of a change in the price of a good on its purchases is called 'Price Effect'. Assuming that the money income, tastes of the consumer and prices of other goods remaining the same, any change in price of a good results into change in consumer's equilibrium position. Like the income consumption curve tracing the income effect the price consumption curve traces the price effect. It is explained in the following diagram 5.19.

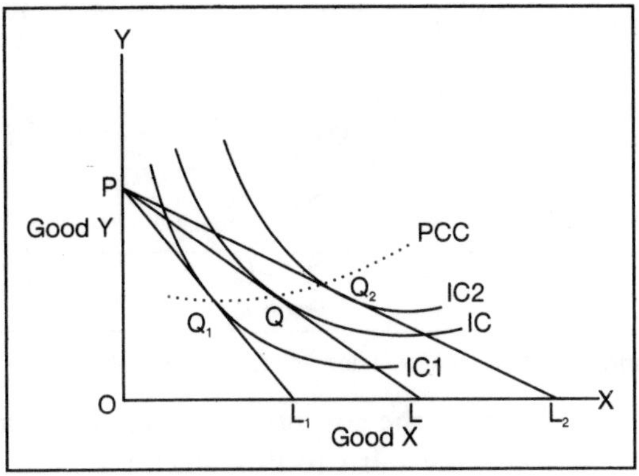

Diagram 5.19: Price Effect

PL is the original budget or price-line, IC is the original indifference curve of the consumer and his equilibrium is at Q. His money income and price of good Y remain constant but change in price of good X will effect on consumer's equilibrium position. The price line moved to PL2 when the price of good X declined and the consumer is place on new equilibrium at Q_2 on higher IC2 or higher level of satisfaction. In contrary, the price-line will be moved to PL1 when the price of good X falls and consumer will be placed at new point of equilibrium i.e. Q_1 which is on lower IC1 or low level of satisfaction. By joining Q_1, Q and Q_2, we get 'Price Consumption Curve' (PCC) which explains the price effect.

The PCC may be upward or downward sloping nature of goods or elasticity of demand for the goods.

It should also be noted that the price effect is the sum total of two effects namely (i) Substitution Effect and (ii) Income Effect. Therefore for a clear study of price effect it can be split into two different parts: one showing income effect and the other showing Substitution effect. It is illustrated in the following diagram 5.20.

PE = QQ_1, IE = QQ_2 and SE = Q_1Q_2

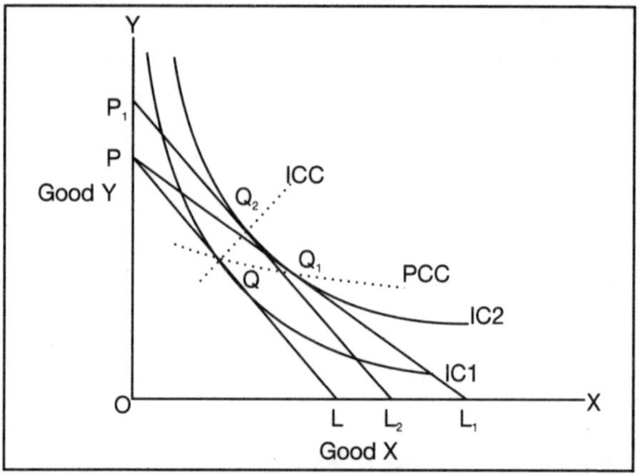

Diagram 5.20: Price Effect: Income Effect + Substitution Effect

In the diagram 5.20 the consumer is in equilibrium at point Q on IC1. The price-line shifts to PL1 when the price of X falls and the consumer attains equilibrium at point Q_1 on IC2. This movement from Q to Q_1 is due to price effect traced by PCC. At the same time due to fall in the price of X, the real income of the consumer rises. Now the price of X being relatively cheaper, he substitutes X for Y. When the consumer's income is reduced by the compensating variation in income, the consumer moves along the same IC2 and substitutes X for Y. With price line P1L2 he is in equilibrium at point Q_2 on IC2. This movement from Q_1 to Q_2 on the same IC2 is Substitution Effect and the movement of the consumer from Q to Q_2 is income effect. The ICC traces the income effect and substitution effect.

In brief, price effect is composed of income effect and substitution effect. The direction in which quantity demanded will change as a result of the fall in price will depend upon the direction and strength of income and substitution effects.

5.4.4 Superiority of Indifference Curve Technique Over Utility Approach: Indifference Curve Approach is superior over Utility Approach in following respect:

(i) IC analysis is based on more realistic assumption i.e. the consumer tells his scale of preference between goods instead of numerical measurement.

(ii) IC analysis is a more general approach because it is applicable to more than one goods.

(iii) IC approach assumes that the marginal utility of money to the consumer does not remain constant. Any change in price of good results into change in real income or purchasing power of the consumer.

(iv) IC analysis clearly brings out the distinction between income effect and substitution effect.

(v) It is a more objective approach because it takes into account of the related goods like substitutes and complementary goods.

(vi) It makes fewer assumptions.

5.4.5 Criticisms: In spite of IC analysis superiority over utility approach, it is criticized by many economists as under:

(i) **It is old wine in new bottle:** D.H. Robertson said that IC analysis tells nothing new. It told the same thing that is told by the utility analysis.

(ii) **It is based on wrong assumption:** It assumed that the consumer is aware of the various combinations of two goods that give him same level of satisfaction. But it is unrealistic assumption because it is difficult to say that all combinations of two goods will give same level of satisfaction, for ex: the satisfaction from 4 apples and 4 banana combination may be different from the satisfaction given by 1 apple and 6 banana combination.

(iii) **IC analysis deals with only two goods:** In real life the consumer spends his income on more than two goods. So it is inapplicable in real context.

(iv) **It too depends upon the assumption of 'Consumer behaves rationally':** All consumers do not behave rationally. There are many consumers who spend their income on goods irrationally.

(v) **It is a microeconomic analysis:** Since it is based on certain assumptions, it is based on microeconomic analysis. So it neglected macroeconomic analysis.

(vi) **It is based on introspective method:** It studies consumer behaviour on the basis of imaginary indifference curve but it is not applicable to the real world conditions.

(vii) **It is difficult to undertake empirical research work:** Since utility is not measurable quantitatively under IC analysis, it is difficult to draw the relation between price and demand.

5.5 MODEL QUESTIONS

2 Marks Questions

(a) What do you mean by Indifference Curve?

(b) What is Indifference Schedule?

(c) What is Indifference Map?

(d) Name any two assumptions of Indifference Curve Analysis.

(e) State Marginal Rate of Substitution.

(f) What is Price-line?

(g) Write any two properties of Indifference Curve.

(h) What is Consumer's Equilibrium?

(i) What do you mean by Price Effect?

(j) What do you mean by Income Effect?

(k) What do you mean by Substitution Effect?

5 Marks Questions

1. Give the brief account of Indifference Curve Analysis.
2. Write a short note on Assumptions of Indifference Curve Analysis.
3. Write a note on Indifference Map.
4. Write a note on Indifference Schedule.
5. Discuss in brief consumer's equilibrium under IC Approach.
6. Write a note on Price Effect.
7. Write a note on Income Effect.
8. Write a note on Substitution Effect.

9. Discuss in brief Price Effect = Income Effect + Substitution Effect.
10. Write a note on Marginal Rate of Substitution.

10 Marks Questions

1. Define Indifference Curve. Explain its properties.
2. Define Indifference Curve. Explain consumer's equilibrium.
3. Explain Price Effect, Income Effect and Substitution Effect.
4. Explain in detail Indifference Curve Analysis.

6

Theory of Production

6.1 PRODUCTION ANALYSIS

Production is another important branch of economics. Production is the source of supply and thereby it plays important role in theory of value. It is also considered as the theory of production that has the various aspects.

6.1.1 Meaning and Definition of Production: Since consumption means the destruction of utility, production means the creation of utility. In other words, production refers to the process of physical transformation of inputs into output and value addition to the output. For ex: A farm takes fertilizer, seed, land and labour and turns them into wheat or corn. Modern factories take inputs such as energy, raw materials, computerized machinery and labour and use them to produce goods like tractors, TV's, etc. Thus, production can be defined as "a process by which inputs are transformed (produced or processed) into output". The following are the main points to be noted from the above definition of production:

(i) It is a process of physical transformation of basic materials or inputs into output.

(ii) It is a process of creation of utility in goods and services.

(iii) It includes all the activities that amount to addition of value to the output.

6.1.2 Types of Creation of Utility: There are four types of utility-creation:

(i) **Form Utility:** The physical transformation of basic material into a commodity creates utility in it. For ex: Row cotton converted into cotton-cloth.

(ii) **Place-Utility:** The shifting or transporting a thing from one place to another place creates utility in it. For ex: Transporting the iron-ore from mining-place to steel factory.

(iii) **Time-Utility:** The climatic condition or season creates utility in a thing. For ex: Use of cotton cloth in summer.

(iv) **Service Utility:** The services like education, training, etc. services create utility in the persons. For ex: Bed training makes a student a capable teacher.

6.1.3 Factors of Production: Basic materials are necessary to produce goods or services and without them production is impossible. The basic materials use in production process is called 'Factors of Production or Inputs'. For ex: Land, labour, water, time, minerals, forest, etc. They are also called 'Resources'.

There are two types of classification of inputs. They are:

(A) Traditional Classification: The classical economists have classified inputs into four types:

(i) **Land:** The resources on the earth, above the earth and under the earth are called land.

(ii) **Labour:** The mental and physical exertion of human-being is called labour.

(iii) **Capital:** It is man-made. The produced means for further production is called capital. It is in form of fund as well as capital goods like machines, tools, etc.

(iv) **Organizer:** It is also known as 'Entrepreneur'. One who organizes the other three factors of production and undertakes other production activities is called 'Organizer'.

The classical economists have difference of opinion about the classification of inputs. Some classical economists argue that originally there are only two factors of productions *viz.* land and labour.

(B) Modern Classification: On the basis of nature, modern economists classified inputs into two types:

(i) **Fixed Factors:** The factors of production used in production process but that are not related to the level of production are called 'Fixed Factors'. These are essential in production process but their quantity remains same at various levels of output or at zero level of output. For ex: Factory Building, Machines, Managerial Staff, Security Staff, etc.

(ii) **Variable Factors:** The factors of production used in production process but that are related to the level of production are called 'Variable Factors'. The use of their quantity depends upon the level or quantity of output. They are zero when the level of output is zero. That is why they are called variable factors. For ex: Row materials, labour, fuel, etc.

6.1.4 Production Function: (a) Meaning: The Production of a commodity or service depends upon the inputs. For ex: The production of cotton cloth depends upon the row cotton, machines, labour, fuel, managerial staff, etc. So the output is the function of inputs. Thus the functional relation between input and output is called 'Production Function'. It can be expressed in algebraic form as:

$$Q = f(L, K \ldots)$$

Q = Output, f = Functional Relation and L, K ... are inputs.

It can be read as 'output is the functional outcome of inputs L, K,' etc. It can also be written equation-form as:

$$Q = \alpha L + \beta K, \ L = \text{Labour}, \ K = \text{Capital}.$$

α and β are the constants. a indicates the ratio or proportion between change in output to change in labour i.e. $\Delta Q/\Delta L$ and β indicates the ratio or proportion between change in output to change in capital i.e. $\Delta Q/\Delta K$.

For ex: L = 10, K = 100, $\alpha = 0.75$ and $\beta = 0.25$. The value of Q can be calculated as:

By substituting the values in above 'Production Function Equation', the output can be calculated as:

$$Q = 0.75 \times 10 + 0.25 \times 100$$
$$= 7.5 + 25 = 32.5$$

(b) Features of Production Function: The production function has the following main features:

(i) It indicates the technical and logical relation between inputs and output i.e. input: output ratio.

(ii) It differs from industry to industry. For example, handloom is labour intensive and powerloom is capital intensive.

(iii) It may be fixed factors proportion or variable factors proportion.

(iv) It is a flow concept.

(v) It is a physical concept.

(vi) It will be influenced by change in technology, time and quality and quantity of inputs.

(c) Production Function Schedule: The technology or technique of production determines the proportion of inputs require to produce a certain quantity of output. For example, either 4 units of labour plus one unit of capital or 3 units of labour plus 2 units of capital are required to produce 100 units of output. The tabular statement showing the same amount of output at various combinations of labour and capital is called 'Production Function Schedule'. It is explained in table 6.1.

Table 6.1: Production Function Schedule
(in Units)

Combination	Capital (K)	Labour (L)	Output (Q)
A	4	1	100
B	3	2	100
C	2	3	100
D	1	4	100

Each combination has different amount of units of labour and capital but it produces the same amount of units of output. The input-output ratio is differing from combination to combination, it depends on technology.

(d) Equal Product Curve: Equal Product Curve is also called 'Production Indifference Curve' or 'Isoquant' or 'Production Possible Curve'. It is an important tool to analyze the production behaviour.

The curve that explains the relation between combination of inputs and output is called 'Equal Product Curve'. It helps to explain the production function. On the basis of Table 6.1, equal product curve is illustrated in the following diagram 6.1.

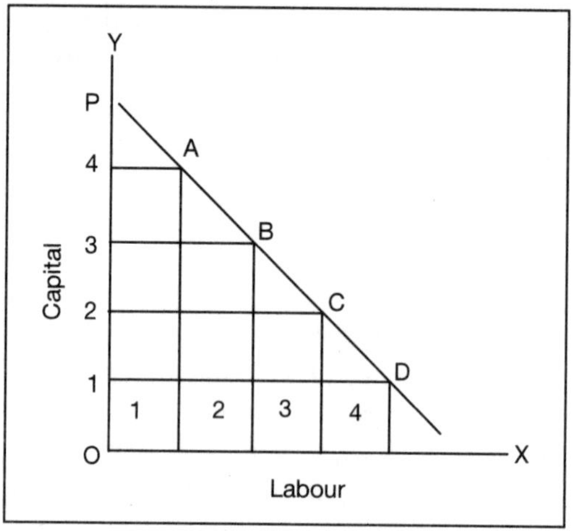

Diagram 6.1: Equal Product Curve

Units of labour are measured along 'OX' axis and units of capital are measured along 'OY' axis. 'PP' is the 'Equal Product Curve'. It shows the functional relation between inputs (units of labour and capital) and output. All the combinations on same 'PP' curve give same quantity of output, i.e. 100 units.

(e) **Properties of 'Equal Product Curve':** Production possible curve is governed by some properties and they are also considered as characteristic features of equal product curve. They are as follows:

(i) **Isoquant slopes downward from left to right:** In combinations of inputs, as producer increases the units of one input (labour) the units of other input (capital) declines in order to get same amount of output. So the shape of isoquant is neither rises upward nor horizontal nor vertical, if so, it is absurdity. No firm does like to employ more units of inputs than before to get same quantity of output.

(ii) **Isoquant is convex to the origin 'O':** The firm wants to use cheap input in place of dear input to reduce the cost of production so the rate of substitution between cheap dear inputs must decline. As the units of labour increases in same quantity, the given up quantity of units of capital must decline because no one input is complete substitute of another input. The right featured isoquant is shown in the following diagram 6.2.

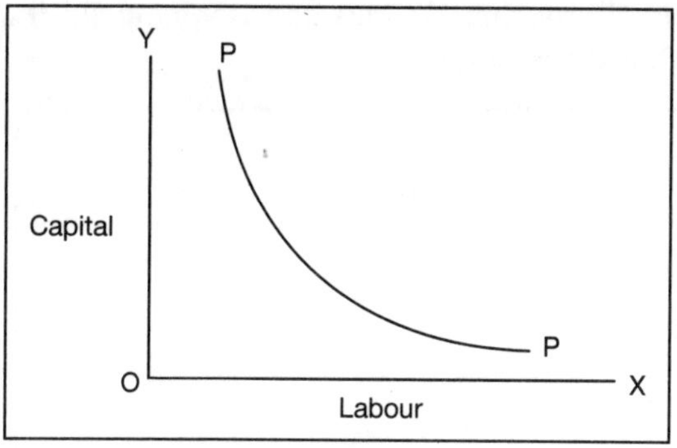

Diagram 6.2: Isoquant

'PP' is the isoquant which slopes downwards to right and convex to the origin 'O'.

(iii) **No two or more isoquants intersect each other:** Two different isoquants show two different quantities of output and combinations of inputs. No combination of inputs lies on two different isoquants giving same quantity of output. The intersection of isoquants 'PP' and 'P_1P_1' at the point 'E' explain the same absurdity situation. It is illustrated in the diagram 6.3.

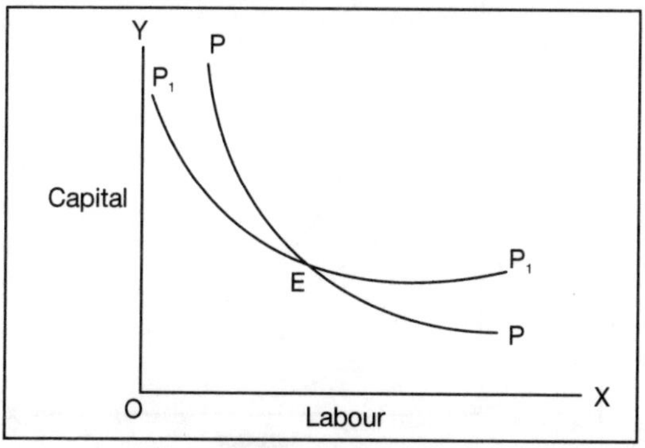

Diagram 6.3: Isoquants

(iv) **Isoquants should not touch either axis:** If any isoquant touches either 'X' or 'Y' axis, it shows the quantity of one input is zero in combination. It is absurdity because without the co-operation of two inputs production is not possible. It is illustrated in the diagram 6.4.

Isoquant 'P' touches 'Y' axis and isoquant 'P_1' touches 'X' axis so both are absurdities.

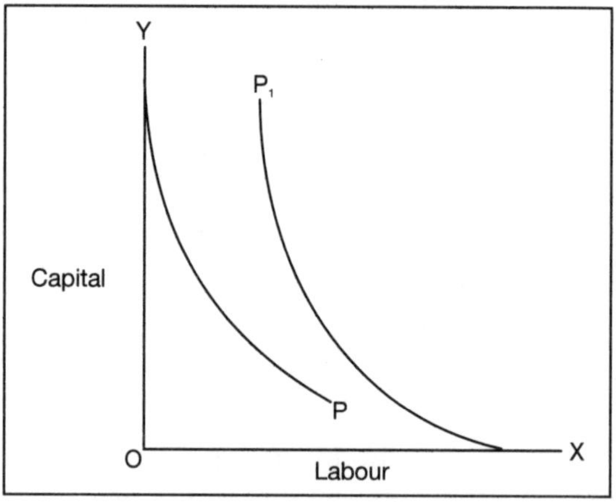

Diagram 6.4: Isoquants

(v) **Higher isoquant represents higher level of output:** Each isoquant shows different level of output. The higher isoquant shows higher level of output and the lower isoquant shows the lower level of output. It is illustrated in the following diagram 6.5.

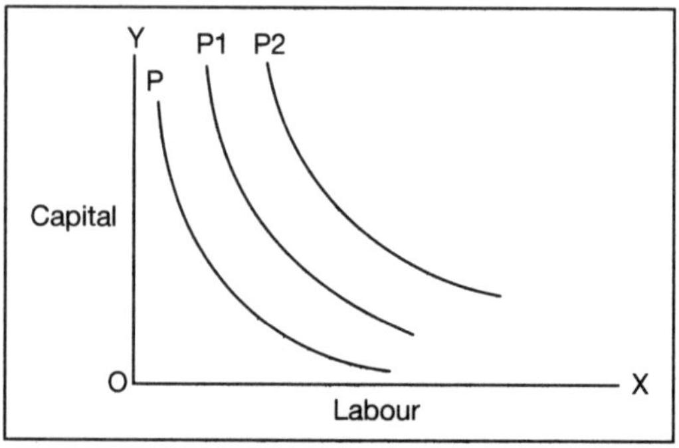

Diagram 6.5: Isoquants

'P' isoquant is lower to P_1 and P_2 isoquants; P_2 is higher than P and P_1 isoquants.

(F) Use of Isoquant: It helps producer to attain equilibrium where the producer could produce maximum output at minimum cost.

(G) Forms or Types of Production Function: There are two types of production function. They are discussed as under:

(i) On the basis of factor proportions the production functions can be classified in two forms. They are:

(a) **Fixed Factor-Proportions Production Function:** If the input-output ratio and input-input ratio are constant at all levels of output, it will be called 'Fixed Factor-Proportions Production Function'. For ex: 10 units of labour plus 5 units of capital are used to produce 100 units of output. 20 units of labour plus 10 units of capital are used to produce 200 units of same output. The input-output ratio is 15:100 at both levels of output. It is illustrated in the following diagram 6.6.

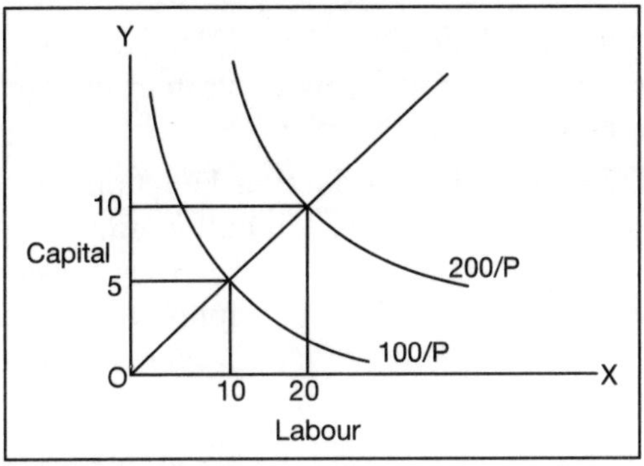

Diagram 6.6: Fixed Factor-Proportions

'OT' line shows input-output ratio as well as input-input ratio and it is determined by technology; it also decides input intensity. Input-output ratio is also called 'Technical Co-efficient of Production'. P, P1 are isoquants. The input-output ratio is 15:100 at both levels of output.

The fixed factor-proportions production function is also known as 'Homogeneous or Linear Production Function'.

(b) Variable Factor-Proportions Production Function: If the input-output ratio and input-input ratio are variable or changeable at all levels of output, it will be called 'Variable Factor-Proportions Production Function'. For ex: 10 units of labour plus 5 units of capital are used to produce 100 units of output. 20 units of labour plus 5 units of capital are used to produce 150 units of same output. The input-output ratio was 15:100 at 100 units of output and 25:150 at 150 units of output. It is the subject matter of short-run production function.

It is also known as 'Non-Homogeneous' or 'Non-Linear Production Function'.

(ii) On the basis of inputs used the production functions can be classified as:

(a) **Single Variable Production Function:** The functional relation between one input and output is called 'Single-Variable Production Function'. It can be algebraically expressed as:

$Q = f(L) \therefore Q = \alpha L$ Q = output,

f = functional relation, L = Labour and a = $\Delta Q/\Delta L$. It is the subject matter of 'Law of Variable Proportions' or 'Short-run Production Function'.

(b) **Two Variables Production Function:** It explains the function relation between output and two variables. It is classical economists' model. They considered labour and capital are the two inputs using in production process. It is more popular in economic analysis. It can be written as:

$Q = f(L, K) \therefore Q = \alpha L + \beta K$ L = Labour, K = Capital. $\alpha = \Delta Q/\Delta L$ and $\beta = \Delta Q/\Delta K$.

(c) **Multi-Variables Production Function:** It explains the functional relation between output and more than two variables. It can be expressed as:

$Q = f(N, L, K, E, U)$, N, L, K, E and U are the inputs.

(iii) On the basis of time-elements the production functions can be classified as:

(a) **Short-run Production Function:** In short-run, technology and inputs like capital remain constant. Only the variable inputs like labour are changeable. So the single-variable production function is short-run production function. . It is the subject matter of 'Law of Variable Proportions'.

(b) **Long-run Production Function:** Since there is sufficient time in long-run, the technology, scale of production and all inputs are variable or changeable. It is the subject matter of laws of returns to scale.

6.1.5 Cobb-Douglas Production Function: American economists P.H. Douglas and C.W. Cobb had conducted an empirical study on manufacturing industries to know the functional relation between inputs and output. Now it is popularly known as 'Cobb-Douglas Production Function'. They took two inputs namely labour and capital to explain the functional relation between inputs and output. They proved that to produce one unit of output labour contributes 75 per cent (3/4) and capital contributes 25 per cent (1/4) to the production. The sum of total contribution is ¾ + ¼ = 1 (or 75% + 25% = 100%). The contribution of labour is denoted by α (= $\Delta Q/\Delta L$) and the capital's contribution is denoted by β (= $\Delta Q/\Delta K$). Hence they explained the production function in form of following equation:

$$Q = f(L^{\alpha} K^{\beta})$$

Q = output, f = functional relation, L = labour, a = labour's contribution, K = capital and b = capital's contribution.

Cobb-Douglas had used it as a tool to analyses the constant returns to scale. It means to double the quantity of output; the inputs should be doubled in same proportions. In other words, the proportionate change in output should be equal to the proportionate change in inputs. For ex: 100 per cent change in quantity of inputs must lead to 100 per cent change in output. It can be expressed as:

Proportionate Change in Inputs = Proportionate Change in Output

$$\frac{Fn-Fn-1}{Fn-1} = \frac{Qn-Qn-1}{Qn-1}$$

Q = Output, F = Inputs, n = After Change Quantity, n–1 = Before Change Quantity. It can be also written as:

k = Fn– Fn–1/Fn–1, h = Qn–Qn–1/Qn–1

or

$k = \Delta F/F$, $h = \Delta Q/Q$

Therefore, according to Cobb-Douglas, the value of

$$h = k$$

It can be proved with the help of the following numerical example:

Q_1 = 100 units, F_1 = 50 units, Q_2 = 200 units and F_2 = 100 units. By substituting these values in above equation,

$h = Q_2 - Q_1/Q_1 = 200–100/100 = 1$ and

$k = F_2 - F_1/F_1 = 100 - 50/50 = 1$

$\therefore h = k = 1.$

Hence, the Cobb-Douglas production-function can be written as:

$h(Q) = k\ (L_\alpha\ K_\beta)$

With the help of this equation the laws of returns can be identified as:

If, h = k it is 'Law of Constant Returns to scale;

h > k it is 'Law of Increasing Returns to scale;

h < k it is 'Law of Decreasing Returns to scale;

Since Cobb-Douglas production function explains the proportionate relations between change output to change in input, it is also called 'Linear or Homogeneous Production-Function'.

6.1.6 Laws of Production: Like the laws of consumption, there are certain laws to explain the production and its behaviour. On the basis of time-element, the laws of production can be classified into two types: (a) Law of Returns to a factor and (b) Laws of Returns to scale.

(A) **The Law of Variable Proportions or Law of Returns to a Factor:** The Law of variable proportions is an important law of production. It explains the short-run production function. All factors of production are not variable in short-run because the inputs like machines, buildings, etc. need longer time for their change and by the by the technology or methods of production too need sufficient time for change. So only the variable factors like labour, raw material, fuel, etc. are changeable in short-run. Thus, in short-run, output is the functional outcome of variable factors. The law explains the short-run output behaviour in relation to a single factor of production i.e. labour. It is also called 'single variable production-function'. It can be explained as under:

(i) **Statement of the Law:** The law explains the production-function with one variable factor while the quantities of other factors of production are fixed. It describes the input-output relation in short-run. In short-run the variable factor is variable and fixed factors are constant. In such a situation the output can be increased by employing more and more equal amount of a variable factor with a given quantity of fixed factors. The resultant output will increase initially at increasing rate, then it will start increasing at diminishing rate up to a certain point, beyond that point it will also start diminishing. Under such circumstances the input-input ratio and input-output ratio will be changed. Thus the law is called 'law of variable proportions'.

Prof. Stigler defined the statement of the law as "As equal increments of one input are added, the input of other productive services being held constant, beyond a certain point the resultant increment of product will decrease i.e. the marginal product will diminish." In brief, the law states that "The Marginal Productivity of a variable input, which is being added to other inputs that are fixed in quantity, will eventually decline." For example, assuming labour is a variable input, as more units of labour in same quantity is added to a fixed amount of capital the resultant output of additional labour or the marginal production of labour starts declining. Of course, initially the total production, average production and marginal production will increase up to a certain point but beyond that point they will start falling. The point is decided by technique of production that determines the optimum combination of the fixed and variable inputs.

(ii) **Assumptions:** The statement of the law depends upon the following assumptions:

(i) Only a single variable input is changeable and all other inputs should remain constant. A variable input should be increased in same quantity.

(ii) The technique of production should remain unchanged.

(iii) The scale of production, size of plant and efficiency of the firm should remain constant.

(iv) All the units of a variable input are homogeneous or identical.

The statement of the law holds good only under these assumed conditions.

(iii) **The Explanation of the Law:** The statement of the law can be expressed in form of the following equation:

Q = f (L); Q = Output, L = Labour and f = Functional Relation.

As the quantity of labour is increased in same amount the resultant output will increase initially then start falling. So it can be expressed with the help of following quadratic equation:

$$Q = aL^1 + a_1L^2 - a_2L^3 \qquad \ldots(1)$$

Q = Output, L = Units of Labour, 1, 2, 3 = Exponential Power and a = Ratio between change in output to change in labour i.e. $\Delta Q/\Delta L$.

For example, if a = 5, a_1 = 4 and a_2 = 1, calculate the value of Q when the unit of labour is increased as 1, 2, 3, 4, 5 and 6 on 100 units of capital.

By substituting values in equation (1), the resultant output is calculated as:

When $L = 1, Q_1 = 5\times1 + 4\times1\times1 - 1\times1\times1\times1 = 08$

$L = 2, Q_2 = 5\times2 + 4\times2\times2 - 1\times2\times2\times2 = 18$

$L = 3, Q_3 = 5\times3 + 4\times3\times3 - 1\times3\times3\times3 = 24$

$L = 4, Q_4 = 5\times4 + 4\times4\times4 - 1\times4\times4\times4 = 20$

$L = 5, Q_5 = 5\times5 + 4\times5\times5 - 1\times5\times5\times5 = 00$

$L = 6, Q_6 = 5\times6 + 4\times6\times6 - 1\times6\times6\times6 = -42$

On the basis of these values, Total Production (TP), Average Production (AP) and Marginal Production (MP) are calculated to explain the statement of the law as:

(a) **Total Production (TP):** It is the sum of total of output of all labour units. It is worked-out as:

$$TP = Q_1 + Q_2 + Q_3 + Q_4 + Q_5 + Q_6 \ldots Q_n = \Sigma\, Q_n$$

(b) **Average Production (AP):** The output per unit of labour or average production of labour can be calculated as:

$$AP = \Sigma Q_n / \Sigma\, L_n$$

(c) **Marginal Production (MP):** It is output of additional unit of labour. It can be worked-out as:

$$MP = Q_n - Q_n - 1$$

By using above values and the example, the statement of the law is explained in the following table 6.2.

Table 6.2: Law of Variable Proportions
(Quantity in Units)

Capital	Labour	TP	AP	MP	Stage
100	1	08	08	08	Increasing (I)
100	2	26	13	18	
100	3	50	16.67	24	Decreasing (II)
100	4	70	17.5	20	
100	5	70	14	00	Negative (III)
100	6	28	4.67	-42	

By keeping capital constant, as units of labour are increased the resultant total output increased at increasing rate till 2 units of labour; it increased at diminishing rate from 2 to 4 units of labour then it declined from 5 to 6 units of labour. Similarly AP and MP too increased initially then they started falling but MP became zero when labour is 5 units thence it became negative. Thus, stage-I is increasing returns stage, stage-II is diminishing returns stage and stage-III is negative returns stage.

With the help of the above example and Table 6.2, the law is illustrated in the following diagram 6.7.

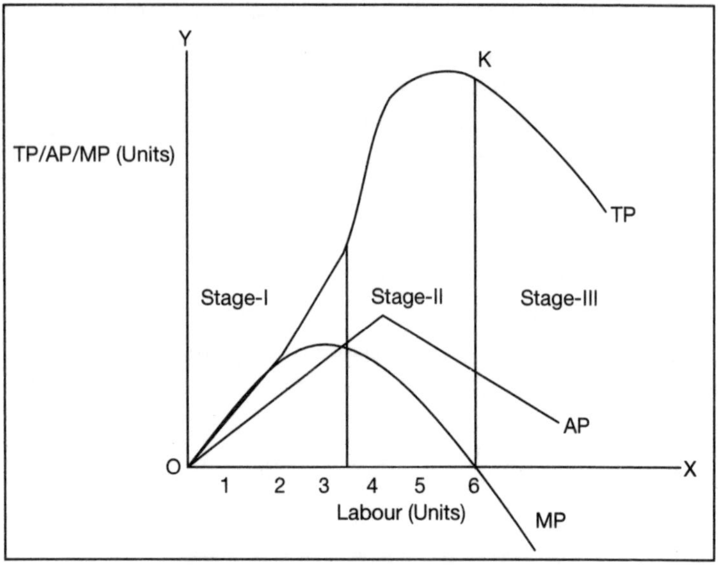

Diagram 6.7: Law of Variable Proportions

Total production (TP), average production(AP) and marginal production (MP) are measured along 'OX' axis and labour-units along 'OY' axis. TP is total production curve. OH on TP curve shows that total production increases at increasing rate thus it is called 'increasing returns stage'; HK on TP curve shows that total production increases at decreasing rate thus it is called 'diminishing returns stage'; beyond K on TP curve shows that total production is decreasing thus it is called 'negative returns stage'.

AP curve shows average production and MP curve shows marginal curve. The output increases as units of labour are increased by same quantity and it passes three stages. They are studied as:

(i) **Stage–I:** Stage–I is called 'Increasing Return Stage' because under this stage the total output increased at increasing rate till 'H'. Meanwhile marginal product and average product are also increasing. Marginal production is greater than the average production. They increased because (a) the efficiency of both variable input and fixed inputs is increased as units of labour increased, (b) the fixed factor cannot be divided, and (c) the quantity of labour is less than the quantity of capital.

(ii) **Stage–II:** Stage–II is also called 'Diminishing Return Stage' because under this stage the total output increased at diminishing rate till 'K'. Meanwhile marginal product and average product are falling but positive. According to Mrs. Joan Robinson the output declines because of two reasons: (a) fixed factors of production are indivisible, (b) factors are imperfect substitutable, (c) fixed and variable factors have attained optimum combination, and (d) as units of labour increased the efficiency of both labour and capital declined.

(iii) **Stage–III:** Stage–III is also called 'Negative Return Stage' because under this stage total production also declined. Meanwhile average production and marginal production are declining but marginal product became negative. It is shown beyond 'K'.

Stage–I and Stage–III are called 'Non-economic Region' because (i) under Stage–I both average production and marginal production are increasing and (ii) under Stage–III average production is declining and marginal production is negative.

Stage–I is called 'Economic Region' because under this stage both average production and marginal production are positive thus it is profitable stage.

(iv) **Importance or Application of the Law:** The law is applicable to agriculture and mining operations. The importance of the law can be briefed as:

(a) **The law is helpful to the producers:** The law suggests the producers to decide the level of output at 'Economic Region' because it is a profitable region. It may help them to select economic combinations of factors.

(b) **It is helpful to the government to solve the economic problems:** The law advises the labour-rich country to use labour intensive technique. It may help them to solve their unemployment problem.

(v) **Criticisms and Limitations of the Law:** The law has certain limitations thus it is criticized as under:

(a) **The old wine in new bottle:** (i) The statement of the law of variable proportions is as same as the statement of Marshall's Law of Diminishing Returns. So it is criticized as the old wine in new bottle.

(ii) The theory assumed that the technology should remain constant but since the present world is dynamic world, the technology cannot remain constant.

(iii) The law ignored the non-substitutable factors, for example, there is no substitute to the lime-stone to produce cement.

(iv) The law is applicable only to the short-run. it explains the output behaviour in the short-run. In long-run, all factors are variable. So it is not applicable to the long-run.

(B) **Laws of Returns to Scale:** In long-run, all factors of production are variable factors; the technique of production is changeable and the scale of production is also changeable. The laws of returns to scale explain the production behaviour in long-run due to change in the scale of production. The change in technology brings the changes in factor-combinations as well as the factor-proportions. These changes may result into either increase or diminish or constant returns to scale. They are discussed as under:

(i) **Law of Constant Returns to Scale:** The law of constant returns to scale states any change in inputs leads to a proportionate change in output. For example: if labour, land, capital and other inputs are changed by 100 per cent (k) then the resultant output would also change by 100 per cent (h). Many handicraft industries show constant returns. It can be denoted as: h = k or h/k = 1. It is explained in the following table 6.3.

Table 6.3: Law of Constant Returns
(Quantity in Units)

Inputs	TP (Total production)	AP (Average production)	MP (Marginal production)
01	10	10	10
02	20	10	10
03	30	10	10
04	40	10	10

When a firm doubles inputs from 01 to 02 units, the resultant output will also become double i.e.10 to 20 units and so on. The proportionate change in output to inputs is equal to one at all levels of changes. It is as under:

$h = Q_2 - Q_1/Q_1 = 20 - 10/10 = 1$ and

$k = F_2 - F_1/F_1 = 02 - 01/01 = 1$

$\therefore h = k = 1$ or $h/k = 1/1 = 1$.

Average Production and Marginal Production will remain constant thus they are equal to each other (AP = MP).

(ii) **Law of Increasing Returns to Scale:** The law of increasing returns to scale states any change in inputs leads to more than a proportionate change in output. For example: if labor, land, capital and other inputs are changed by 100 per cent (k) then the resultant output would also change by 110 per cent (h). It can be denoted as: $h > k$ or $h/k > 1$. Chemical plants are the best examples of the law. It is explained in the following table 6.3(a).

Table 6.3 (a): Law of Increasing Returns
(Quantity in Units)

Inputs	TP (Total production)	AP (Average production)	MP (Marginal production)
01	10	10	10
02	21	10.5	11
03	33	11	12
04	46	11.5	11

When a firm employs inputs from 01 to 02, 03 and 04 units, the resultant output will also increase from 10 to 21, 33 and 46 units. The proportionate change in output to inputs is greater than one at all levels of changes. It is as under:

$h = Q_2 - Q_1/Q_1 = 21 - 10/10 = 1.1$ and

$k = F_2 - F_1/F_1 = 02 - 01/01 = 1$

$\therefore h \neq k$ thus $h/k = 1.1/1 = 1.1 > 1$.

Average Production and Marginal Production are also increasing but MP > AP.

(iii) **Law of Diminishing Returns to Scale:** The law of diminishing returns to scale states any change in inputs leads to less than a proportionate change in output. For example, if labour, land, capital and other inputs are changed by 100 per cent (k) then the resultant output would also change by 90 per cent (h). It can be denoted as: $h < k$ or $h/k < 1$. Electricity generation plants are the best examples of the law. It is explained in the following table 6.3(b).

Table 6.3(b): Law of Diminishing Returns
(Quantity in Units)

Inputs	TP (Total production)	AP (Average production)	MP (Marginal production)
01	10	10	10
02	19	9.5	09
03	27	9	08
04	34	8.5	07

When a firm employs inputs from 01 to 02, 03 and 04 units, the resultant output will also increase from 10 to 19, 27 and 34 units. The proportionate change in output to inputs is less than one at all levels of changes. It is as under:

$h = Q_2 - Q_1/Q_1 = 19 - 10/10 = 0.9$ and

$k = F_2 - F_1/F_1 = 02 - 01/01 = 1$

$\therefore\ h \neq k$ thus $h/k = 0.9/1 = 0.9 < 1$.

Average Production and Marginal Production are also declining but MP < AP.

The laws of returns to scale are depending upon the economies (advantages) and diseconomies (disadvantages) that occur due to change in scale of operation. If economies are greater than diseconomies, there will be increasing returns and *vice versa*. All the three laws of returns are illustrated in the diagram 6.8.

In diagram 6.8, 'OX' axis measures inputs and 'oy' axis measures output. "P" is the output curve. The –20 'ab' on 'P' curve shows law of increasing returns; 'bc' the constant returns and 'cd' the diminishing returns.

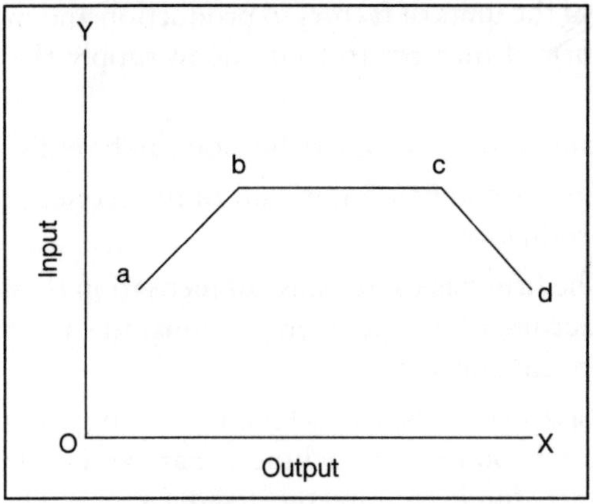

Diagram 6.8: Laws of Returns

6.2 COS T ANALYSIS

6.2.1 Nature, Meaning and Definition of Cost: As law of diminishing marginal utility governs the demand, the cost of production governs the supply. Output is the source of supply. The cost of production is the result of output. Cost controls supply of output and size of firms in the market through influencing on the size of profits. When cost declines, the size of profits will be increased; the new firms will be attracted; thus the size of firms and supply of output will increase in the market. The relation between cost and supply is more complex.

For production of a commodity or service, we have to employ various factors of production, viz. land, labour, capital, etc. Some compensation or price have to be paid by the firm to the owners of factors of production for continuing their services in production process. The price or compensation paid to the owners of factors of production by the firm is known as cost of production. In brief, the expenditures incurred in production of output of a commodity or service is called cost of production. For example: A firm spent ₹ 100 for purchase of raw cotton, fuel, payment wages and interest, etc. and produced a meter of cotton cloth. The cost of production of a meter of cloth is ₹ 100.

To know the precise meaning of cost and its nature, we have to refer a correct definition on cost. Prof. Due defines cost of production as "Cost is the compensation which must be received by owners of the units of factors of production and money capital used by a firm if they are to continue to supply the units to the firm."

The main points from the definition can be enlisted as under:

(i) Cost is compensation paid to the services of factors of production.

(ii) The firm has to pay this compensation to the owners of factors of production to continue their service in production process.

(iii) Raw materials, fuels, labour, etc. are variable factors. Land, building, machines, managerial staff, security staff, fund, etc. are the fixed factors. The owners of these factors of production must receive some compensation to continue the supply of their service to the firm in production process.

(iv) The firm should also receive some compensation to the service of his own money or capital employed in the production process.

6.2.2 Concepts of Cost: The various concepts of cost are used in the theory of production. They play a significant role in theory of product pricing. They enable to identify the output behaviour in short-run as well as in long-run. They help us to know the efficiency of factors of production and the productive efficiency of the technique of production.

(a) Kinds of Cost-Concepts: On the basis of nature, we can classify the cost-concepts into the following kinds:

(i) **Explicit Costs:** For production of output of a commodity or service, the firm involves in contract with the owners of various factors of production like land, labour, capital, entrepreneur, etc. Accordingly the firm has to pay them the contractual payments like rent, wages, interest, etc. Such contractual payments made by the firm to the owners of various factors of production are called 'Explicit Cost'. It is also known as 'Expenditure Cost' or 'Outlay Cost'. Since the explicit costs are recorded in books of accounts, they are also known as 'Accounting Costs'. The contractual payments are made to the outsiders so they are called 'Explicit Costs' or 'Expenditure or Outlay Cost'.

(ii) **Implicit Costs:** In production process, the firm employs his own money or capital or factors of production. So the firm has no any contractual obligations. But compensation should be paid to the service of his own money or capital or factors. Thus the expenditures incur directly to the firm itself for use of its own money or capital or factors of production without any contractual obligations are known as 'Implicit Cost'. For example: If the firm as used his own car to the service of the production unit, the compensation or price will be paid to the firm. The money spent on such expenses goes to the firm itself. The implicit costs are also known as 'Non-Expenditure Costs'. These are not recorded in books of accounts.

(iii) **Economic Cost:** Usually the firm takes into account only explicit cost while calculating profits. But according to economists, the real economic profit is the excess of revenue over both explicit and implicit costs. Hence the sum total of explicit costs and implicit costs is called 'Economic Cost'. Thus economic cost can be calculated as:

$$C_e = C_x + C_m$$

where, C_e= economic costs, C_x= explicit costs, C_m= implicit costs.

(iv) **Money Cost:** The monetary expenditures on purchases of various factors of production required for production of a commodity or service are called 'money costs'. The cost measured in terms of money is also known as 'money cost'. In modern context all costs are money costs. Money cost plays a vital role in pricing of both products and factors. It means price of products or factors is fixed in terms of money. For example, the price of a unit of 'X' commodity is ₹ 10 or the price of a unit of labour is ₹ 15.

(v) **Real Cost:** 'Real cost' is a subjective term, so it is difficult to measure the real cost in terms of money. The firm has to put some efforts; it has to bear some troubles, pains and toils and has to make some sacrifice in production of output of a commodity or service. The sacrifice made and the troubles and toils undertaken by the firm in production of a commodity or service is called 'Real Cost'. Prof. Alfred Marshall defines real cost as "all exertions taken directly or indirectly, in making commodity". At the establishment stage and operation stage of the plant, the firm has to sacrifice its valuable time. The entrepreneur has to visit the government offices and other places often and has to spare his resources.

(vi) **Opportunity Cost:** Meaning and definition: Opportunity cost has a significant position in modern economic analysis. It is a notional idea. It is not actual expenditure incurred by the firm. It is measured in terms of the opportunity lost. For example: A firm has ₹ 100 capital. It has two alternative uses or opportunities: (a) it can be used in his own business and earn profits of ₹ 12 or (b) it can be lent to the other and earn interest thereon of ₹ 10. The firm has to choose one use or opportunity. If it chooses investing the money in his own business, it will have to give up the next best alternative use i.e. lending money to others. The opportunity cost of investing in business is forgoing of money lending to others. Hence, the opportunity cost of any things is sacrifice or forgone of its next best alternative use or opportunity. It is also known as 'Alternative cost'.

Prof. Benham defines opportunity cost as "The opportunity cost of anything is the next best alternative that could be produced instead by the same factors or by an equivalent group of factors costing the same amount of money."

The main points of the definition are:

Opportunity cost of anything is sacrifice of its next best alternative use.

The same amount of factor or money is used to produce alternative uses.

Importance of opportunity cost: The following are the importance of opportunity cost in economic analysis:

(i) It is useful to determine the price of a commodity. For instance, the firm determines the price of 'X' commodity not less than its opportunity cost. If the opportunity cost of X commodity is forgoing ₹ 10 worth Y commodity then the price of X commodity should be minimum ₹ 10.

(ii) It is useful to determine the factor-price. For example: A labourer has two opportunities, either to work in factory or in agriculture. The wages per day is ₹ 50 in agriculture. So the firm has to pay more than ₹ 50 to retain the labourer in factory.

(iii) It is useful to decide the allocation of resources. For instance: steel is resources, steel has several uses. Steel should be allocated to that use which has less opportunity cost. Construction of dam and production of car are two alternative uses of steel. The construction of dam has less opportunity cost; the production of car has more opportunity cost.

(iv) It is useful concept in international trade. For Instance: A country decides to produce and export that commodity which has less opportunity cost. Thus the opportunity cost determines the gains from international trade.

(b) Types of Cost Concepts Related to Behaviour of Output: There are cost concepts which are related to behaviour of output. Some costs are independent of level of output; some costs are dependent of level of output. They are as follows:

(i) **Fixed Costs: Meaning and Nature:** The firm employs various fixed factors in production of a commodity. Land, building, machine, equipment and tools, managerial staff, security staff, etc. are the fixed factors. The amount spent on fixed factors of production in short-run by the firm are called 'Fixed Costs'. Fixed costs remain constant in short-run. Fixed costs are independent of change in level of output. Fixed costs remain unchanged at all levels of output. Hence fixed cost is positive (>0) even at zero level of output. Therefore Marshall called fixed cost or 'supplementary cost' or 'overhead cost'. Rent, interest, insurance premium, salary of managerial staff, security staff, property tax, depreciation charges, etc. are the examples of fixed costs.

Illustration of fixed cost: Fixed cost is explained in the following table:

Table 6.4: Fixed Cost

Quantity of output of X commodity (units)	Fixed cost (₹)
0	20
1	20
2	20
3	20

Either increase from 0 to 3 or decrease from 3 to 0 in level of output makes no change in fixed costs. To understand it more effectively, the fixed cost is illustrated in the following diagram 6.9.

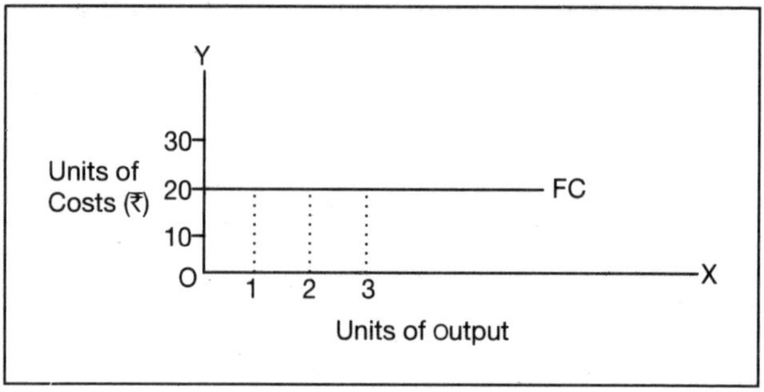

Diagram 6.9: Fixed Cost

Units of output are measured along 'OX' axis and Fixed cost (₹) is measured along 'OY' axis. ₹ 20 is fixed cost. It remains same at 0, 1, 2 and 3 unit of output. So the fixed cost is shown by FC horizontal straight-line which is parallel to 'OX' axis.

Fixed Cost can be calculated by using following equation:

Fixed Cost = Total Cost – Variable Cost

FC = TC – VC

Or a = C – b (q) where, a = Fixed Cost, c = Total Cost and b (q) = Variable Cost (VC), q = Output.

For example, Total costs = ₹ 250, variable costs = ₹ 50, Fixed costs is:

FC = TC – VC

FC = 250–50 = ₹ 200 is Fixed cost.

Types of Fixed Costs: The fixed costs are classified into two types:

(a) **Recurrent Fixed Costs:** The fixed costs appear repeatedly to the firm are called 'Recurrent Fixed Costs'. For example, payment of rent, interest, insurance premium, salaries of managerial, office and security staff, taxes, license fees, etc. The firm has to pay them at a regular time-interval.

(b) **Allocable Fixed Costs:** The fixed costs incur once but are used in successive time or years are called 'Allocable Fixed Costs'. For example Depreciation cost or Replacement cost.

Average Fixed Cost (AFC): Fixed cost per unit of output is called Average Fixed Cost (AFC). Dividing total fixed costs by total output, we get average fixed cost. It is shown as:

AFC = TFC/q, Where, AFC = Average Fixed Cost, TFC = Total Fixed Costs, Q = Total Output

For example: A firm spent ₹ 1000 on fixed factors to produce 100 units of output of a commodity. Then

AFC = TFC/q = ₹ 1000/100 units = ₹ 10 is Average Fixed Cost

Average Fixed Cost is related to the level of output. As the level of output increases, the average fixed cost declines; as the level of output declines, the average fixed cost increases. But at one unit or zero level of output, the average fixed cost will be positive, i.e. equal to the total fixed cost. It is explained in the following table 6.5.

Table 6.5: Average Fixed Cost

Total Fixed Costs TFC (₹)	Total Output q (Units)	Average Fixed Cost AFC (₹) AFC=TFC/q
20	0	–
20	1	20
20	2	10
20	4	5

As output (q) increases from 0 to 4 units, the Average Fixed cost (AFC) declines from ₹ 20 to ₹ 5. In contrary, as the output (q) declines from 4 to 0 units, the average fixed cost (AFC) increases from ₹ 5 to ₹ 20.

By using the above example, Average Fixed Cost (AFC) is illustrated in following diagram 6.10.

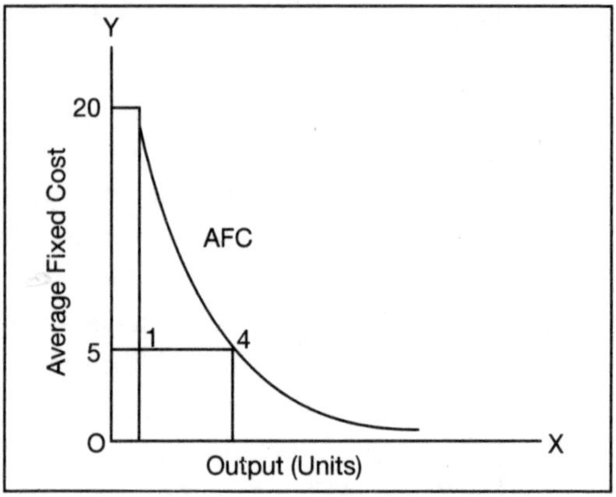

Diagram 6.10: Average Fixed Cost

AFC is the Average Fixed Cost curve. It declines from left to right. It shows the inverse relation between level of output and average fixed cost. As output increases from 1 to 4 units, the average fixed cost declines from ₹ 20 to ₹ 5. In contrary, it is *vice versa*.

(ii) **Variable Costs: Meaning and Nature:** Like fixed factors, the firm employs various variable factors (inputs) in production of a commodity. Raw materials, labour, fuel, power, transport service, etc. are the variable factors of production. The amount spent on variable factors of production by the firm for production of a commodity or service is called 'variable cost'. The variable cost incurs regularly in production process. The variable cost depends on level of output. As the level of output increases, the variable cost increases; as level of output declines, the variable cost also declines. The variable cost becomes zero when the level of output becomes zero.

Alfred Marshall called Variable Costs are 'Prime Costs'. Price of raw materials, wages, fuel and power charges, transport expenditures, sales taxes, etc. are the examples of variable cost.

Illustration of Variable Costs: The variable costs are explained in the following table 6.6.

Table 6.6: Variable Costs

Quantity of Output (Units)	Variable Costs (₹)
0	0
1	15
2	20
3	27
4	40
5	80
6	120

As the output increases from 0 to 6 units, the variable cost also rises from ₹ 0 to ₹ 120. In contrary, decline in output froms 6 units to 0 unit, the variable cost declines from ₹ 120 to ₹ 0. The variable cost depends upon the level of output. The variable cost is illustrated in the following diagram 6.11.

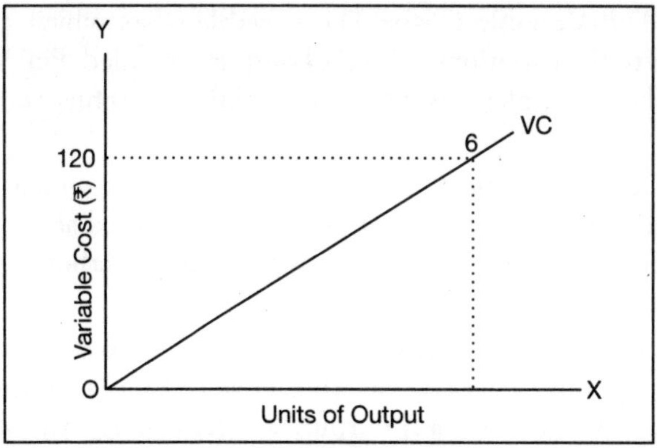

Diagram 6.11: Variable Cost

Units of output are measured along 'OX' axis. The variable cost is measured along 'OY' axis. When the units of output increased from 0 to 6, the variable costs increased from ₹ 0 to ₹ 120. In contrary when the units of output decreased from 6 to 0 units, the variable costs also decreased from ₹ 120 to 0. The variable costs will be zero, when the level of output becomes zero. The variable cost curve starts from zero and rises upwards from left to right which is shown by VC curve. The variable costs can be calculated as under:

Variable Costs = Total Costs – Fixed Costs

VC = TC – FC

Or b(q) = c – a; Where, c = Total Costs; a = Fixed Costs, b(q) = Variable Costs (VC)

Since variable costs depend upon level of output, it is denoted as b(q). 'b' denotes the ratio between change in output (q) to change in variable cost. 'q' denotes units of output.

$\therefore$ VC = b(q)

For example, Total Cost = ₹ 250 and Fixed Costs = ₹ 200, variable costs is:

VC = TC–FC

VC = ₹ 250 – ₹ 200 = ₹ 50. The variable costs is ₹ 50.

Types of Variable Costs: The variable costs can be classified into two types:

(a) **Full-Variable Costs:** The variable costs which are fully variable to the variations in level of output are called 'Full Variable Costs'. For example: Cost of raw material, cost of fuel and power, etc.

(b) **Semi-Variable Costs:** The variable costs which are not changeable to change in level of output are called semi-variable costs. For example: Transport costs, wages of labour, sale tax rates, etc.

Average Variable Cost (AVC): Variable costs per unit of output is called average variable cost (AVC). Dividing total variable costs by the total output, we get average variable cost (AVC). It is calculated as under:

$$AVC = TVC/q$$

Where, AVC = Average Variable Cost, TVC = Total Variable Cost, q = Total Output.

For example, a firm has spent ₹ 200 on variable factors to produce 100 units of output. Then the Average variable cost is:

AVC = TVC/q = ₹ 200/100 = ₹ 2 is average variable cost.

Average variable cost is also related with level of output. When the level of output is increased, initially, average variable cost declines up to a certain point, beyond that point, the average variable cost also rises. The behaviour and calculation of average variable cost are shown in the following table 6.7.

Table 6.7: Average Variable Cost

Units of Output (q)	Total Variable Costs (₹) (TVC)	Average Variable Cost (₹) AVC=TVC/q
0	0	–
1	15	15
2	20	10
3	27	09 (Lowest point 'S')
4	40	10
5	80	16
6	120	20

Average variable cost declines up to 3 units of output. It is the lowest average variable cost point. Beyond the lowest point 'S', the average variable cost will be increased as level of output rises. The behaviour of average variable cost is shown in the following diagram 6.12.

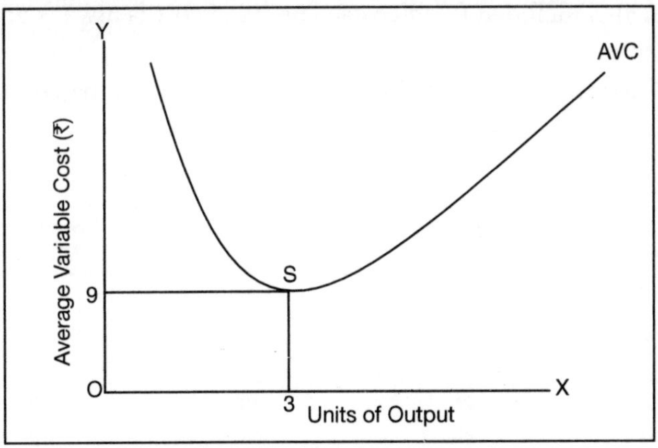

Diagram 6.12: Average Variable Cost

Up to 3 units of output (or point 'S'), the average variable cost declines because of the reasons:

(a) When we use more and more variable factors, the productivity of variable factors increases and (b) As number of variable factors increases, the productivity of fixed factors also increases. At this stage output increases more than increase in variable factors.

At 'S' point the average variable cost is minimum i.e. ₹ 9. The increase in unit of output beyond point 'S', results into increase in average variable cost. This behaviour of average variable cost related to behaviour of output is shown by avc curve.

(iii) **Total Costs: Meaning and Nature:** The sum total of total fixed costs and total variable costs is called 'Total Cost'. The total cost can be calculated as under:

$$TC = TFC + TVC$$

Where, TC = Total Cost TFC = Total Fixed Costs, TVC = Total Variable Costs.

The firm has to employ various fixed factors and variable factors to produce a commodity or service. The total money spent on fixed factors and variable factors is total cost. Total cost is also related to with behaviour of output. The total cost increases, when the level of output rises. It declines, when the level of output falls. But total costs never become zero. It is because the total cost is also included fixed costs. The fixed cost is always greater than zero.

Illustration of Total Cost: The calculation and behaviour of total cost are explained in the following table 6.8.

Table 6.8: Total Costs

Output (units) (q)	Fixed Costs (₹) (FC)	Variable Costs (₹) (VC)	Total Costs (₹) (TC=FC+VC)
0	20	0	20
1	20	15	35
2	20	20	40
3	20	27	47
4	20	40	60
5	20	80	100
6	20	120	140

As total cost includes fixed costs, it is ₹ 20 at zero level of output. The Total Cost increases, with increases in level of output and decrease with decline in level of output.

In short-run, as fixed costs remain constant, the total cost varies due to variations in variable costs. In long-run, as both fixed costs and variable costs are changeable, the total cost varies due to variations in both fixed costs and variable costs. But total costs never become zero.

The calculation and behaviour of total cost are illustrated in the following diagram 6.13.

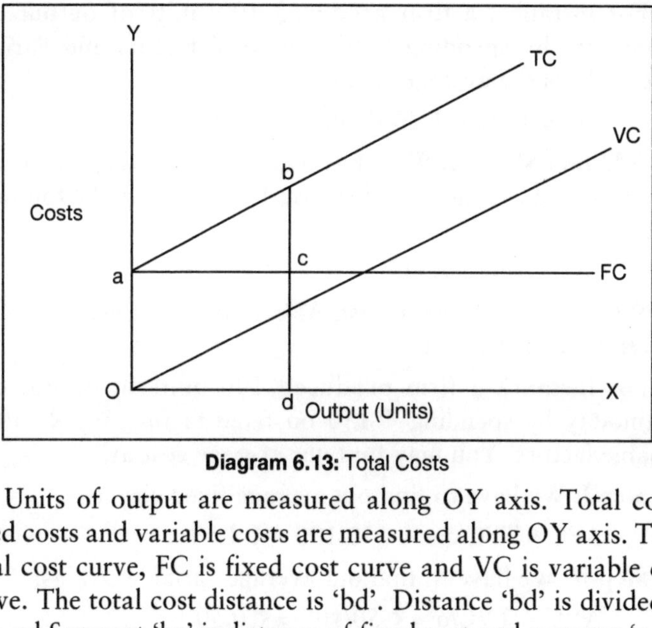

Diagram 6.13: Total Costs

Units of output are measured along OY axis. Total costs, fixed costs and variable costs are measured along OY axis. TC is total cost curve, FC is fixed cost curve and VC is variable cost curve. The total cost distance is 'bd'. Distance 'bd' is divided as bc + cd Segment 'bc' is distance of fixed cost and segment 'cd' is distance of variable cost.

As output increases the total and variable cost will increase but fixed cost will remain same. At zero level of output (i) Fixed cost is 'Oa' i.e. ₹ 20 shown on OY axis and (ii) Variable cost is zero. i.e. variable cost curve starts from origin 'O' or zero.

The total cost curve starts from 'a' on OY axis because the total cost includes 'oa' fixed cost at zero level of output, So 'a' becomes the starting point of total cost curve.

(iv) **Average Cost (AC): Meaning and Nature of Average Cost:** The overall cost per unit of output is called

'Average Cost'. It is also known as per head cost of the output. There are two methods of calculating average cost:

Division Method: Dividing total cost by corresponding total output, we get average cost. It is shown in the following equation.

$$AC = TC/q$$

Where, AC = Average cost, TC = Total cost, q = Total output.

For instance, a firm produced 100 units of output of a commodity by spending ₹ 200 on fixed factors and variable factors. Thus the average cost is:

AC = TC/q = ₹ 200/100 units = ₹ 2

Addition Method: We get average cost by adding up average fixed cost and average variable cost. It is shown in the following equation.

$$AC = AFC + AVC$$

Where, AC = Average cost, AFC = Average fixed cost, AVC = Average variable cost.

For instance a firm produced 100 units of output of a commodity by spending ₹ 150 on fixed factors and ₹ .50 on variable factors. You may find out average cost as:

Step-I: We have to find out average fixed cost as:

AFC = TFC/q = ₹ 150/100 = ₹ 1.50

Step-II: We have to find out average variable cost as:

AVC = TVC/q = ₹ 50/100 = ₹ 0.50

Step-III: To get average cost, we have to add up both average fixed cost and average variable cost.

AC = AFC + AVC = ₹ 1.50 + ₹ 0.50 = ₹ 2

Average cost is related to the level of output. As output increases, (i) initially average cost declines up to a minimum point because the average productivity and marginal productivity of both fixed factors and variable factors are rising. (This aspect is explained in details in law of variable proportions) and (ii) beyond a minimum point, the average cost starts increasing. The average cost is lowest at a minimum point.

Average cost determines the size of per unit profits. The per unit profits is the excess of price of output over average cost. It is shown as:

$$PU\Pi = P–AC$$

Where, PUΠ = Per Unit Profit. P = Price per unit of output. AC = Average cost.

For example, the price per unit of output is ₹ 5 and average cost of that output is ₹ 3, then the per unit profits of that output is:

$$PU\Pi = P - AC = ₹\ 5 - ₹\ 3 = ₹\ 2$$

Given the price of output, as AC increases, the per unit profit of output declines; as AC declines, the per unit profits increases. Average cost is popularly known as 'Unit cost'.

Illustration of Average Cost: The average cost and its behaviour are explained in the following table 6.9.

Table 6.9: Average Cost Schedule

Units of Output (q)	Total fixed cost (₹) (TFC)	Total variable costs (₹) (TVC)	Total costs (₹) (TC = TFC +TVC)	Average fixed cost (₹) (AFC = TFC/q)	Average variable costs (₹) (AVC=TC/q)	Average costs (₹) $AC=\frac{TC}{q}$ or AC = AFC + AVC
0	20	0	20	–	0	20
1	20	15	35	20	15	35
2	20	20	40	10	10	20
3	20	27	47	06.67	9	15.67
4	20	40	60	05	10	15
5	20	80	100	04	16	20
6	20	120	140	03.33	20	23.33

The various average costs at various level of output is known as 'Average Cost Schedule'. As output increased from 0 to 4 units, initially, the average cost declines from ₹ 35 to ₹ 15. At output 4 units, the average cost is at minimum i.e. ₹ 15. As output increased beyond a minimum point i.e. 4 units, the average cost increased to ₹ 20 and ₹ 23.33, when output is 4 and 5 units respectively. When output is zero, like fixed cost and the total cost, the average cost is also positive, Average cost will be equal to fixed cost at zero level of output. Average cost its relation to level of output and its behaviour are illustrated in the following diagram 6.14.

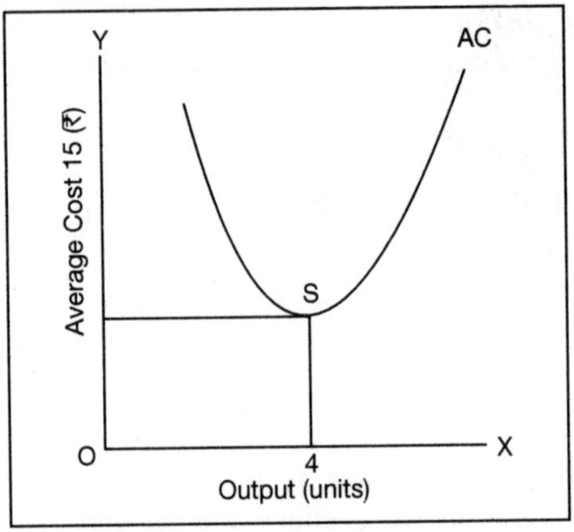

Diagram 6.14: Average Cost Curve

Units of output are measured along 'OX' axis. Average Cost is measured along 'OY' axis. 'S' is the minimum point on AC curve. AC is the Average cost curve. At 'S' point the average cost is minimum, i.e. ₹ 15.

As units of output increased to 1, 2, 3 and 4, the average cost declined respectively from ₹ 35 to ₹ 20, ₹ 15.67 and ₹ 15, respectively. Beyond 4 units, as output increased to 5 and 6 units, the average cost increased to ₹ 20 and ₹ 23.33 respectively. At zero level of output average cost is positive i.e. ₹ 20. It equal to fixed cost or average fixed cost. The shape of average cost curve is usually like English letter 'U'. Thus average cost curve is called U-shape average cost curve. But generally the shape of average cost curve depends upon time-elements. The average cost curve has different shapes in long-run. It is studied in details in the next section when we study short-run costs and long-run costs.

(v) **Marginal Cost: Meaning and Nature:** The cost of additional unit of output of a commodity or service is called 'Marginal cost'. For instance: A firm produced 10 units of output of a commodity by spending ₹ 100 as Total cost. Further the firm produced one more unit of output, thus the total production increased to 11 units. On account of this his total cost of 11 units of output gone up to ₹ 110. Thus to produce additional one unit of output, the firm spent ₹ 110 – ₹ 100 = ₹ 10. Hence ₹ 10 is spent to produce one additional unit of output so it is marginal cost. Thus 'marginal cost' is defined as the change in cost resulting from a unit change in output.

Prof. Ferguson defined 'Marginal cost' as "Marginal cost is the addition to the total cost attributable to the addition of one unit of output." In brief 'Marginal Cost' is the cost of additional unit of output. Marginal cost can be calculated by using the following formula.

(A) Marginal Cost can be calculated on the basis of the difference between total costs of present and previous units of output. It is:

$$MC = TC_n - TC_{n-1}$$

Where, MC = Marginal cost, TC_n = Total costs of 'n' units of output (Present), TC_{n-1} = Total costs of 'n–1' units of output (Previous).

For example: A firm produced 10 units, 11 units, 12 units and 13 units in time period 1, 2, 3 and 4 respectively. The firm spent total costs of ₹ 100, ₹ 110, ₹ 118, and ₹ 120 on 10 units, 11 units, 12 units and 13 units respectively.

Now we may calculate 'Marginal cost' of each additional unit of output:

Marginal cost of 11th unit of output can be calculated as:

At time period 2, $MC_n = TC_n - TC_{n-1}$

$$MC_{11} = TC_{11} - TC_{10}$$
$$= 110 - 100 = 10$$

₹ 10 is marginal cost of 11th unit.

Marginal cost of 12th unit of output:

At time period 3, $MC_n = TC_n - TC_{n-1}$

$$MC_{12} = TC_{12} - TC_{11}$$
$$= 118 - 110 = ₹\ 8$$

₹ 8 is 'Marginal cost' of 12th unit of output.

Marginal cost of 13th unit of output:

At time period 4, $MC_n = TC_n - TC_{n-1}$

$$MC_{13} = TC_{13} - TC_{12}$$
$$= 120 - 118 = ₹\ 2$$

₹ 2 is 'Marginal cost' of 13th unit of output.

(B) Marginal Cost can be calculated on basis of ratio between changes in Total cost to change in Total output:

$MC = \Delta c/\Delta q$

Where, MC = Marginal cost

Δc = Change in Total costs, it can be worked out as: $\Delta c = TC_n - TC_{n-1}$

Δq = change in total output, it can be worked out as $\Delta q = q_n - q_{n-1}$

q_n = 'n' units of output (present time)

q_{n-1} = 'n-1' units of output (previous time)

For instance: A firm previously produced 100 units of output by spending ₹ 100 as total costs. Now at present time firm produced 101 units by spending ₹ 110 as total costs. Thus marginal cost can be calculated as:

$MC = \Delta c/\Delta q = TC_n - TC_{n-1}/q_n - q_{n-1}$

= ₹ 110 – ₹ 100/101 – 100 units = ₹ 10

Where, TC_n = ₹ 11, TC_{n-1} = ₹ 100, q_n = 101 q_{n-1} = 100. ₹ 10 is marginal cost or cost of one addition unit of output.

Marginal cost is related to additional unit of output.

As output increases: (a) initially marginal cost declines up to a minimum point because initially marginal productivity of both fixed factors and variable factors are increasing. And (b) beyond the minimum point, marginal cost increases as output increases because the marginal productivity starts falling. At the minimum point, marginal cost is minimum: The behaviour of Marginal cost is also related to the level of output.

Illustration of marginal cost and its behaviour: Generally the marginal cost calculation and its behaviour in relation to level of output and total costs are explained in the following table 6.10.

Table 6.10: Marginal Cost Schedule

Units of Output (q)	Total Costs in ₹ (TC)	Marginal costs in ₹ ($MC = TC_n - TC_{n-1}$)
0	20	–
1	35	15=35–20
2	40	5=40–35
3	47	7=47–40
4	60	13=60–47
5	100	40=100–60

The marginal cost at various levels of output is called 'Marginal Cost Schedule'. When output increased from 0 unit to 1, 2, 3, 4 and 5 units, the total cost increased from ₹ 20 to ₹ 35, ₹ 40, ₹ 47, ₹ 60 and ₹ 100, respectively. The marginal cost initially declined from ₹ 15 to ₹ 5 then it started rising from 3rd unit to 5th unit. It increased to ₹ 7, ₹ 13 and ₹ 40, respectively. The marginal cost is lowest at 2nd unit of output i.e. ₹ 5. The marginal cost and its behaviour are illustrated in the following diagram 6.15.

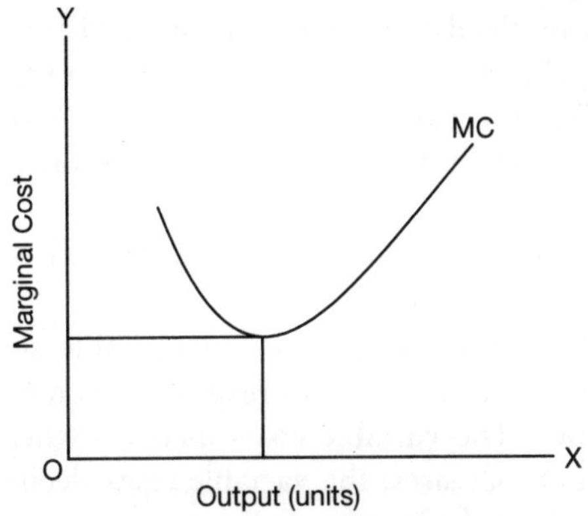

Diagram 6.15: Marginal Cost Curve

Units of output measured along 'OX' axis and marginal cost is measured along 'OY' axis. MC is marginal cost curve. As the output increased from 0 unit to 1, 2, 3, 4 and 5 units, marginal cost declined to ₹ 5. It is a minimum at point 'k', and then it started increasing due to increase in output. When output increased from 1 unit to 2 units, the marginal cost of additional unit is ₹ 5; as output increased from 2 units to 3 units, the marginal cost of additional unit increased to ₹ 7 and so on. The behaviour of marginal cost differs from short-run to long-run.

(c) Short-Run Costs Analysis

Time-elements play important role in cost analysis. For convenience of the study, the time periods are classified as: (a) short-run or short period and (b) Long-run or long-period.

The duration of short-run may be few days or few months say up to 15 months. The output behaviour in short-run is typical. In short-run, as there is insufficient time, the technology, size of firm, scale of operation and fixed factors remain constant. The output behaviour depends upon variable factors only. The short-run costs depend upon short-run behaviour of output.

Meaning and Nature of Short-run Costs: The expenditures incurred in association with change in output in short-run are called 'short-run costs'.

In short-run, fixed costs remain unchanged but variable costs are changeable in response to change in level of output. Generally short-run costs increase due to increase in level of output. The behaviour of short-run costs depends on the following assumptions:

(i) Since fixed factors remain unchanged, the fixed cost remains constant.

(ii) Only variable factors are changeable so the variable costs are changeable in response to change in level of output. The variable costs increase when the level of output increases; the variable costs decline when level of output declines.

(iii) All units of variable factors are equal in efficiency, for instance, units of labour like L_1, L_2, L_3...L_n all are equal in efficiency.

(iv) Technology or Method of production assumed to be constant. For example: if a firm is using handloom, it must use handloom only in short-run.

(v) The price of variable factors must remain constant, for example: If the wages per unit of labour is ₹ 10, it remains same in the short-run.

The short-run output and short-run costs behaviour is governed by 'Law of variable proportions'.

Types of Short-run Costs: The short-run costs are classified into three types. They are:

(a) Short-run Total Costs (STC)

(b) Short-run Average Costs (SAC), and

(c) Short-run Marginal Cost (SMC).

(i) **Short-run Total Cost (STC):** The total expenditures incurred to the firm in production of a commodity or service in short-run are called 'short-run total costs'. The short-run total costs are divided into (a) Short-run Total Fixed Costs (STFC) and (b) Short-run Total Variable Cost (STVC). We can calculate short-run total costs (STC) as:

STC = STFC + STVC

(a) **Short-run Total Fixed Costs (STFC):** Prof. Benham defined fixed costs as "The fixed costs of a firm are those costs that do not vary with a size of its output." Fixed costs are unavoidable contractual costs. They are positive even when the output is zero. They remain unchanged. They are independent of change in output for example: investment in plant and machine, insurance premium property taxes, remuneration of managerial staff, etc. Short-run Total Fixed Cost (STFC) can be calculated as:

STFC = STC – STVC

(b) **Short-run Total Variable Cost (STVC):** Prof. Benham defined variable costs as "The variable costs of a firm are those costs that do vary with the size of its output." The short-run total variable costs are directly related to level of output. These costs fall to Zero when output becomes zero. Wages to the labourer, purchase of raw materials, fuel, power, transport cost, etc. are variable costs. Short-run total variable cost can be calculated as:

STVC = STC – STFC

The short-run total costs, fixed costs and variable costs are illustrated in the following table 6.11.

Table 6.11: Short-run Costs

Units of Output (q)	STFC (₹)	STVC (₹)	STC (₹)
0	100	0	100
1	100	100	200
2	100	180	280
3	100	220	320
4	100	300	400
5	100	400	500
6	100	520	620

The points from Table 6.11: (i) When output is zero: STVC = 0 but STFC = ₹ 100 and so also STC = ₹ 100 short-run total costs never be zero. (ii) When output increased, STVC and STC increases but STFC remains constant. The behaviour of short-run costs is illustrated in the following diagram 6.16.

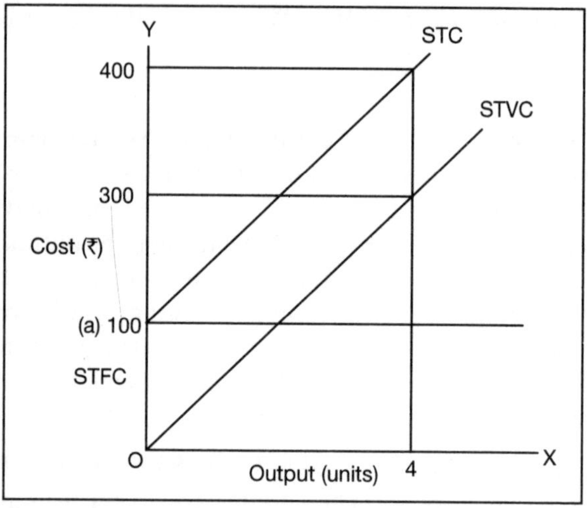

Diagram 6.16: Short-run Total Cost Curves

Units of output are measured along 'OX' axis, and costs in ₹ are measured along 'OY' axis. STFC curve represents short-run total fixed costs. STFC curve is independent of level of output. It is positive when output is zero. 'Oa' is the size of short-run total fixed cost. STVC curve represents short-run total variable cost. STVC increases as output increases. STVC depends upon level of output. STVC becomes zero when output is zero. STC curve represents short-run total costs. It is sum of STFC plus STVC. Therefore,

STC = STFC + STVC

STC varies in the same proportion of change in STVC. It is because STFC remain constant.

$$\Delta STC = \Delta STFC + \Delta STVC$$

Where, Δ = change

When ΔSTFC = 0,

$$\Delta STC = 0 + \Delta STVC$$

$$\Delta STC = \Delta STVC$$

For example: When STC increased from ₹ 280 to ₹ 320 due to increase in STVC from ₹ 180 to ₹ 220, but STFC remained ₹ 100 only, ΔSTC=ΔSTVC can be proved as:

$\Delta STFC = 100 - 100 = 0$

$\Delta STVC = 220 - 180 = 40$

$\Delta STC = \Delta STFC + \Delta STVC$

$= 0 + 40 = 40$

$\therefore \Delta STC = \Delta STVC$

$40 = 40$

(ii) **Short-run per unit costs:** There are four types of short-run per unit costs in short-run. They are:

(a) **Short-run Average Fixed Cost (SAFC):** The short-run fixed cost per unit of output is called Short-run Average Fixed Cost (SAFC). It can be calculated as:

SAFC = STFC/q

Where, SAFC=Short-run Average Fixed Cost, STFC = Short-run Total Fixed and q = Total Output. Dividing STFC by q, you get SAFC.

(b) **Short-run Average Variable Cost (SAVC):** The short-run variable cost per unit of output is called 'Short-run Average Variable Cost'. It can be calculated as:

SAVC = STVC/q

Where, SAVC = Short-run Average Variable Cost STVC = Short-run Total Variable Cost and q = Total Output. Dividing STVC by q, we get SAVC

(c) **Short-run Average Cost (SAC):** The Short-run Total cost per unit of output is called Short-run average Cost. It can be calculated as:

SAC = STC/q = (STFC + STVC)/q

where, SAC = Short-run Average Cost, STC = Short-run Total Cost, which is equal to sum of Short-run total fixed costs (STFC) plus short-run total variable costs (STVC)q = Total output. Dividing STC by q, we get SAC.

(d) **Short-run Marginal Cost (SMC):** The short-run total cost of an additional unit of output produced is called Short-run Marginal Cost (SMC). It can be calculated as:

$$SMC = STC_n - STC_{n-1}$$

Where, SMC = Short-run Marginal Cost, STC_n = Short-run Total Cost of 'n' units of output, STC_{n-1} = Short-run Total cost of n–1 units of output. By deducting STC_{n-1} from STC_n, we get SMC.

Short-run Marginal Cost (SMC) can also be calculated as:

$$SMC = \Delta c / \Delta q$$

Where, SMC = Short-run Marginal cost. $\Delta c = STC_n - STC_{n-1}$ means the difference between short-run total cost of 'n' units of output and short-run total cost of 'n–1' units of output. $\Delta q = q_n - q_{n-1}$ means the difference between 'n' units of output (q_n) and 'n-1' units of output (q_{n-1}).

Short-run marginal cost is independent of short-run total fixed cost. It can be proved as:

Step-I: STC = STFC + STVC

Since STFC is constant, the change in STFC =0

STC = 0 + STVC

STC = STVC

Step-II: $SMC = STC_n - STC_{n-1}$

Since ΔSTC = ΔSTVC

$SMC = STVC_n - STVC_{n-1}$

Thus SMC is independent of short-run total fixed cost.

Output and Short-run Cost Behaviour: All short-run total costs and per unit costs are depend upon change in level of output. It is illustrated in the following table 6.12.

Table 6.12: Short-run Costs of per Unit of Output

Units of (q)	Short-run Cost (₹) (STFC)	Short-run Costs (₹) (STVC)	Short-run Cost (STC)	SAFC (₹)	SAVC (₹)	SAC (₹)	SMC (₹)
0	50	0	50	–	0	–	–
1	50	10	60	50	10	60	10
2	50	16	66	25	8	33	6
3	50	18	68	16.7	6	22.7	2
4	50	28	78	12.5	7	19.5	10
5	50	42	92	10.01	8.4	18.4	14
6	50	66	116	8.3	11.0	19.3	24

The important points from the table 6.12 are:

(a) Units of output increased from 0 to 1, 2, 3, 4, 5 and 6.

(b) Short-run total fixed cost (STFC) remained ₹ 50 at all level of output.

(c) But SAFC declined continuously from ₹ 50 to ₹ 25, ₹ 16.7, ₹ 12.5, ₹ 10.0, and ₹ 8.3 as output units increased.

(d) Short-run total variable costs (STVC) increased from ₹ 0 to ₹ 10, ₹ 16, ₹ 18, ₹ 28, ₹ 42 and ₹ 66 as units of output increased respectively.

(e) SAVC declined up to 3 units of output as output increased, after that SAVC increased with increased in level of output.

(f) STC short-run total cost STC increased from ₹ 50 to ₹ 60, ₹ 66, ₹ 68, ₹ 78, ₹ 92 and ₹ 116. It remained ₹ 50 even at 0 unit of output as it includes the STFC.

(g) As STFC remained constant, the change in STC is same proportion to change in STVC. For example: when STVC increased from ₹ 10 to ₹ 16 as units of output increased from 2 units to 3 units, the STC also increased from ₹ 60 to ₹ 66. But the difference of STVC and STC are equal to ₹ 6 i.e.

$\Delta STVC = 16 - 10 =$ ₹ 6 and

$\Delta STC = 66 - 60 =$ ₹ 6

$\Delta STC = \Delta STVC =$ ₹ 6

(h) Both STC and STVC increased at low rate or slowly at initial stage, after that both increased at high rate.

(i) The short-run average cost (SAC) falls initially as level of output increases up to a point, beyond that point, it is increased as output increases. It declined up to 5 units, after that it increased continuously.

(j) Short-run marginal cost (SMC) falls initially, up to 3 units, then started rising continuously.

(k) SAC and SMC behaviours governed by 'Law of variable proportions' or short-run production function.

The behaviour of all short-run per unit costs are illustrated in the following diagram 6.17.

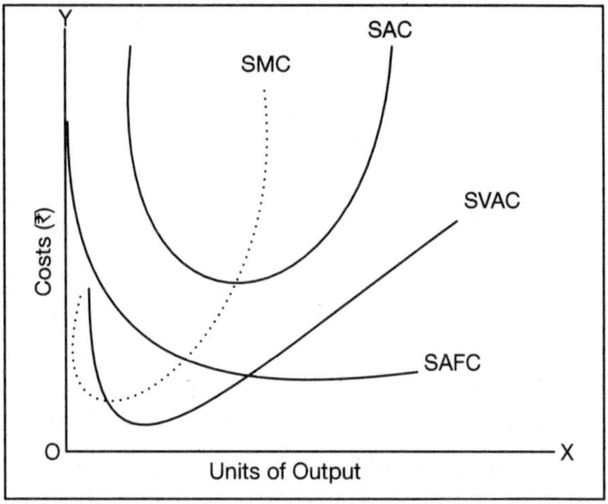

Diagram 6.17: SAFC, SAVC, SAC, and SMC Relations.

On the basis Table 6.12 SAFC, SAVC, SAC, and SMC curves are drawn in diagram 6.17. Units of output are measured along 'OX' axis. Costs (₹) are measured along 'OY' axis.

(d) Long-Run Costs Analysis

The duration of more than five years is called the long-run or long-period. There is sufficient time in long-run. Firm undertakes all possible adjustments in long-run. Firm adjusts supply with demand. Size of firm, scale of returns and technology are changeable in long-run. All fixed factors and variable factors are variable in long-run. There is no difference between fixed costs and variable costs. Hence there are only average cost and marginal cost in long-run. The long-run costs behaviour depends upon the output behaviour in the long-run.

Long-run is a planning horizon. The long-run is perspective view for future course of action. Actually all economic activities operate in short-run. Thus the long-run includes all short-run situations. So the long-run costs depend upon the short-run costs.

Meaning and Nature of Long-run Cost: The costs associated with the change in scale of returns or output and alterations in the size of plants are called 'long-run costs'. In long-run the scale may change from small to large or large too small to increase or decrease the level of output. It results into change in costs. Change in size of plant or firm and technology may result in to change in level of production. For example: When a firm becomes small too big and uses new technology to produce output at large scale, it results into increase in production. Thus it also changes cost of production. Whether costs increase or decrease in long-run depends upon scale of returns, size of firm and technique of production. For example: Handloom is the example of small scale, small firm and traditional technique of production, thus the costs are higher. On the other hand: Automatic looms are the example of large scale production, big firm and modern technique of production, thus the output is higher and costs are lower. Thus the behaviour of long-run costs depends upon scale of production, size of firm and technique of production. Since long-run includes all short-run situations, the long-run costs depend upon the short-run costs.

Types of Long-run Costs and Their Behaviour: The long-run costs can be classified and studied as under:

(i) **Long-run Total Cost (LTC) and Its Behaviour:** In long-run firm spends money on all variable factors. There is no difference between fixed factors and variable factors. All are changeable or variable in long-run. Thus the total expenditures incur on all factors by the firm for production of output of a commodity in the long-run are called long-run total costs (LTC). It can be calculated as:

Long-run Total Costs (LTC) = Costs on All Variable Factors

Total costs depend upon the change in scale of production, size of firm and technique of production in long-run. So it is difficult to draw the exact shape of long-run total cost curve; it is difficult to identify the total costs behaviour in long-run: It may rise or fall or remain constant. However it governs by laws of returns.

(ii) **Long-run Average Cost (LAC) and Its Behaviour:** The long-run total costs per unit of long-run output is called long-run average cost (LAC). Dividing Long-run total cost (LTC) by long-run total output (q), we get long-run average cost (LAC).

Thus it can be calculated as: LAC = LTC/q

Where, LAC =Long-run average cost, LTC = Long-run total cost and q = Long-run total output.

The derivation of long-run average cost curve, the features of LAC curve and LAC's relation with SAC are discussed as under:

(A) **Derivation of Long run Average Cost Curve:** In long-run, firm adjusts the production to the demand of long-run. Thus firm chooses the size of plant or scale in long-run, which is the size of plant having short-run average cost curve and it operates at one of its point. So, to derive the long-run average cost curve, the points on short-run average cost curves should be found out. By joining these points on SAC curves by the tangent curve, we get long-run average cost curve. Thus Joe S. Brain defined, LAC curve as "The long-run average cost curve shows for each possible output the lowest cost of producing that output in the long run." The derivation of LAC curve is illustrated in the following diagram 6.18.

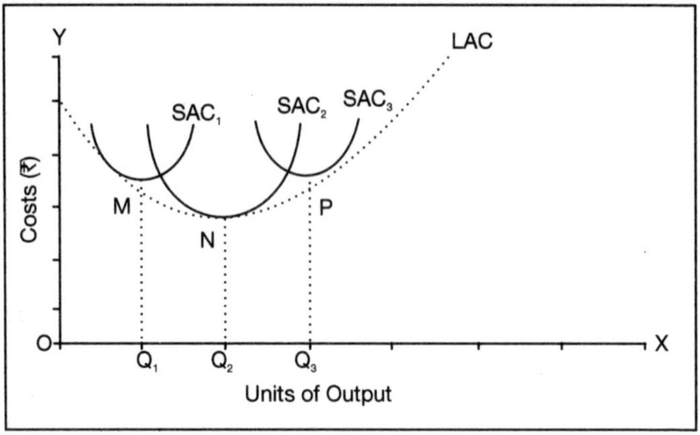

Diagram 6.18: Derivation of LAC Curve

Units of output are measured along 'OX' axis; units of cost are measured along 'OY' axis. SAC_1 is the short-run average cost curve of the size of plant which the firm chooses to operate at M point in long-run. SAC_2 is the short-run average cost curve of the size of plant the firm chooses to operate at 'N' point in long-run. SAC_3 is the short-run average cost curve of the size of plant the firm chooses to operate at 'P' point in long-run. By joining M, N and P points on short-run cost curves 1, 2 and 3 by a tangent curve, we derive a long-run average cost curve i.e. LAC, shown in the diagram 6.18. The firm selects the scale or level of output which has minimum average cost i.e. N point. As firm increases-level of output, the long run average cost declines up to 'N' point, at N point LAC is minimum; after 'N' point increase in level of output raises the LAC. But in long-run the behaviour of LAC with output depends upon laws of returns to scale.

(B) **Features of LAC Curve:** The features of long-run average cost curve are as follows:

(i) LAC curve is a tangent curve of short-run average cost curves. It is shown in diagram 6.10.

(ii) LAC curve is an envelope of a group of short-run average cost curves at different level of output. So LAC curve is also called 'Envelope curve'.

(iii) LAC curve denotes that the firm selects the least cost of producing each possible level of output. Thus LAC curve is a long-run planning decision. So LAC curve is called 'Planning curve'.

(iv) The firm selects to operate at optimum scale of plant. The minimum point of SAC is tangent to minimum point of LAC when plant is an optimum Scale plant.

(v) LAC curve represents the minimum cost-combination. In long-run, the firm operates at the minimum point on SAC and LAC curves.

(vi) LAC curve never intersects SAC curve because LAC curve is always below SAC curves. In long-run, firm always thinks of reducing cost to minimum level. Thus LAC curve is always tangent to SAC curves.

(vii) The behaviour of long-run average cost depends upon the operation of law of returns to scale. So the shape of LAC curve is shown by 'Saucer shape'. It is illustrated in the following diagram 6.19.

(viii) Long-run average cost curve is a flatter U-shape curve. LAC U-shape is flatter than SAC U-shape. It is because of release of some economies and diseconomies due to change in scale of production and change in size of firm.

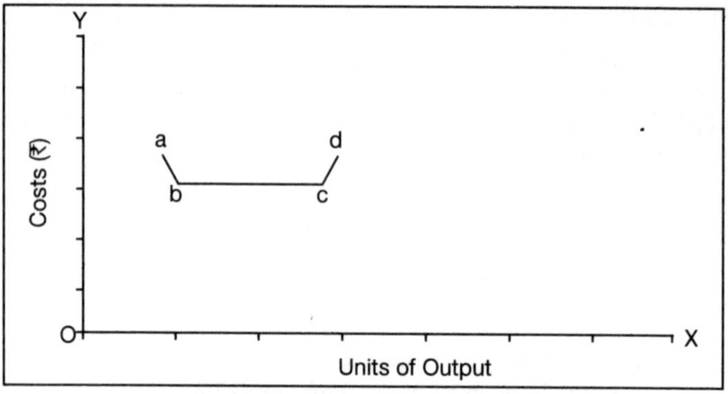

Diagram 6.19: Saucer Shape LAC Curve

(ix) LAC declines at initial stage because at this stage economies are more than diseconomies.

(x) LAC becomes constant at the minimum because at this stage economies are equal to diseconomies.

(xi) LAC starts increasing after the minimum point because at this stage economies are less than diseconomies.

(xii) LAC curve is a family or group of SAC curves.

$$\therefore LAC = SAC_1 + SAC_2 \ldots SAC_n$$
$$= \Sigma SAC_i$$
$$i = 1$$

(xiii) Shifts in LAC Curves: LAC curve shifts above or below the base LAC curve depends upon change in conditions of Total costs in long-run. It is shown in following diagram 6.2.

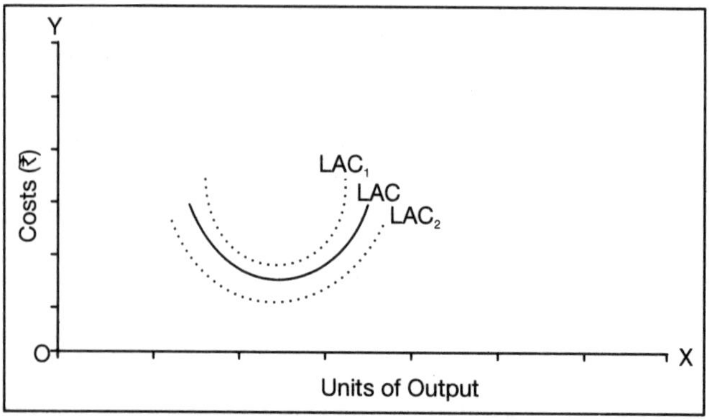

Diagram 6.20: Shifts in LAC Curve

LAC curve represents base LAC. When total costs increase in long-run due to rise in price of factors of production, etc. the LAC curve shifts above the base LAC curve. It is shown by LAC_1. When total costs decline in long-run due to fall in price of factors of production, etc. the LAC curve shifts below the base LAC curve. It is shown by LAC_2.

(iii) **Lang-run Marginal Cost and Its Behaviour:** The long run total costs of an additional unit of output produced in long-run is called long-run marginal cost (LMC). It can be calculated as:

$$LMC = LTC_n - LTC_{n-1} \text{ or } LMC = \Delta c/\Delta q$$

The long-run marginal cost curve can be derived from long-run total cost curve. The behaviour of LMC curve is same as the behaviour of LAC curve, LMC curve falls initially up to a point, then it starts rising faster than LAC as units of output increase: Generally LMC cuts LAC at its minimum point. Thus, LMC is equal to LAC when the firm selects the optimum scale of plant to produce a given level of output.

LMC curve, its behaviour and relation with LAC curve are illustrated in the following diagram 6.21.

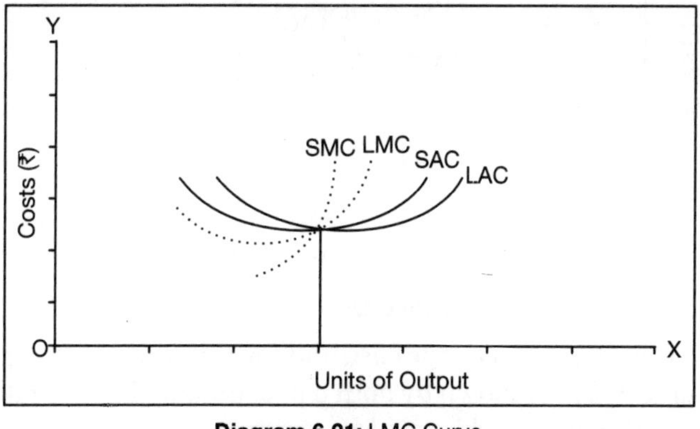

Diagram 6.21: LMC Curve

Units of output are measured along OX axis. Costs are measured along OY axis. LAC is long-run average cost curve which it tangent to SAC.

SAC is short-run average cost curve. At point 'R' on SAC curve the average cost is lowest so the firm decides to operate at that scale of plant in long-run. SMC is short-run marginal cost curve which intersected SAC at point R.

LMC curve tangent SAC curve at point 'R' LMC is long-run marginal cost curve, which is also U-shape LMC intersected LAC at its minimum point 'R' because firm wants to operate the size of plant to produce a given level of output in long-run at minimum average cost. Thus at point R, SMC = SAC = LAC = LMC. OM is the level of output decided by the firm in the long-run.

LMC declines initially up to point 'S', beyond 'S', it starts increasing because initially both marginal productivity and average productivity of the plant are rising up to a certain point. Beyond that point both are falling.

Like LAC, the LMC is also governed by the laws of returns to scale. LMC is falling when output is increasing; LMC is constant when output is constant; LMC is increasing when output is falling. Like LAC, the LMC curve is also 'Saucer shape' under these three conditions. It is shown in the following diagram 6.22.

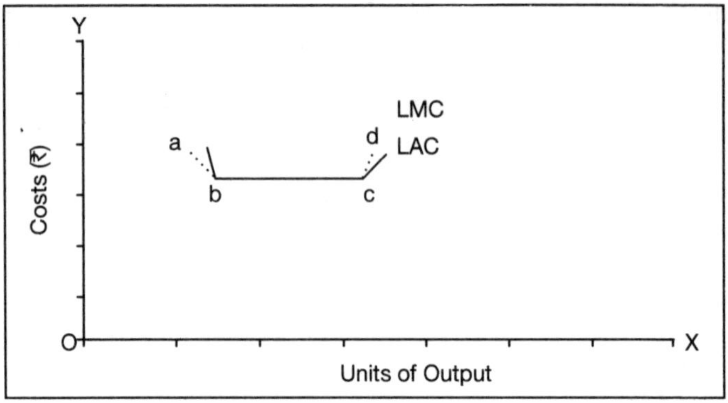

Diagram 6.22: LMC Curve

LAC is long-run average cost, and LMC is long-run marginal cost curve which is shown by dotted line. Initially LMC is falling, which is shown by 'ab' on LMC curve, as output increasing. LMC is below LAC when both are falling. LMC became constant when LAC is constant and LMC=LAC. LMC is rising when LAC is rising but, LMC is above LAC. LMC curve intersects LAC curve whether to the left of minimum point on LAC or at the minimum point of LAC depends upon type of commodity market.

Under perfect competition market, the firm's LMC cuts its LAC at the minimum point of LAC because of optimum utilization of plant capacity.

(e) Relation Between Average Cost and Marginal Cost

Marginal cost and average cost play an important role in determination of price of output and level of output. Firm takes decision regarding fixation of price and level of output in short-run as well as in long run on the basis of average cost and marginal cost. AC and MC are useful to know firm's equilibrium. There is unique relation between AC and MC. The relationship between AC and MC are discussed as under:

(a) **When AC is falling, MC is also falling but MC is less than AC.** MC Curve lies below AC curve. It is explained in the following table 6.13.

Table 6.13: Both AC and MC are Falling

Units of Output (q)	Total cost in ₹ (TC)	Average costs in ₹ (AC)	Marginal cost in ₹ (MC)	Position of MC and AC
1	8	8	–	Both are falling
2	14	7	6	MC < AC
3	18	6	4	MC < AC
4	20	5	2	MC < AC

As output increased from 1 to 2, 3 and 4 units. AC is falling from 8 to 7, 6 and 5 and MC is also falling from 6 to 4 and 2. At this stage, MC is less than AC i.e. MC = 6 < AC = 7 and so on.

(b) **When AC is constant, MC is also constant but MC=AC.** Both MC and AC are shown by same horizontal straight-line curve. It is explained in the following table 6.14.

Table 6.14: Both AC and MC are Constant

Units of Output (q)	Total cost in ₹ (TC)	Average costs in ₹ (AC)	Marginal cost in ₹ (MC)	Position of MC and AC
1	8	8	8	Both are constant
2	16	8	8	MC = AC
3	24	8	8	MC = AC
4	32	8	8	MC = AC

As output increased from 1 unit to 2, 3 and 4 units, the total cost increased from 8 to 16, 24 and 32. But AC and MC both remained constant and equal to each other at all level of output i.e. AC = 8, MC = 8. Therefore MC = 8 = AC = 8.

(c) When AC is rising upwards, MC also rises upwards but MC is greater than AC: MC Curve lies above AC curve. It is explained in the following table 6.15.

Table 6.15: Both AC and MC are Rising

Units of Output (q)	Total cost in ₹ (TC)	Average costs in ₹ (AC)	Marginal cost in ₹ (MC)	Position of MC and AC
1	8	8	-	Both are increasing
2	18	9	10	MC > AC
3	30	10	12	MC > AC
4	44	11	14	MC > AC

As output increased from 1 to 2, 3 and 4 units, the total cost increased from 8 to 18, 30 and 44, AC increased from 8 to 9, 10 and 11 and MC increased from 10 to 12 and 14. Thus both AC and MC are increasing but MC > AC at all level of output.

In brief Table 6.13, Table 6.14 and Table 6.15 explained the relationship between AC and MC under different cost conditions viz. increasing cost, decreasing cost and constant cost, as result of law of returns to scale in long-run. The relationship between AC and MC is illustrated in the following diagram 6.23.

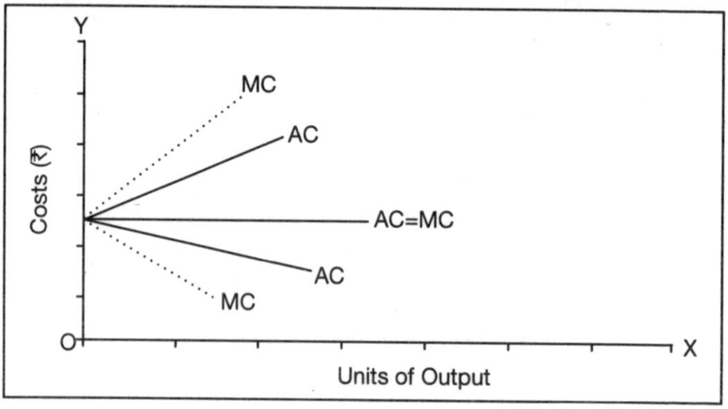

Diagram 6.23: Relation between AC and MC Under different cost Conditions

Points from the diagram 6.23.

(i) When AC is constant, MC is also constant and AC = MC.

(ii) When AC is increasing, MC is also increasing but MC > AC.

(iii) When AC is falling, MC is also falling but MC < AC.

(iv) When firm is governed by: (a) Constant returns to scale, MC and AC are constant and MC = AC. (b) Increasing returns to scale, MC and AC are falling and MC < AC. (c) Decreasing returns to scale, MC and AC are increasing upwards and MC > AC.

6.2.3 Determinants of Cost of Production: There are various factors, which influence on cost of production viz. price of factors of production, the level of output, price of relative factors, efficiency of factors and technology. The factors which influence on cost of production are called 'determinants of cost'.

They can be discussed as under:

(i) **Price of factors of production:** The cost of production of output depends upon the price of factors which are employed in production process. For example labour is input. When the wages rate increases, the cost of production also increases.

(ii) **Price of relative factors of production:** Some factors of production are competitive to each other for example wood and steel. Wood or steel can be used to produce chair. If the price of wood increases, the price of steel will rise.

Some factors of production are complementary to each other. For example cement and steel. Both are used in construction of building so when the price of cement increases, the price of steel also increases.

(iii) **Efficiency of factors of production:** If the factors are more efficient, more output will be produced at low cost. If the factors are less efficient, the output will be low and cost will be more. So the change in efficiency of factors of production results into change in cost.

(iv) **Level of output :** Cost of production depends upon level of output produced. General the cost will be more when the output is produced at large scale; the cost will be less when the output is produced at low scale.

(v) **Technique of production or technology:** The size of cost depends upon technique of production for example: cost of 1 meter cloth produced by handloom is more than the cloth produced by automatic loom. Change in technology or improvement in technique of production generally reduces the cost of production.

6.2.4 Cost Function: The functional relation between cost and level of output is known as 'cost function'. It can be explained as:

$C = f(q)$

Here, C = Cost of production, f = functional relation and q = level of output.

Further cost function can be explained as:

$C = f(q)$

Or $C = \alpha(q)$ here $\alpha = \Delta C/\Delta q$; ΔC = Change in cost; Δq = Change in output

For example: $\alpha = 2$ and $q = 10$, then Cost $= 2 \times 10 = 20$.

Cost equation can be drawn from cost function as:

Since $C = f(q)$

$q = f\ (FF, VF)$

Here q = output, f = functional relation, FF = Fixed Factors and VF = variable factors.

$\therefore$ C = FC + VC, here C = total cost, FC = fixed cost and VC = variable cost. It can be written as:

$C = a + b\ (q)$ (Cost equation)

Here C = total cost, a = Fixed cost, b (q) = variable cost.

Cost function can be classified as:

(i) Single-variable cost function and

(ii) Multi-variables cost function.

(i) **Single variable-cost function:** The functional relation between output and a variable factor or determinant is known as 'Single variable cost function'. For example:

$$C = f(q)$$

Here C = cost, f = functional relation and q = output, a single variable.

It can be explained as:

$C = \alpha(q)$, here C = cost, $\alpha = \Delta C/\Delta q$, q = output, Δ = Change.

(ii) **Multi variables cost function:** The functional relation between cost and its determinants is called 'Multi variable cost function'. It can be explained as:

C = f (q, Pf, Pr, Ef, T)

Where, C = cost, f = functional relation, q = level of output, Pf = price of factors of production Pr = price of relative factors, Ef = efficiency of factors and T = technique of production.

6.3 REVENUE ANALYSIS

6.3.1 Nature and Meaning of Revenue: Firm plays dual role. It acts as producer as well as seller of a commodity. Firm takes decisions about what to produce and how much to produce. Firm produces a commodity demanded in the product market. Firm expects at least a fair price to his commodity or produce. The fair price brings the firm the fair revenue to keep him in the market. Firm determines the level of output possible at minimum cost of production. The revenue and cost enable the firm to attain equilibrium. At equilibrium, firm gets maximum profits and determines price and level of output of a commodity.

Like cost, revenue plays equally important role in the study of the behaviour of the firm. The firm produces and sells more when the price of commodity is higher; the firm produces and sells less when the price of commodity is low.

The revenue is replica of price of commodity. Higher the price, higher the revenue; lower the price, lower the revenue. The firm sells the commodity at a price and gets sales proceeds. For example: A firm sells a chair at the price ₹ 500 and gets sale proceeds of ₹ 500. The total sales proceeds that a firm gets by selling its output of a commodity at a prevailing price are called 'Revenue'.

Revenue is also known as 'receipts' or 'earnings' from selling of a commodity at a prevailing price. Revenue is equal to the price paid to the commodity or output. The price paid by the buyer for the commodity of the firm is revenue of the firm. For example: If a buyer bought a pen by paying ₹ 10 as price to the seller, then ₹ 10 is revenue of the seller.

Hence, Prof. Dooley defined revenue as, "The revenue of a firm is its sale receipts or income."

Revenue varies with variations in price as well as quantity sold of a commodity. Given the price, the increase or decrease in quantity sold of a commodity increases or decreases the revenue. For example: At a given price ₹ 2 per pen, the seller's sale increased from 10 pens to 20 pens, then the revenue increases from ₹ 20 (2 × 10) to ₹ 40 (2 × 20).

The revenue behaviour also depends upon the time elements. The revenue is more in short-run because short run price is higher. The revenue is less in long-run because long-run price is lower.

The nature of revenue also depends upon the types of market situations. The revenue is higher in monopoly than in monopolistic competitive and perfect competitive market.

6.3.2 Determinants of Revenue: Revenue depends upon certain factors. It is resultant outcome of these factors. They determine the size or value of revenue and its behaviour. Price per unit of output and quantity of output sold are the main determinants of revenue.

(i) **Price per Unit (P):** Revenue depends upon the price at which the firm sells its output. The change in price results into change in revenue. For instance: A firm sold same quantity of output, say 10 units at different prices, say ₹ 2, ₹ 3 and ₹ 4. the calculation of revenue is done in the following table 6.16.

Table 6.16: Revenue Schedule

Price (₹) (P)	Output sold (Units) (q)	Revenue (₹) (R = P × q)
2	10	20
3	10	30
4	10	40

As price increases, given the quantity of output sold, revenue also increases. In contrary, as price declines, given the quantity of output sold the revenue also declines.

(ii) **Quantity of Output Sold (q):** Like price, the quantity of output sold also determines the revenue. At a given price, as output sold (q) increases, the revenue also increases; as output sold (q) declines, the revenue also declines. For instance: A firm sold different quantity of output say, 10 units, 20 units and 30 units, at the same or given price ₹ 2 per unit. The revenue is calculated in the following table 6.17.

Table 6.17: Revenue Schedule

Price (₹) (P)	Output sold (units) (q)	Revenue (₹) (R = P × q)
2	10	20
2	20	40
2	30	60

At a given price ₹ 2, as output sold (q) increased to 10 units, 20 units, 30 units, the revenue also increased to ₹ 20, ₹ 40, and ₹ 60 respectively. In contrary, it is *vice versa*. Any variation in price and quantity of output sold results into variation in revenue. It is explained in the following table 6.18.

Table 6.18: Revenue Schedule

Price (₹) (P)	Output sold (units) (q)	Revenue (₹) (R = P × q)
2	11	22
3	10	30
4	8	32

As price increased to ₹ 2, ₹ 3, ₹ 4, the quantity sold declined to 11, 10 and 8 units, but the revenue increased to ₹ 22, ₹ 30 and ₹ 32 respectively. In contrary, as price declined to ₹ 4, ₹ 3, ₹ 2, the quantity sold increased to 8, 10 and 11 units respectively. The main aim of the firm is to maximize profits through increasing revenue and reducing cost. The firm maximizes the revenue either by raising price or by sale maximization. The firm maximizes the revenue either by selling same quantity of output at higher and higher price or by selling more and more quantity of output at same price.

Totally, the revenue (Total Revenue) depends on price per unit and quantity of output sold. The various level of revenue at different price and quantity of output sold is called 'Revenue Schedule'.

6.3.3 Revenue Function: Revenue or total revenue is resultant outcome of price per unit and quantity of output sold. The functional relation between revenue and price and output sold is called 'Revenue function'.

Revenue function can be written as:

$R = P(q)$ or $P \times q$

R = Total Revenue, P = Price per unit, q = quantity of output sold.

It can be read as "Revenue is the function of quantity of output sold at a price."

An eminent economist Mrs. Joan Robinson in her book, *The Economics of Imperfect Competition* stated the revenue function as:

Total revenue = selling price times the quantity sold = F(x y)

F = Functional relation, x = quantity sold, y = price

The revenue function, $R = P \times q$ is also called revenue equation.

Using the revenue equation $R = P \times q$, we can calculate the total revenue. Thus, revenue is the resultant outcome of quantity of output sold at price times.

6.3.4 Concepts (Types) of Revenue: It is essential to know concepts of revenue. They can help the firm to take decisions like maximization of profits and determination of price and level of output under different market situations. The firm's revenue can be classified into three concepts, viz. (i) Total Revenue, (ii) Average Revenue (iii) Marginal Revenue. They are studied in next sub-sections.

(I) Total Revenue (TR): Total Revenue is an important concept of revenue. It shows total revenue position of the firm. It helps the firm to identify the area of maximum profits by finding the maximum difference between total revenue and total cost. Thus, it plays important role in 'total cost and total revenue analysis' to find out firm's equilibrium. Total revenue helps the firm to identify the 'average revenue' and 'marginal revenue'.

The firm offers to sell his output of a commodity at a given price. The total receipts or sale proceeds the firm received by selling its units of output of a commodity at a given price over a given period of time is called 'Total Revenue' (TR). For example: A firm sells 100 units of output of a commodity at a price of ₹ 10 per unit, its total revenue (TR) = ₹ 10 × 100 units = ₹ 1000. Total revenue depends upon two factors: (a) Price per unit of output and (b) number of units of output of a commodity sold.

Total revenue can be calculated by using following formula or equation:

$TR = P \times q$

Here, TR = Total Revenue, P = price per unit of output and q = number of units of output of a commodity sold.

For example: A mango seller sold 10 mangoes at the price of ₹ 5 per mango then TR = ₹ 5 per mango × 10 number of mangoes sold = ₹ 50. Total revenue is generally denoted by 'TR' or 'R'.

Total revenue varies with variation in price (P) and quantity of output sold (q).

At given price, the total revenue varies with variations in quantity sold. It is explained in the following table 6.19.

Table 6.19: Total Revenue Schedule

Price (₹) (P)	Output sold (units) (q)	Revenue (₹) (R = P × q)
10	10	100
10	20	200
10	30	300

Price per unit is constant i.e. ₹ 10. Quantity sold increased from 10 units to 20 and 30 units. Thus total revenue increased from ₹ 100 to ₹ 200 and ₹ 300.

At a given price, as quantity of output sold increases the total revenue increases: the total revenue decreases when the total quantity of output sold declines.

The total revenue and its behaviour are illustrated in the following diagram 6.24.

Units of output sold measured along OX axis; the revenue is measured along OY axis. TR is total revenue (TR) curve. TR curve explains that: (i) TR = 0, when q = 0, (ii) TR will be increased to R1 and R2 when q increases from Q units to Q1 units and Q2 units respectively. In contrary, TR will be declined, when q declines. TR varies directly with variations in q, when P is constant, because of (a) increase in demand for the output and (b) sellers policy of sale maximization to maximize profits.

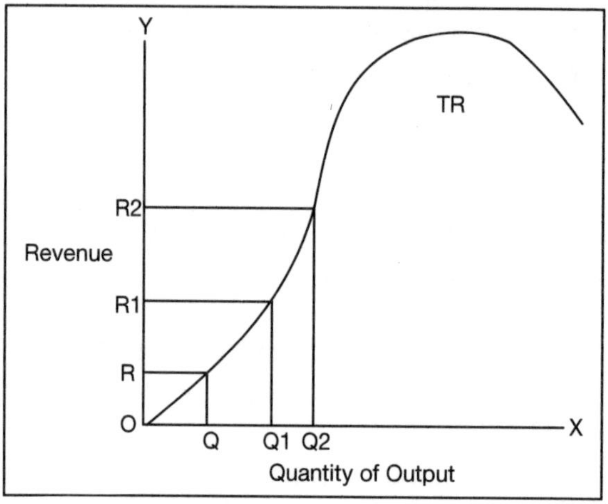

Diagram 6.24: Total Revenue Curve

Thus in brief, total revenue varies with variation in price and quantity sold.

(II) Average Revenue (AR): 'Average Revenue' is another important concept of revenue. Average revenue (AR) is derived from total revenue. It helps the firm to calculate the size of profits. The shape of 'average revenue' curve helps you to understand the market situations. It helps to measure the degree of monopoly. The revenue received per unit of output sold is called 'Average revenue'. It is generally denoted by 'AR'. 'Average revenue' can be calculated by using following equation:

AR = TR/q

AR = Average revenue, TR = Total revenue and q = quantity of output sold. For example: A firm received total revenue ₹ 1000 by selling 5 chairs. Then the average revenue is:

AR = = TR/q = ₹ 1000/5 chairs = ₹ 200

We get 'AR' dividing total revenue by the number of units of output sold.

(a) **Average Revenue and Price:** Average Revenue and price per unit of output sold is one and same when the number units of output are sold at same price. In such case Average Revenue is equal to the price. For example: If a seller sold 10 chairs at the price of ₹ 200 each , then the Average Revenue is:

AR= TR/q = P × q/q Here TR = P × q

AR = ₹ 200 × 10 chairs/10 chairs = ₹ 200

Here, price per chair is ₹ 200 and Average Revenue is ₹ 200

Thus, AR = P

By definition, 'Average Revenue' is price. It can be proved by the following equations:

(i) Total Revenue (TR) equation is:

TR = P × q P = price per unit q = quantity sold

P= TR/q ...(1)

(ii) Average Revenue (AR) equation is:

AR=TR/q ...(2)

TR = Total Revenue (P.q), q = quantity sold

Since P = TR/q and AR = TRq

P = AR = = TR/q

∴ P = AR

AR = P when the number of units of output are sold at same price. Price is always per unit of output.

If different quantities of output are sold at different prices, the average revenue is not equal to price. For example: If a firm sold 10 chairs at ₹ 200 each and 15 chairs at ₹ 220 each. Of course, the total quantity sold is 10 chairs + 15 chairs = 25 chairs, but they are sold at different prices. So AR is not equal to price. It is proved as:

TR = 10 chairs × ₹ 200 + 15 chairs × ₹ 220

= ₹ 2000 + ₹ 3300 = ₹ 5300

AR = TR/q = ₹ 5300/25 chairs = ₹ 212

Thus AR = ₹ 212 is not equal to price. The prices are ₹ 200 and ₹ 220.

(b) **Average Revenue, Price and Demand:** Demand for a commodity depends upon its price. Demand is always at price. The quantity demanded will be low, when price is high; the quantity demanded will be high when price is low. Since average revenue is equal to price and price is shown on demand curve, the demand curve becomes average revenue curve.

The shape of average revenue curve and its behaviour are depending upon the market situations and shape of demand curve.

(c) **Derivation of Average Revenue (AR) Curve:** Total Revenue (TR) and quantity of output sold are the determinants of average revenue (AR). Therefore average revenue (AR) curve can be derived from total revenue (TR) curve. First, we should calculate total revenue of the different quantities of output sold at different prices. And then, we should calculate average revenue (AR). It is explained in the following table 6.20.

Table 6.20: Revenue Schedule of a Firm.

Price (₹) (P)	Quantity sold (Units)	Total Revenue (₹) (TR = P × q)	Average Revenue (₹) (AR = TR) q
1	30	30	1
2	20	40	2
3	10	30	3

Points from the table 6.20:

When Price = ₹ 1, q = 30 units TR = 30, then AR = ₹ 1.

When P = ₹ 2, q = 20 units, TR = 40 then AR = ₹ 2

When P = ₹ 3, q = 10 units, TR = ₹ 30, then AR = ₹ 3

With the help of this information, we can derive AR curve from TR curve as shown in the diagram 6.25.

Part (A) of the diagram explains total revenue curve. Part (B) of diagram explains the derivation of AR curve from total revenue curve shown in part A. In part 'A', plot the, b, c points. Point 'a' should show total revenue ₹ 30, when output sold is 10 units. Point 'b' should show total revenue ₹ 40,when output sold is 20 units and point 'c' should show total revenue ₹ 30 when output sold is 30 units. Similarly, in part 'B', plot points a_1, b_1 and c_1. Point a_1 should show average revenue ₹ 3, when output sold is 10 units at price ₹ 3 per unit. Point b_1 should show average revenue

₹ 2 when output sold is 20 units at price ₹ 2 per unit and point c_1 should show average revenue ₹ 1 when output sold is 30 units at price ₹ 1 per unit. Join a_1, b_1 and c_1 point by drawing a straight line, you get average revenue curve AR. Thus AR curve derives from TR curve. At each level of output sold, AR = Price.

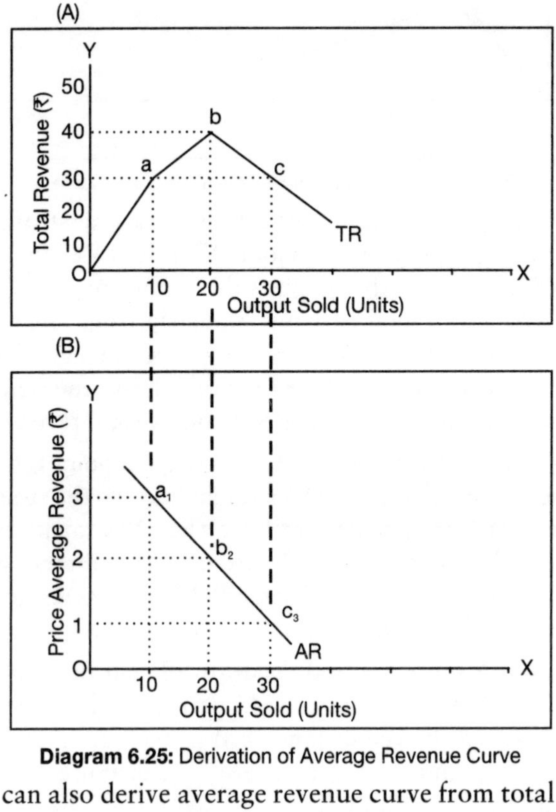

Diagram 6.25: Derivation of Average Revenue Curve

We can also derive average revenue curve from total revenue curve by using the Geometric Method (Diagram 6.26).

Revenue is measured along OY axis. Output sold (units) measured along OX axis. TR is total revenue curve. To derive AR curve from TR curve following steps are to be followed.

STEP-I: Draw 'AA' and 'BB' two separate straight lines to tangent TR curve at two different places. 'AA' line tangent TR curve at R point and 'BB' line tangent TR curve at S point.

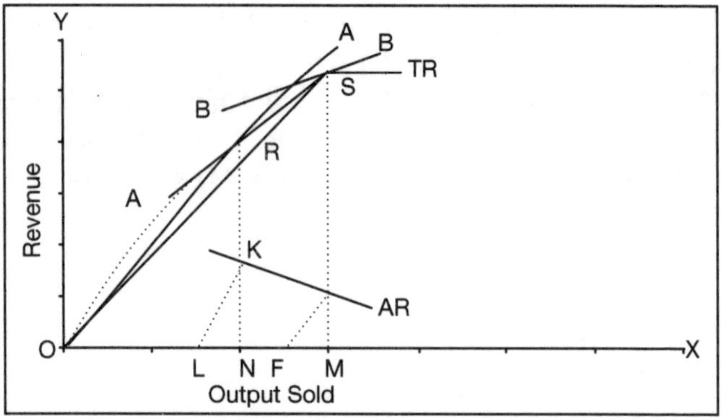

Diagram 6.26: Geometrical Derivation of AR Curve

STEP-II: From tangent point 'R' draw a straight line downwards or perpendicular to join OX axis at 'N', the distance ON at OX axis shows the output sold at tangent point 'R'. The distance RN shows total revenue. Similarly from tangent point 'S' draw a straight line downwards or perpendicular to join OX axis at 'M'. the distance OM at OX axis shows the output sold at tangent point 'S'. the distance SM shows total revenue.

STEP-III: Draw a straight line from tangent point R to the left to join the origin 'O' you get OR straight line. To the straight line 'OR' draw 'LK' parallel straight line. The LK straight line joins 'RN' perpendicular at K and OX axis at L. The distance between LN shows a unit of output and distance KN shows average revenue. When output sold is ON and total revenue is RN.

Follow the same method to draw FE parallel line to OS straight line. FE parallel line join SM perpendicular or TR line at E and OX axis at F. The distance EM is average revenue of the output sold OM and total revenue SM. The distance FM is a unit of output.

STEP-IV: Join K and E points by a straight line, we get average revenue curve A.

The geometrical method helps you to identify the average revenue or to measure average revenue at different points on total revenue curve.

(d) **Shape of Average Revenue Curve and Its Behaviour:** The shape of average revenue curve generally depends upon the shape of demand curve. The shape of demand curve for the output of a firm depends upon market situations or forms. The shape of average revenue curve under different market forms is studies as follows:

(a) **Horizontal Straight line AR Curve:** Under perfect competitive market the demand curve for the output of a firm is horizontal straight line. It is because the firm is price-taker. The price is single and constant. The firm sells different quantity of output at same price. It is explained in the following table 6.21.

Table 6.21: Revenue Schedule of a Firm in Perfect Competition

Price (₹) (P)	Quantity sold (Units)	Total Revenue (₹) (TR = P × q)	Average Revenue (₹) (AR = TR) q
2	1	2	2
2	2	4	2
2	3	6	2
2	4	8	2

Points from the table 6.21:

Price is same and constant.

Quantity sold increased from 1 unit to 2, 3 and 4 units.

Total revenue also increased from ₹ 2 to ₹ 4, ₹ 6 and ₹ 8.

But, the average revenue at all level of output is same i.e. ₹ 2 and AR = P = ₹ 2.

On the basis of table 6.21, you can derive average revenue curve as shown in diagram 6.27.

In diagram 6.27.

Part 'A' explains total revenue. TR is total revenue curve. a, b, c and d are the points on TR curve. Point 'a' shows total revenue is ₹ 2 when output sold is 1 unit. In similar way points b, c and d show the total revenue ₹ 4, ₹ 6 and ₹ 8, when output sold is 2, 3 and 4 units respectively.

Part 'B' explains the derivation of average revenue curve on the basis of total revenue. The average revenue is ₹ 2 when level of output 1, 2, 3 and 4 units. The average revenue is same at all level of output. You plot the points a_1, b_1, c_1 and d_1 to show averages revenue ₹ 2 at all level of output. Join a_1, b_1, c_1 and d_1 points by a straight line, you get horizontal straight line parallel to OX axis. It is average revenue curve. It is possible only in perfect competitive market. The AR curve coincides with demand curve. It means in perfect competition the average revenue curve and demand curve of the firm is one and same.

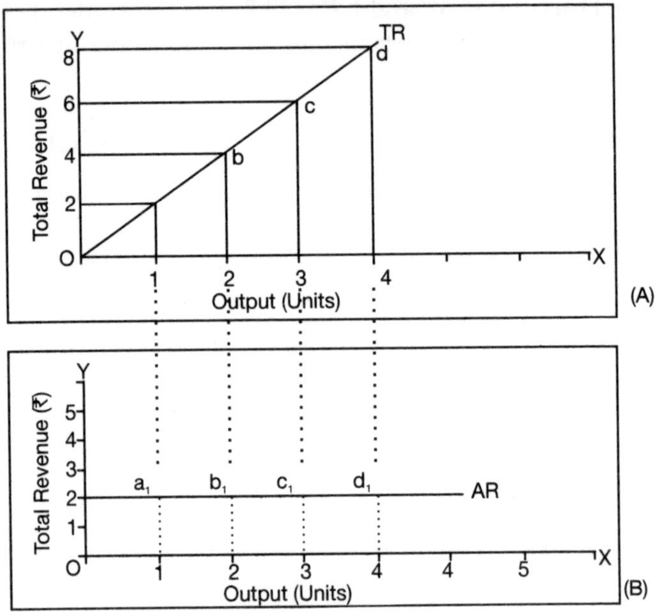

Diagram 6.27: Horizontal Straight line AR Curve

(b) **Steeper Downwards Sloping AR Curve:** In monopoly market, the demand curve for the output of the firm is sloping downwards from left to right and which is steeper. In monopoly market, since there is only one seller, the buyers are less sensitive to change in price. So the demand curve is steeper. Since 'Demand curve' is average revenue curve, the AR curve is steeper downwards sloping curve. The revenue schedule of a firm in monopoly is explained in the following table 6.22.

Table 6.22: Revenue Schedule of Firm in Monopoly

Price (₹) (P)	Quantity Sold (Units)	Total Revenue (₹) (TR = P × q)	Average Revenue (₹) (AR = TR) q
6	1	6	6
4	2	8	4
3	3	9	3

By using the table 6.22, we can draw AR curve in the following diagram 6.28.

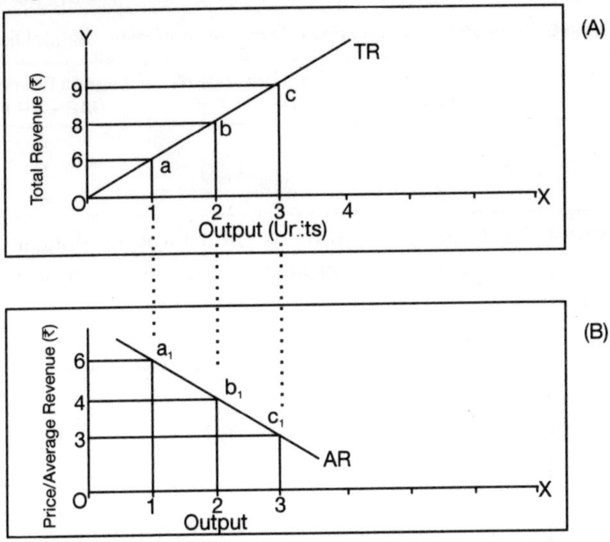

Diagram 6.28: Steeper Downward Sloping AR Curve in Monopoly

In part 'A' you plot a, b and c points on TR curve to show total revenue ₹ 9, ₹ 8 and ₹ 6, when output is 1 unit, 2 units and 3 units, respectively.

In part 'B' you plot a_1, b_1 and c_1 points to show average revenue ₹ 6, ₹ 4 and ₹ 3, when output sold is 1 unit, 2 units and 3 units, respectively.

Join a_1, b_1, c_1 points by drawing a straight line, you get steeper downwards sloping AR curve. At each point AR = P.

Like demand curve, AR curve slopes downwards from left right because (i) demand is at price and P = AR, so demand curve and average revenue curve is one and same, (ii) when price increases, quantity demanded declines and when price falls, quantity demanded rises and (iii) as price falls, AR declines; as price rises, AR also rises.

(c) **Flatter Downwards Sloping AR Curve:** In monopolistic competition or imperfect competitive market, the firm has a flatter downwards sloping demand curve for its output. The buyers are more sensitive to price changes in monopolistic competitive market. The revenue schedule of a firm in monopolistic competition is explained in the following table 6.23.

Table 6.23: Revenue Schedule of a Firm in Monopolistic Competition

Price (₹) (P)	Quantity Sold (Units)	Total Revenue (₹) (TR = P × q)	Average Revenue (₹) (AR = TR) q
6	1	6	6
5	2	10	5
4	3	12	4

Using table 6.23, you can draw the following diagram 6.29 to explain the derivation of average revenue curve in monopolistic competition.

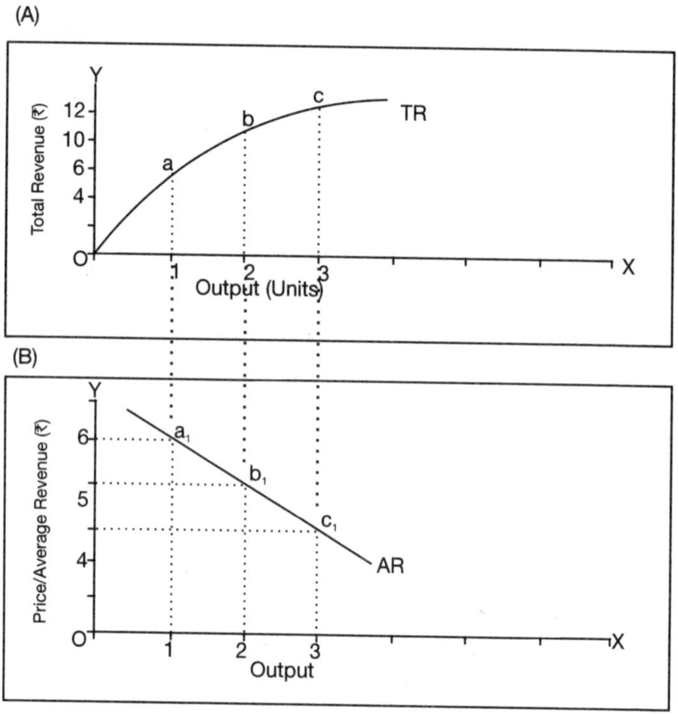

Diagram 6.29: Flatter Downward Sloping Average Revenue Curve

Part 'A' explains the deriving of TR curve. The points a, b and c on TR curve show that the total revenue is ₹ 6, ₹ 10 and ₹ 12 at 1 unit, 2 units and 3 units of output, respectively.

Part 'B' explains the deriving of AR curve. The points a_1, b_1, and c_1 show that AR is ₹ 6, ₹ 5 and ₹ 4 at 1 unit, 2 units and 3units of output, respectively.

Join a_1, b_1 and c_1 points by a straight line, you get AR curve. It is flatter downwards shaping in shape.

(d) **Upwards Rising AR Curve:** The shape of demand curve decides the shape and nature of average revenue curve and its behaviour. There is exception to the law of demand. In case of prestigious goods, the rich buy more when price rises of prestigious goods. In case of prestigious goods, the shape of demand curve is rising upwards from left to right. Since AR curve is demand curve. AR curve also rising upwards from left to right. It is shown in the following diagram 6.30.

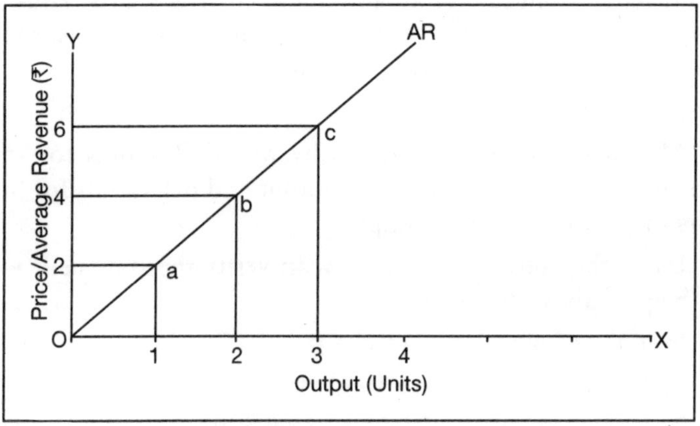

Diagram 6.30: Upwards Rising AR Curve

The diagram explains (i) As price of prestigious commodity increases from ₹ 2 to ₹ 4 and ₹ 6, the quantity of output sold will be increased from 1 unit to 2 and 3 units. (ii) Points a, b and c show that the average revenue is ₹ 2, ₹ 4 and ₹ 6 at the 1 unit, 2 units and 3 units of output sold respectively. (iii) Price = AR (iv) By joining points a, b and c you get rising upwards AR curve. Thus the shape of AR curve depends upon the shape of demand curve under different market forms and nature of commodity.

(III) Marginal Revenue: 'Marginal Revenue' is another important concept of revenue. It is calculated from total revenue. Its curve can be derived from total revenue curve. Marginal revenue is related to production of additional unit of output. Its behaviour and shape of curve depend upon average revenue and shape of average revenue curve. Marginal revenue concept is very useful to the firm. The firm decides (i) Price determination, (ii) level of output determination and (iii) size of profits or firm's equilibrium with the help of marginal revenue. It plays a very important role in marginalist analysis.

The sale proceeds or revenue received by the firm through selling an additional unit of output is called 'Marginal Revenue'. For instance, A chair-seller sold 10 chairs and received ₹ 2000, then by selling one more chair the seller received ₹ 210. The total chairs sold increased to 11 chairs (10 + 1 = 11) and the total amount revenue received increased to ₹ 2210 (₹ 2000 + ₹ 210). The revenue from sale of an additional chair is ₹ 210. Thus the marginal revenue is ₹ 210. Marginal revenue can be measured or calculated by using following formula:

$$MR = TR_n - TR_{n-1}$$

Marginal revenue is denoted by MR, TR stands for total revenue, n stands for 'n' units of output and n-1 stands for 'n-1' units or previous units of output.

Using the above example, we can verify the statement with the help of above formula:

'n' units of output are 11 chairs

'n-1' units of output are 10 chairs

The total revenue of 'n' units of output i.e. 11 chairs is ₹ 2210. The Total Revenue of n–1 units of output i.e. 10 chairs is ₹ 2000.

Substitute the numerical values into formula.

$$MR = TR_n - TR_{n-1}$$
$$= ₹\ 2210 - ₹\ 2000 = ₹\ 210.$$

Marginal revenue or the revenue of additional unit of output or chair sold is ₹ 210.

Marginal revenue can also be calculated by using following formula:

$$MR = \Delta R/\Delta q$$

MR stands for marginal revenue, DR stands for change in total revenue which means the difference between total revenue of 'n' units of output sold and 'n–1' units of output sold

$\therefore \Delta R = TR_n - Tr_{n-1}$

Dq stands for change in total output sold or produced by the firm which means the difference between 'n' units of output and 'n-1' units of output

$\Delta q = q_n - q_{n-1}$

By using the above example, we can verify the formula:

$MR = \Delta R/\Delta q = TR_n - TR_{n-1}/q_n - q_{n-1}$

By substituting the numerical values of the said example,

$MR = TR_n - TR_{n-1}/q_n - q_{n-1}$ = ₹ 2210 – ₹ 2000/11 chairs –10 chairs = ₹ 210/1.

Therefore the marginal revenue of the additional one chair sold is ₹ 210. In brief, marginal revenue is the revenue accrue to the firm from the sale of additional unit of output.

(a) **Derivation of Marginal Revenue Curve:** Marginal revenue is also related with total revenue. The marginal revenue schedule can be prepared on the basis of total revenue and total output sold. It is explained in the following table 6.24.

Table 6.24: Marginal Revenue Schedule

Price (₹) (P)	Quantity sold (Units) (q)	Total Revenue (₹) ($TR = P \times q$)	Marginal Revenue (₹) ($MR = TR_n - TR_{n-1}$)
3	1	3	3
2	2	4	1
1	3	3	–1

The marginal revenue at various quantities of output sold is called 'Marginal Revenue Schedule'.

Points from the above table 6.24: (a) At different level of price ₹ 3, ₹ 2 and ₹ 1, the quantity of output sold is 1 unit, 2 units and 3 units respectively. (b) Total revenue is ₹ 3, ₹ 4 and ₹ 3 when output sold is 1 unit, 2 units and 3 units, respectively, (c) Marginal revenue at 1 unit is ₹ 3 (₹ 3 – ₹ 0), at 2 units is ₹ 1 (₹ 4 – ₹ 3) and at 3 units ₹ – 1 (₹ 3 – ₹ 4).

By using the table 6.24 and marginal revenue schedule, we can derive 'Marginal revenue curve' in the following diagram 6.31.

(A)

(B)

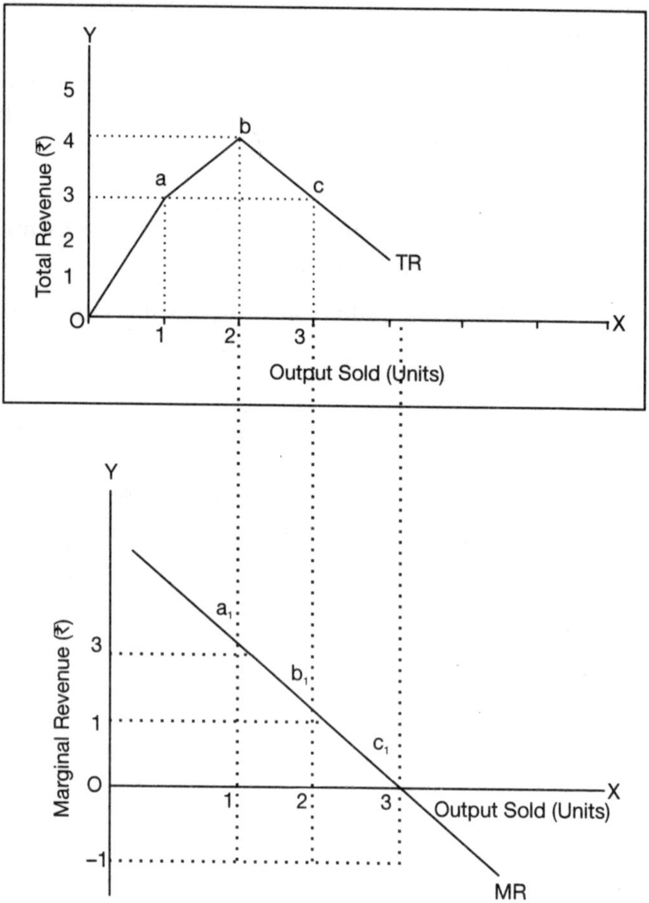

Diagram 6.31: Derivation of Marginal Revenue Curve

Part (A) explains total revenue curve. TR is the total revenue curve. Point a, b and c show total revenue ₹ 3, ₹ 4, ₹ 3 at output 1 unit, 2 units and 3 units respectively.

Part (B) explains the deriving of marginal revenue curve from marginal revenue schedule. Point a_1, b_1 and c_1 show the marginal revenue ₹ 3, ₹ 1 and ₹ –1 at output 1 unit, 2 units, and 3 units, respectively. Joining points a_1, b_1, c_1 through a straight line, we derive marginal revenue curve MR. We can also derive MR curve on the basis of TR curve by using Geometric method as follows:

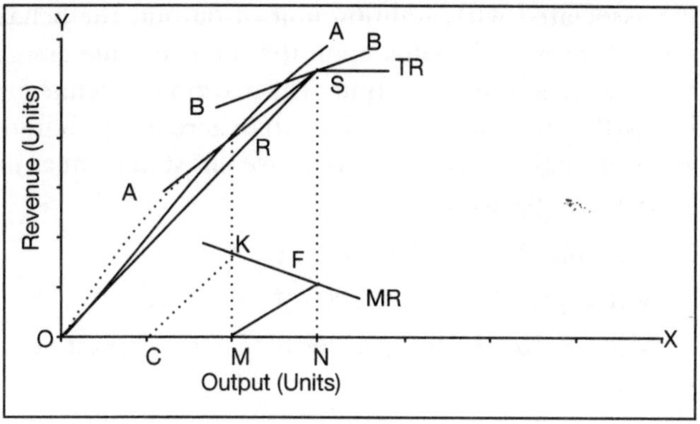

Diagram 6.32: Derivation of MR Curve

Units of output are measured along OX axis. Units of revenue are measured along OY axis. TR is the total revenue curve. On the basis of TR curve, we can derive MR curve and measure unit of marginal revenue by following the following steps:

STEP-I: Draw 'AA' and 'BB' straight lines to tangent TR curve at two different points. 'AA' straight line tangent TR curve at point 'R' and 'BB' straight line tangent TR curve at point 'S'.

STEP-II: Draw 'RM' perpendicular from tangent point 'R' and 'SN' perpendicular from tangent point 'S'. 'RM' perpendicular join OX axis at 'M' point. So the total output is 'ON' units and total revenue is the distance 'RM'. 'SN' perpendicular joins OX axis at 'N' point. So the total output is 'ON' units and total revenue is the distance 'SN'.

STEP-III: Draw 'CK' straight line parallel to 'AA' tangent line. 'CK' line joins perpendicular 'RM' at K point and OX axis at 'C' point. The distance 'CM' is a unit of output and 'KM' is marginal revenue. Similarly draw 'MF' straight line parallel to 'BB' tangent line. 'MF' line joins 'SN' perpendicular at 'F' point and OX axis at 'M' point. The distance 'MN' is a unit of output and 'FN' is marginal revenue.

STEP-IV: Draw a straight line to join point K and 'F', you get MR marginal revenue curve.

Thus marginal revenue curve is derived from TR curve.

(b) Shape of MR Curve and Its Behaviour: Since marginal revenue associated with addition unit of output, the behaviour of marginal revenue depends upon the total revenue associated with the change in level of output. The marginal revenue may be positive (MR > 0) or negative (MR < 0) or zero depends upon the behaviour of total revenue. We can prove this statement as under:

(a) MR > 0 (Positive)

For example: TR_n = ₹ 100, TR_n–1 = ₹ 90

MR = TR_n–TR_n–1 = ₹ 100 – ₹ 90 = ₹ 10

MR = ₹ 10 which is greater than zero or positive

(b) MR = 0

For example:

TR_n = ₹ 100, TR_n–1 = ₹ 100

MR = TR_n–TR_n–1 = ₹ 100 – ₹ 100 = ₹ 0

Hence MR = 0

(c) MR < 0 (negative)

For example:

TR_n = ₹ 90, TR_n–1 = ₹ 100

MR = TR_n–TR_n–1 = ₹ 90 – ₹ 100 = –₹ 10

MR = – ₹ 10 which is less than zero or negative.

The marginal revenue may or may not be equal to price per unit of output, it depends upon the shape of marginal revenue curve. The shape of marginal revenue curve depends upon the nature of demand curve and market forms.

6.3.5 The Relation between AR and MR Curves: Both AR and MR curves are derived from Total Revenue (TR) curve. Average revenue curve is denoted by AR curve and Marginal revenue curve is denoted by MR curve. Market forms or situations, linearity and non-linearity of the curve and price elasticity of demand determine the relationship between AR and MR curves. The relationship between AR and MR curves is traced as under:

(a) **MR Curve Coincides with AR Curve:** In perfect competitive market, the demand curve for the output of the firm is horizontal straight line which is parallel to OX axis. Since 'Demand Curve' is the AR curve, it is horizontal straight line. AR curve shows that price is equal to AR and AR is constant or same at all quantities of output sold. Since AR is constant MR is also constant, it means MR remains same at all level of output sold. Thus AR = MR and MR curve coincides with AR curve. In perfect competition, demand curve, AR curve and MR curve are shown by a same horizontal straight line. It is illustrated in the following diagram 6.33.

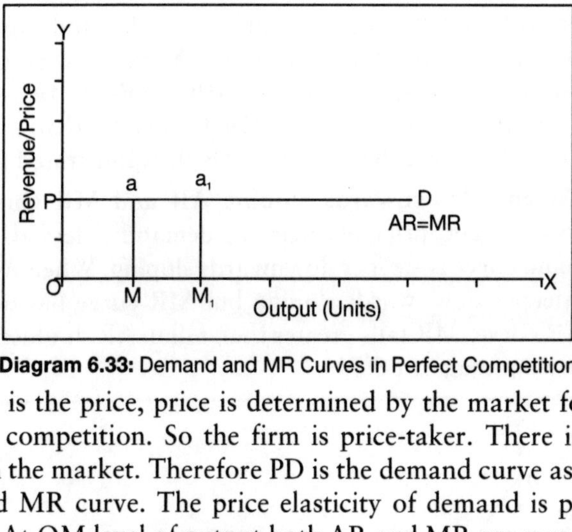

Diagram 6.33: Demand and MR Curves in Perfect Competition

OP is the price, price is determined by the market forces in perfect competition. So the firm is price-taker. There is single price in the market. Therefore PD is the demand curve as well as AR and MR curve. The price elasticity of demand is perfectly elastic. At OM level of output both AR and MR are same so AR = MR = aM. Similarly at oM_1 level of output AR = MR = a_1M_1 and aM = a_1M_1. AR and MR both are constant or same and equal to each other. It is explained in the following table 6.25.

Table 6.25: Revenue Schedule for a Firm in Perfect Competition

Price (₹) (P)	Quantity sold (Units) (q)	Total Revenue (₹) (TR = P × q)	Average Revenue (₹) (AR = TR) q	Marginal Revenue (₹) ($MR = TR_n - TR_{n-1}$)
6	1	6	6	6
6	2	15	6	6
6	3	18	6	6

Points from table 6.25: (i) Price is same or constant ₹ 6 at all level of output sold. (ii) As quantity sold increased to 1, 2, 3 units the total revenue increased to ₹ 6, ₹ 12, ₹ 18 respectively. (iii) But AR and MR remain constant or same ₹ 6 at all level of output. When AR is constant, MR is also constant and AR = MR, thus both are shown by a same horizontal straight line which is parallel to OX axis.

(b) **When AR Curve is falling, MR Curve is also falling from left to right but MR Curve is below the AR Curve:** In monopoly and monopolistic competitive market both AR and MR curves are falling or sloping downwards from left to right. It is because in both market situations the demand curve is falling or sloping downwards from left to right. As price falls, demand expands; as price rises, demand contracts. So also the Average Revenue. When AR is falling, MR is also falling but MR < AR or MR curve lies below or to the left of AR curve. MR falls faster than AR when price falls. MR is less than price or AR. It is illustrated as:

(i) **Steeper Downwards Sloping AR and MR Curves:** In monopoly market, price elasticity of demand is less elastic. So the demand curve is steeper downwards sloping. When AR curve is also steeper downwards sloping but MR curve lies below or left of AR curve. MR falls greater than fall in AR. It illustrated in the following diagram 6.34:

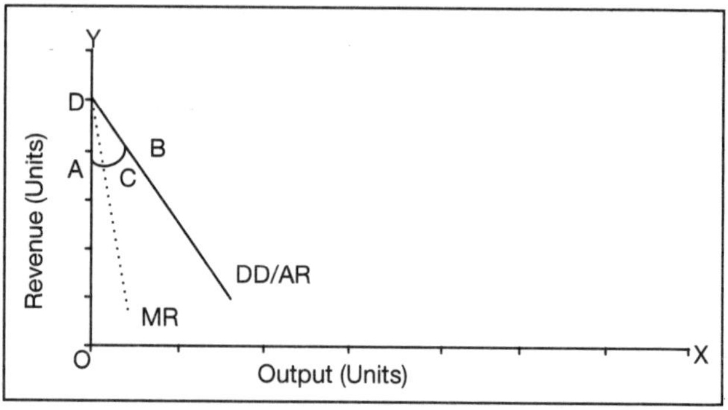

Diagram 6.34: DD, AR and MR Curve in Monopoly

DD/AR is the demand curve as well as AR curve. AR curve is a steeper downwards sloping curve. It explains the price-elasticity of demand is less elastic. MR is the marginal revenue curve which is also steeper downwards sloping curve. MR curve is more steeper than AR curve because MR falls faster than AR. MR curve lies below or left of AR curve which shows MR is less than AR (MR < AR). In monopoly market, the distance between AR and MR curve is larger. To measure the distance between AR and MR, you draw a 'AB' perpendicular to OY axis. AB straight line is horizontal and parallel to OX axis. Plot the point 'C' at the middle of AB line. MR curve cuts AB line to the left of 'C' point. It means the distance between AR curve to MR curve is more than ½ the distance between AR curve and OY axis or AB line. It shows that the market situation is a monopoly market.

According to Mrs. Joan Robinson, greater the distance between AR and MR curves, higher the degree of monopoly and greater the extent of monopoly profits. The relation between AR and MR in monopoly market can be explained in the following table 6.26.

Table 6.26: Revenue Schedule of a Firm in Monopoly

Price (₹) (P)	Quantity sold (Units) (q)	Total Revenue (₹) (TR = P × q)	Average Revenue (₹) (AR = TR) q	Marginal Revenue (₹) ($MR = TR_n - TR_{n-1}$)
8	1	8	8	–
5.50	2	11	5.50	3
4	3	12	4	1
3	4	12	3	0

Points from the table 6.26: (a) When AR falls to ₹ 5.50, ₹ 4, ₹ 3, MR also falls to ₹ 3 ₹ 1 ₹ = 0, respectively. (b) AR is equal to price (AR = P) but MR is not equal to price. MR is less than AR and price. (c) MR falls faster than AR. (d) MR becomes zero even when AR is greater than zero.

(ii) **Flatter Downwards Sloping AR and MR Curves:** In imperfect competition or Monopolistic competition market, price elasticity of demand is more elastic. Thus the demand curve is as usual but flatter. Therefore, the AR curve is flatter downwards sloping curve.

When AR is falling and AR curve is flatter downwards sloping, MR is also falling and MR curve is flatter downwards sloping but MR is less than AR and MR curve lies below or left of AR curve. The rate of fall in MR is greater than the rate of fall in AR. It is illustrated in the following diagram 6.35.

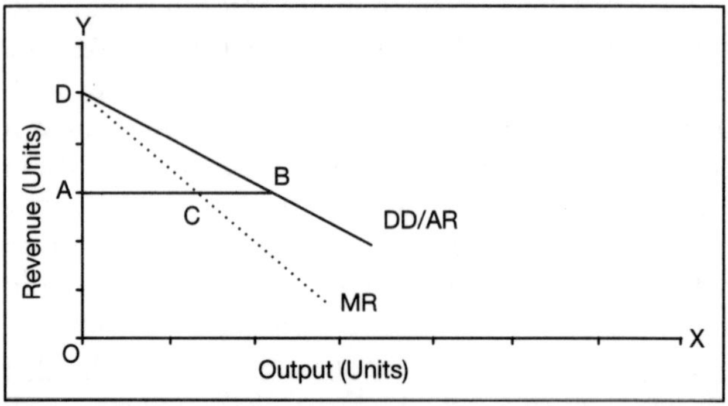

Diagram 6.35: DD, AR and MR Curves in Monopolistic Competition

DD/AR is the demand curve as well as AR curve. AR curve is falling and flatter. When AR curve is falling and flatter, MR curve is also falling and flatter but MR curve lies below or left of AR curve. It means MR is less than AR. The distance between AR and MR is less. Draw AB perpendicular to OY axis to measure the distance between MR and AR curves. AB straight line is parallel to OX axis. 'C' point should be plotted at the middle of AB line. When MR curve is flatter, it cuts AB line somewhere between CB segment or right of point 'C'. The distance from AR to MR is less than ½ of AB line from AR to OY axis. It is because there is imperfect competition in the market. According to Mrs. Joan Robinson, as the distance between AR and MR curve is less, the degree of monopoly will be lesser and the size of profits will be less than the size of monopoly profits. The relation between AR and MR in monopolistic competition is also explained in the following table 6.27.

Table 6.27: Revenue Schedule of a Firm in Monopolistic Competition

Price (₹) (P)	Quantity sold (Units) (q)	Total Revenue (₹) (TR = P × q)	Average Revenue (₹) (AR = TR) q	Marginal Revenue (₹) (MR = $TR_n - TR_{n-1}$)
7	3	21	7	–
5	5	25	5	4
4	7	28	4	3

Points from table 6.27: (a) When AR falls to ₹ 7, ₹ 5, ₹ 4, the MR falls to ₹ 4, ₹ 3 respectively. The rate of fall in MR is more than AR. (b) MR is less than price or AR.

The nature of slope of MR curve depends upon the nature of slope of AR curve.

(c) **When AR Curve is Rising Upwards, MR Curve is also Rising Upwards but MR is greater than AR:** There are exceptions to the law of demand. For instance prestigious goods like diamond ornaments, car etc. The rich people purchase more prestigious goods when their price increases to show their prestige. In case of prestigious goods, the demand curve is rising upwards. As DD curve is as well as AR curve, the AR curve is rising upwards. When AR curve rises upwards, the MR curve also rises upwards but MR is greater than AR. It is illustrated in the following diagram 6.36.

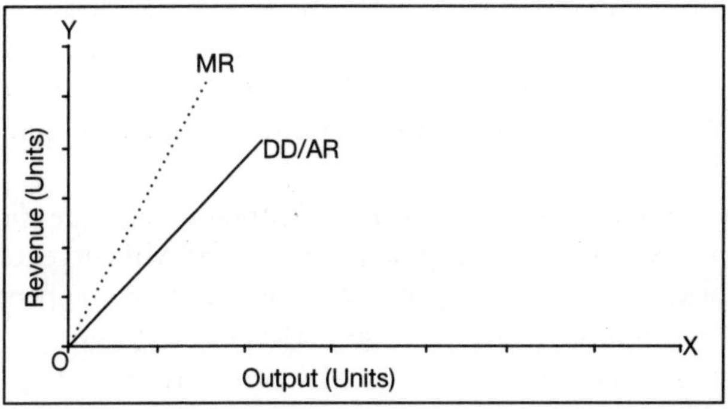

Diagram 6.36: Upwards Rising Demand or AR and MR Curve

DD/AR curve is demand as well as AR curve when AR curve is rising upwards, MR curve is also rising upwards but MR curve lies above the AR curve. It means MR is greater than AR. The following table 6.28 enables you to understand the rising upwards AR and MR curves more correctly.

Table 6.28: Revenue Schedule of a Firm Selling Prestigious Goods

Price (₹) (P)	Quantity sold (Units) (q)	Total Revenue (₹) (TR = P × q)	Average Revenue (₹) (AR = TR) q	Marginal Revenue (₹) ($MR = TR_n - TR_{n-1}$)
10	1	10	10	–
20	2	40	20	30
30	3	90	30	50

Point from table: (i) MR and AR are increasing as price increases. (ii) MR is greater than AR. (iii) Rate of increase in MR is greater than the rate of increase in AR. When price increased from ₹ 20 to ₹ 30 and the resultant output sold increased from 2 units to 3 units, (a) AR increased by 50 per cent (30–20/20) × (100). (b) MR is increased by 67 per cent (50–30/30) × (100).

(d) **Degree of Competition in the Market and AR and MR Curves:** The distance between AR curve and MR curve depends upon the degree of competition in the market. The degree of competition depends upon the number of firms in the market. The shape of demand or AR curve is determined by the degree of competition among the firms in the industry. Accordingly AR moves or inclines either to OY axis (left side) or to right side. As AR moves or inclines towards OY axis the distance between AR and MR curves becomes large. It happens when the degree of competition in market is zero. It is in monopoly market. As AR curve moves away from OY axis or moves towards right, the distance between AR curve and MR curve is less. It happens when the degree of competition is more. It appears in imperfect competition or monopolistic competition.

As AR curve became horizontal straight line, the distance between AR and MR curves disappears. AR and MR curves become one and same curve. It happens when the degree of competition is perfect or infinite. It exists only in perfect competition.

As AR curve raises upwards MR curve also rises but MR is above AR curve. It appears in case of sale of prestigious goods.

The relation between AR and MR curves based on degree of competition in the market is shown in the diagram 6.37.

As AR curve moves from AR_4 to AR_3, AR_2 and AR_1 the distance between AR and MR widens. It is because the degree of competition declines from perfect to imperfect and zero. As AR curve moves from AR_1 to AR_2, AR_3 and AR_4, the distance between AR and MR curves becomes less and less, ultimately it disappears (or $AR_4 = MR_4$). When AR rises upwards once again the distance between AR and MR curves appears but MR_5 is greater than AR_5. MR curve behaves in correspondence with AR curve and the relation between them is determined by degree of competition in the market.

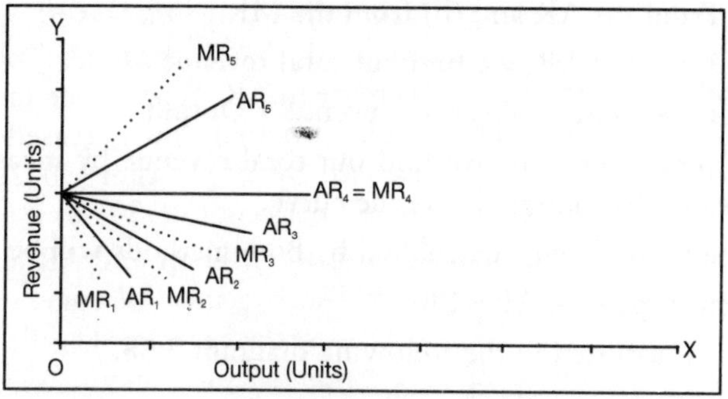

Diagram 6.37: Distance between AR and MR Curve Related with Degree of Competition in the Market

6.8.6 Geometrical Relation between AR and MR Curves: Mrs. Joan Robinson in her book *The Economics of Imperfect Competition* explained the relationship between AR and MR through price elasticity of demand for the firm's output. She expressed the relation between AR and MR in the following formula:

AR = MR (e/e-1)

Or

MR = AR (e-1/e)

Where AR = Average Revenue

MR = Marginal Revenue

e = Price elasticity of demand

Mrs. Joan Robinson's formula can be used to find out Price elasticity of demand on demand or average revenue curve and thereby further we have to find out the relationship between AR and MR.

(a) **Linear Demand or AR Curve and Corresponding MR Curve:** When both AR and MR curves are straight line, the MR curve cuts at the middle point 'P' of AB line a perpendicular from point 'A' on AR curve. The segments of AB line, AP and PB are equal to each other. It can be easily proved that:

AP = PB

To prove it, first you have to find out total revenue. There are two methods to find out total revenue:

(i) From the AR and (ii) from the MR

(i) From the AR, we find out total revenue as

Total Revenue = Average revenue × Output

(ii) From the MR, we find out total revenue by measuring the area under marginal revenue curve.

The total revenue calculated by both methods will be same.

Thus it proves: AP = PB

It is illustrated in the following diagram 3.68.

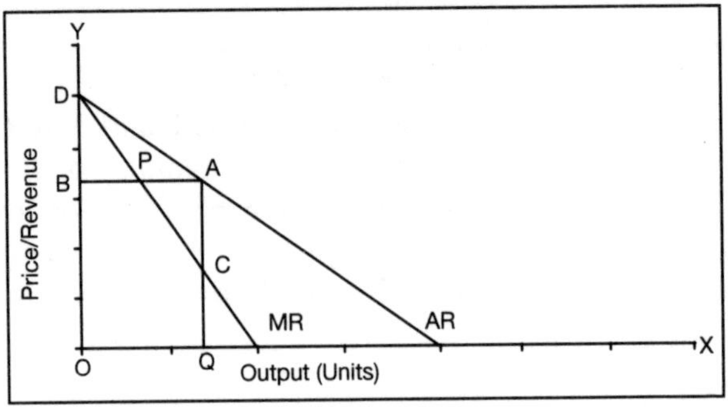

Diagram 6.38: Relation between AR and MR Curves

AB line at the middle is shown as point 'P'. AB line is a perpendicular from point 'A' on AR curve which measures the distance between AR curve and Y axis. Since MR curve cuts AB line at middle, the Segment PA is equal to the segment PB. Therefore PA = PB.

It can be proved as: First we have to find out total revenue by the following methods:

(i) Total revenue from AR curve:

Total revenue = Average revenue × Output

= AR × OQ = Area OBAQ

(ii) Total revenue from MR curve:

Total revenue = Area under MR curve = Area DPCQO

The total revenue calculated through both methods (i) and (ii) are same:

Area OBAQ = Area DPCQO

Subtract area BPCQO from both sides. It is common to both.

After subtraction, we get:

Area OBAQ – BPCQO = Area DPCQO – BPCQO

Therefore Triangle PAC = Triangle DBP

ΔPAC and ΔDBP are also similar angles as both are right angles.

The opposite angles CPA = DPB in all respect. Therefore,

PA = PB

Hence point 'P' lies exactly at middle of AB line. It means MR is half the distance between AR and Y axis.

Since the corresponding sides of two similar triangles bear the same ratio.

Price elasticity of demand = e = AQ/DB = AQ/AC

Since AC = AQ – CQ,

e = AQ/AQ – CQ

When AQ = Average Revenue, CQ = Marginal Revenue

Therefore e = AR/AR – MR

Or e (AR – MR) = AR

Or e AR – e MR = AR

Since AR shifted to one side,

e AR – AR = e MR

Or AR (e-1) = e MR

Or AR (e-1)/e = MR

Or (e-1/e) AR = MR

Or AR = MR (e/e-1)

This formula can help us to know MR curve or corresponding MR and size of MR. For instance, if price elasticity of demand = e = 2, then we calculate MR as

MR = AR(e-1/e) = AR(2-1/2) = AR1/2

If value of AR = 4 then:

1 1 4

MR = AR(1/2) = 4 × (1/2) = 4/2 = 2

When AR and MR curves are linear and falling downwards, the MR is half of AR. Marginal revenue falls twice of fall in price or average revenue.

(b) **Non-linear Demand or AR Curve and Corresponding MR Curve:** When demand or AR curve is non-linear, we can find out MR curve by using geometrical proof of the formula suggested by Mrs. Joan Robinson. It is illustrated in the following diagram 6.39.

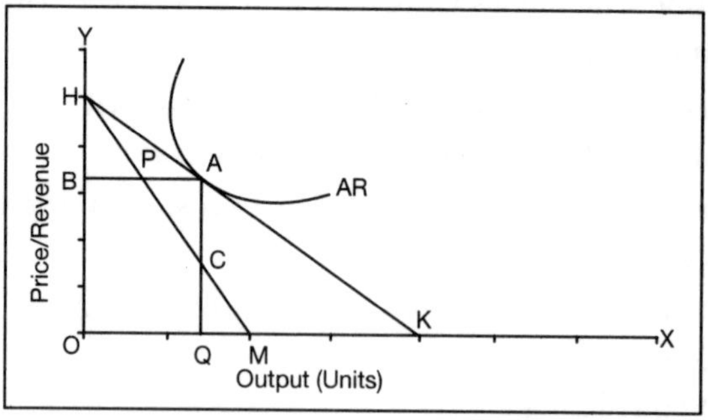

Diagram 6.39: Relation between AR and MR through Price Elasticity of Demand

AR is non-linear average revenue curve. The output is OQ. Average revenue is AQ when the output is OQ. Draw HK tangent line at the point A to find out marginal revenue at this point. Draw a perpendicular AB to Y axis from point 'A' and a straight line HM which bisects AB line at 'P' point and AQ line at C point HM is the marginal to the tangent HK. CQ is the marginal revenue corresponding to average revenue AQ at output OQ. Now, we find price elasticity of demand at point A.

Price elasticity of demand at point A = AK/AH

Triangle AQK = Triangle HBA are similarly (right angles)

The corresponding angles are also similar.

DHAB = DAKQ

The corresponding sides of these two similar triangles (i) ΔAQK = ΔHBA (ii) ΔHAB = ΔAKQ and the ratio they bear is same:

AK/AH = AQ/HB

Therefore Price elasticity of demand is:

e = AK/AH = AQ/HB ...(1)

And ΔHBP and ΔPAC are equal to each other and similar in all respects.

∴ HB = AC

By substitute this in equation (1), we get price elasticity of demand = e = AQ/HB = AQ /AC.

Since AC = AQ – CQ, we can write

e = AQ/AC = AQ/AQ – CQ

When AQ = Average Revenue(AR) and CQ=Marginal revenue(MR) we can write:

e = AR/AR – MR

Or AR = e(AR – MR)

Or AR = e AR – EMR

Or e MR = e AR – AR

Or e MR = AR (e-1)

Or MR = AR (e-1/e)

Or AR = MR (e/e-1)

To find the MR, we may assign different values to price elasticity of demand (e):

When value of

(i) e= 2 then MR = AR (e–1/e) = AR (2–1/2) = AR (1/2)

(ii) e = 1 then MR = AR (e–1/e) = AR (1–1/1) = ARXO = O

(iii) e = 1/2 then MR = AR(e–1/e) = AR (1/2–1 ÷ 1/2) = –1

Similarly, we may find out MR when,

(i) e = 2 AR = 4

(ii) e = 1 AR = 3

(iii) e = 1/2 AR = 5

we may find out MR as: When

(i) e = 2, AR = 4 then MR = AR (e–1/e) = 4 × 2–1/2 = 2

(ii) e = 1, AR = 3 then MR = AR (e–1/e) = 3 × (1–1/1)

= 3 X 0 = 0

(iii) e = 1/2, AR = 5 then AR(e–1/e) = 5 × (½–1/½)

= 5 (–½/½)

$= 5(-\frac{1}{2} \times 2/1) = 5 \times -1 = -5$

When price elasticity of demand or elasticity of average revenue curve is:

e = 1 then MR is zero

e = 2 or >1 then MR is greater than zero (Positive)

e = ½ or < 1 then MR is less than zero (Negative)

The relation between AR and MR corresponding to price elasticity of demand is illustrated in the following diagram 6.41.

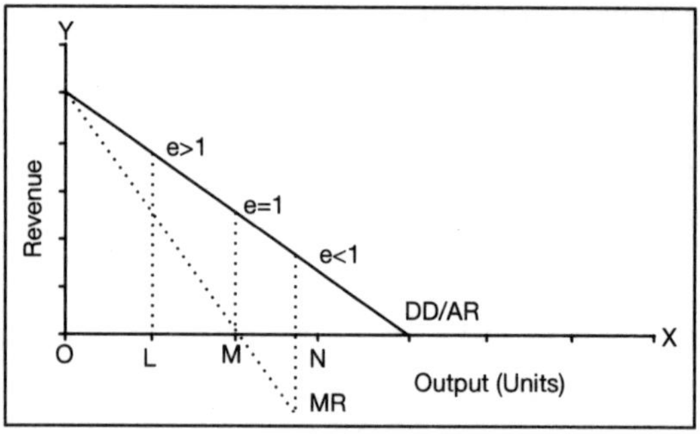

Diagram 6.41: Price Elasticity of Demand and Corresponding Relation between AR and MR

DD/AR is average revenue curve, MR is marginal revenue curve. L, M, N is quantities of output.

e = price elasticity of demand.

(i) When e > 1 (greater than one) at output OL

MR is positive (MR > 0); AR is also positive (AR > 1) but AR > MR

(ii) When e = 1 at output OM

MR is zero but AR is positive

(iii) When e < 1 at output ON

MR is negative (MR < 0) but AR is positive. The rate of fall in MR is higher than rate of all in AR.

6.4 MODEL QUESTIONS

2 Marks Questions

(a) Give the meaning of Production.

(b) What is 'Production Function'?
(c) Name any two laws of production.
(d) Give the meaning of economies.
(e) Name any two diseconomies.
(f) What do you mean by cost of production?
(g) Give the meaning of fixed cost.
(h) Give the meaning of variable cost.
(i) Name any two determinants of cost.
(j) What do you mean by marginal cost?
(k) Give the meaning of revenue.
(l) What do you mean by marginal revenue?
(m) Prove P = AR.
(n) Name any two determinants of Revenue.

5 Marks Questions

(1) Write a note on Cobb-Douglas production function.
(2) Give a brief account of properties of isoquant.
(3) Write a short note on opportunity cost.
(4) Write a note on economies of scale.
(5) Write a note on diseconomies of scale.
(6) Write in brief the relation between average cost and marginal cost.
(7) Write a note on types of costs.
(8) Give a brief account of total revenue, average revenue and marginal revenue.

10 Marks Questions

(1) Explain the law of variable proportions.
(2) Discuss the laws to returns to scale.
(3) What is equal product curve? Explain its properties.
(4) Discuss the economies and diseconomies to scale.
(5) What is cost of production? Discuss its determinants.
(6) What is revenue? Explain the relation between average and marginal revenues.

7
Markets

7.1 PERFECT COMPETITION

7.1.1 Meaning and Definitions: A perfect competitive market is a market situation in which the number of buyers and sellers is very large. The buyers and sellers are engaged in buying and selling a homogeneous product. Demand for output of each producer in the market is perfectly elastic. It means the number of sellers in this market is so large that a single seller is not in a position to influence the price. Hence perfect competition is defined as under:

(i) Mrs. Joan Robinson defined perfect competition as "Perfect Competition prevails when the demand for the output of each producer is perfectly elastic. This entails, first that the number of sellers is large so that the output of any one seller is negligibly small proportion of the total output of the commodity, and second, that buyers are all alike in respect of their choice between rival sellers so that the market is perfect."

(ii) According to Robert Triffin "In perfect competition, the cross elasticity of demand for product of a single firm with respect to a change in price of the rest of the industry will be infinite."

These definitions enable to identify the various essential conditions or features of the perfect competition.

7.1.2 Features or Essential Conditions. The market situation which fulfills the following essential conditions or has the following features is called perfect competitive market.

(i) **Large Number of Buyers and Sellers:** The number of buyers and sellers in this market is so large that individual buyer or seller is not in a position to influence the price or output in the market. The position of the individual buyer or seller in this market is insignificant. The demand of the individual buyer and the supply of the individual seller in the market are very small compared to the total market demand and supply. Both the buyer and the seller should accept the price prevailing in the market. Therefore perfect competition is the market of 'price takers'. The seller should adjust the supply of his output depending on the market price control is zero.

(ii) **Homogeneous Product:** All the firms in the industry produce the homogeneous product. Buyers do not have the choice of products, as all the products produced are identical or same. Identical products or goods mean the products or goods which are same in all respect like, shape, design, quality, etc. Since the product is identical, the price elasticity of demand for the product of firm is infinite. The market which fulfills these two conditions is called 'Pure Competition'. The demand curve for the product of firm is shown in the following diagram 7.1.

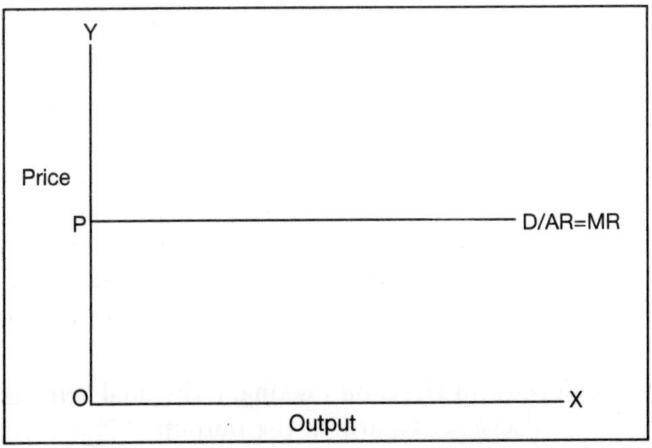

Diagram 7.1: Demand Curve in Pure Competition

(iii) **Free Entry and Exit of Firms:** There is no restriction to entry or exit of the firm. New firms are free to enter in to the industry, if there is profit. Old firms are free to leave the industry, if there is loss. No restrictions are imposed either by the government or any other organization for entry or exit of firms.

(iv) **Same Price or Single Price:** Since all the firms in this market are price takers and produce identical goods, there is single price throughout the market demand for and supply of goods determines the price.

(v) **Perfect mobility of Factors of Production:** The factors of production are free to move from firm to firm and industry to industry where they get higher price. It means there is perfect competition in the factors of production market. The perfect mobility of factors of production results into identical price of factors thus it results into identical cost conditions in the market. It means all firms in the market have identical cost conditions.

(vi) **Perfect Knowledge About Market Conditions:** All the sellers and buyers have complete knowledge regarding the conditions prevailing in this market. The buyers and sellers in this market have complete knowledge about the purchase and sale price of the output. This does not allow the sellers to exploit the consumers either with respect to the price or quality of the output sold in market. Buyers are also alike in their choice.

(vii) **Absence of Transport Cost:** The perfect competitive market assumes that the various firms operating in this market are so closely established that there is absence of transport cost. This condition is essential as the price prevailing is uniform throughout the market. If the transport cost is added even the homogeneous product will have different prices depending on the cost of transport.

(viii) **Independent Decision-making:** Individual firm takes its own decisions regarding the output.

The features or conditions from 3 to 8 make the competition perfect.

7.1.3 Equilibrium of Firm and Industry. Equilibrium refers to state of balance. Firm is a unit of production whereas industry is a group of firms producing identical goods. The point of equilibrium helps to measure the profit or loss position of firm and industry under perfect competition. Time-elements play a vital role to study the equilibrium of firm and industry. Equilibrium explains the determination of price and output.

(A) Equilibrium of Firm: Under perfect competition firm attains equilibrium where the following conditions are fulfilled:

(i) Marginal Cost = Marginal Revenue (MC = MR). (ii) Marginal Cost Curve (MC) must cut Marginal Revenue Curve (MR) from bellow and MC Curve must be rising at the point of intersection.

The equilibrium of firm under perfect competition is illustrated in the following diagram 7.2.

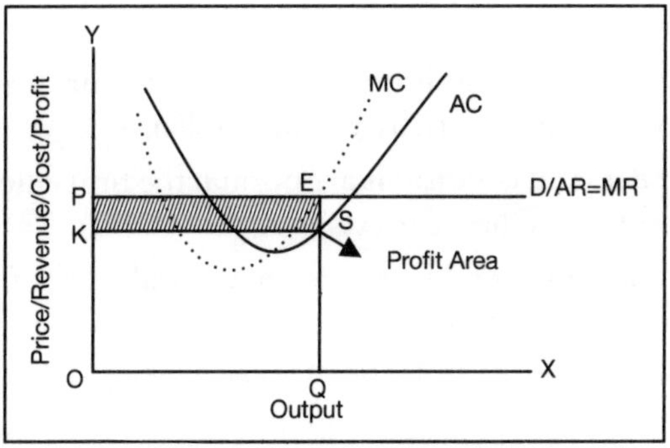

Diagram 7.2: Firm's Equilibrium

Units of output are measured along 'OX' axis and Price/Revenue/Cost/Profit is measured along 'OY' axis. Since firm is price-taker under perfect competition, the prevailing price is OP, it is shown by PD line so the demand curve for the output of the firm is PD which is horizontal and parallel to OX axis. Since average revenue curve is the demand curve, PD is also average revenue curve. When average revenue is constant marginal revenue is also constant, i.e. AR = MR thus MR curve coincides with AR curve.

Both the conditions of equilibrium are fulfilled at point 'E' thus the firm attains equilibrium at point 'E'. It is point of firm's equilibrium.

At the point of equilibrium 'E' the firm determines to produce 'OQ' quantity of output at 'OP' price Thus 'OQ' is equilibrium level of output

Average cost curve (AC) is used to measure the profit or loss at the point of equilibrium.

From point 'E' downward a perpendicular 'EQ' is drawn which joins 'OX' axis at 'Q' so 'OQ' is the determined level of output. EQ perpendicular intersects AC curve at 'S' thus 'SQ' distance is the average cost so the total cost = average cost x total output, i.e. SQ (=OK) × OQ (=KS) =OKSQ.

'EQ' distance is the average revenue so total revenue =Price X total output i.e. TR=OP (=EQ) × OQ (=PE) =OPEQ.

Thus Profit =TR–TC i.e.

Profit = OPEQ – OKSQ = PESK. It is shown by shaded area. Whether the firm enjoys profits or suffers losses depends upon the demand conditions:

- If demand conditions are more favourable, the firm enjoys supernormal profits. (When P > AC)
- If demand conditions are normal the firm enjoys normal profits. (When P = AC)
- If demand conditions are unfavourable, the firm suffers losses. (When P < AC)

(B) **Equilibrium of Industry:** Under perfect competition the industry said to be at equilibrium at that level of output where the quantity demanded is equal to quantity supplied. In other words, under perfect competition, the point of intersection between demand and supply curves is the point equilibrium of industry. At intersection on point demand (DD) = Supply (SS). At the point of equilibrium:

(i) There is no tendency of either increase or decrease the level of output.

(ii) There is no tendency of either entry or exit of the firms.

(iii) All the firms in the industry are at equilibrium.

The equilibrium of industry is shown in the following table 7.1.

Table 7.1: Equilibrium of Industry

Price (₹)	Quantity Demanded (Units)	Quantity Supplied (Units)
1	50	10
2	40	20
3	**30**	**30**
4	20	40
5	10	50

Demand is governed by law of demand and supply is governed by law of supply. As price increases from ₹ 1 to ₹ 5, the quantity demanded declined from 50 units to 10 units, on the other hand, as the price increases from ₹ 1 to ₹ 5, the quantity supplied is increased from 10 units to 50 units.

Both quantity demanded and supplied are equal to each other at price ₹ 3.

The equilibrium between demand and supply is illustrated in the following diagram 7.3.

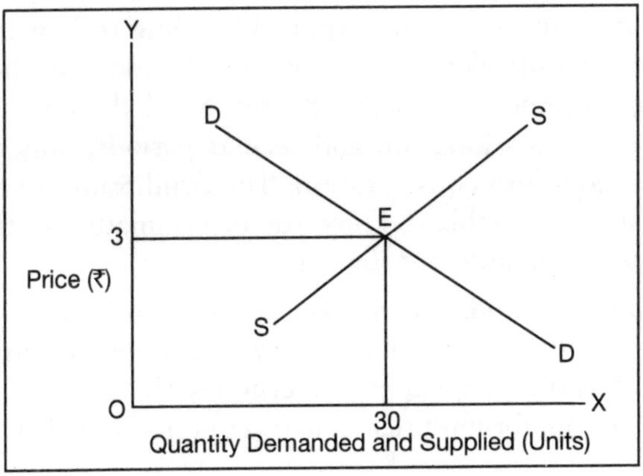

Diagram 7.3: Equilibrium of Industry

Quantity demanded and supplied are measured along OX axis and price is measured along OY axis. DD is demand curve and SS is Supply curve. DD curve and SS curve interested each other at point 'E'. Thus, 'E' is the equilibrium of industry. At 'E' point demand (30 units) is equal to supply (30 units).

The equilibrium between demand and supply determines the price i.e. 'E' or ₹ 3. So the price determined at equilibrium is called 'Equilibrium Price'. The price other than ₹ 3 disturbs the equilibrium between demand and supply.

If price is more than ₹ 3, the quantity demanded will be less than quantity supplies in contrary it is *vice versa*.

In brief, the industry attains equilibrium where the following conditions are fulfilled:

(a) Demand = Supply.

(b) All the firms in the industry should be at equilibrium.

(c) There is no tendency of either increase or decrease the quantity of output either by exiting firm or by increasing the size of firms.

(d) There is no tendency of either entry of exit of firms.

7.1.4 Importance of Time-Element: Price and Output Determination: Even though the price and output under the conditions of perfect competition are determined by demand and supply, their relative influence depends on the elements of time. Marshall has explained the importance of time-elements in the determination of price and output. According to him there are four types of time elements: (i) Market Period, (ii) Short-run, (iii) Long-run, and (iv) Secular Period. Since there is no much difference between long-run and secular periods, only the first three are taken into consideration. The equilibrium of the firm and industry can enable to know the determination of the price and output in the different time periods.

(i) Market Period: The market period is too short time; say few hours or few days. A momentary or temporary equilibrium between demand and supply determines the price in market period. The equilibrium price in market period is called 'Market Price'.

'Market Price' is the price of a commodity which prevails at any given time. Thus market price is also known as 'Prevailing Price'.

In market period, the demand for commodity is changeable, but the supply of commodity is fixed or constant. Whether whole stack of commodity or part of it is offered to sell is depend upon the nature of goods. Goods can be classified as:

(a) Perishable goods like, milk, vegetable egg, meat, etc. and (b) Non-Perishable goods like durable goods.

(a) **Perishable Goods:** The supply of perishable goods is fixed or constant in market so supply curve is vertical. The demand plays important role in determination of market price. It is illustrated in the following diagram 7.4.

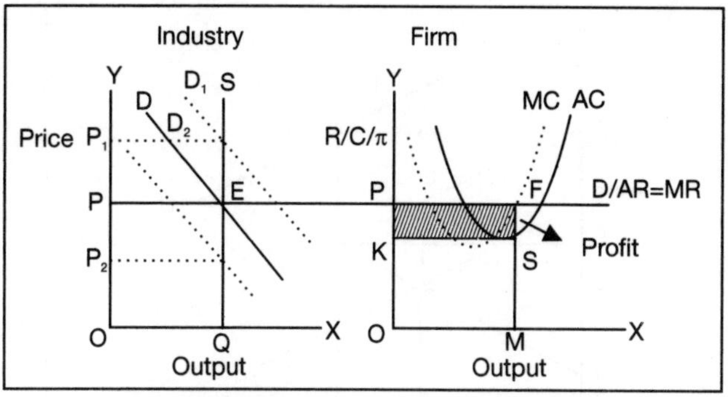

Diagram 7.4: Equilibrium of Firm and Industry

In the diagram 7.4 'S' is the market supply curve, which is perfectly inelastic. The supply of output is fixed at OQ. The price depends upon the demand for output. The original quantity demanded is OQ at the price OP. When the demand increases to D_1 the price increases to P_1.On the other hand when the demand decreases to D_2 the price decreases P_2.Thus in the market period the price depends upon the demand for the commodity. The firm is at equilibrium on 'F' point and determined to produce 'OM' quantity of output at 'OP' price thereby he gets 'PFSK' area-size of profits.

(ii) **Non-Perishable Goods:** Unlike perishable goods, the supply curve of non-perishable goods is rising upwards up to point 'R' beyond that it becomes vertical-line. In case of Non-Perishable goods also the demand plays important role in determination of Market Price.

Till point 'R' on supply curve any increase in demand also accompanied with increase in supply, thus the increase in Market Price will be in small proportion but beyond point 'R', any increase in demand results into proportionate increase in market price because the supply becomes constant or the supply curve becomes vertices. This explanation is given in the following diagram 7.5.

Output demanded and supplied is measured along OX axis and price is measured along OY axis. TRS is Market period Supply Curve of Non-perishable goods. The supply of output is flexible from T to R, after R, it becomes fixed or vertical.

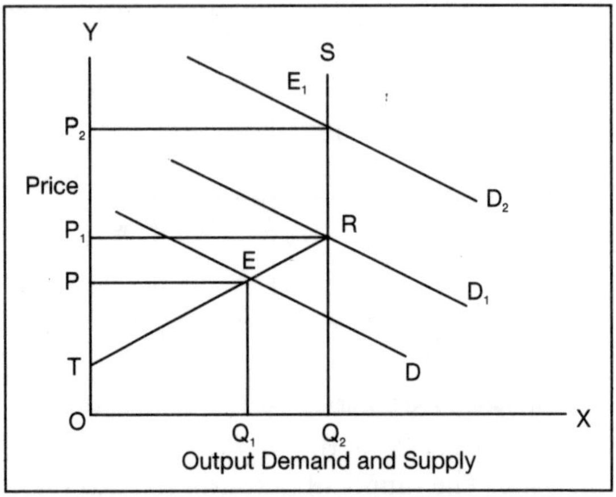

Diagram 7.5: Equilibrium of Firm and Industry

DD curve intersected TRS supply curve at 'E' point, the determined market price is OP. As Demand curve increases to D_1, the supply also increased by Q_1Q_2. At 'R' both D_1 and supply curve are intersected and determined market prices is 'P_1'. Output increased by Q_1Q_2 and price increased by PP_1. The change in price-size is smaller than change in demand-size. It is because of the increased supply reduced the effect of change in demand on price.

When demand further increased to D_2, the equilibrium moved to E_1 and the market price increased by P_1 P_2. The price increased in proportion to increased-demand because the supply became fixed or constant i.e. OQ_2.

If demand conditions are unfavourable or demand decreases, the market price declines so also supply of output declines. The seller continues selling output under declining price situation till price declines to T. He stops further selling of output when price declined below T because the price is very small to cover the average variable cost. Thus T is the 'Minimum Price' or 'Reserve Price' for non-perishable goods. Since goods are durable, the firm stops selling at too low price and waits the increase in price in future. That is why the minimum price is called reserve price.

Factors Influencing Reserve Price: The size of reserve price depends upon various factors as follows:

(a) **Seller expectation regarding future price:** If firm expects high price is future, the reserve price will be higher. In contrary, it is vice versa.

(b) **Seller's preference to liquidity:** If seller is badly in need of money, he sells out his goods at low price, then, the reserve price will be low.

(c) **Storage-Cost:** if cost of storage of goods is higher, the firm will sell goods at low price, thus, reserve price is low.

(d) **Durability of goods:** Longer the durability of goods, higher will be the reserve price and lesser the durability, lower will the reserve price.

(e) **Production Cost:** If present or future cost of production is higher the reserve price will be higher. In contrary, it is *vice versa*.

However, generally in market period, all the firms in industry enjoy abnormal profits.

(i) **Short-run:** According to Marshall the supply of the output in the short period is adjusted without changing the size of the plant and machinery. The existing plant and machinery will be used intensively with the application of variable factors of production to meet the increased demand. The fixed factors are not altered, as the demand is likely to be short-lived.

The short period equilibrium of the firm and industry is presented in the diagram 7.6.

The left-hand side diagram (Industry) explains the determination of the price and output by the interaction of industry demand and industry supply curves in the short period. D_1 is the demand curve and S_1 is the supply curve. Both the curves intersect at the equilibrium point 'E'. At this point the equilibrium price is OP and the output produced is OQ.

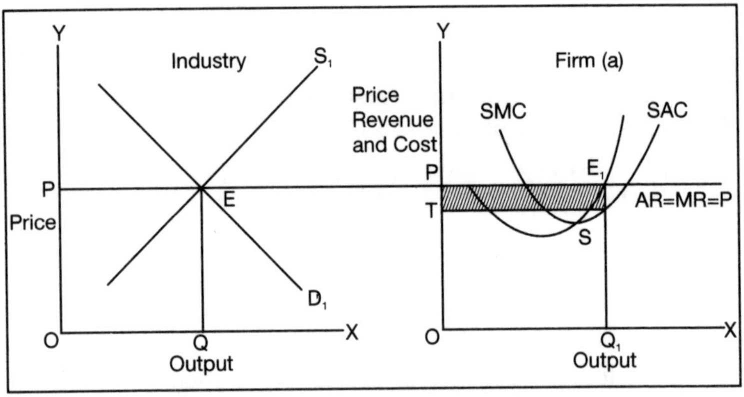

Diagram 7.6: Equilibrium of Firm and Industry

The right-hand side diagram (Firm) describes the equilibrium of the firm. SMC is the short-run marginal cost curve and SAC is the short-run average cost curve. All the firms have to accept the equilibrium price, as they do not have control over the price. The equilibrium price fixed by the industry is 'OP'. The parallel line drawn to the 'X' axis is the price line and it is equal to the Average Revenue and the Marginal Revenue of the firm. Therefore in the perfect competition AR = MR = P. All the firms have to accept the price fixed by the industry and adjust their output accordingly. The equilibrium price in shorten is also called 'short-run price'. Area 'PE_1ST' is the size of profit enjoyed by the firm in short-run.

Both the conditions of equilibrium are satisfied at E_1 so the firm equilibrium in the short-run.

The output produced by the firm is OQ_1 at the price OP. The firm earns supernormal or abnormal profit of PE_1ST (shaded area).

During the short period the firm may also earn normal profit or suffer loss depending on the demand conditions.

Firm earns abnormal profits when the demand condition is more favourable. It is explained in the diagram 7.6.

If demand condition is normal, the firm earns the normal profits in short-run. It is shown in the diagram 7.7.

In diagram 7.7 the SMC is equal to the SMR at the point 'S'. Here the AR (Price) curve is tangent to the AC curve of the firm. Thus, when the AR is equal to the AC, the firm earns normal profit in the short period.

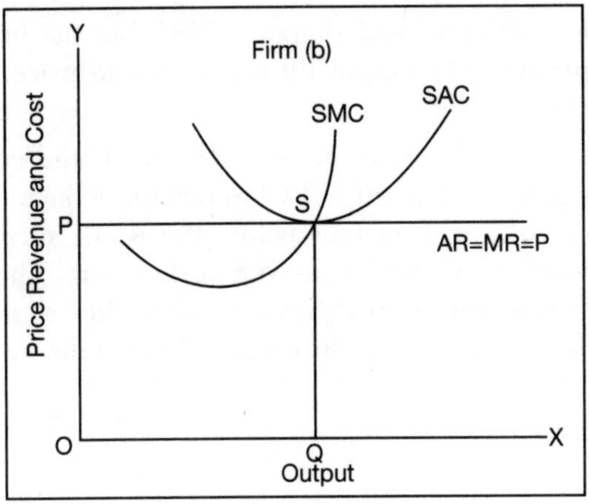

Diagram 7.7: Equilibrium of Firm

If the demand condition is unfavourable, the firm will suffer loss in the short period. It is explained in the following diagram 7.8.

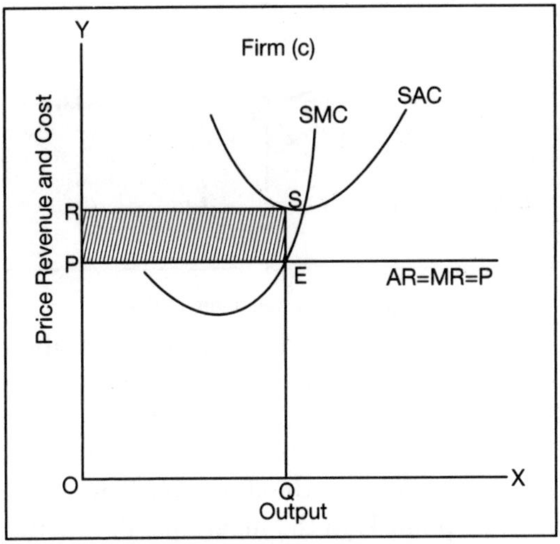

Diagram 7.8: Equilibrium of Firm

In the diagram 7.8 the AR curve or the price line is below the short-run AC curve. The equilibrium is established where the SMC curve cuts the MR curve. 'E' is the point of equilibrium. The firm is suffering a loss of 'ES' for each unit of output produced. The total loss made by the firm after producing OQ units of output is shown with the shaded area 'PESR'. But the firm still continues to produce the output till the short-run price covers average variable cost.

The firms suffering loss in the short period should cover at least the Average Variable Cost (AVC) to remain in the industry. If the AR curve of any firm falls below the AVC, such firms should close down their operations even in short-run. The point at which the firm is able cover its AVC is called the "shut down point". The shut down point is shown in following diagram 7.9.

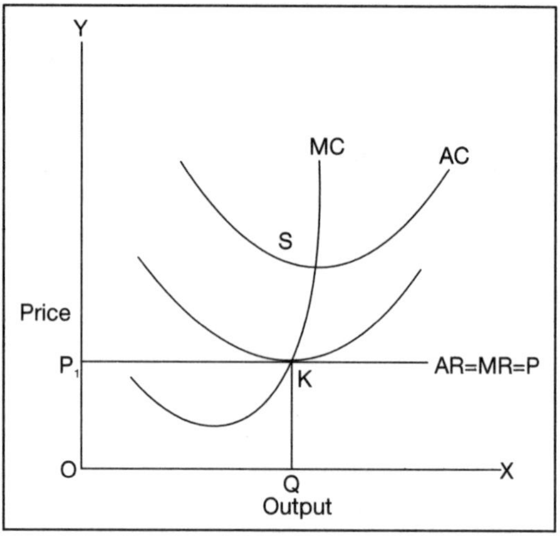

Diagram 7.9: Equilibrium of Firm

In the diagram 7.9 the AVC is the average variable cost curve. AR is the average revenue curve or it is the price line. The AR curve or the price line is tangent to the AVC curve at the point K. If the price (AR) falls below OP_1 it is feasible to shut down the operations of the firm even in the short-run. The shut down point is denoted by the point K in the diagram. AVC is the minimum limit to short-run price.

In short-run, only existing firm adjusts in the level of output but number of firms remains same.

(ii) **Long-run:** The long period is defined as that period where the industry has sufficient time to adjust its output to the changes in demand. There is scope for new firms to enter the industry and also existing firms may leave the industry. It results into adjustment of supply with demand in the long-run.

If the short-run equilibrium price is higher than the short-run average cost, the firm earns supernormal profit. Thus existence of supernormal profit in the short run will attract new firms in to the industry. Entry of new firms will result in increased competition and increase the output of the industry. This causes for a fall in the price. This process continues as long as the price (LAR) is equal to the average cost of the firm. Therefore in the long run the LAR or the price line is always tangent to the LAC curve. Thus all the firms in the long-run earn only normal profits.

If the short-run price is less than short-run average cost, firms suffer the loss in short-run. Some firms exit form market which reduces the level of output in the long-run thus supply adjusts with demand and long-run prices increases to the level of minimum of LAC. Thus all firms enjoy only normal profits in the long-run.

In long-run, the change in demand and supply are permanent. The long-run equilibrium between demand and supply determines the long-run price and long-run level of output. The long-run price is called 'natural price' or 'normal price'.

Prof. Alfred Marshall defined normal price as "Normal or Natural value of a commodity is that which economic forces would tend to bring about in the long-run."

Normal price is not actual price or not equal to average price but is likely to be market price or prevailing price revolves around normal price.

The long-run equilibrium of the firm and industry is explained in the diagram 7.10.

In diagram 7.10 (Industry) point 'E' shows the long-run equilibrium of the industry. The long-run demand for output and the supply of output will determine the equilibrium long-run price. The equilibrium price determined by the industry is OP and the output is OQ. All the firms have to accept the equilibrium price, as they do not have control over the price. All the firms have to adjust their output to the price, OP, fixed by the industry.

The long-run equilibrium price is called long-run price or normal or natural price.

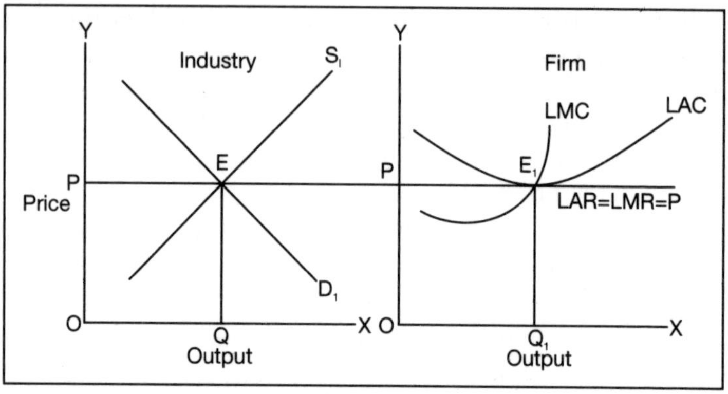

Diagram 7.10: Equilibrium of Firm and Industry

In the diagram 7.10 (Firm) the firm is in equilibrium at that point where the long-run marginal cost curve (LMC) cuts the long-run average revenue (LAR) curve from left and below at the minimum point. Thus the equilibrium is at the point 'E_1' and all the firms are producing OQ_1 output. At this point the long-run marginal revenue (LMR) is equal to the long-run marginal cost (LMC) of the firm. And the long-run average revenue (LAR) is also equal to the long-run average cost (LAC). Thus the firms in the long-run produce at the minimum point of their LAC and earn just normal profits. The long-run equilibrium conditions of the firm are:

(i) LMC = LMR = P

(ii) LMC = LMR = LAC = LAR = P

The output produced at this point is the 'optimum output'; and all those firms producing the maximum output at the least cost are the 'optimum firms'.

In the perfect competition all the firms producing the homogeneous product have identical cost conditions the equilibrium of a firm represents the equilibrium of all the firms in industry under perfect competition. Thus all the firms in the industry will be in equilibrium and earn normal profits. The industry as a whole will also be in equilibrium at the point 'E'.

The long-run equilibrium conditions of the industry are: (i) Demand = Supply, (ii) All firms should be at equilibrium, and (iii) There is no tendency of either entry or exit of the firm.

The slope or nature of supply curve depends upon cost conditions the cost conditions may change in long-run due to expansion of the firm or scale of production. So three cost conditions entail in long-run namely (a) increasing cost conditions, (b) decreasing cost conditions, and (c) constant cost conditions.

When there is increasing cost conditions, the industry has from left to right upwards rising supply curve or usual supply curve.

When there is decreasing cost conditions, the industry has from left to right sloping downwards supply curve. It is like usual demand curve.

When there is constant cost conditions the industry has a horizontal parallel line supply curve. To know the equilibrium of industry and price and output determination in long-run, we should assume the increasing cost conditions.

Comparison: The price and output determination in market-period, short-run and long-run under perfect competition is illustrated in following diagram 7.11.

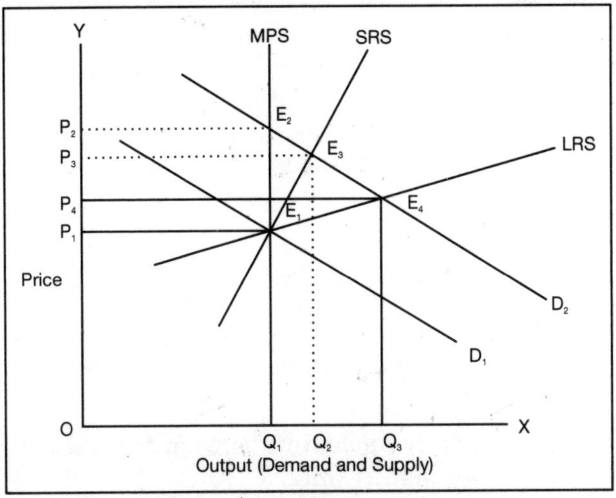

Diagram 7.11: Equilibrium of Industry

The level of output (Demand and Supply) is measured along 'OX' axis and price is measured along 'OY' axis.

When demand is D_1, in market period the supply curve is MPS. The output is OQ_1. E_1 is market period equilibrium and OP_1 is market price.

When demand increased to D_2, market period equilibrium and price gone up to E_2 and OP_2, respectively. But level of output remained same i.e. OQ_1.

In response to increased demand D_2, in short-run the level of output increased by Q_1Q_2, thus SRS is the short-run supply curve which intersected new demand curve at E_3 i.e. short-run price is OP_3 and output is OQ_2.

In long-run, the supply adjusts with new demand D_2, the long-run output is OQ_3 or the long-run supply is shown by LRS curve. The long-run supply curve intersected demand curve (D_2) at E_4 which is equilibrium of Industry. Thus OP_4 long-run price and OQ_3 long-run output is determined by the equilibrium.

When we join equilibrium points E_1 and E_4, you get LRS, long-run supply curve. Long-run price OP_4 is less than short-run price OP_3 and market price OP_2 because the long-run supply of output is OQ_3 which is greater than short-run output OQ_2 and market period output OQ_1.

The increased supply of output reduces the effect of increased demand on price in long-run. In long-run all firms in the industry enjoy only normal profits. Normal profit is profit which is just sufficient to induce the firm to stay in industry and when no firm outside the industry thinks that he could earn at least normal profit if he were to enter it. Firm get normal profit when price is just equal to average cost.

Difference between Market Price and Normal Price

Market Price

(a) Market is actual prevailing price at a particular point of time.

(b) The temporary equilibrium between demand and supply determines market price.

(c) Market price is influenced by the temporary changes.

(d) Market price changes day by day.

(e) All commodities have Market price.

Normal Price

(a) Normal price is not actual price; it is likely to be in the long-run.

(b) The long-run equilibrium between demand and supply determines normal price.

(c) Normal price is influenced permanent changes.

(d) Normal price remains constant.

(e) Only reproducible commodities have Market price.

7.1.5 Is Supernormal Profit Possible?: Is supernormal profit possible in long-run under perfect-competition? This question is answered in positive by Prof. J.A. Schumpeter. In above analysis, we have studied that only normal profit is possible in long-run under identical cost conditions in perfect competition. But non-identical or differential cost conditions supernormal profit is possible even in long-run under perfect competition, says J.A. Schumpeter. According to him, the main function of the firm is to undertake innovations like new method of production or technique. The new method of production may reduce the average cost of the firm. This makes the cost conditions differ from firm to firm is industry. The Firms who maintain the secrecy of new technique, his average cost will be less than the average cost of the rest in the industry. Thus he enjoys supernormal profits even in long-run. It is illustrated in the following table 7.2.

Table 7.2: Differences in Size of Profit

Firms	Price (₹)	AC (₹)	Profit (n=P-AC)
A	1	0.50	0.50
B	1	0.75	0.25
C	1	0.90	0.10
D	1	1.00	00

Assuming there are A, B, C and D firms in the market, the long-run price is ₹ 1.00. The average cost differs from firm to firm. It is assumed that the cost difference is due to differ in technique of production. Firm 'A' is more efficient than the rest.

Firm D is marginal firm. Thus Firms A, B, and C enjoy super-normal profits even in long-run.

7.2 MONOPOLY

7.2.1 Meaning and Definitions: The Monopoly is opposite extreme of perfect competition. Monopoly is a market situation in which there is a single seller. He is the sole producer of the product that has no close substitutes. As there is a single seller in this market the distinction between the firm and industry disappears. The word monopoly is derived from two distinct Greek words—*mono* and *poly*. Mono means single and poly implies selling. The monopoly market has been defined as:

(i) According to A.P Lerner "Who is having downward sloping demand curve for his product."

(ii) Robert Triffin defined monopoly as "a market situation where a firm is independent of price changes of others."

(iii) E.H. Chamberlin defined monopoly as "as complete control over supply of commodity."

(iv) According to Stonier and Hague, "The monopolist is the sole producer of a product which has no closely competing substitutes."

In brief, monopoly is a market situation in which there is a single seller. There are no close substitutes for the commodities produced by the monopolist. Monopolies do not face any competition generally fix a high price. The monopoly firms are 'price makers' and not 'price takers'. Pure monopolies are a myth.

7.2.2 Features of Monopoly: Monopoly market has following features:

(i) **One Seller and Large Number of Buyers:** There is only one firm/seller in the monopoly market. The distinction between the firm and industry in the monopoly market disappears, as there is a single producer. The number of buyers in this market is large.

(ii) **No Close Substitute:** There are no close substitutes for the output produced by the monopolist. The cross elasticity of the demand for the product produced in this market is zero. It means the monopoly does not face any competition.

(iii) **Barriers to Entry:** Monopoly is Single Seller's Market. He prevents the entry of others by barriers like economic barriers (controlling output or price) and institutional barriers (creating government department's corporations or business combinations).

(iv) **Price Giver:** The seller in this market has the freedom to fix a fantastic price. The monopoly firms are 'price makers' and not 'price takers' as in perfect competition. They have absolute control over the supply of output. But he cannot dictate the price as well as the amount sold. He can either fix the price or the output. Such monopolies are called as pure monopolies. They are also known as perfect or absolute monopolies. But pure monopolies are a myth. They do not generally exist in the practical world.

In reality we find imperfect or limited monopolies. These firms face the competition from alternative sources, for example: the Indian Railways is facing competition from the road, air and water transport. The electricity has the substitutes in the form of kerosene oil, cooking gas, fire wood, candle, etc.

7.2.3 Types of Monopoly: The monopolies may be classified as follows:

(i) **Natural Monopoly:** The natural monopolies arise due to the natural factors like climate, availability of natural resources like land, minerals, etc. For example Gulf countries have the natural monopoly in oil extraction; South Africa has monopoly in gold mining, etc.

(ii) **Social Monopoly:** The social monopolies are created by the intervention of the government to protect the interest of the consumers. E.g. the public utility services like Railways, distribution of cooking gas, electricity, water, etc. Social Monopoly is also known as Public Monopoly or Government Monopoly.

(iii) **Legal Monopoly:** The legal support of the government also creates monopolies. E.g. patent rights in the production of goods with the brand names like Maruti Suzuki, Hero Honda, Infosys, Lux, Bajaj, and Tata, etc. are the legal monopolies. Other firms are not allowed to use these brand names/trademarks. The trade secrets in the production of a commodity and intellectual property rights also give birth for monopolies.

(iv) **Voluntary Monopoly:** Few firms manufacturing identical product voluntarily agree to regulate their price and output. This helps them to maximize profits by eliminating possible competition e.g. Oil extracting Gulf countries have formed monopoly organization by the name Organization of Petroleum Exporting Countries (OPEC). These agreements fall under the category of Trusts, Cartel and Holding company. In all these cases many firms come together to form a single selling unit to maximize the profits. The consumer is always at the receiving end in the monopoly market.

(v) **Simple Monopoly:** The Monopoly firm which charges a uniform price for its sold to all buyers is called 'Simple Monopoly'. The Simple Monopoly firm operates in the single market.

(vi) **Discriminating Monopoly:** The Monopoly firm who charges different prices for its same output to different buyers. Discriminating Monopoly firm operates in more than one market.

(vii) **Private Monopoly:** The Monopoly firm which is owned and controlled by a private individual or body is called Private Monopoly.

7.2.4 Demand Curve, Average Revenue and Marginal Revenue Curves: The Monopoly firm has downwards sloping demand curve for his output. It means the monopoly will be able to sell more only at a reduced price or he has to reduce the size of his output to raise the price. Since demand for output is at price, the demand curve and average revenue curve become one and same. When average revenue curve is falling from left to right, MR curve is also falling but it is below average revenue curve.

The average revenue curve and the marginal revenue curve in monopoly market are illustrated in the following diagram 7.12.

In the monopoly market the elasticity of the Average Revenue (AR) or the Demand curve influences the determination of price.

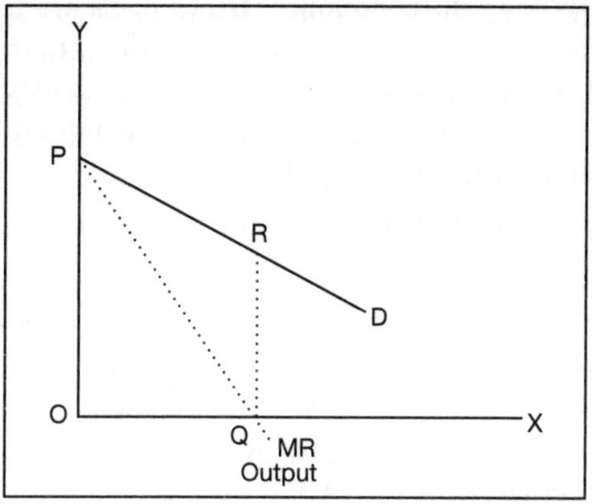

Diagram 7.12: Demand Curve of Monopoly

The monopoly will always fix the output at a level where the elasticity of his Average Revenue curve is equal to one or greater than one. In the diagram 7.12 at the point 'R' the elasticity of demand (AR) is equal to one and MR is zero. Between R and P the elasticity of AR is greater than one and MR is positive. It is always profitable for the monopoly firm to fix the output between these points.

7.2.5 Does Monopoly Minimize Profits?: The monopoly firm has two alternative ways to maximize profits. It follows any one of the following ways:

(i) The monopoly firm can fix up the level of output and leave the price to determine by demand conditions in the market: When supply is fixed or given naturally the demand for output will rise, thus the price will rise automatically. The higher price brings the firm maximizes the profits.

(ii) The Monopoly firm can fix up the price and leave the level of output to determine by demand conditions in the market: When the price is fixed at low level and remained constants naturally the demand for output with increase, thus the sale will be more. The sale maximization brings maximum profits to the monopoly firm.

7.2.6 Monopoly Equilibrium: Price and Output Determination: Monopoly firm is a price maker, not price taker. He controls entire market. Since he is the only seller or producer in the market there is no difference between firm and industry. He has downward sloping demand curve for his output. The main aim of monopoly firm is to get maximum profits. He gets maximum profits when he attains the equilibrium.

Monopoly firm attains equilibrium where the following conditions are fulfilled:

(i) Marginal Revenue (MR) = Marginal Cost (MC).

(ii) MC curve must cut MR from left and below, at intersection point MC must be rising.

(iii) Price must be greater than MR and Price (P) is equal to Average Revenue (AR).

The equilibrium of firm and price and output determination in monopoly market is illustrated in the following diagram 7.13.

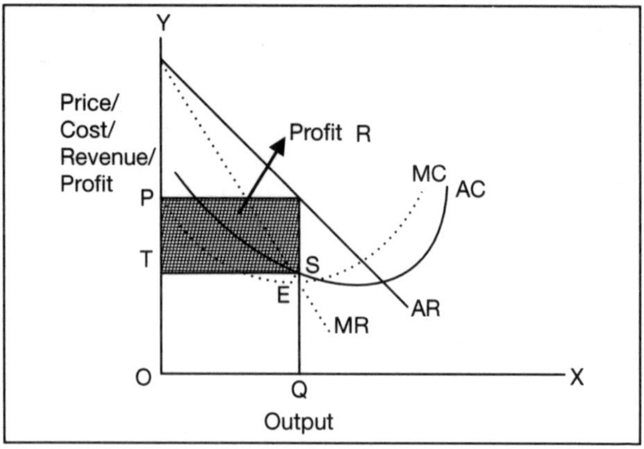

Diagram 7.13: Equilibrium of Monopoly Firm

Output is measured along 'OX' axis and price, revenue, cost and profits are measured along 'OY' axis.

AR is average revenue curve and MR is marginal revenue curve. AC is average cost curve and MC is marginal cost curve.

The monopoly firm attained equilibrium at 'E'. Where both the conditions of equilibrium are fulfilled viz. MC = MR and MR < P.

At equilibrium point 'E' the firm determines RQ or OP level of price. Draw RQ perpendicular passing through the 'E' point and it joins AR curve at R, so RQ is the determined price. It can also be shown along 'OY' axis as OP, here OP = RQ.

The perpendicular RQ joins 'OX' axis at Q, thus the firm determines the OQ level of output.

Thus the monopoly firm determines 'OP' price and 'OQ' output at equilibrium 'E'.

To measure the size of profits, we have to use AC curve. The perpendicular RQ intersects AC curve at 'S'. Thus the size of AC is QS whereas AR is RQ. The Profit is the excess of Total Revenue (TR) over Total Cost (TC):

$\pi = TR - TC > 0$

Where π = Profits, TC = Total Cost and TR = Total Revenue.

We can calculate monopoly profit on the basis of above diagram 7.3 as:

$\pi = TR - TC > 0$; Where TR = Price (P) × Output (Q)

$\therefore \pi = (P \times Q) - (AC \times Q)$. TC = Average Cost (AC) × Output (Q).

= OP (= RQ) × OQ (= PR) – OT (= SQ) × OQ (= TS)

= OPRQ – OTSQ

= PRTS area.

Thus area PRTS is the size of total profit. It is shown by shaded area in the diagram 7.3.

In brief, the Monopoly firm attain equilibrium at 'E' where MC = MR and determines 'OP' price and OQ level of output thus he gets PRTS profit.

7.2.7 Importance of 'Time-Elements': Like in perfect competition, time elements play a vital role in price and output determination in monopoly market. It is studied as under:

(i) **Short Period:** In the short period, a monopoly firm earns supernormal profit or normal profit or makes loss depends upon demand condition for his product. The firm attains equilibrium at the level of output where both the order of equilibrium conditions is fulfilled.

(a) **Supernormal Profit:** The monopoly firm does get supernormal profit when the demand condition is more favourable. It is illustrated in the following diagram 7.14.

The firm in short-run attains equilibrium at 'E_1' where both the conditions of equilibrium are fulfilled.

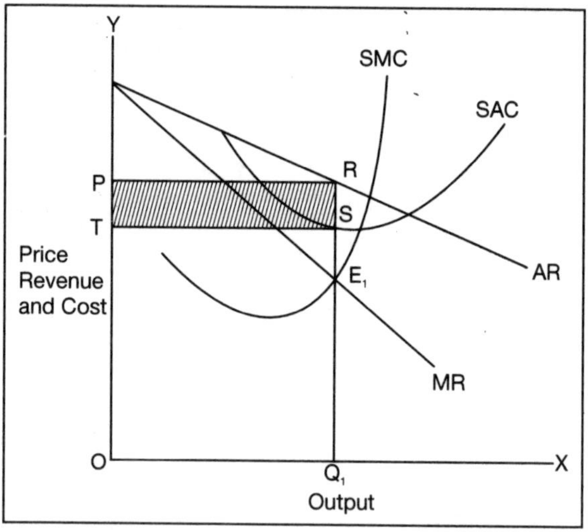

Diagram 7.14: Equilibrium of Monopoly Firm

In the diagram 7.14 AR and MR are the average and marginal revenue curves respectively. SMC is the short-run marginal cost curve and SAC is the short-run average revenue curve. At the equilibrium point E_1 the output produced is OQ and the determined price is 'OP'. As the AR curve is above the SAC curve the monopolist is earning supernormal profit denoted by the shaded area PRST. SR is the per unit profit earned by the monopoly, i.e. the difference between the SAC curve and the AR curve.

(b) **Normal Profit:** When demand condition is normal the monopoly firm does earn only normal profit in short period. If the Average Revenue (Price) is equal to the Average Cost the monopoly earns normal profits. It is shown in the following diagram 7.15.

In the diagrame 7.15 the AR curve is tangent to the SAC curve at the point 'T'. The monopolist attains the equilibrium at the point 'E' where the MC curve is equal to the MR curve. OQ is the equilibrium output and the price is OP. Price OP is equal to the average cost. Thus the monopoly firm is earning only normal profits.

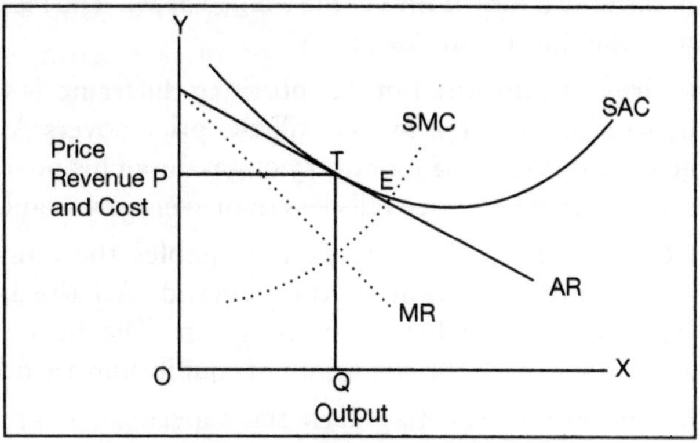

Diagram 7.15: Equilibrium of Monopoly Firm

(c) **Loss:** When demand condition is unfavourable the Average Revenue (Price) is less than the Average Cost so the monopoly suffers loss. This is shown in the following diagram 7.16.

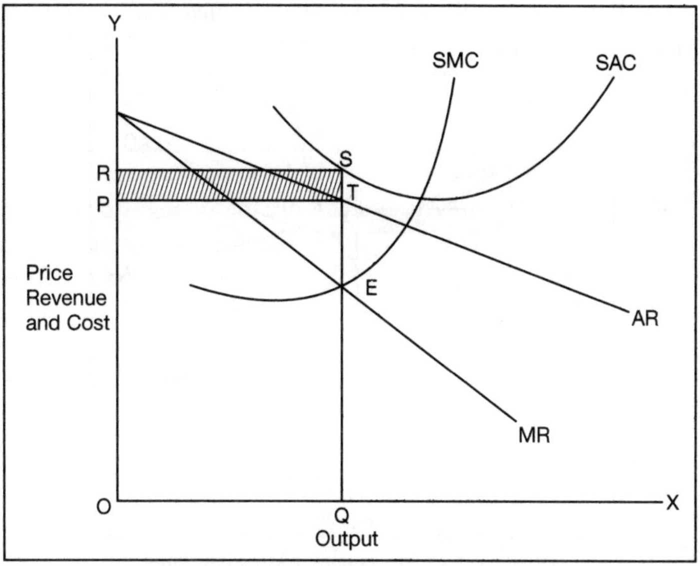

Diagram 7.16: Equilibrium of Monopoly Firm

The firm has attained equilibrium at the point 'E'. OQ is the equilibrium output and 'OP' is the price. The AR curve in this case is found below the SAC curve. It means the revenue earned by the monopoly is less than his cost. Therefore the monopoly firm has suffered a loss of PRST (the shaded area). The loss made per unit of the output produced 'TS'.

The firm earning the normal profit or suffering loss may continue to remain in the market till the price covers Average Variable Cost (AVC). The monopoly closes down his operations even in short-run when price falls less than average variable cost.

(ii) **Long Period:** The long period enables the monopoly to adjust supply of output to the demand. All the factors of production are variable in the long-run. The firm attains equilibrium where both the conditions of equilibrium are fulfilled.

The monopoly firm may earn the supernormal profit or normal profits in the long-run depend upon demand conditions continued in long-run. If short-run losses continue in long-run due to unfavourable demand conditions, the firm shutdown the production unit or stop production in long-run.

The long-run equilibrium of monopoly firm and its price and output determination is illustrated in the diagram 7.17.

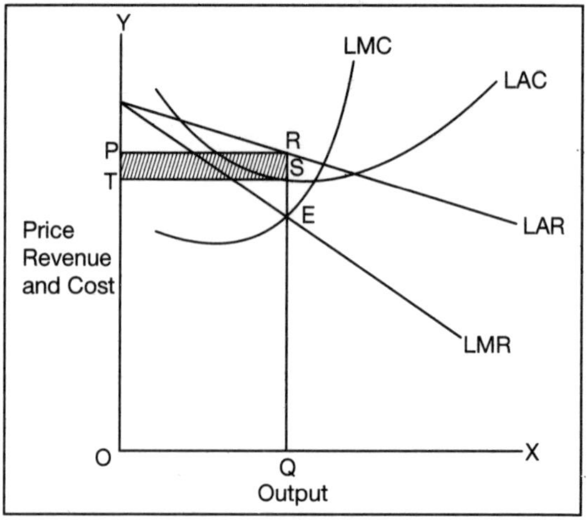

Diagram 7.17: Equilibrium of Monopoly Firm

In the diagram 7.17 the point of equilibrium of firm is at E, where Long-run Marginal Cost (LMC) is equal to Long-run Marginal Revenue (LMR). The output produced OQ is sold at the price OP. Since the Long-run Average Revenue exceeds the

Long-run Average Cost of the firm the monopoly earns a supernormal profit of PRST (the shaded area).

The LMC is the sum of Short-run marginal cost curves where as LMR is the sum of Short-run marginal revenue curves. OP is the determined Long-run monopoly price and OQ is the determined long-run output.

7.2.8 Merits and Demerits of Monopoly: The monopoly is generally considered as exploitative as he has the opportunity to fix a high price for his output. But it has both merits and demerits:

(i) **Merits of Monopoly:** The existence monopoly is also justified on the following grounds of it merits:

(a) **Benefits of Internal and External Economies:** The monopoly concerns are generally large in size and are in a position to secure the advantages of internal and external economies associated with large-scale production. The decrease in the cost of production ultimately is beneficial to the consumer.

(b) **Ability to Withstand Business Uncertainties:** The monopolies are in a position to withstand the business uncertainties and depression owing to their strong financial resources. On the other hand the small sized firms may not be in a position to withstand the onslaught of business uncertainties.

(c) **Better Suited for Public Utility Services:** Monopoly concerns are better suited for public utility services like, supply of cooking gas, electricity, rail transport, etc. Forming social monopolies in the field of public utility services will protect the interests of the consumers.

(d) **Ability to Face Global Competition:** If the domestic firms are weak they may not be able to face international competition. Such firms have to opt for mergers and amalgamations and organize themselves on monopolistic basis. Thus various firms coming together in the form of a monopoly will help them to face the threat of global competition effectively. Unifying Monopoly does improve efficiency.

(e) **Over-Production is not Possible:** Monopoly firm produces less than the production capacity. Supply of output is low so there is no scope for over-production. It avoids or prevents over-production.

(f) **No Selling Cost:** There is no selling cost in monopoly marked. Thus it saves the cost and prevents inflation.

(g) **Less or No Transport Cost:** Monopoly firm use to supply his output to near market or place. It also saves cost.

(ii) **Demerits of Monopoly:** The monopoly has been considered as a social evil. The monopolist uses every opportunity to exploit the consumers. The demerits of monopoly are also known as disadvantages or evils or dangers of monopoly.

(a) **Charge Exorbitant Price:** Monopolists charge exorbitant price for their products and exploit the consumers. The price charged by the monopolist is generally higher than the price prevailing under competitive conditions. To this extent the monopolist is in a position to exploit the consumers.

(b) **Use Obsolete Methods of Production:** As the monopolist is not faced with competition the monopolist continues to use the obsolete techniques and methods of production. He may not adopt the advanced techniques and methods of production, which will help in bringing down the cost of production. As result of this consumer will be forced to purchase low quality product at a higher price.

(c) **Discriminatory Pricing Policy:** The monopolist has the opportunity to charge different prices for different consumers for the same product. The monopolist tries to extract the maximum price from each of the customer depending upon their capacity to pay. This discriminatory pricing policy of the monopolists is against the interest of the consumers and is exploitative.

(d) **Influence the Political and Administrative Set up:** Monopoly results into concentration of economic and political power in a few hands. The monopolists with large financial resources under their control may influence the political and administrative set up of the country to promote their self-interest. Sometimes they use their monopoly power to acquire political power. This will help them to exploit the administrative set up in promoting their self-interest. In such cases the consumers will be forced to pay a high price for low quality products. It is danger to the nation.

(e) **Excess Capacity:** The monopoly concerns generally have an excess and unutilized capacity. The monopolists generally do not use their full capacity in the production of the output. The main objective of the monopolist is to restrict the output and to raise the price to maximize profits. Such under utilization of capacity reduces the benefits to be enjoyed by the community.

(f) **Ignorance of Common Welfare:** Monopoly neglects needs of common people. They produce private goods which bring them more profits.

The monopolies for these reasons are considered as social evils and need to be controlled and regulated.

7.2.9 Causes and Limitations of Monopoly: There are various factors like natural factors, law, etc. which create monopoly in the economy. Monopoly market also operates under certain limitations.

(i) **Cause of Monopoly:** There are various factors which create monopoly in the economy. They are:

(a) **Natural Factors:** Natural factors like climate, geographical distribution of natural resources, etc. create monopoly in the economy. For ex: Oil deposits— rich countries became monopoly in oil and petroleum production.

(b) **Legal Factors:** The Government laws like Patents Act, Copy Rights Act, etc. create Monopoly. The legal measures of the government also create monopolies like Central Bank as Monopoly of Note-Issue, Post and Telegraph, etc.

(c) **Public Utility Services:** Governments set up some bodies like water board, electricity board, etc. to render public utility services. Such bodies become monopolies.

(d) **Voluntary Combinations:** Voluntary business combinations are formed to eliminate competition among the group as well as to prevent the entry of new firms. Business cartels, syndicates, trusts, pools, holding-companies, etc. are the examples of voluntary combinations.

(e) **Central of a Secret Process:** So far the firm maintains the secrecy of a new process of manufacturing or production, he becomes the monopoly.

(ii) Limitations on Monopoly: The following factors limit in the scope and operation of monopoly market.

(a) **Public Opinion:** If the public opinion is against monopoly market the operation of monopoly cannot survive. The existence and the degree of monopoly depend upon the degree of public resistance against monopoly.

(b) **Potential Competition:** In modern context absolute monopoly is not possible. There are rival firms or sellers in the market. So the existence and degree of monopoly dependants upon the existence of the degree of potential competition by rival firms or sellers.

(c) **Existence of Substitutes:** The production of close substitutes prevents concentration of monopoly power.

7.2.10 Control and Regulation of Monopoly: As the monopolist has the opportunity to exploit the consumer by charging exorbitant prices, it is necessary to regulate such firms. The government may adopt the following measures to regulate monopolies:

(i) **Encouraging Potential Rivals:** The government should encourage entry of new firms in those areas where the monopolists charge exorbitant prices to earn maximum profits. The government should encourage the entry of rival firms into the market by providing them the necessary concessions and facilities. This may force the monopolist to charge reasonable price to avoid entry of new firms.

(ii) **Production of Substitutes:** The firms producing substitutes should be encouraged to prevent the monopolies from charging high prices. Promotion of innovations to produce substitutes helps in regulating monopoly firms.

(iii) **Nationalization:** To protect the interest of the consumers the governments may also take over the ownership and management of monopoly firms. E.g. the government generally owns and manages the public utility services like supply of water, electricity, cooking gas, etc. Existence of monopolies in these areas is socially desirable, as it has cost advantages.

(iv) **Consumers' Associations:** The government should encourage the formation of Consumers' Associations to improve their bargaining strength. These associations should keep a watch on the unfair trade practices of monopolies and insist on the production of quality products.

(v) **Publicity:** There is need to give wide publicity to the unfair trade practices adopted by the monopolies to earn exorbitant profits. Such measures prevent the monopolists from charging high prices for their products.

(vi) **Anti-Monopoly Legislation:** The government may also take legislative steps to regulate monopoly firm. The new monopoly firms may be prevented from coming into existence, and the old and existing firms may be dissolved and split into competing firms. At the same time monopolies should be barred from adopting unfair trade practices leading to exploitation of consumers.

(vii) **Regulation of Monopoly Price and Taxation Policy:** It is also known as 'Government Methods' to regulate monopoly. The monopolies, if not regulated, would exploit the consumers by charging an exorbitant price. In such cases the government should impose a ceiling on the price, which is socially beneficial. A price or rate tribunal can be appointed for this purpose.

The government should also force the monopolies to increase their output according to their excess capacity. This not only helps in reducing the price but also increases the supply of the output. 'Price Regulation' is useful method to regulate the monopoly.

Another effective method to be adopted by the government is to impose tax on the monopoly profits. This measure not only regulates the monopoly profit but also helps in augmenting government revenue.

7.3 PRICE DISCRIMINATION

7.3.1 Meaning and Definition: Price discrimination means the practice of selling the units of same commodity at different prices to different customers. The monopoly who sells its output at different prices to different consumers is called 'Discriminating Monopoly'. For example: a telephone company may charge higher rates for a day time and lower rates for night trunk calls. An electricity concern charges higher rates for industrial purpose and cheaper rate for domestic purpose. Hence price discrimination has come to be associated with monopoly. It is a technique by which the monopolist makes the consumers pay according to their ability. Mrs. John Robinson defines price discrimination as, "the act of selling the same article produced under a single control at different prices to different customers".

7.3.2 Types of Price Discrimination: There are various types of price discrimination. They are:

(i) **Personal Discrimination:** In this case, monopolist will charge different prices to different customers on the basis of their ability to pay. Rich customers will be asked to pay more and poor customers to pay less. This is possible in specialized personal services like doctors, lawyers, etc. For ex: lawyers may charge different fees to different types of clients on the basis of status of their income.

(ii) **Place Discrimination:** Monopolist having different markets in different regions may charge different prices for the same commodity in the different region. The locality in which his market is situated will be the criterion in fixing up the price. For instance, a monopolist has a shop in an aristocratic (rich) locality and also in a slum. He will charge higher prices to the customers of aristocratic locality and lower charge to the customers of aristocratic locality sometimes. A monopolist charges lower prices in a foreign country and higher prices at home. This is commonly described as 'dumping'.

(iii) **Trade Discrimination:** Here the monopolist will charge different prices for different types of uses of the same commodity. For instance, the electric company may charge higher price for domestic lighting, a lower price for industrial use.

(iv) **Age Discrimination:** Price discrimination may be done on the basis of age of the buyers. Usually the buyers are grouped into children and adults. For instance, a barber may charge lower rates for children's haircuts than those for adults. In railways and bus transport services, it is a commonly adopted form of price discrimination that person below 12 years of age is charged at half the rate.

(v) **Sex Discrimination:** In selling certain goods, producers may discriminate between male and female buyers by charging low prices to females. For instance, a tour organizing firm may provide seat to ladies at concessional rates.

(vi) **Quality Variation Discrimination:** On the basis of some qualitative differences, different prices may be charged for the same product. For instance, a publisher may sell a deluxe edition of the same book at a higher price. Quality variation may be in the form of material used, the nature of packing, colour, style, etc.

(vii) **Special Service or Comforts:** Price discrimination may also be resorted on the basis of special facilities or comforts. Railways, for instance, change different fares for the first class and second class travel.

(viii) **Time Discrimination:** On the basis of the time of Service, different rates may be charged. For ex: The telephone company charges half rates for trunk-calls at night.

Pigou's Classification

Prof. A.C. Pigou in his book *Economics of Welfare* describes three degrees of in discrimination. They are:

(a) **Price Discrimination of the First Degree:** Price discrimination of the first degree is also known as perfect price discrimination because this involves maximum possible exploitation of each buyer in the interest of a sell's profits. In this case the monopolist is able to sell each separate unit of the output at a different price. Under discrimination of the first degree, every buyer is forced to pay the price which is equal to the maximum amount he is willing to pay rather than go without the good all together. In other words, the seller leaves no consumer's surplus to any buyer. For examples: charges for doctors services.

An important point about perfect price discrimination is worth noting is that under simple monopoly, marginal revenue curve of the seller lies below the demand curve of the buyer whereas under perfect price discrimination the demand curve of the buyer also becomes the marginal revenue curve of the seller.

(b) **Price Discrimination of the Second Degree.** In this case buyers are divided into different groups and for each group a different price is charged is the low or minimum demand price. Monopolist leaves certain consumer's surplus to the buyer. For example: Railway fares. This is done to keep the consumers satisfied and prevent the entry of potential rivals.

(c) **Price Discrimination of the Third Degree:** Price discrimination of the third degree takes place when the seller divides his buyers into two or more than two sub-markets or groups and charges a different price is each sub-markets. The size of output sold in that sub-market is based on price elasticity of demand. Third degree price discrimination is practicable as well as most commonly found in the real world. For example: Theatres.

7.3.3 Essential Conditions: Discriminating monopoly will become successful where the following conditions are fulfilled:

(i) **Sub-Markets:** Price Discrimination is possible when the total market is divided into sub-market; each sub-market acquires a separate identity, so that one sub-market has no connection with others. Again consumers have no inclination to move from high priced market to a low priced on due to either ignorance or absence of inertia.

(ii) **Differentiated Products:** Discrimination is possible when buyers need the same service in connection with differentiated products. For example, railways charges different freights for transport attain of coal and copper. For, they know that it is physically impossible for a copper merchant to convert copper into coal for the purpose of transporting it cheap.

(iii) **Ignorance of Buyers:** Discrimination becomes possible due to ignorance and laziness of buyers. If a seller discriminates between the two markets, but the buyer of the dearer market may be ignorant of the fact that the same commodity is being sold at lower price in cheaper market.

(iv) **Geographical or Tariff Barriers:** Discrimination is possible when markets are separated by wide distance or tariff barriers. So that it is very expensive to transfer goods from a cheaper market to dearer market. For example, a monopolist in Karnataka may sell his goods in Kerala at ₹10 and in another city say Delhi at ₹ 15. If transport cost is more than ₹ 5 per unit then it will not be worthwhile for the buyers in Kerala to transfer the goods to Delhi.

(v) **Preferences or Prejudices of the Buyers:** Price discrimination many become possible due to prejudices of the buyers. The same good is generally converted into different varieties by providing different packing, different names or labels in order to convince the buyer that certain varieties are superior to others. Different prices are charged for different varieties, although they differ only in name or label.

(vi) **Legal Sanction:** In some cases government permits the price discrimination. For example, the Electricity Department is permitted to charge different prices to different consumers. Similarly Railway is permitted to charge high fare for First class passengers and a lower fare for Second class passengers. Public monopolies have the legal sanction of price discrimination.

(vii) **Let-Go-Attitude of Buyers:** When price differences between two markets are very small, the consumers do not think it worthwhile to consider such discrimination. For instance, in the distribution of vanaspati-ghee, there is a zonal price differential which is a marginal one, so that we hardly pay any attention to such differences of 5 to 10 paise per kg in different zones.

7.3.4 When is Price Discrimination Profitable: Price discrimination is profitable under the following situations:

(i) Elasticity of demand in one market is different from elasticity of demand in other.

(ii) The cost-differential of supplying output to different markets should be same.

7.3.5 Price and Output Determination: Under simple monopoly, a single price is charged for the whole output; but under price discrimination the monopolist will charge different prices in different sub-markets. First of all, the monopolist has to divide his total market into various sub-markets on the basis of elasticity of demand for the product. After dividing the market, the producer has to decide the supply of each sub-market. Here the decision of output for each sub-market depends on equilibrium conditions of each sub-market with the total cost condition and the revenue curves of the sub-market.

In order to reach the equilibrium position, the discriminating monopoly has to take two decisions: (i) How much total output should be produced? (ii) How the total output should be shared between the two sub-markets and what price should be charged in the two sub-markets?

For the sake of simplicity, we shall take that a discriminating monopoly divides his market into two sub-markets: sub-market A and B and finds the AR curve different in these two.

How price discrimination is done in these two sub-markets can be illustrated in the following diagram 7.18.

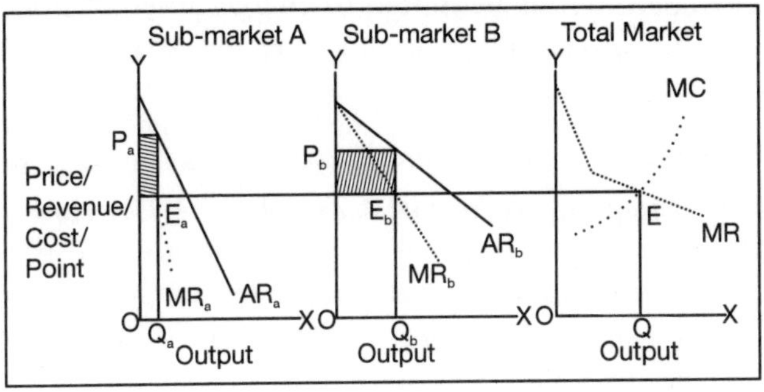

Diagram 7.18: Equilibrium of Discriminating Monopoly

The diagram 7.18 illustrates the revenue curves of the two sub-markets A and B and the aggregate situation in the entire market under his control. In sub-market A, AR_a is the demand curve or the average revenue. In sub-markets B, AR_b is the demand drive or the average curve of the market. It should be noted that the elasticity of demand in these two sub-markets is different. In sub-market A the demand curve shows less-elastic nature and in sub-market B the curve shows more-elastic nature. In the two sub-markets the respective marginal revenue curves are shown as MR_a and MR_b which lie below the evaluated revenue cause of the respective sub-markets. The figure on the extreme right shows the total market where the aggregate conditions of the revenue curves are shown. The MR is aggregate marginal revenue curve and MC is aggregate marginal cost curve.

Since output is under single control we have shown the marginal cost for the entire production. The level of production is determined at a point where MR=MC. In the total market the aggregate MR curve cuts the MC curve at E and the total output is determined at OQ. Now this output OQ has to be sold in the two sub-markets. How much of OQ goes to each of these markets? To find out this, we draw from E_a line parallel to 'X' axis. Therefore quantify OQ_a will be sold in sub-market A and quantity OQ_b in sub-market B. Thus, the monopolist producing OQ quantities of commodity and will sell OQ_a quantities in sub-market A at a price P_a and OQ_b quantity in sub-market B at a price P_b. We can see from the figure that the price is higher in sub-market A and lower in B. He has discriminated the two and charges different prices for the same commodity. E_a is equilibrium of firm in sub-market A and E_b in sub-market B.

Total Output = OQ = $OQ_a + OQ_b$

The shaded area in both sub-markets shows the size of profits.

7.3.6 Dumping—A Special Case of Price Discrimination: Dumping is a special type of price discrimination in which monopolist fixes a higher price for his product in the home market and a lower price for the same product in the foreign market so as to capture the foreign market.

It is assumed that the producer is a monopolist in the home market and there is perfect competition in world market. In the home market, demand is inelastic while in the foreign market it is perfectly elastic. The condition of equilibrium and price determination is illustrated in the following diagram 7.19.

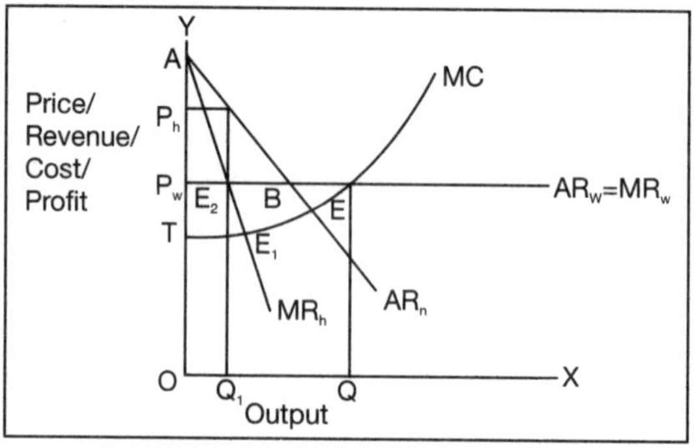

Diagram 7.19: Equilibrium of Discriminating Monopoly

Output is measured along 'OX' axis and price, revenue, cost and profit are measured along 'OY' axis. AR_h and MR_h are average and marginal revenue curves of home market. AR_w and MR_w are average and marginal revenue curve of world market. MC is marginal cost curve. In world market the firm's equilibrium is at 'E' where MC=MR_w so the price in the world market is 'P'.

In domestic market the firm selects equilibrium at 'E2' which is higher than 'E_1' so the firm fixes 'P_h' price in domestic market. Further the firm determines to produce 'OQ' size of output and sells 'OQ_1' quantity of output at 'P_h' in domestic monopoly market meanwhile he sells 'Q_1Q' at 'P' price in the world competitive market. Thus he makes the total profit 'ABET'.

7.3.7 Economic Effects of Price Discrimination: It is mixed with both good and bad effects. The following are the major economic effects of price discrimination:

(i) According to Mrs. John Robinson, total output under price discrimination tends to be larger than the output under a simple monopoly.

(ii) Total profits of discriminating monopoly will be higher than the simple monopoly because price discrimination helps the monopoly to convert the consumer's surplus into profit.

(iii) Price discrimination helps to increase sales and output that leads to large scale of production and minimization of costs.

(iv) It is socially justified because the price discrimination helps the poor buyers to get output at lower prices. It helps to improve the economic welfare of the community at large.

(v) The dumping helps the firm to export output to foreign countries and enjoy the advantage of economies of large scale.

(vi) Price discrimination of the first and second degree obstructs the maximization of utility by a consumer.

(vii) Price discrimination leads to inefficient allocation of resources in a market economy.

7.3.8 Is Price Discrimination Beneficial?: Prof. A.C. Pigou and Mrs. John Robinson have analyzed the circumstances under which price discrimination is beneficial to the society as a whole. It is explained as under:

(i) Price discrimination promotes economic welfare of the people. Government usually permits or encourages price discrimination for instance, rail transportation, etc. In public utility services, the higher income groups are charged higher prices and the funds so collected may be used to subsidies the goods meant for the poor.

(ii) Price discrimination is also beneficial to society in reducing inequalities of personal incomes when higher fees are charged to the rich than to the poor.

(iii) Some of the commodities and services may not be produced in the absence of the priced discrimination. The best example is that of a doctor in a village. If a doctor charges uniform fee to all his patients, his income may be low as to induce him to leave his private practice.

According to Mrs. Joan Robinson "It may happen, for instance, that a railway would not be built or a country doctor would not set up his practice, if discrimination were forbidden. It is clearly desirable that price discrimination should be permitted in such cases."

(iv) Price discrimination is not only beneficial but is also justified when a country sells a commodity cheaper abroad than at home.

(v) Average cost of production may be lowered on account of larger output and economies of scale.

Price discrimination, however, does not receive social and moral justification when its main motive is profit maximization.

7.4 MODEL QUESTIONS

2 Marks Questions

(a) Give the meaning of perfect competition.

(b) Name any two features of perfect competition.

(c) Mention the difference between firm and industry.

(d) Give the meaning of equilibrium of firm.

(e) What do you mean by normal profits?

(f) What is monopoly?

(g) Name any two features of monopoly.

(h) What is price discrimination?

(i) What do you mean by dumping?

5 Marks Questions

(1) Write a note on features of perfect competition.

(2) Discuss in brief the equilibrium of industry.

(3) Write a note on merits and demerits of monopoly.

(4) Give the brief account of causes and limitations of Monopoly.

(5) Write a note on control of monopoly.

(6) Discuss in brief the types of price discrimination.

(7) Is Price Discrimination Beneficial?

(8) Write a note on dumping.

10 Marks Questions

(1) Define perfect competition and explain its features.

(2) Explain the price and output determination in perfect competition.

(3) Define monopoly and explain its features.

(4) Explain the price and output determination in monopoly.

(5) Explain the price and output determination in discriminating monopoly.

8

Markets (Contd.)

8.1 MONOPOLISTIC COMPETITION

8.1.1 Meaning and Definition: Mrs. Joan Robinson (UK) and Prof. E.H. Chamberlin (USA) independently had conducted empirical study on market situation in 1933 thereby found out that the market is neither perfect competitive nor monopoly but a blend of both situations. Mrs. Joan Robinson called it 'Imperfect Competition' and Prof. E.H. Chamberlin called it 'Monopolistic Competition'.

According to Mrs. Joan Robinson it is imperfect competitive market because each firm has his own group of costumers who make him monopoly. Prof. E.H. Chamberlin called monopolistic competition because it is a market situation where there are many sellers of a differentiated product. "There is competition which is keen, not perfect between many firms, making very similar products." No seller can have any perceptible influence on the price-output policies of the other seller nor can be influenced much by their actions. Thus monopolistic competition refers to competition among many sellers producing close but not perfect substitute products. So Prof. E.H. Chamberlin defined monopolist competition as "Where there is product differentiation, there is neither monopoly nor competition but monopolistic competition."

Monopolistic competition is commonly found in many fields, especially in retail trade, in service industries and in some branches of manufacturing field we also find it in the garment industry, shoe making industry, cosmetic products, furniture manufacturing units, etc. For example, toothpaste of different brand names like Colgate, Babool, Pepsodent and other.

8.1.2 Features: Monopolistic competition is a version of imperfect competition. It has many sellers and a large number of buyers, but what differentiates it from pure competition is the product differentiation by sellers. The products of different sellers are close but not complete substitutes. The main features of monopolistic competition are:

(i) **Existence of Many Firms:** Under monopolistic competition the number of firms producing a commodity will be large but less than the number in perfect competition. Each will be acting independently in determination of price and output. Any action of the individual firm in increasing or decreasing output will have little or no effect on other firms.

(ii) **Product Differentiation:** The important feature of monopolistic competition is the existence of product differentiation. The products produced by the firms are relatively close substitutes but not perfect substitutes, for instance, in India there are various tooth paste manufactures producing different brands such as Colgate, Pepsodent, Forhens, Babool, etc.

Product differentiation means a commodity serving the same purpose being produced under different brand-name, trade-mark, wrapper, colour, quality, etc. by different firms. Product differentiation may also be effected by offering customers some benefits with the sale of the product. Facilities like free servicing, home delivery etc., would make the consumers to demand that particular brand of product. Thus product differentiation is attempted through (a) physical differences; (b) quality differences; (c) imaginary differences by advertisements; and (d) purchase benefit differences.

The ultimate aim of product differentiation is to capture a large number of customers.

(iii) **Selling Cost:** Selling cost a unique feature of monopolistic competition. Since products are differentiated, advertising and other forms of sales promotion becomes an integral part of selling-efforts. Expenses incurred on advertisement and salesmanship or selling-efforts are called selling costs. The purpose of selling costs is sales promotion. Selling-cost exists only in monopolistic competition. Selling-costs are included in total cost of production.

(iv) **Non-Price Competition:** Another important feature of monopolistic competition is non-price competition. There are different methods of competing with rivals other than price. It may be a guarantee for repairs within a particular time, after sale service, a gift scheme with particular purchases, a discount not declared in the price list or transport free of cost, etc.

(v) **Shape of Revenue Curve:** The shape of revenue curve in monopolistic competition is not same as in monopoly and perfect competition. So it should be noted that the average revenue curve of the firm is neither a horizontal straight line as under perfect competition nor a downward sloping steep-line as under monopoly but lies in between. It is shown in the following diagram 8.1.

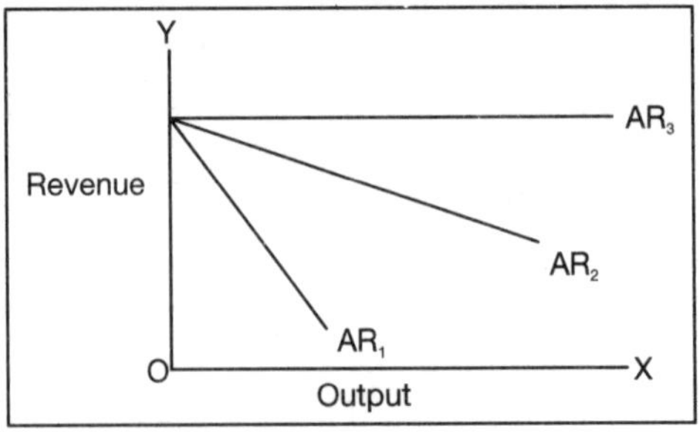

Diagram 8.1: Revenue Curves

AR1 = Average Revenue Curve in Monopoly.

AR2 = Average Revenue Curve in Monopolistic Competition.

AR3 = Average Revenue Curve in Perfect Competition.

(vi) **Freedom of Entry and Exit of Firms:** Like perfect competition, there is no difficulty for a new firm to enter into the market or an existing firm to leave the market. This makes the competition stiff because of the close substitutes produced by the new entrants with their own brand names. Thus all firms earn normal profits in long-run.

(vii) **Difference between Industry and Group:** E.H. Chamberlin has used the word group instead of industry in order to draw distinction between pure competition and monopolistic competition. The word industry is generally used in economics in context of pure or perfect competition and refers to a collection of firms that produce homogeneous products. But under monopolistic competition we have product heterogeneity and not product homogeneity. Therefore the word 'industry' loses its significance under monopolistic competition. Thus, Prof. Chamberlin used the word 'group'. By group he means "a number of producers whose goods are fairly close substitutes". Prof. Chamberlin's 'group' refers to a collection of firms that produce closely related but not identical products.

(viii) **Excess Capacity:** The theories of both Chamberlin and Joan Robinson indicate that a firm under monopolistic competition in the long-run equilibrium produces the output which is less than the socially optimum or ideal output. This means that firms under monopolistic competition operate at that point on the falling portion of long-run average cost that is why they do not produce the level of output at which long-run average cost is at minimum. The difference between actual long-run output of a firm and socially ideal output is a measure of 'excess capacity'. In brief, the firm uses less than the installed production-capacity.

(ix) **Large Number of Buyers:** There are a large number of buyers in the market. However each buyer has a preference for a specific brand of the product. He, thus, becomes patron of a particular seller. Unlike perfect competition, here buying is by choice and not by chance. It makes the seller monopoly.

8.1.3 Price and Output Determination: In Monopolistic Competition, the firm is price-maker. The firm's main aim is to get maximum profits. In monopolistic competition firm's market is isolated of his rivals. Firm's equilibrium depends upon its (i) Price, (ii) Variety of product and (iii) Selling cost.

When explaining firm's equilibrium under monopolistic competition, of these three, any two variables should be assumed constant, otherwise it becomes very difficult to explain firm's equilibrium.

(A) Price Variation and Firm's Equilibrium: Like perfect competition and monopoly, the firm under monopolistic competition also uses marginalist approach to attain the equilibrium. The firm attains equilibrium where (i) Marginal Cost (MC)= Marginal Revenue (MR) and (ii) MC Curve cuts MR Curve from left below and at intersection point MC must be rising, these two conditions are full-filled. Variety of product and selling cost are assumed constant to explain firm's equilibrium.

The shape of demand curve for the product of monopolistic competitive firm is unlike the shape of demand curve is neither horizontal straight line nor steeper downward sloping demand curve but a flatter sloping demand curve. Marginal Cost and Marginal Revenue Curve are used to explain firm's equilibrium. At the point of equilibrium, the firm determines price and output.

Demand Curve is the average revenue curve. Average Cost (AC) Curve is used to measure the profits or loss of the monopolistic competitive firm at the point of equilibrium.

Time-elements play important role in price and output determination in monopolistic competition also:

(i) **Short-run Equilibrium or Individual Equilibrium:** Prof. E.H. Chamberlin used the term individual equilibrium in place of short-run equilibrium, of the firm. In short-run firm attains equilibrium where the conditions of equilibrium are fulfilled. The firm determines price and output at the point of equilibrium. This analysis is based on the following assumption:

(a) All firms should be similar in all respect like demand and cost conditions.

(b) Demand and cost conditions should be constant.

The firm's equilibrium in short-run is illustrated in the following diagram 8.2.

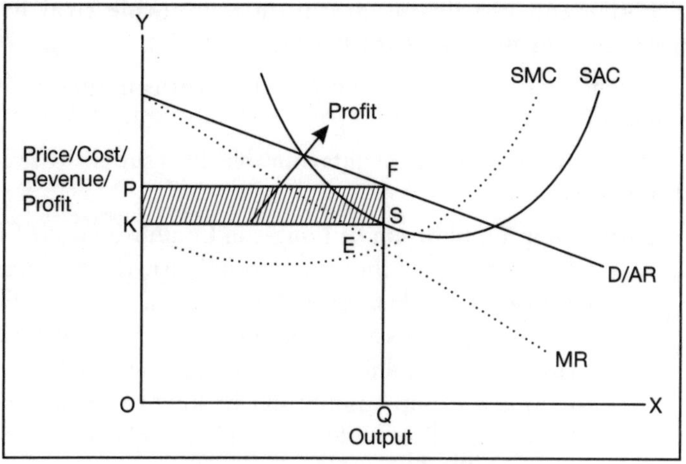

Diagram 8.2: Individual Equilibrium

Output is measured along OX axis and price, revenue, cost and profits are measured along OY axis. D/AR is demand/average revenue curve and SAC is short-run average cost curve. SMC is short-run marginal cost curve and MR is marginal revenue curve.

MC curve intersected MR curve at 'E' where both conditions of equilibrium are fulfilled. Thus the firm is in equilibrium at point 'E' and he determines OP (= FQ) price and OQ output.

AC and AR curves are used to measure size of profit at point of equilibrium FQ. Perpendicular cuts AC curve at S, thus average cost is SQ. Since the determined price is OP or FQ, the average revenue is FQ. Therefore the profits are calculated as:

Π = TR–TC > 0. Where Π = Profits

TR = Total Revenue = Price × output.

TC = Total Cost = AC × output.

By substituting the values in the equation

Π = OP (= FQ) × OQ (= PF) – SQ (= OK) × OQ (= KS)

= OPFQ × OKSQ

= PFSK area

The area PFSK is profit which is shown by shaded area.

In short-run whether the firm earns supernormal profit or normal profits or suffers loss depends upon demand condition and its price policy.

If demand conditions are more favourable firm earns supernormal profits, i.e. when P > AC.

If demand conditions are normal, firm earns normal profits, i.e. when P = AC.

If demand conditions are unfavourable, firm suffers losses, i.e. when P > AC.

(ii) **Group Equilibrium or Long-run Equilibrium:** Prof E H Chamberlin used the term 'Group' instead of 'Industry' because of the heterogeneity of firms. Since all firms are heterogeneous and interdependent, it is very difficult to explain the equilibrium of firms in long-run. However to explain group equilibrium or long-run equilibrium of the firms Prof. E.H. Chamberlin used two sets of assumptions. They are:

(a) **Uniformity Assumptions:** It is also called Heroic Assumptions. It is assumed that demand and cost conditions of all firms are alike.

(b) **Symmetry Assumptions:** It means, an individual action regarding price and output is small and negligible so it cannot be adjustment by others.

In long-run supply of output will be adjusted with demand conditions through free-entry or exit of the firms. If there is supernormal profits in short-run, the new firms enter the market and share away the abnormal profits. The supply of output increases through entry of new firm and reduces the long-run price.

In contrary, if there is loss in short-run, the marginal firms exit from the market in long-run thus supply of output declines and price rises.

The adjustment in supply of output through entry or exit of firms makes the firms to earn normal profits in long-run. The group equilibrium is illustrated in the diagram 8.3.

D/AR is demand/average revenue curve and MR is marginal revenue curve. LMC and LAC are long-run marginal and average cost curves. Point E is the equilibrium point where both the conditions of equilibrium are fulfilled and the determined output is OQ and price is OP. At the equilibrium, since price is equal to average cost (P = AC), the firm makes only normal profit. The diagram shows that the AR curve just touches the AC curve at F point. Thus in long-run under monopolistic competition every firm will earn only normal profit. Since all firms are producing on no-profit no loss condition (normal profit), there will be no tendency for neither the new firms enter nor existing firms exit the market. The group has come to equilibrium.

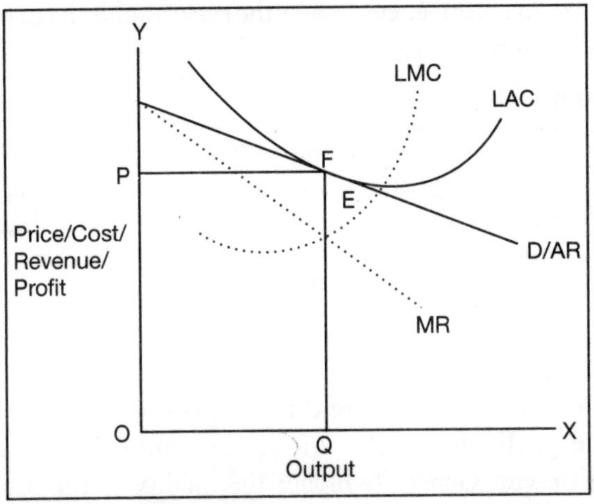

Diagram 8.3: Group Equilibrium

(B) Product Differentiation and Firm's Equilibrium: A very important feature of monopolistic competition is product variation or differentiation. Product differentiation is generally brought out in two ways: (i) through change in quality and (ii) through sales promotion.

Change in quality may refer either to the physical aspects of the commodity such as the material, workmanship, durability, shape; size, colour, smell, etc. or it may refer to differences in service associated with the sale such as pleasantness of the surroundings, the courtesy and consideration, shown by the personally attending to the customers, promptness of delivery and above all, convenience of the location of the shop. The purpose of quality variation is to adopt particular brand of a product as far as possible to the tastes and preference of consumers. This gives a firm monopoly power over the price of its brand by widening the gap between its product and the brands of other products.

The second method to bring about differentiation in products is through sales promotion. It brings out the describe-able qualities of a particular brand of product possesses, distinct from and superior to those of other brands of the same product. The purpose of sales promotion is to retain existing consumers and attract new consumers. Product differentiation is very common in the case of manufactured goods. But it is also found in case of food grains like wheat, rice, tea, coffee, etc. when they are sold in bags or packets with label or trademarks.

Equilibrium

Under monopolistic competition the quantity which a firm produces and sells depends upon three factors, viz. price, nature of the product and selling costs. Assuming price and selling cost are constant, under the product variation the equilibrium of firm in monopolistic competition can be studied as under:

A firm may accept a price generally prevalent or the one established by tradition. The firm has now the problem of finding out the exact variety or quality of product which will yield maximum profit. For each variety, cost and demand conditions will be different. Generally higher the quality of the product, the greater will be the average cost and larger will be the potential sales. The product variation and firm's equilibrium is illustrated in the following diagram 8.4.

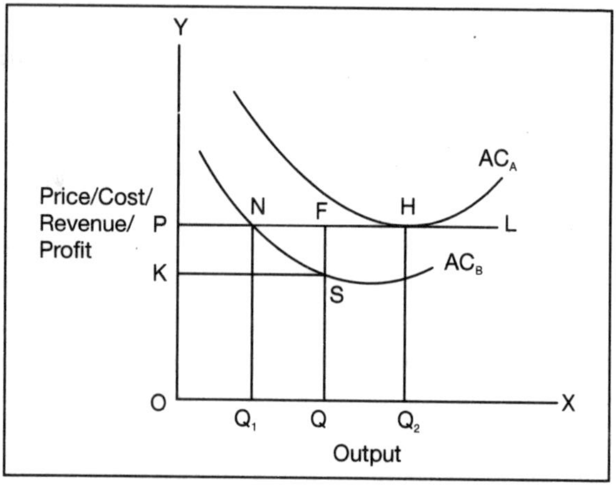

Diagram 8.4: Product Differentiation

Output is measured along OX axis and price, revenue, cost and profits are measured along OY axis. The firm prefers to produce two verities of product, viz. A and B.

A is improved variety than B. AC_A curve is average cost curve of A variety and ACB is average cost curve of B variety. The given price is OP and PL is the price line. Revenue curves are not drawn in order to avoid confusions.

At OP price, the firm determines to produce OQ level of output of B variety and to make profit of PFSK area. When the firm introduces the A variety product its average cost curve ACA tangents price line at 'H'. The total output increased to 'OQ_2', the output of B variety declined from OQ to OQ_1 and the output of A variety is 'Q_1Q_2'. Both varieties will get normal profits because $P = AC_A = AC_B$.

The change in price of the products definitely results into change in price of its substitute. The increase in demand for cheap substitute or improved variety of a product may reduce price and profits.

In short-run equilibrium or individual equilibrium, the firm with products variation is explained in above diagram. But the long-run equilibrium or group equilibrium with product variation is different from individual equilibrium.

In long-run, the new firms enter the group so the output of the old firms declines. The demand curve or average revenue curve will shift left. Thus all firms earn only normal profits.

(C) **Selling Cost and Firm's Equilibrium:** Under monopolistic competition, a firm has many variables to consider before it can attain equilibrium. The problem is extremely complicated because of many possible combinations. The problem before a firm is for which product (of many possible varieties) at which price, and at what selling costs can minimum profits be realized? The other two variable viz. price and variety of product are assumed to be constant the variation in selling cost is taken into account to explain firm's equilibrium in monopolistic competition. It is illustrated in the following diagram 8.5.

D/AR curve is demand/average revenue curve and MR is marginal revenue curve. AC is average cost curve before selling cost. AC_1 is average cost including selling cost (SC) i.e. $AC_1 = AC + SC$. The distance between AC and AC_1 is the size of selling cost. MC is marginal cost curve. Price, cost, revenue and profits are measured along 'OY' axis and output is measured along 'OX' axis.

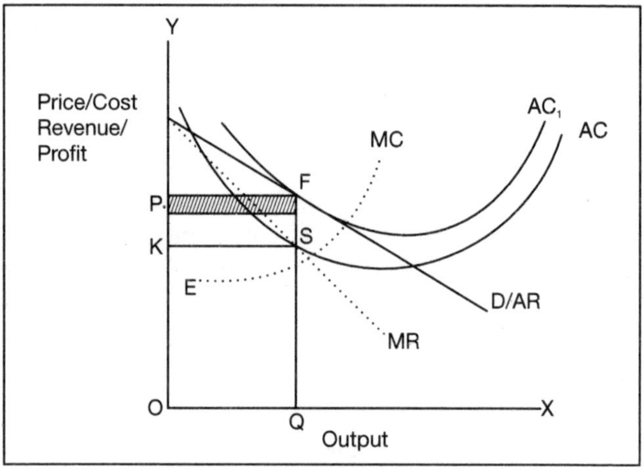

Diagram 8.5: Selling Cost and Firm's Equilibrium

The firm attained equilibrium at 'E' where the both conditions of equilibrium are fulfilled. Before selling cost, the firm determined to produce OQ level of output at OP price so he does get PFSK area of profit. After selling cost, the average cost increased to the extent of selling cost but price and output remain same thus his profit declines which is shown by shaded area.

The selling cost would bring more profits to the firm only when it raises the demand for the product, otherwise, the selling cost reduces the size of profits.

8.1.4 Selling Cost: Expenditure incurred by a firm on advertisement, sales promotion, etc. selling efforts of its product is known as selling costs. Thus, the selling costs include the items of expenses: (a) Advertising and publicity expenditure of all sorts. (b) Expenses of sales departments, such as commissions and salaries of sales manager, sales executives and other staff. (c) Margin granted to dealers in order to increase their efforts in favour of particular goods. (d) Expenses for window displays, demonstration of goods, free distribution of samples, etc.

Economists, however, define selling costs as "costs incurred in order to alter the location or shape of the demand curve or sales curve of a product". The effect of advertisement-expenses is to shift the demand curve for a given product to the right by making known to the perspective buyers its availability, by describing it, and by suggesting the uses it can be put to. In brief, the aim of any producer, who incurs advertising expenses, is to sell larger output at a given price than that he can sell in excess of these costs.

Under monopolistic competition, extensive advertising expenditure becomes essential to highlight the features of product differentiation of the firm's product from that of his rivals. Through a successful advertising campaign, the firm may establish the buyers' preference, patronage and brand legal for its product.

Sales promotion is based on two important factors: (i) imperfect knowledge on the part of the consumers and (ii) the possibility of changing their wants through advertising or selling appeal.

To Chamberlin, ignorance of products on the part of consumer is an important reason for advertisement. Buyers are ignorant of different sellers in a given line of product and the difference in the quality. They are also not aware of relative prices for similar goods. In this regard a seller may resort to "Informative advertisement", i.e., describing the quality and price of his product, their comparative prices, etc., and thereby try to influence the shape and location of the demand curve. By spreading information about the product through appropriate advertisement, sellers market may increase the demand and it leads to a shift in demand curve to the right basic demand curve. Indeed the demand curve will be higher when more people are informed about the product through advertising.

There can also be "manipulative advertisement" which affects the consumer demand by altering, the wants or preferences of the people.

When a product is constantly advertised, the buyers become familiar with the particular brand name or trade mark and goes in for it in preference to many other which are not advertised. Here advertisements have not given any information to buyers but have made the buyer familiar with a particular brand name.

Manipulative advertising generates demand for the product by its influence on consumer's psychology, by playing upon human weakness such as fear, flattery, demonstration effect, prestige, so that the consumers preferences is altered in favour of the advertised product.

Types of Selling Cost: There are two types of selling costs. They are:

(i) **Informative Selling Cost:** The expenses on selling efforts like product advertisement in news-paper, radio, TV etc that gives information regarding the price, quality, uses, etc of the product are called 'informative selling costs'. They are useful to the buyers and raise the demand for the product.

(ii) **Wasteful Selling Costs:** The selling costs that simply raise the price of the product or bring inflation in the country are called wasteful selling costs.

Illustration of Selling Cost: The selling cost is illustrated in the following diagram 8.6.

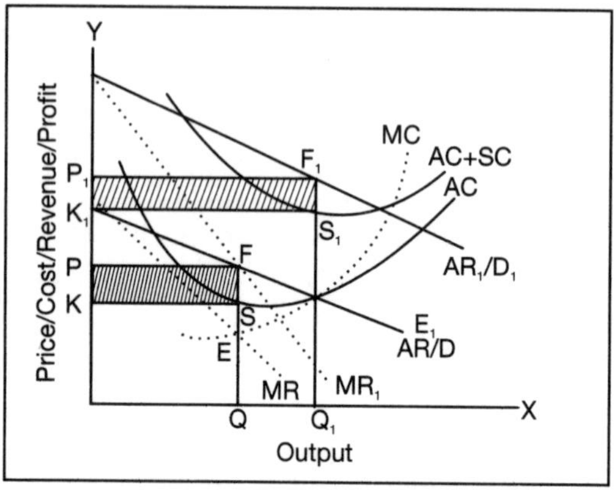

Diagram 8.6: Selling Cost

Price, cost, revenue and profits are measured along 'OY' axis and output is measured along 'OX' axis.

Before Selling Cost: AR/D is average revenue/demand curve; MC is marginal cost curve and AC is average cost curve. The equilibrium point is 'E' where the both conditions of equilibrium are fulfilled so the firm by selling 'OQ' output at 'OP' price gets 'PFSK' size profit which is shown by shaded area.

After Selling Cost: When cost incurs the average cost increased to the extent of selling cost so the average cost curve moved upward right i.e. 'AC + SC' curve. The distance between AC and AC + SC is the size of selling cost. As a result of selling cost the demand for the product increased so the demand/average revenue curve moved upwards right above the basic AR/D curve. The new equilibrium takes place at 'E_1' so the firm determined to sell OQ_1 size of output at OP_1 price to get '$P_1F_1S_1K_1$' size profit which is shown by shaded area.

After incurring of selling cost the size of output, price and profits are increased more than before.

8.1.5 Wastes of Monopolistic Competition or Criticisms: Monopolistic competitive market suffers from a number of wastes. So it is criticized as under:

(i) **Unemployment:** The firms of monopolistic competition put resources to under utilization. So it will result into unemployment of resources in the economy.

(ii) **Waste of Advertisement:** One of the important wastes of monopolistic competition is the expenditure on advertisement by firms. Expenditure on advertisement on media like the TV, the radio, the Cinema, the newspaper, etc. creates unnecessary product differentiation. As a result, irrational preferences for certain brands of products are created in the minds of the consumers which tend to push the sales of one firm at the cost of others. But all such expenditure is socially wasteful. Such selling costs result into inflation in the country which is not desired by the society.

(iii) **Too Many Varieties:** Another waste of competition is the production of varieties of product. This is done by creating artificial or imaginary differences so as to distinguish the goods of one seller from other. This is done by changing colour, design, packing, etc., of the same product by the same producer. This leads to wastage of resources and to loss of economic efficiency.

(iv) **Cross Transport:** The existence of Cross Transport is another waste of monopolistic competition. If firms want to cater the needs of the locality, transport expenditure must be minimized. For instance, cloth produced in Bangalore will be sold at Delhi and cloth produced in Delhi will be sold at Bangalore. Hence the cost of cloth will be increased unnecessarily due to transport cost.

(v) **Excess Capacity:** All the firms under monopolistic competition possess excess capacity. All firms work under less than optimum capacity and all charge higher than competitive price. In other words, they produce less quantity and charge high price. It is underutilization of resources and installed capacity. It is economic waste.

(vi) **Inefficient Firms:** A monopolistic competitive market accommodates many inefficient firms whose cost structure is high. The buyers' irrational preference and attachment to product differentiation make it possible for inefficient firms to survive by charging high prices to cover up the high costs. In the long-run in a perfectly competitive market inefficient firms are automatically driven out. But in monopolistic competition this does not happen.

8.2 OLIGOPOLY

8.2.1 Meaning and Definitions: Oligopoly is a term derived from two Greek words 'oligos' means few, and 'polien' means selling. Thus Oligopoly means few sellers. They produce either homogenous product or products which are close substitutes but not perfect substitutes. When the products of the few sellers are differentiate but close substitutes each other, such a situation is called oligopoly with product differentiation or differentiated oligopoly. The simplest form of oligopoly is duopoly where there are only two producers or sellers in the market.

Oligopoly is also known as 'limited competition', 'incomplete monopoly', 'multiple monopolies', etc. But the term oligopoly is used popularly now-a-days to refer to competition among the few. It is most realistic market situation and many economists believe that it is most prevalent market form, extensively prevails in capitalist economies.

Prof. Paul Samuelson defines oligopoly as "a situation of imperfect competition in which as industry is dominated by a small number of suppliers....the actions of one affect the actions of all other firms in the industry".

Prof Stiggler defines oligopoly as "situation in which a firm bases its market policy in part on the expected behaviour of a few close rivals".

The best examples of oligopoly in India are steel industry, automobiles, cement, petroleum, etc.

8.2.2 Types of Oligopoly: Oligopoly may take any of the following forms:

(a) Pure (homogenous) and differentiated oligopoly, (b) Open and closed oligopoly, (c) Collusive and competitive oligopoly, (d) Full and partial oligopoly, and (e) Syndicated and organized oligopoly.

(a) **Pure (homogenous) and Differentiated Oligopoly:** In Pure/homogenous oligopoly there is no product differentiation. For ex: cement, aluminum industry. But in a differentiated oligopoly there is product differentiation. The stronger the differentiation, the weaker will be the feeling of mutual dependence. For ex: talcum powder.

(b) **Open and Closed Oligopoly:** In open oligopoly the new firms can enter the market and compete with the existing firms. But in a closed oligopoly, new firms cannot enter the oligopoly market.

(c) **Collusive and Competitive Oligopoly:** In collusive oligopoly, the producers come together to fix a common price and output.

But in competitive oligopoly there is no such agreement among producers.

(d) **Full and Partial Oligopoly:** In full oligopoly, each producer fixes the price independently. In other words the market will be conspicuous by the absence of price leadership.

But in partial oligopoly, there is a price leadership. That is one of the dominant firms fixes the price and others follow the dominant producer with regard to price and output.

(e) **Syndicated and Organized Oligopoly:** In syndicated oligopoly the firms sell their product through a centralized syndicate. But in organized monopoly the firms organize themselves into a central association for fixing prices, output, quotas, etc.

8.2.3 Features of Oligopoly: The following are the main features of oligopoly:

(i) **Interdependence:** The most striking feature of an oligopoly is the interdependence in decision-making among the few firms. The price and output decisions of one will affect the other firms. As the number of firms is few, a change in price and output by a firm will directly affect the fortunes of its rivals who retaliate by changing their own price and output policies. Decision-making is closely connected with the price, output policies of other firms. Hence, in oligopolistic market, a firm cannot act independently in fixing the price. This interdependence between firms is a special feature of oligopoly.

(ii) **Group Behaviour:** The theory of oligopoly is a theory of group behaviour and not of mass or individual behaviour. The profit maximization assumption may not be very valid. All firms in an oligopoly market will be acting and reacting on the basis of behaviour of each other. However, there is no generally accepted theory of group behaviour. Do the firms agree to pull together to promote their common interest or will theory fight to promote their individual interest? Does the group possess any leader? If so, how does he get the others to follow him? These are some of the questions that need to be answered by the theory of group behaviour.

(iii) **Importance of Selling Cost:** Indeterminate demand leads to the condition of aggressive advertisement to bring more customers into the fold of the firm. A direct effect of interdependence and indeterminateness of demand of various firms lead to enormous selling cost incurred by the competing firms. To make the average revenue curve (Demand curve) decisive and also favourable, each firm will be employing various advertisement techniques and consequently the selling cost will be very high. The significance of advertisement and selling costs is so high is a differentiate oligopoly so Prof Boumal calls it a "life and death question" for firms. The success of a differentiated oligopoly is determined by its expenditure on advertisement and selling cost.

(iv) **Indeterminate Demand Curve:** Mutual interdependence of firms in an oligopoly market creates an element of uncertainty for all firms.

The demand curve of an oligopoly firm cannot be definite or determined because no firm can predict accurately the reactions of its rivals to its price and output policy. For ex: If a firm reduces the price of its product, it is not sure whether the other firms will retaliate by reducing the prices of their products. It is possible that the other firms may not reduce their prices. Or if they reduce their prices they may not reduce them to the same extent. As a result, the demand curve (AR curve) facing can oligopolistic firm loses its definiteness and determinateness since its changes depending upon rival action. Consequently, the general rule of profit maximization, namely, MR = MC cannot be applied to an oligopoly market without making certain assumptions.

(v) **Price Rigidity:** In an oligopoly market with product differentiation, there is price rigidity. This means the price will be kept unchanged. If any firm reduces its price, it will attract the customers from its rivals. But the rival firms retaliate by cutting down their prices. The result is a price-war between the firms but such a price war benefits none of them. Therefore, no firm desires to resort to price-cutting policy.

(vi) **Kinked Demand Curve:** According to Paul Sweezy, firms in oligopolistic market have a kinky demand curve for their products. It is illustrated in diagram 8.7.

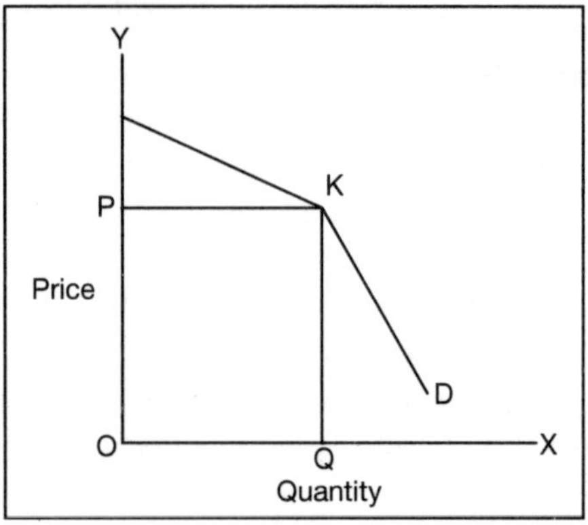

Diagram 8.7: Kinked Demand Curve

'D' is kind demand curve. 'K' is point of kink on demand curve. Oligopoly firm fixes up the price at 'K', i.e. OP Price. To left of 'K' any increase in price by firm, he loses the buyers or decline price below 'K', firm has to take price cut war.

8.3 DUOPOLY

The simplest case of oligopoly is duopoly. It prevails only when there are two producers or sellers of a product. The basic features of duopoly are same as the features of oligopoly.

Like oligopoly, there are two types of duopoly. They are:

(a) **Duopoly without Product Differentiation:** When both the producers produce same product, there must be agreement between them regarding fixation of price, size of production and sharing of market. Such agreement is possible only when both have identical cost and demand conditions; the demand must less price-elastic. If there is no agreement between them, it will lead to price-war; so nobody will get maximum profits.

(b) **Duopoly with Product Differentiation:** If there is product differentiation, the each producer will take independence decision regarding price and output. One who produces best quality product will get maximum profits.

8.4 MODEL QUESTIONS

2 Marks Questions

(a) State the meaning of Monopolistic Competition.

(b) Give any two features of Monopolistic Competition.

(c) What do you mean by 'Product Differentiation'?

(d) Name any two wastes of monopolistic competition.

(e) Define selling cost.

(f) Give the meaning of oligopoly.

(g) What do you mean by duopoly?

5 Marks Questions

(1) Write a note on features of monopolistic competition.

(2) Explain briefly selling cost.

(3) Write a note on product differentiation and firm's equilibrium.

(4) Write a note on oligopoly and its types.

(5) Discuss in brief the wastes of monopolistic competition.

10 Marks Questions

(1) Define monopolistic competition and explain its features.

(2) Define monopolistic competition and discuss price and output.

(3) Define oligopoly and explain its types and features.

9

Theories of Distribution

9.1 THEORY OF DISTRIBUTION

The theory of distribution refers to the distribution of national income among the various factors of production. It deals with the pricing of the productive resources. It determines the share of the owners of factors of production in the national income. The basic factors of production, namely land, labour, capital and organization by acting upon country's natural resources produce certain amount of goods and services. Sum of these goods and services is called the "National Income". Therefore the national income is the outcome of the joint effort of all the four factors of production; it must be distributed among them on the basis of certain principles. This aspect is studied in the theory of distribution. From the national income, land gets its reward in the form of rent, labourers reward in wages, capital gets interest and finally the reward of the entrepreneur is called profits. National income is distributed in the form of rent, wages, interest, and profit amongst the factors of production.

The distribution of National Income is analyzed in two ways: (a) Personal Distribution and (b) Functional Distribution.

9.1.1 Personal Distribution of Income: It refers to the study of individual incomes. It analyses how much is earned by individuals of the nation. But the difficulty is that we cannot explain individual incomes adequately as individuals earn their incomes from various sources. Suppose the income of a person is five hundred rupees per month. This income may be from many services rendered, in the form of interest from capital or form profit. It also depends on social and political structure system of ownership of property and the laws of inheritance. Personal distribution, therefore, is a technical concept.

9.1.2 Functional Distribution of Income: The functional distribution deals with the study of factor-incomes. It describes how much income is earned by each factor of production, namely land, labour, capital and organization. In other words, it studies the pricing of the factors of production in terms of functions performed by each factor. Therefore, it is also described as the study of the pricing of the productive resources. In brief, in functional distribution we are no longer concerned with individuals and their individual incomes, but with factors of production, labour, capital, land and something also that may, perhaps best be called 'entrepreneurial activity'. The theory examines how these factors of production are remunerated. It is primarily concerned with the price of a unit of labour, a unit of capital, a unit of land and being an extension of price theory, it is sometimes called the theory of 'factor-pricing'.

9.2 MARGINAL PRODUCTIVITY THEORY

The Marginal productivity theory is merely an extension of the marginal principle to the theory of distribution. This theory is very much helpful in explaining the determination of the income of the factors. The theory was developed by J. B. Clark, Wicksteed, Walras and Jevons during the end of 19th century.

The demand for the factors of production is derived demand. It is created by the producers. Factors are demanded because they help in the process of production. Hence factors are demanded depending on their productivity i.e. based on the contribution they make to the production process. Higher the productivity of a factor, greater will be its price.

9.2.1 Meaning and Definitions: According to J.B. Clark, "Under static conditions, every factor including the entrepreneur would get remuneration equal to its marginal product."

Prof. Mark Blaug defines "The marginal productivity theory contends that in equilibrium each productive agent will be rewarded in accordance with its marginal productivity." In other words, the theory states that every factor of production receives its price or reward just equal to its marginal productivity in production process.

9.2.2 Concepts of Productivity: In order to understand the theory, it is necessary to understand the various concepts of productivity:

(i) **Marginal Physical Productivity (MPP):** Marginal physical productivity refers to the addition made to the total physical product by employing one more unit of a factor, the quantity of other factors remaining constant. For instance, if five workers produce 20 feet of cloth and when six workers are employed they produce, say 25 feet. The addition made to the total production of cloth in (25 – 20 = 05) feet by the employment of one more worker (6 – 5 = 1) is known as marginal physical productivity. It can be calculated as:

$MPP = TPP_n - TPP_{n-1}$

Where MPP = Marginal Physical Productivity,

TPP = Total Physical Productivity and n, n-1 are units of a factor of production.

(ii) **Marginal Value Product (MVP):** The MVP is the monetary representation of marginal physical productivity. Hence the value of marginal physical productivity at market price of a factor is called Marginal Value Productivity. When we multiply price by MPP we get MVP i.e. MVP = MPP × Price.

In the above example, the 6th worker has produced 5 feet of cloth. If the price of cloth is ₹ 10 per feet, then MVP = 5 × 10 = ₹ 50.

(iii) **Marginal Revenue Productivity (MRP):** Marginal Revenue Productivity is the addition made to total revenue productivity (TRP) by employing an additional unit of a factor, quantity of other factors remaining constant. For example if 10 workers produce cloth worth ₹ 1000 and 11 workers make cloth worth ₹ 1100 then MRP of the 11th worker is ₹ 1100 – 1000 = ₹ 100

$\therefore MRP = TRP_n - TRP_{n-1}$

In other words, when the marginal physical productivity is multiplied by the market price of that product we get marginal revenue productivity i.e. MRP = MPP × Price.

(iv) **Average Revenue Productivity (ARP):** Average Revenue Productivity (ARP) is the average revenue per unit of a factor of production. If total revenue productivity is divided by total production, we get average revenue productivity i.e.

ARP = TRP/Q Q means total output.

9.2.3 Assumptions of the Theory: The classical economist assumed that the marginal productivity theory of distribution is based on the following assumptions:

(i) There prevails perfect competition both in the factor and the product market.

(ii) All the units of a factor are identical, uniform or homogeneous. In other words all the units of a factor are equally efficient.

(iii) The employer is interested in getting optimum profits. In other words the aim of every entrepreneur is to get maximum amount of profits. Therefore, he employs units of each factor up to a point at which the reward paid to a factor is equal to its marginal productivity.

(iv) There is existence of full employment in the economy. All the units of each factor of production are fully employed means there is no unemployment and under-employment of units of factor.

(v) Substitution of one factor for another is possible so that the production can be increased or decreased by changing the factor units by small quantities. This is necessary so that the marginal productivity can be found out by increasing or decreasing the quantities of the factor of production.

(vi) The factors of production are completely mobile as between different regions and employments. Therefore, the marginal productivity of a factor unit will be the same in all occupations and at all places. If the marginal productivity of a factor is higher in one occupation than in another, then it will move from the latter to the former occupation. So the marginal productivity remains the same in all occupations or in all places.

(vii) The theory is based on the law of diminishing marginal productivity.

(viii) The theory assumes a long-period to prove that the remuneration paid to a factor will be equal to both average and marginal productivity.

Only under these assumptions the marginal productivity theory holds good.

9.2.4 Explanation: The entrepreneur buys the services of the various factors of production. Since he works for profit, he can only pay a price for a factor, which he finds just worthwhile. Obviously he cannot afford to pay more than its marginal productivity. Since there is open competition, nobody will accept less than marginal productivity. That is how marginal productivity determines the remuneration or the price of a factor of production. Thus the theory states that the each factor of production involved in production process will be paid price or reward just equal to its marginal productivity.

At the margin of employment, the payment made to the factor concerned is just equal to the value of the addition made to the total production on account of the employment of the additional unit of a factor. If for instance, the prevailing wage is less than the marginal productivity, then more labour will be employed. Competition among employers will raise the wage to the level of marginal productivity. If on the other hand, the marginal productivity is less than the wage, the employers are losing and they will reduce their demand for labour. As a result, the wage will come down to the level of marginal productivity. In this way, by competition wage tends to equal the marginal productivity. This also applies to the other factors of production and their rewards. The entrepreneur, in employing the various factors production, acts on the principle of substitution. He substitutes one factor for another till the marginal productivities of all the factors he uses are equalized. Thus, he maximizes his profits. It is illustrated in the diagram 9.1.

The quantity of a factor of production is measured along 'OX' axis and 'OY' axis measures price of a factor. MP is the marginal productivity curve. It is the demand curve for a factor of production. At the price OP, the quantity of the factor employed is OM, because at this level of employment, marginal productivity equals price. If the employment is more than OM, the marginal productivity will be less than the price i.e. E′ M′ < EM. He will thus be a loser. Similarly if the employment is less than OM, the marginal productivity is more than the price i.e. E″ M″ > EM, and the employer can add to his profit by employing more, i.e. till at OM when marginal physical productivity equals price.

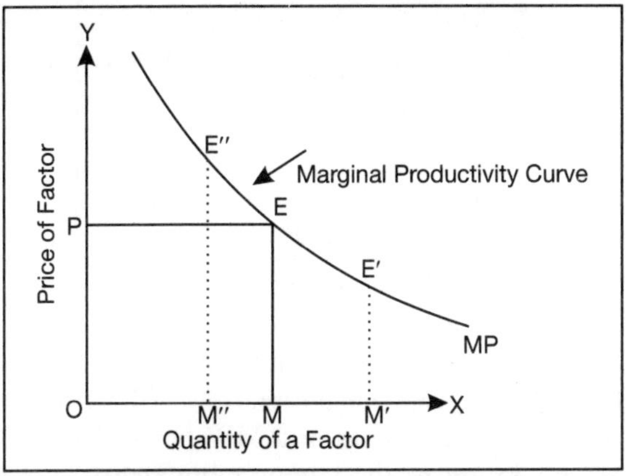

Diagram 9.1: Marginal Productivity Curve

Thus, under perfect competition, every entrepreneur employs and pays each factor according to the marginal productivity of each factor. He pays neither more nor less. He goes on employing more and more units of a factor until a point where payment made to the factor is equal to the value of the marginal productivity of that factor. Therefore under perfect competition, the price paid to each factor is equal to its marginal productivity. Further, the marginal productivity of each factor will be the same in all the employments and in all the places and the marginal productivities of all the factors will be proportional to their respective prices.

The reward or price paid to a factor unit should also be equal to the average revenue productivity. When reward given is more than the average revenue productivity, the firms will suffer losses. In case the reward is less than average revenue productivity, the firms will be getting profits. In the first instance, the firms will reduce the demand for the factor units whose average remuneration is higher than its average revenue productivity. As a result, the reward for such a factor will be reduced. In the second instance, new firms will be attracted to enter the industry. With the entry of new firms, the demand for the factor unit will increase resulting in the increased remuneration for that factor. The theory is shown in the following diagram 9.2.

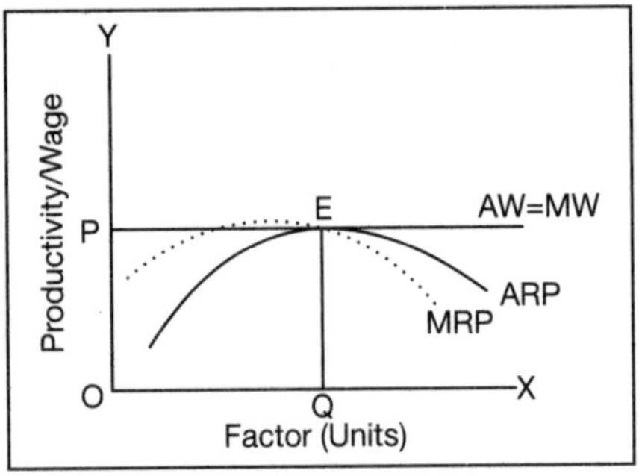

Diagram 9.2: Marginal Productivity Theory

In the diagram 9.2 labour is taken as a factor and its price is wage-rate. 'OX' axis measured units of labour and 'OY' axis measured productivity and wage-rate. AW = MW is price or wage line. AW means Average Wage and MW means Marginal Wage. Wage is remuneration to the labourer but cost to the producer so AW and MW are also considered as Average Cost (AC) and marginal Cost (MC) respectively. ARP is average revenue productivity curve. MRP is marginal revenue productivity curve. At point E, equilibrium is established in the long-run where the reward paid is equal to the marginal revenue productivity. Here the marginal wage is also equal to the average revenue productivity. Therefore the reward of the factor unit will be equal to the average and marginal product of that factor of production.

In brief, the price of a factor is determined at the point where MRP = MC.

9.2.5 Criticisms: The marginal productivity theory is an elegant piece of analysis, time honoured and built by contributions of many writers. But recently it has been under attack due to its unrealistic assumptions. The main criticisms against the theory are as under:

(i) **It is difficult to measure marginal revenue productivity of each factor:** The eminent economists Taussig and others maintained that every final product is the joint product of all the factors of production hence it is difficult to find out the separate production for of a factor. But this sort of a criticism can be easily avoided by defining the term marginal product in a more suitable fashion. Even though we cannot physically separate the product of a particular factor, we can measure a separate productivity of each factor by using the concept of marginal revenue productivity.

(ii) **The theory is based on unrealistic assumptions:** The critics have pointed out that the assumptions, on which the theory is based, do not hold well in the real world. Therefore, the theory has little importance. The assumption of perfect competition is unrealistic similarly; to assume all the factors are perfectly mobile is wrong. In reality, there are so many obstacles in the way of factor mobility like family attachment, language problem, etc. the assumption of perfect divisibility of the factors is also wrong. The entrepreneurs cannot be divided. The assumption of full employment is also criticised. Actually, almost every country of the world is faced with the problem of unemployment.

(iii) **Factors cannot be substituted freely:** Hobson criticized the theory on the ground that factors cannot be varied or substituted as the factors are always used in a certain fixed ratio. They cannot be changed freely. For instance, in a bus only one driver can be employed. This cannot be increased or decreased.

(iv) **It is difficult to measure marginal revenue productivity:** In reality, it is difficult, to measure MRP. As the theory explains, by changing the units of factor employed we can measure MRP. But actually we are unable to measure it. For example, in large-scale industry if the work of one labourer is decreased it does not induce any fall in total production. Therefore, according to theory, the marginal productivity of the factor will be zero and he will not be given any price for his services. But it is absurd; similarly the Marginal Revenue Productivity (MRP) of the entrepreneur cannot be estimated because quite often, there is a single entrepreneur in a firm.

(v) **The theory holds good only in the long period:** The theory does not throw any light on the short period determination of the price of a factor.

(vi) **The theory ignored that wage improves productivity:** The theory states that the reward of a factor is determined by its marginal productivity. Hence MRP is the cause and the reward is the effect. But Prof. Sydney Webb says the law is also applicable when it is reversed. When a labourer is given higher wages, his standard of living will increase, he will have good health and his productivity will increase. Hence reward is the cause for productivity and not its effect.

(vii) **The marginal productivity theory does not show how the reward is determined:** It only explains how much of the factor will be employed, given their prices. Hence, it does not determine the price of factors but determines only their demand.

(viii) **The theory ignored supply-side:** The theory is also criticized because it only explains the demand side of factors. The supply side is ignored. The law tells us that the demand for a factor is determined by its productivity. But it does not explain the factors affecting the supply of the factors.

(ix) **The theory ignores the powerful influence of selling costs:** Prof. Chamberlin criticized the theory on this ground the theory is neither theoretically complete nor practically helpful as it failed to take selling cost into consideration.

(x) **The marginal productivity theory neglects the problem of technical change:** It is a static theory. It ignored that technical changes cause shifts in production function. Marginal productivity theory assumes technology as given. Therefore it is not a complete theory.

Thus, in conclusion, the marginal productivity theory is not an adequate explanation of the determination of the pricing of factor services.

9.3 RENT

9.3.1 Meaning and Definitions: In the ordinary language, the term 'Rent' means a periodical payment made for the hiring of, say a plot of land, a house, a machine, a car, etc. It is a payment made for the use of a fixed factor of production. But in economics the term rent is used in a special sense. In economics rent means the reward or price paid to the land for its utilization or service in production of output. Therefore Ricardo defined rent as "Rent is that portion of the produce of earth which is paid to the landlord for the use of the 'original and indestructible power of soil'." But modern economists such as Mrs. Joan Robinson did not admit that the rent derived from land only so according to them rent is the surplus earnings of all the factors of production. Hence, Mrs. Joan Robinson defined rent as "The essence of the concept of rent is the conception of a surplus earned a particular part of a factor of production over and above the minimum earnings necessary to induce it to work."

In brief, under modern context rent means the surplus payment paid to a factor necessary to keep it in work and it is applicable to all the factors of production like land, labour, capital, etc.

9.3.2 Concepts of Rent: There are three concepts of rent namely:

(i) **Contractual Rent:** The total payment made by a tenant to the landlord is called contract rent. Therefore, contractual rent is different from economic rent. The contractual rent includes: (a) Interest which is payment for use of capital, (b) Wages which is a payment for the labour, engaged in the maintenance of accounts, collection of rent and management of the land, (c) Depreciation and repairs charges. It is also known as Layman's concept of contractual rent.

(ii) **Economic Rent:** Economic Rent is a payment for the use of land only. Ricardo and Marshall used the concept of economic rent as an income derived from the land, the free gift of nature. The payment made by an agriculturist to his landlord need not be equal to economic rent. A part of this payment may consist of interest on capital invested in the land by the landlord in the form of buildings, fences, drainage, well, etc. The part of the payment, which is made for the use of land only, is called economic rent.

But modern economists generally call for hiring of land as 'Land Rent' and surplus over and above its transfer earnings as 'Economic Rent'. What is true of land is also true of other factors. The modern economists hold that rent is not peculiar to land alone but it can arise even in the case of other factors namely labour, capital and organization. Economic rent can arise when the supply of any factor is less than perfectly inelastic. In the words of Marshall "The rent of the land is not a thing by itself, but the leading species of a large genus."

According to modern economists, not only land can earn a surplus but other factors can also earn a surplus income. Whenever any factor of production receives an income over and above what is necessary to induce it to remain in its present occupation, a surplus or extra earnings arises. This surplus or extra income is called economic rent.

Professor Kenneth Boulding defines "Economic rent is any payment to a unit of a factor of production, in any industry in equilibrium, which is in excess of a factor of production, in any industry in equilibrium, which is in excess of the minimum amount necessary to keep that factor in its present occupation."

Let us take few examples to understand the meaning of economic rent. If a worker is ready to work for ₹ 5000 per month but if he gets ₹ 7000 per month, the extra amount of ₹ 2000 is economic rent. According to Mrs. Joan Robinson, the root cause for the emergence of economic rent is the scarcity of the factor of production. It means that the transfer earning of a factor unit is determined by the elasticity of supply. If the elasticity of supply is zero, that is supply of a factor of production is perfectly in elastic, the transfer earnings will be zero. This will be so because the factor of production cannot be transferred to any other use. The same amount of factor units are supplied irrespective of its price, in this case the minimum supply price is zero. It is shown in the following diagram 9.3.

Demand for and supply of a factor is measured along OX axis and price of a factor is measured along OY axis. Demand curve 'D' indicates demand for a factor. The supply is perfectly inelastic as shown by a vertical line SQ parallel to OY-axis. The total earnings are shown by shaded area OPEQ. Transfer earnings being zero, all earnings indicate economic rent. Economic rent is thus a surplus remaining with the farmer after he has paid all the expenses of cultivation and has remunerated himself for his own labour. In this sense, it is the excess of the crop value over the expenses. Therefore, economic rent is a surplus income earned by the owners of the land and other free gift of nature.

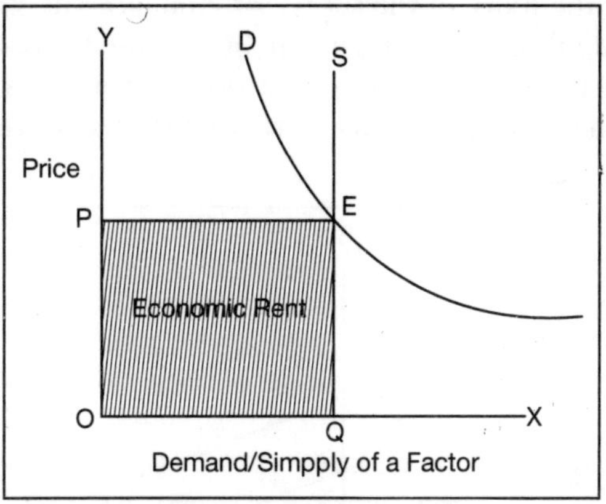

Diagram 9.3: Economic Rent

Thus according to modern economists, economic rent means any surplus or excess earnings over the transfer earning. This sort of surplus is not peculiar to land alone but it may be found even in other factors of production.

(iii) **Scarcity Rent:** According to Ricardo, rent is a differential surplus. It arises on account of differential fertility of different grades of land. Ricardo did not explain scarcity rent which arises due to scarcity of land in relation to its demand. When the population is increasing and consequently the demand for land, even the least fertile land called as no-rent land or marginal land by Ricardo would yield rent. The rent arises because of scarcity and hence this is called scarcity rent. It is a price paid for the use of land when it is scarce in relation to the demand for it. In the words of Marshall, "In a sense all rents are scarcity rents, and all rents are differential rents."

The scarcity theory of rent enunciated by Malthus assumes that all land is homogeneous and specific. But they are scare. The scarcity rent arises due to inflexible or rigid supply of land. The supply of land is slightly different from the supply of other factors of production. In other factors a rise in price would cause an increase in their supply, at least in the long period. But in the case of land an increase in price (i.e. rent) cannot bring about any increase in the supply of land at all as the supply of land is already fixed. It is because of the fixity of the supply of land, scarcity rent emerges. Since the supply of other factors can be increased in response to the increase in prices, the scarcity rent does not arise as in the case of land. The concept scarcity rent is illustrated in the following diagram 9.4.

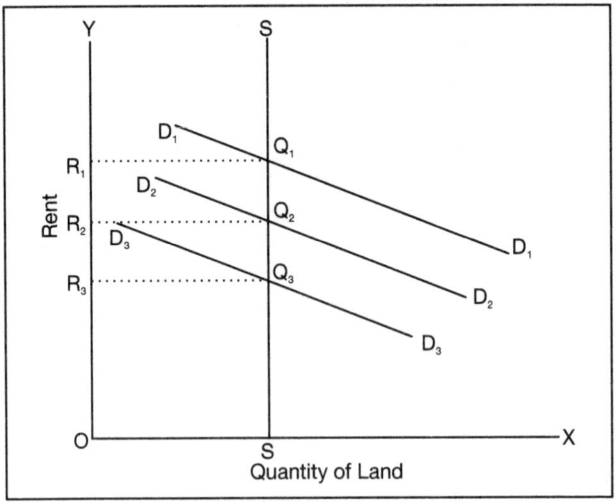

Diagram 9.4: Scarcity Rent

The supply of land is assumed to be fixed so it is shown by SS line and D_1, D_2 and D_3 are demand for land curves. D_2D_2 curve cuts the supply curve at Q_2 so, assuming perfect competition, the rent is OR_2. When the demand increases to D_1D_1 the rent is increases to OR_1 and when demand decreases to D_3D_3 rent decreases to OR_3. Thus rent arises due to increase in demand and scarcity of land.

However, the other factors may be fixed even in the long period. In such cases, scarcity rent may also arise to such factors. Therefore, scarcity rent arises not only in the case of land, but also in the case of talented and skilled labour like film-stars, technicians, etc.

(iv) **Quasi-Rent:** The concept of 'Quasi-Rent' was introduced and popularized by Alfred Marshall. It is an extension of Ricardian concept of rent. According to Marshall, Quasi-rent refers to short-run earnings of capital equipment, such as machinery, building, plant, etc. which are inelastic in supply in short period.

Ricardo said that land is fixed in its supply. Alfred Marshall opined that man-made factors are also fixed in supply in the short period. So their inelastic supply in the short-run earns rent which he named as 'Quasi-Rent'. The supply of land remains constant in the short period as well as in the long period. So it always earns rent. Thus, the rent earned by land is permanent. Since the supply of man-made appliances like machines and certain types of labour which are fixed in the short period and changeable in the long-run, they earn rent only in the short period. Marshall called it 'Quasi-rent'.

Silverman defines, "Additional payment of those agents of production the supply of which, though alterable in the long period but is fixed in the short period, is technically known as Quasi-rent."

The Quasi-rent of Marshall can be illustrated in many ways. During the World War II, there was a sudden increase in the demand for shipping and the supply of ships, as we know, could not be increased over-night. Since there was acute shortage of shipping in the wartime, the freight charges went up. Not only the existing ships earned enormous income, but also old and discarded ships, which were pressed into services, earned abnormal freight. Thus the ships earned a surplus over their normal income. The additional income was due to shortage of supply of ships and the surplus earnings were only a short period phenomenon. In the long-run, new ships were constructed and shipping charges came down. Hence the Quasi-rent earned by the ships in the initial period of the war, disappeared altogether.

In short-run production is possible when a fixed factor is combined with some variable factors. Therefore quasi-rent is defined as "the excess of total revenue in short-run over and above the total variable cost". So it can be calculated as:

Quasi-Rent (QR) = Total Revenue (TR) – Total Variable Cost (TVC)

The concept of Quasi-rent is illustrated in the following diagram 9.5.

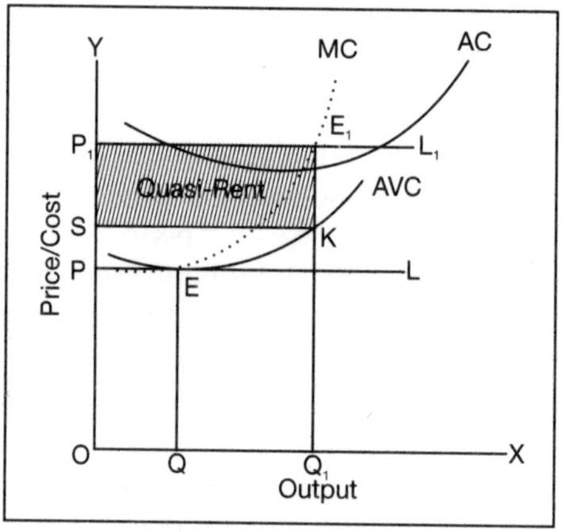

Diagram 9.5: Quasi-Rent

Output is measured along OX axis; price and cost are along OY-axis; AC is average cost curve and AVC is average variable cost curve. When demand is PL and price is OP, the quantity produced is OQ; the price is equal to AVC at equilibrium point E. As demand for output increased to P_1L_1, the price increased to OP_1; equilibrium moved to E1 and the firm increased production to OQ_1. E_1Q_1 vertical line intersected AVC at K so the area P_1E_1KS, shaded area, is quasi-rent.

Similarities and Differences between Rent and Quasi-rent: The followings are the main similarities and differences between rent and quasi-rent:

(A) Similarities: The similarities between Quasi-rent and the rent are:

(i) Ricardian rent and Quasi-rent both are surplus or excess earnings.

(ii) Ricardian rent and Quasi-rent arise due to rise in demand for land and man-made factors or products.

(iii) Ricardian rent and Quasi-rent are also similar because both accrue due to the fixed or inelastic supply of factors.

(iv) Ricardian rent and Quasi-rent both are measured by the difference between the actual earning and transfer earnings of a factor.

(B) Differences: The differences between Quasi-rent and the Ricardian rent are:

(i) According to Ricardo, rent is the peculiarity of land alone. According to modern economists, rent is earned by other factors as well Quasi-rent is basically related to the surplus earnings of capital. It can, however, be applied to other, special categories of factors, as well. Thus, Quasi-rents are ubiquitous.

(ii) Economic rent is earned by a factor when its supply is less than perfectly elastic irrespective of time-period. But Quasi-rent is earned by a factor when its supply is inelastic only in the short-run.

(iii) Ricardian concept of rent is differential surplus of super-marginal land over marginal land, which is demand-determined. Marshall's concept of Quasi-rent is a differential surplus, by way of extra income over the normal earnings through use of man-made appliances in the short period.

(iv) Ricardian rent is natural, real and permanent. Marshallian Quasi-rent is artificial and temporary.

(v) Economic rent is payment made to a factor to induce it to remain in a particular industry. Quasi-rent is not meant for such inducement.

(vi) Ricardian rent is the result of differential fertility, Quasi-rent is the result of relative short-term scarcity of a factor in relation to its demand.

(vii) Rent is never zero. But Quasi-rent becomes zero when price is equal to average variable costs.

9.3.3 The Ricardian Theory of Rent:

(i) **Statement and Explanation:** David Ricardo was a brilliant 19th century economist of England. He propounded a systematic theory of rent. It is in many ways the basis of the modern concept of rent. But his

> ideas on rent have a distinct place in economic theory. His views are known as the 'Ricardian Theory of Rent'. Ricardo said that rent is a 'Surplus' which accrues to the owners of land by reason of relative merits of fertility or situation or both which a particular grade of land enjoys over 'less-productive' land.

According to Ricardo "Rent is that portion of the produce of the earth which is paid to the landlord for the use of the original and indestructible powers of the soil". Hence, rent is the price for use of land. It is paid to the owner of the land. Land gets rent for its natural non-perishable powers. The theory says that rent can arise due to two important reasons namely: (a) Differences in the productivity of various grades of land, and (b) Situational difference.

David Ricardo considered rent as a surplus which arises due to the differences in fertility of grades of land and situation. He took the assumption of 'Marginal land', for explaining the origin of rent. Marginal land is also termed as 'No rent land'. The land which is just covering costs of production is called 'No-Rent Land'.

There are two techniques or methods of farming, i.e. (i) Intensive cultivation and (ii) Extensive cultivation. Rent arises in both the techniques of cultivation. It can be explained as follows:

(A) **Rent under Extensive Cultivation:** Extensive cultivation is the type of farming under which production is increased by using more and more strips of land. Ricardo was able to explain the emergence of rent under extensive cultivation.

David Ricardo took the case of an island where people go to settle. It is believed that no one is living before on this island. The land is surplus in relation to the number of people who want to settle there. Since land is a free gift of nature, nothing has to be paid for its use. We suppose that there are four 'grades' of land i.e. A, B, C and D which have been used in the diminishing order of their fertility. It means that 'A' grade land is the most productive than 'B', 'C' and 'D' the least.

According to theory the people cultivate 'A' grade land to meet their demand of food. 'A' grade land produces 25 quintals of food grains. When the demand for food grains increases, say due to increasing population, the whole of land of grade A will be utilized for farming. In order to meet the rising demand, people use cultivation of B grade land which yields them 20 quintals of food grains. A grade land gets a surplus, i.e. Rent which is equal to the fertility difference (25 – 20 = 5 quintals). 'A' grade land is called 'Intra Marginal Land' and 'B' grade land is called 'Marginal Land'. The difference of produce between the marginal and intra-marginal land is called rent. Now if the demand for food grains increases further, the people will start cultivating the C grade land also. Suppose it produces 15 quintals because it is less fertile than grade A and B lands. Now C grade land is the marginal land, A and B grade lands are intra-marginal lands. A and B grade lands will earn rent equal to the difference between the output on C grade land and the output on these lands. Later 'D' grade land will also be brought under cultivation to meet further rise in demand for food grains; say, 'D' grade land gives 10 quintals of output. Since it is the last to be cultivated, it will be called 'Marginal land' and A, B and C grades of land will be the 'Intra-marginal lands'. These will be entitled to earn rent which is a surplus production over and above the production of the marginal land D. The process discussed above is shown in the following table 9.1.

Table 9.1: Ricardian Theory of Rent

Grade of Land	Production(Quintals)	Surplus (Quintals)
A	25	25-10= 15
B	20	20-10= 10
C	15	15-10= 05
D	10	10-10= 00

Table 9.1 shows that A, B and C lands earn rent of 15, 10, and 05 quintals of produce respectively. The D. grade land earns no rent. It is called Marginal land. The rent earned by A, B and C grades of land are the surplus, which they produce in relation to D grade land.

The same idea can be illustrated in the following diagram 4.6. The amount of rent earned by A, B and C grades of land are shown by the shaded areas. D grade land just covers its costs or is the marginal land. Therefore it is 'No-Rent' land. Hence rent under extensive cultivation is a surplus between the production of the marginal and the intra-marginal lands.

(B) **Rent Under Intensive Cultivation:** Under intensive cultivation, on the same grade or piece of land, more units of labour

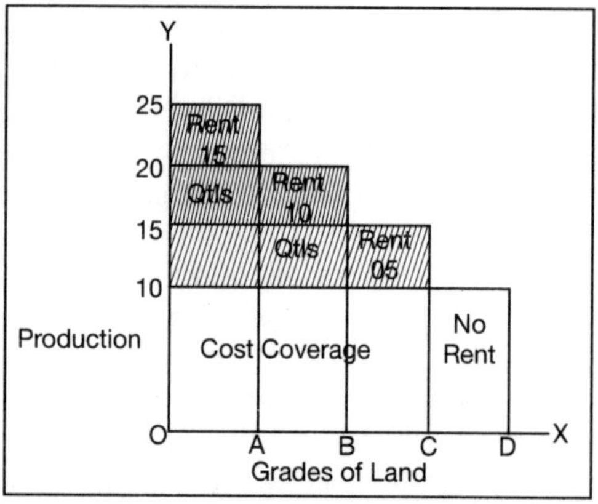

Diagram 9.6: Ricardian Theory of Rent

and capital are employed to increase production. It is necessary to note that Ricardo used the assumption of the operation of the law of 'diminishing returns' on agriculture. It means that production increases at a diminishing rate when more and more units of labour and capital are employed on the given grades of land. Hence marginal product will go on diminishing. We suppose that four units of labour and capital i.e. 1st, 2nd, 3rd and 4th are put to use and they produce 25, 20, 15 and 10 quintals of output respectively. When the 1st unit of labour and capital is used it makes an addition of 25 quintals to total production. By using 2nd, 3rd and 4th units, additions to total production of 20, 15 and 10 quintals are made respectively. As the 4th unit of labour and capital is the last to be used, it is known as the marginal unit of labour and capital. It is also called as 'No Rent Unit'. The other units i.e. 1st, 2nd, 3rd are producing more compared to the marginal units. They earn rent and are called the Intra-Marginal units. Their rent is equal to the difference between their production and that of the last unit i.e. the 4th. It can be explained in the following table 9.2.

Table 9.2: Ricardian Theory of Rent

Labour and Capital (Units)	Production (Quintals)	Surplus (Quintals)
1st	25	25 – 10 = 15
2nd	20	20 – 10 = 10
3rd	15	15 – 10 = 05
4th	10	10 – 10 = 00

Table 9.2 explains that 1st, 2nd and 3rd units of labour and capital earn rent, not due to the differences of the fertility of land, but due to diminishing returns, to variable factors on the same piece of land. This is due to the operation of the law of diminishing returns.

Thus, according to Ricardo, rent is a surplus which the intra-marginal lands and units of labour and capital earn over the above the production of marginal units of labour and capital or marginal lands.

(ii) **Assumptions:** Ricardian theory of rent is based on the following assumptions:

(a) The supply of land is fixed.

(b) The fertility differs from land to land so the land is classified in different grades like A, B, C, and so on.

(c) People use first more fertile land for cultivation and move to lesser and lesser fertile lands as the demand for food grains increase.

(d) More fertile land always gets rent over less fertile land. Thus the differential surplus is rent.

(e) The productivity of land is governed by law of diminishing returns.

(f) Rent is not included in price of output.

(g) The powers or qualities of land are original and non-perishable.

(h) There is existence of perfect competition.

(iii) **Criticisms:** The Ricardian theory of rent has faced criticism for its assumptions and implications.

(a) **The assumption of the original and indestructible powers of the soil is unrealistic:** Ricardian theory is based on the assumption that the powers or qualities of land are original and non-perishable but it is completely absurd in the modern age. The fertility of land can be improved through human efforts like by using adequate and proper manures, fertilizers, by rotation of crops and so many other technical measures. Therefore powers of land are not original, they are the result of human efforts, similarly, the idea that the powers of land never diminish is also not correct. In fact, when we use a piece of land again and again its fertility diminishes.

(b) **Ricardo's order selection of land on basis of fertility is not true:** Historical facts do not always testify to the assumption of David Ricardo that the best land is cultivated first. People usually select the land which is near and convenient to them. However, the defenders of Ricardo pointed out that the order of cultivation is not the critical part of the theory; it is used only for the illustration of the differential nature of rent. The reverse order of cultivation does not disprove Ricardo's theory.

(c) **The assumption of perfect competition is unrealistic:** Ricardo assumed the prevalence of perfect competition. But it never exists in the real world. Since there is imperfect competition for land, the rent charged by the landowners is more than the economic rent.

(d) **The concept of 'no-rent land' is wrong:** Ricardian theory is also criticized on the ground that it assumed the existence of 'no-rent land'. But, in actual world no land, even the barren piece of land, is available without rent. It is because, firstly, demand for land is much more than its supply; secondly, land has several other uses than farming.

(e) **Ricardo used narrow concept of rent:** Modern economists criticized this narrow concept of rent. According to them rent is not the income of land only but also the earnings of other factors of production.

(f) **'Rent does not enter into price' is wrong:** Modern economist disagree with Ricardo's statement that rent does not enter into price. Ricardo wrongly argued that rent is not a component of the cost of production. In the modern view, rent determines price. Land is a factor of production. So its price, i.e. rent, becomes a part of the cost of production. Thus, when price is based on the cost of production, rent does affect price. From society's point of view land may be a free gift of nature, but to an individual farmer, it is certainly not a free gift. So, when price for land i.e. rent, is paid, it cannot be price determined but it is price-determining.

(g) **The law of diminishing returns is not a perennial feature of farm production:** The law of diminishing returns is a basic postulate of Ricardian theory. Technical progress and organizational improvements have tended to offset the operation of the law in England and Europe and improved farm productivity tremendously. Green revolution in India has enhanced productivity of food grains in a significant way. Hence, the law of diminishing returns can be held in abeyance, at least postponed.

(h) **Ricardo ignored that scarcity of land is also cause for rent:** Ricardo believed that rent a differential surplus. But he ignored that rent arises not only due to the fertility and situational differences but also due to the scarcity of land. Actually, rent arises because the demand for land is much more than its supply.

However, from the time of David Ricardo, economists have attempted to devise measures by which the unearned increment to the value of land and land rent might be appropriated by the government for the benefit of the community. No wonder that socialists regard the Ricardian theory of rent as "the very corner-stone of collectivist economy".

9.3.4 Modern Theory of Rent: Modern economists like Marshall, Mrs. Joan Robinson and Boulding have contributed to the development of 'Modern Theory of Rent'. The theory also carries the threads of the ideas already given by Ricardo. In other words, modern theory of rent is an improvement or modification over the Ricardian theory of rent.

Modern economic analysis takes the Marshallian framework a step forward. Like the remuneration of the other factors of production, rent is also determined by the equilibrium between demand and supply forces. Even if all lands are equally fertile and equally favourably situated, rent would still arise on account of its scarcity.

(i) **Statement of the Theory:** Ricardian theory explains that the more fertile lands produce more than the cost of cultivation and hence they get a surplus called 'rent'. But 'How is rent determined?' question was not answered by Ricardo. Modern economists have developed 'a demand and supply theory' to answer the question. Therefore modern economists are of the opinion that like the prices of products and other factors, rent is also determined by the forces of demand and supply. The theory explains that rent does not arise due to fertility differences of land alone but due to more demand in relation to the supply of all factors. The more the scarcity of land and the other factors, the higher will be the size of rent earned. Hence the forces of demand and supply together determine rent.

(ii) **Explanation of Theory:** Modern theory of rent states that the equilibrium between demand for and supply of land determines rent. It can be explained in detail as under:

(a) **Demand-Side:** The demand for land is indirect or derived. In fact, land is demanded as it produces something. The higher the demand for the goods produces on land, the demand for land will also go up and therefore the rent of land will be higher. Marginal productivity of land determines the demand for it. As we go on investing more and more on the same land, its marginal productivity goes on declining. So land will be demanded only up to that point where marginal productivity of land equals its cost of cultivation. We can also say that more land will be demanded at lower rent. Hence the demand curve for land slopes downward from left to right.

(b) **Supply-Side:** The supply of land cannot be altered for the community as a whole. Increased rent cannot increase its supply. Nor the fall in its price can decrease its supply. It is gift of the God. We know that land has alternative uses i.e. it can be used in several ways. So far a particular individual or firm or industry, the supply of land can be changed i.e. supply is elastic. Any individual can get more land by bidding up its price. Hence, the supply curves of land for an individual firm or industry in having an 'upward slope'.

Rent is determined at the point where demand for and supply of land curves intersect each other. It is shown in the diagram 9.7 given below:

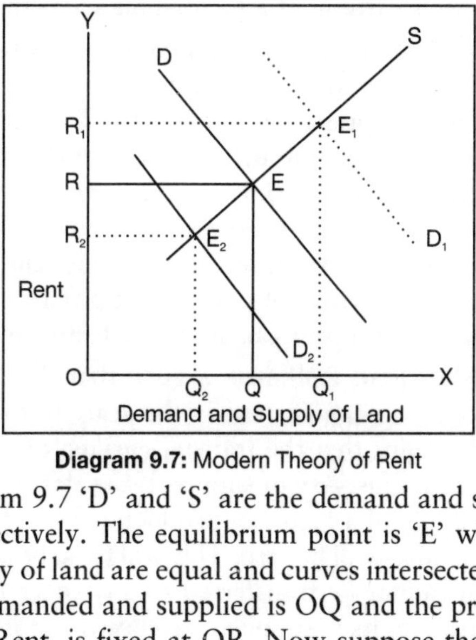

Diagram 9.7: Modern Theory of Rent

In diagram 9.7 'D' and 'S' are the demand and supply curves of land respectively. The equilibrium point is 'E' where demand for and supply of land are equal and curves intersected each other. Here land demanded and supplied is OQ and the price of the use of land, i.e. Rent, is fixed at OR. Now suppose the demand for land increases and its price also goes upward to OR_1 because the higher demand curve D_1 cuts the supply curve at point E_1. On contrary, a fall in demand as shown by D_2 leads to fall in rent to the level OR_2.

Like Ricardo, modern theory is also applicable when lands differ in fertility. Rent of land depends on fertility also. The price of more fertile and better situated land will be higher than those of the others. The equilibrium rent of such lands will also be higher than those of the less fertile and relatively less favourably situated lands.

(C) **Transfer Earnings:** The modern theory of rent has been systematically developed by Mrs. Joan Robinson. She contends that rent is a surplus earned over and above the minimum earnings necessary to induce a factor unit to work. The minimum payment which is necessary to make a factor unit to work is known as 'Transfer Earnings'. Transfer earnings, in other words, is what the factor of production can earn in its next best alternative occupation. When this minimum payment is not made to a factor-unit, it will leave the existing job and transfer itself to another alternative employment. In case payment made to a factor-unit is over and above the transfer earning of a factor-unit arises rent.

Thus, according to Mrs. Joan Robinson, rent is a surplus earned by the factor-unit over and above its transfer earnings. Suppose a software engineer is prepared to work for ₹ 40,000 per month, but he actually gets ₹ 60,000 per month. In this case, the transfer earning of a factor-unit is ₹ 40,000 and actual earning is ₹ 60,000. The factor-unit is earning an excess or surplus of ₹ 20,000 and, therefore, this amount is regarded as economic rent. In the words, according to the modern theory, rent is the difference between the actual earnings and transfer earnings of a factor-unit.

Further Mrs. Joan Robinson argued that the root cause for the emergence of economic rent is the scarcity of the factor of production. It means that the transfer earning of a factor-unit is determined by the elasticity of supply. If the elasticity of supply is zero, that is supply of a factor of production is perfectly inelastic, the transfer earnings will be zero. This will be so because the factor of production cannot be transferred to any other use. The same amount of factor-units is supplied irrespective of its price; in this case the minimum supply price is zero. This may be shown with the help of following diagram 9.8.

In above diagram 9.8, demand for a factor is shown by a downward sloping demand curve 'D'. The employer demands more of factor-unit only at lower price. The supply is perfectly inelastic so it is shown by 'SQ' vertical-line. Both demand and supply curves are intersected at 'E' so the determined price is 'OP'. Since the supply of a factor remains same at zero-price, the transfer earnings is zero so all earnings indicate economic rent. Hence, in this case, the entire earning is in the form of rent which is shown by shaded area i.e. OPEQ.

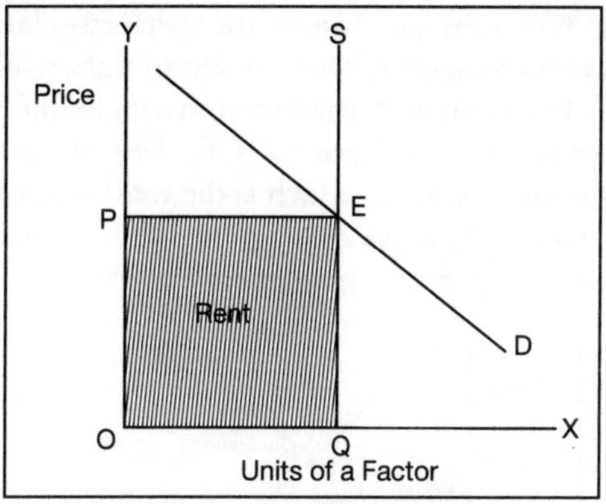

Diagram 9.8: Perfectly Inelastic Supply

But, in contrary, when the supply is perfectly elastic, the factor of production earns no rent. Its entire earning is transfer earning. It is shown in the following diagram 9.9.

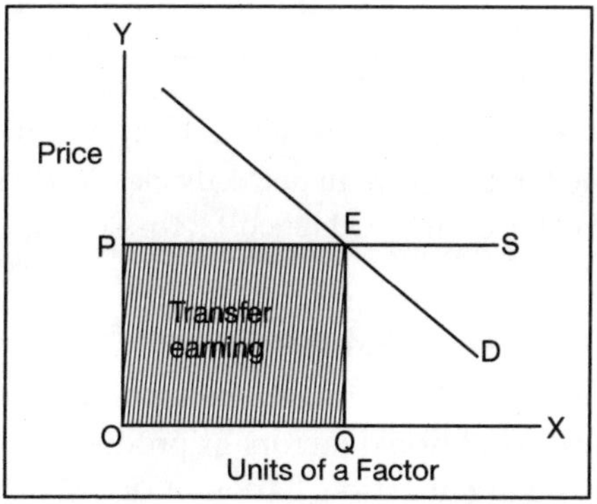

Diagram 9.9: Perfectly Elastic Supply

In the diagram 9.9, the supply curve is shown by 'PS' horizontal-line which indicates perfectly elastic supply. It means any amount of factor-units can be had at the same price. Since supply is perfectly elastic, the entire earning becomes transfer earning of the factor of production. The actual earning is shown by OPEQ. Transfer earning is equal to actual earning. In this case, there is no surplus or economic rent.

But, if the supply of a factor is relatively elastic or less than perfectly elastic, the income of a factor of production will contain, both transfer earning and rent. This is shown in the following diagram 9.10. When the supply is neither perfectly elastic nor zero elastic, its curve is rising upwards from left to right which is shown by 'KS' curve. The demand for factor is shown by 'D' curve. 'E' is the equilibrium point and the price is 'OP'. Thus the total or actual earning of a factor is 'OPEQ' which is the total sum of rent 'KPE' plus transfer earning 'OKEQ'.

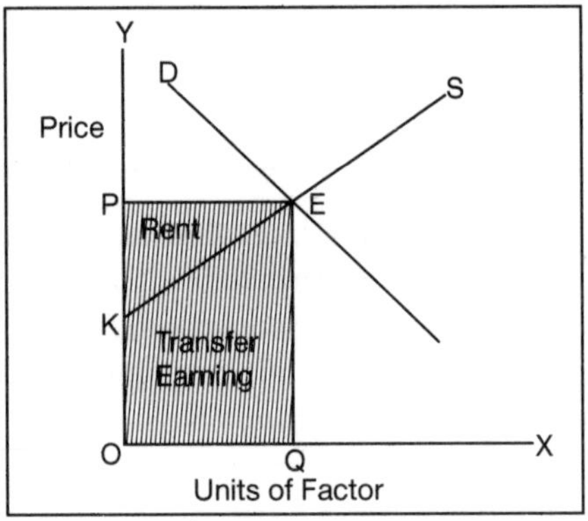

Diagram 9.10: More Elastic Supply

In brief, modern economists pointed out that if the supply of factors including land is less than perfectly elastic, they earn surplus above their transfer earnings. Hence factors other than land can also earn rent.

9.4 WAGES

9.4.1 Meaning and Definitions: Production is the result of the efforts of the four traditional factors of production, namely land, labour, capital and organization. Labour is one of them. Generally, by labour we mean physical or mental work such as the services of a coolie, an ordinary worker working in a factory, etc.

Wages are the remuneration or reward paid to labour for its productive services. Since the term labour refers to various kinds of workers like physical, mental, skilled and unskilled, or blue collar and white collar, educated and uneducated workers, etc. the term wage in economics also has a broad meaning. It includes pay, salary, fees, allowance, commission, emoluments, bonus, etc. all kind of income earned by labour as a factor of production. In fact, wages can be regarded as the price or reward per unit of time for the productive efforts of labour. So, the rewards given to workers, whether mental or physical are termed as wages in economics.

The term 'wage' has been defined by economists in various ways from time to time. Some definitions of wage are given as under:

(i) **Prof. Benham:** Prof. Benham defined wage as "A wage may be defined as a sum of money paid under contract by an employer to a worker for services rendered."

(ii) **Prof. J.L. Hanson:** Prof. Hanson defined wage as "wage is a payment to a labourer for its assistance to production".

In brief, wage is a payment made by the employer to labour as reward for its service in production process.

9.4.2 Concepts of Wages: There are various concepts of wage often used in economic literature and theories. They are as under:

(i) **Kind Wages:** The wage paid to the workers for their services in the form of commodities is called 'kind wages'. Generally it is popular in villages. For example: workers are paid in Rice, Wheat, Maize, etc. for their services.

(ii) **Time Wages:** Wages paid on the basis of time-duration of work done are called time wages. In other words, time wages means the daily wages, monthly wages, half-yearly wages, etc. For instance a worker who white-washes the house is paid ₹ 150 for working eight hours. Here the time taken for doing the work is considered instead of the work done.

(iii) **Task Wages:** The wage paid for the completion of task is called 'task-wage'. For instance, the wage paid for making toys, making a chair, white-washing a building, digging of a well, etc.

(iv) **Piece Wages:** Piece wage is payment made on the basis of the quantity of work done. For example, a weaver is paid on the basis of the quantity of cloth woven by him. For ex: ₹ 150 wage will be given for weaving of 10 metres cloth.

(v) **Service Wages:** The wage paid through a service is called service wage. For example: a barber employs a shoemaker and pays him in the form of his own service.

(vi) **Cash or Money Wages:** Wages paid in money are called cash wages. Nowadays in towns and cities the workers are usually paid in money for their services.

(vii) **Minimum Wages:** Minimum wages refers to the minimum amount of money fixed by a competent authority payable to industrial workers by their employer. The authority fixing the minimum wages may be the government or the trade union. There is a strong case for the fixing of minimum wages in certain selected industries, usually called 'sweated trade' in which there is too much exploitation of industrial labour. The need for fixing minimum wage arises to put an end to the exploitation of workers by their employer. Sweating of labour is now regarded socially unjust. Social justice calls for a wage which would give the worker a reasonable standard of living. Even to maintain moral, social and industrial peace in a country, the fixation of minimum wage is necessary. Minimum wage concept has now received a wide recognition and almost all developed countries accepted it in principle.

(viii) **Need-based Minimum Wage:** The concept of need-based minimum wage was invented at the 15th session of the Indian Labour Conference held at New Delhi in July 1957. The Resolution passed at the conference maintained that the minimum wage should be need-based and must ensure minimum human needs of the industrial worker through this need-based minimum wage, an honest attempt was made to quality in physical terms the needs of an average worker family in terms of food, fuel, housing, clothing, lighting, medical care, etc. The need-based minimum wage concept has been strongly supported by the trade unions. But employers have always disapproved the concept of need-based as their main considerations are productivity and profitability. It is pointed out that the concept of need-based minimum wage is impracticable in a developing country like India.

9.4.3 Distinction between Real Wages and Money Wages: Broadly wages are classified into two types. They are: (i) money wages (WM) or nominal wages and (ii) real wages (WR).

(i) **Money Wages (WM):** Money wages are also called nominal wages. Money wages refer to the wage paid in form of money or cash to a worker for his service. For example: If an accountant of a factory gets ₹ 5000 per month, it is his money or nominal wages. Prof. Thomas defines money wage as "Nominal wages or nominal earnings refer to the amount of the wages as measured in terms of money."

(ii) **Real Wages (WR):** Real wages refer to the purchasing power of money wages. The money wage of an accountant is ₹ 5000 per month but real wages is how much he can purchase goods and services with his money income. Prof. Thomas defined real wage as "Real wages or real earnings refer to the purchasing power of the workers remuneration i.e. the amount of necessaries, comforts, and luxuries which the worker can command in return for his services."

Besides, employees get other facilities, besides their money wages. The total earnings in real terms or the rewards received by an employee for his services are called real wages. For example, the chief accountant of a factory getting ₹ 5000 per month may be getting medical facilities, Tea and Tiffin facilities, free accommodation, vehicle allowance, education allowance for his sons or daughters, festival allowance, entertainment allowance, washing allowance, maid servant allowance, etc. in addition to his salary. Five thousand rupees are his money wages or nominal wages. When we count all the facilities including his money wage given to him, they are called real wages.

Real wages depends upon two important factors, namely (i) amount of money wage and (ii) the price level. Thus, real wage can be measured as below:

$$W_R = W_M / P$$

Where, W_R = Real wages

W_M = Money wages and

P = Price level.

For instance Wm = ₹ 5000, P = 100 then ₹ 5000/100 = ₹ 50.

Any change either in price or money or both will result into the change in real wage. For instance, a rise in the price level, money wages remaining constant, real wages decline. Similarly with a given general price, increase in money wages leads to rise in real wages.

Bedsides, real wages are also defined as the ratio of money wages to cost of living. So it can be measured as:

Real Wage = Money Wage ÷ Cost of living index

Hence, real wages are the true indicator of workers' standard of living and prosperity. If the facilities received in addition to the money wages are more, the real income will be considered to be much more. Similarly if money wages are low but prices are also low i.e. if purchasing power of money is more, the real wages will be higher. Adam Smith defines, "the labourer is rich or poor well or ill rewarded in proportion to the real, not the nominal wages, of his labour".

9.4.4 Factors Determining Real Wages: Real wages are considered to be the best index of measuring the economic welfare of the workers. Even if money wages are very high, real wages may not be high. Money wages may be same in two industries or in two regions but real wages may differ to a great extent. Real wage is determined not only by the money wage or price but also by so many other factors. So let us try to understand the important factors governing or determining real wages as follows:

(i) **Purchasing Power of Money:** If the purchasing power of money is higher, the real wage will be higher. On contrary it is *vice versa*. Thus, real wages are determined by the purchasing power of money. The purchasing power of money means the power of money to purchase goods and services. Purchasing power of money is affected by the price level. If the prices are high, purchasing power will be less and real wages will also be small.

(ii) **Additional Facilities:** In reality real wage consists of both money wages and the facilities received in return for the services from employer. If an employee gets more facilities along with his money wages, his real wages will be more. Sometimes an employee is given dress in a year, free tea, free lunch, free medical facilities, free accommodation, vehicle allowance, festival allowance, pensions, etc. The larger are the facilities the more will be the real wages.

(iii) **Nature of the Job:** Real wages also depend on the nature of the job. If the job is temporary, the real wages are considered lower. If a worker is on a permanent job, even if with lower money wages, his real wages will be more. For instance a worker in an ice cream factory gets work for only six months and gets 5000 rupees per month. On the other hand, a worker working on a sweets shop gets 3000 rupees per month, but his job is permanent. The real wages of the latter will be considered more than those of the former.

(iv) **Nature of Work:** Some jobs are very risky and hazardous to life, but others are very safe. For example an air pilot is paid ₹ 25000 per month while a school teacher is paid ₹ 5000 per month but the real wages of the school teachers are more than the real wages of the air pilot. Because the school teacher's job is very comfortable and safe while the air pilots job is very risky and dangerous to his life. Since the air crashes are very common in air flights. Therefore pilot may not be able to enjoy his life longer with his high salaries.

(v) **Conditions of Work:** The condition under which the worker performs his job is also an important factor in the determination of real wages. Working condition refer the hours of work and the surroundings under which he is working such as the ventilation, recreational facilities, educational facilities, training facilities, medical facilities, number of holidays leave facilities and other facilities provided by the management to the workers. Bad surroundings will definitely reduce the real wages of the workers as they affect directly his/her health and standard of living. Therefore, while calculating real wages allowance should be made for the working condition of the workers.

(vi) **Scope for Extra Earning:** In some jobs where there is a lot of scope for making extra income the real wage is high. For example, tips may be earned by waiters in posh hotels; professors of university may write books and can earn more than their regular salaries. Similarly school teacher's private tuitions, office employee's additional part time jobs, Government doctors' private practice, etc. are the other most appropriate illustrations.

(vii) **Social Status:** Real wages are also determined by the status of a job in the society. Some jobs people think, are better than the others. For instance, a judge of a court and the bank Agent are rewarded nearly with same money wages. But the status or reputation of a judge of a court is surely more than of the latter. Hence the real wages of a judge will be considered more than the real wages of a bank agent. Some jobs which even though comparatively low, their social prestige being very high, the real wage is high. For example teaching service is regarded as a noble profession. Thus, a teacher's psychological satisfaction and real wages are higher than his salary.

(viii) **Future Prospects:** If the chances of promotion of a worker are more his real wages will be more. For instance, a clerk who earns 4000 rupees per month has chances of becoming a manager of a factory. He will be having more real wages than his money wages.

(ix) **Timely Payment:** Real wages are also determined by timely payment of wages. If a worker gets his wages regularly and on the fixed date, his real wages will be considered more. The other worker who gets wages not on any fixed date or always late will be considered as having lower real wages, for ex: teachers of government aided schools and colleges.

(x) **Number of Hours of Work:** Longer hours of work, very short or no interval, absence of holidays, absence of casual leave facilities, absence of medical leave facilities, etc. affect the health of the worker who loses interest in his work. Even though his money wages are higher, his real wages will be low because he cannot enjoy his life with his salary. But short hours of work, frequent intervals, a large number of holidays, medical leave facilities, casual leave facilities, etc. will add to the real wages of a worker. Even though his wages are low a worker is able to enjoy his life. For example, an Information Technology Engineer gets salary ₹ 80,000/ pm compared to the salary of a Junior officer in a Bank who gets ₹ 20,000 per month, the real wage of the IT engineer is lower than that of the latter because he gets daily more hours to enjoy life.

(xi) **Period and Expenses of Training:** When we calculate the real wages, we have to consider the period and the money spent for learning the job. If a worker has to spend more time and money for getting training his real wages are considered lower. For instance, an accountant gets say ₹ 5000 per month. He has learnt accounts in five months. He has not spent much money for its training. On the other hand, an engineer who also earns ₹ 20,000 per month has to pass a course for which he spent a lot of money and time both. Therefore the real wages of the former will be considered much more than the real wages of the latter. Today, there are certain jobs, which require long and expensive training such as medical, computer engineering, company secretary; etc. in such jobs real wages are less.

(xii) **Level of Money Wages:** If other things remain the same, higher is the money wage rate, higher will be the real wage rate. As money wages rise, real wages also tend to go up. Thus money wages will determine the real wages.

In brief, real wages cover over all working conditions, facilities and the purchasing power of money. Nominal wages are the true indicators of a workers position and status whereas real wages are the true indicator of a worker's prosperity.

9.4.5 Differentials in Wage: General observation shows that there are no same wages are paid to the labourers in all occupations, industries and labour markets. There are many wage rates. Wage rates are differing on account of various factors. They are studied as under:

(i) **Differences in Wages in Different Occupations:** There are various factors responsible for differences in wages in different occupations. They are:

(a) **Risk:** There are some jobs which are risky and dangerous to life. For example, Drivers, mine workers, pilots, etc. They are paid higher wages. But there are some other jobs which are not risky e.g. clerks, teachers, etc. They are paid lower wages.

(b) **Responsibility:** The greater the responsibility of workers, the higher will be their wages and the smaller the responsibility of workers the lower will be their wages. A teacher is a paid a lower wage while an officer is paid a higher wage.

(c) **Cost of Training:** Those occupations which require long period and expensive training such as engineers, doctors, etc. they get higher wages, whereas those occupations which do not require any training such as ordinary workers get lower wages.

(d) **Pleasant and Unpleasant Job:** If the nature of work to be done is pleasant the supply of labour is more and the wages paid will be lower. If the nature of work to be done is unpleasant the supply of labour will be less and therefore, the wages paid will be higher.

(e) **Seasonal and Permanent Employment:** seasonal jobs carry higher wages while regular and permanent jobs carry lower wages. This is so because workers prefer permanent jobs to seasonal ones. Therefore temporary occupations carry higher wages and permanent occupations carry lower wages.

(f) **Tools and Equipments Used:** If the tools and equipments with which the labourers work are the most modern and up-to-date, their wages will be higher; whereas if the tools and equipments are old and absolute, their wages will be lower.

(g) **Experience and Education:** Wages differ from person to person also because the experience and education of various workers is different. Naturally those who are more educated and better trained than the others will be paid higher wages.

(h) **Future Prospects:** In some jobs, a worker has bright future prospects. In those jobs wages can be lower than in others where future prospects are brighter. For example a worker can earn ₹ 2000 per month while working in a shop. The same worker earns ₹ 1500 per month in a factory. But in a factory he has the scope for becoming a manager so he prefers job in factory and will accept even lower wages.

(i) **Trade Unions:** In the words of Webb "a trade union is a continuous association of wage earners for the purpose of maintaining or improving the conditions of their employment". In those occupations where there are strong trade unions, the wage will be higher. But in those occupations where there are weak trade unions or where there are no trade unions, the wages will be lower.

(j) **Supplementary Income:** In those jobs where there is enough scope for earning supplementary incomes, the wages are lower, for example, the wages of teachers are lower since they have enough scope to earn supplementary incomes.

(k) **Non-Competing Groups:** In the present Society there are different labour groups which are non-competing. For instance, Goldsmiths do not compete with hair dressers nor can the Hair dressers compete with the carpenters. Wages in these different occupations are fixed on the basis of customs, convention, social tradition, inheritance, training environment and caste.

(ii) **Differences in Wages in the Same Occupations:** Wages may also be different in the same occupations. The reasons for such wages differences are given below:

(a) **Differences in the Ability or Efficiency:** Ability or efficiency of labour affects its wages. We know that a labourer is demanded only due to his productivity. All workers are not alike; some are more efficient than the others. By more efficient workers is meant more productive workers. It is prudent to pay higher wages, to workers who make more contribution to production. Due to this difference of efficiency among workers, wage differences exist.

(b) **Male and Female Workers:** In same occupations wages paid to male workers are higher than those paid to female workers. This is so because employers know that female workers are physically weaker than male workers and therefore they contribute less than male workers in production. Such differences prevail in the wages of construction workers, farm workers, etc.

(c) **Hours of Work:** If the workers work for longer hours their earnings will be higher and if they work for shorter hours, their wages will be lower in the same occupations.

(d) **Differences in Bargaining Power:** Different workers have different bargaining powers. Some workers can strongly and favourably negotiate with the entrepreneurs. Those who have better bargaining power earn wages higher than the others.

(iii) **Differences in Wages in Different Places:** We know that labour is less mobile, due to family affection, language problems, food habits, difference in taste and preferences, and differences in the cost of living in different places, etc., for example, wages in Bombay are higher than those in Belgaum for the same occupation. Wages also differ from country to country. Wages in America are higher than those in India for the same occupation. Wages may also differ in different places if the workers in one place are unaware of the higher wages prevailing in another place.

(iv) **Differences in Wages at Different Times:** Wages generally differ from time to time. There has been a gradual rise in the wage rates of all occupations and in all places. This is due to the factors like rise in the cost of living, economic development and growth, increase in the efficiency of workers, specialization and division of labour, rise in the standard of living of workers, changing conditions of demand for labour and supply of labour, etc. are responsible for differences in wages at different times.

(v) **Unions and Differences in Wages:** Unions uphold the principle of equal pay for equal work. They force the management to pay the same wage to persons doing similar work. They tend to narrow down wage differences between firms in a region as well as those between regions. Unions also tend to narrow differences across occupations. They often raise the floor of wages. Thus, trade unions narrow down the wages differences. Therefore unions are playing a predominant role in the modern society.

9.4.6 Theories of Wages: Labour is an important factor and also a peculiar factor of production. Among all factors, labour alone is perishable and inseparable from the labourer. At any time, the landlord may withhold the supply of land or the capitalist's may withhold supply of capital but the labourer is forced to sell labour at whatever price is available in the market. Because of this peculiarity, there is an always a danger that the labourer shall get less than what actually due to him. It is an account of this important aspect of wage determination, economists have formulated theories explaining the determination of wages. From time to time, various theories have been developed by economists but none of them is adequate and free from criticisms. Let us try to understand the three important theories of wages as under:

(I) The Subsistence Theory of Wages: The subsistence theory of wages has been developed by the physiocrates, a school of economists in France. It received the blessings of such eminent economists such as Adam Smith, Ricardo and Thomas Robert Malthus, Lassalle, a German socialist, called this theory Iron Law or Brazen Law of wages. This theory was popular during the 19th century. It is based on the cost of production of labour and the classical theory of population.

(a) **Statement:** According to this theory, wages paid to the workers always tend to equal to the subsistence level of living. It means that wages paid to the workers are just for the bare maintenance of their families at minimum subsistence level. The wages can neither be more nor less than subsistence level.

Further the theory states, if the wages are paid higher than their minimum subsistence level, the workers will be encouraged to marry at an early age and to have larger size of families. It increases the total population and consequently the supply of labour. The competition for employment will become keener and wages will come down to the subsistence level.

On contrary, if the wages are paid lower than the minimum substance level, the workers postpone their marriages, and married workers will limit the size of the families and even starve due to undernourishment. It reduces the growth of population. As a result, population will start decreasing and the scarcity of labour will increase the level of wages up to subsistence level.

Therefore the wages should be paid just equal to their cost of living or the subsistence level.

The subsistence theory of wage is called the Iron Law of wages or the Brazen Law of wages. Because there is no chance for workers to increase their wages more than their subsistence level. This theory is based on the Thomas Robert Malthusian theory of population according to which a rise in wages above the minimum subsistence level definitely would lead to increase in population which in turn would bring down the wages of worker to the subsistence level.

(b) **Criticisms/Limitations of the Theory:** The benefit of the subsistence theory of wages is that, it is the simplest and also the oldest theory of wages. But it has been criticized on the following grounds:

(i) **It is based on outdated population theory:** The subsistence theory of wages is based on the outdated promise of the popular Malthusian theory of population. This theory assumes that an increase in the wage rate leads to an increase in population. But this is not correct. Modern conditions have proved that increased wages lead to declining population.

(ii) **Difficult to define the subsistence level of labour:** It is difficult to define the subsistence level of labour in a precise and comprehensive manner. The classification of wants into necessaries contorts and luxuries are flexible, for instance, luxuries of one time become necessaries with the passage of time. Past luxuries have become present day necessaries. TV set which was a luxury at one time has become necessary today. Social habits and customs will also exercise their influence on the level of living of the workers. Therefore, these customs and habits are to be taken into consideration while determining the subsistence level of living.

(iii) **It has neglected demand-side:** The subsistence theory of wages approaches the problem of the determination of wages only from the supply side. It is supply theory of wages. This theory does not explain why labour is demanded in the market. It gives due importance to the supply of labour and ignores completely the demand-side of labour.

(iv) **It has ignored wage-differences:** This theory does not explain why wage-differences arise in the society. It completely neglects this aspect of labour. A satisfactory theory of wages should take into consideration the wage differences.

(v) **It failed to consider the role of trade-union:** Trade unions through collecting bargaining are capable of influencing the wage-rates. These trade unions can succeed even in increasing the wages beyond the subsistence level. Therefore, it is necessary to account for the influence of trade unions on wages. But unfortunately the subsistence theory of wages has neglected the influence of trade unions on wages.

(vi) **It is too pessimistic:** This theory is highly pessimistic for the working class. It presents a very dark picture of the future of the community. If wage rates were to be equal to the subsistence level, then they would have been uniform for everyone. This is also a proof that the theory is unrealistic and pessimistic.

(vii) **It neglected efficiency of labour:** According to this theory, wage rate for all workers tend to be equal to the minimum subsistence level. But it need not be so because workers differ in efficiency and productivity. Therefore, theory has not given attention to efficiency and productivity which is the most important factor in the determination of wages.

The discussion given above shows that subsistence theory of wages is not a sound doctrine as it fails to present a correct empirical description of actual facts in the labour market and it does not adequately explain the determination of wages.

(II) Wage-Fund Theory: Wage fund is that amount of capital which is set apart by the entrepreneurs for the purchase of the services of labour.

The wage-fund theory was propounded by J.S. Mill. It was more popular in mid-nineteenth century. This theory is a definite improvement over the subsistence theory because it allows the influence of demand as well as supply of labour.

(a) **Statement:** According to this theory "wages depend upon the proportion between population and capital, or rather between the number of the labouring class who work for hire and the aggregate of what may be called the wage fund which consists of that part of circulating capital which is expanded in the direct hire of labour". Wages, according to Mill, depend upon the ratio between the number of workers and the wage fund. Wages can increase only when there is a change in these two factors namely the number of workers and the wages fund. Greater the number of working population i.e. numbers workers, smaller is the share in the wages fund. Smaller the number of working population, i.e. number of workers, larger is the share in the wages fund. Therefore, general level of wages is equal to the wages fund by the number of workers. The theory can be stated in the form of the following equation:

$$\text{Wages} = \frac{\text{Wages Fund}}{\text{Number of workers (working population)}}$$

According to this theory, the wages fund can be expanded in the long period. But at a particular point of time wages fund is more or less fixed. Given the wages fund, wages in one industry can increase only at the cost of wages in another industry. When wages in all industries rise, profits of entrepreneurs will fall. Reduced profits will lead to smaller wages fund or stock of capital which in turn leads to lesser wages. Therefore, wages will rise only when its population decreases or the wages fund increases.

(b) **Assumptions:** This theory of wages is based on four important assumptions. They are:

(i) Wages are paid out of capital.

(ii) Capital available for payment of wages is predetermined and fixed.

(iii) Wages depend upon the number of workers.

(iv) Labourers are homogeneous.

(c) **Criticisms or limitations:** In England, the theory was popular during the mid-nineteenth century and it was used to discredit the influence of trade unions on wage-determination. This theory has been disproved by the facts and has been criticized on many grounds:

(i) **Wages fund theory fails to distinguish between stocks and flows:** This theory assumes that wages are paid from out of a fund which is predetermined and fixed. It means the theory has considered that there is fixed stock of capital to pay the wages. But in reality wages are paid from out of national dividend which is not a stock of goods and services, but the flow of goods and services in a given period of time. In short, national income is a flow and not a fund or stock. Therefore, it is unscientific and illogical to assume that wages are paid out of capital which is predetermined and fixed.

(ii) **It has ignored non-conflict between wages and profit:** The wage fund theory contends that there is a conflict between wages and profits. J.S. Mill argued that an increase in wages will necessarily bring down profits. However, this may not happen. For instance, during the inflationary conditions both profits and wages increase. Thus, this theory does not hold well in real life.

(iii) **This theory fails to explain the existence of wage differentials among workers:** This weakness makes the theory highly unrealistic. Critics argued that if the wage fund is fixed and the wage rate depends upon the number of workers seeking employment then it follows that wage rate throughout the country must be uniform. But in real life, it is not so.

(iv) **Assumption of homogeneity is unrealistic:** The theory depends upon the assumption that labour is homogeneous. But this assumption is not in conformity with the facts of life. Workers differ in efficiency and productivity. In fact labour is highly heterogeneous.

(v) **It has ignored the role of trade unions:** In modern times, trade unions are able to affect a rise in the wage levels. But the wage fund theory is incompetent to explain this phenomenon.

(vi) **Wage-fund is also variable:** The theory is based on the concept of a fixed fund. Critics pointed out that there does not exist anything like a fixed fund. Even if it exists in the mind of entrepreneurs, it is subject to variations. It cannot remain fixed forever. It can be increased or decreased in accordance with the requirements for it.

(vii) **It failed to explain the effect of productivity on wages:** A main defect of the theory is that it completely ignores the effect of productivity on wages. Critics pointed out that the wage fund comes from labour. Wages are no doubt drawn out of a reservoir of capital but this reservoir is constantly fed by the products of labour. Higher the efficiency, higher will be the wages. But the wage fund theory cannot take note of this fact. Thus wages fund theory suffers from many weaknesses.

(III) Marginal Productivity Theory of Wages: The marginal productivity theory of distribution has been extended to wages and this has come to be known as marginal productivity theory of wages. A general theory was given by (Marginalist) thinkers to determine the prices of the four basic factors of production. The same marginal productivity theory has been specially applied to determine the wages. This theory was first put forward by Von Thunen, a German Economist, in his famous book, *The Isolated State*. The Marginal productivity theory has been developed by Wicksteed, J.B. Clark, Walras and many others.

(a) **Statement:** According to S.E. Tomas, "As a result of the competition between employers for labour and between workers for employment, a wage rate is determined that is equal to the marginal productivity of the labour force, when the employers as a whole are willing to employ."

The Marginal productivity theory states that a worker is given wages equal to his marginal productivity. Marginal productivity is the addition made to total production by employing one more unit of a worker. A worker is paid in terms of money, therefore the marginal productivity of a worker is also calculated in terms of money. This is called marginal revenue productivity. In other words, marginal revenue productivity (MRP) is the addition made to the total revenue (income earned by an entrepreneur by employing one more unit of a worker). The marginal revenue productivity (MRP) is the addition to total productivity by employing one more unit of labour when other factors remain constant, namely land, capital and organization.

The marginal productivity theory proposes that wages of a worker tend to be equal to his marginal productivity. We can explain it through an example: Suppose an entrepreneur by employing four workers with the other factors of production, he gets ₹ 300 as total revenue i.e. income from the sale of output. If he employs one more workers thereby increasing the number of workers from 4 to 5, other factors of production remaining constant, the total production increases, say, to ₹ 400. Thus by employing an additional worker an addition of ₹ 100 (400–300) is made to the firm's total revenue. This addition to the firm's revenue is called the marginal revenue productivity of a worker.

Under conditions of perfect competition, in the long-run, a worker gets wages equal to his marginal revenue productivity (MRP). The worker in our example will get ₹ 100 as wages. Suppose he wants more than ₹ 100, the organizers will employ lesser number of workers since their new wage will exceed their marginal productivity. When fewer workers will be employed, unemployed workers will bring down the wages. Ultimately wages will tend to equal marginal productivity of workers.

Similarly if the workers are given less than ₹ 100 their reward will be less than their marginal productivity. In this situation, a producer will think of increasing his profits and production by employing more workers since they are contributing more to total production than they are paid when demand for workers increases, their wages also increase. This process of adjustment will go on until wages become equal to the workers marginal productivity. Therefore wages are determined by the marginal productivity of workers. Marginal productivity theory of wages explains that under perfect competition and in the long-run workers wages are always equal to marginal as well as average revenue productivity. In other words, marginal productivity (MRP) and average revenue productivity (ARP) of a worker determine his wages. The process of wage determination as given in this theory can be explained through the diagram 9.11.

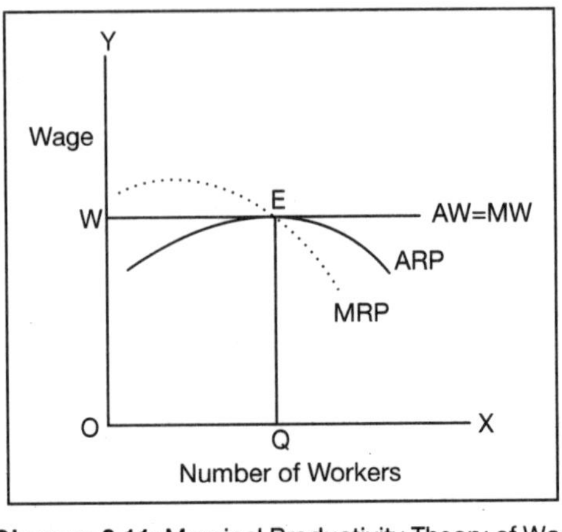

Diagram 9.11: Marginal Productivity Theory of Wag

In the diagram 9.11, the number of workers is measured along OX-axis. Wages are measured along OY-axis. ARP and MRP are the average revenue productivity and marginal revenue productivity curves respectively. OW is the wage rate at which average wage and marginal wage are equal because of the perfect competition in the labour market. Under perfect competition there are a large number of buyers and sellers. No single firm can influence the market wage rate. The price of labour is fixed by the industry which is equal to marginal productivity of labour. A firm required to decide the number of workers to be employed at this given wage level. As is shown in the diagram 9.11 at point E, ARP and MRP are equal. This is the point of equilibrium for a firm. In other words, at OW wage-rate, a firm will employ OQ workers. If more workers than OQ are employed the firm will have added more to its costs and less to its revenue which means less profits. So the equilibrium situation for a firm is to employ workers up to the point where MRP (and ARP) is equal to the wage rate.

(b) **Assumptions:** Marginal productivity theory of wages is based on the following important assumptions.

(i) Existence of perfect competition in both product market and factor market.

(ii) Labour is homogeneous i.e. all the labourers are equally efficient.

(iii) Labour is perfectly mobile.

(iv) There exits full employment in the economy.

(v) The theory is based on the Law of Diminishing Returns.

(vi) The theory is based on the assumption of long-run.

(v) It assumes technology to be constant.

(c) **Criticisms:** The marginal productivity theory of wages states that wages tend to equal the value of the marginal productivity of labour. The marginal productivity of labour is the amount added to the total output by the marginal labourer. The theory is not a complete theory of wages. It constitutes only one part of the whole theory which determines wages. It refers only to the demand side of the theory. It explains the factors that given the demand side of labour and their effect on wage determination. Therefore it has been criticized by critics on many grounds. The important criticisms are below.

(i) **This theory is based on the unrealistic assumption of perfect competition:** In reality we come across imperfections in the market. Because perfect competition does not exist in reality, the theory has been regarded as impracticable and unrealistic.

(ii) **It has ignored the productivity of other factors:** Production is the result of combined efforts of the four basic factors of production. So it is absurd to say that production is increased by increasing only one worker. In big manufacturing industries when we increase or decrease one unit of a worker, it has no effect on the total production. Even then the last employed worker is paid wages. In this way, the wage determination on the basis of this theory is impracticable and impossible.

(iii) **It is a long-run analysis:** The theory explains that wages will be equal to MRP and ARP in the long-run. Its concern is with the long-run. We know that long-run like tomorrow that never comes. If we build a theory in the assumption of long-run which is unseen, it cannot be practical.

(iv) **It is indeterminate:** The theory concludes that wages are determined on the basis of marginal productivity of workers. But actually, productivity is determined by wages. Higher wages improve the standard of living of workers and so their efficiency. It again increases their productivity. Hence, wages determine productivity and are not determined by productivity. In other words, wages are the cause and not the effect of productivity.

(v) **It has ignored that the factor-proportion is given:** It is sometimes noticed that labour is used in a certain fixed proportion with the other factor of production. In this situation we cannot increase or decrease the number of workers. And we cannot find the marginal productivity of a worker.

(vi) Keynes criticized the theory on the ground that it is based on static conditions: It applies only when no change occurs in the economy. The theory failed to solve unemployment problem during 1930s great depression.

(vii) **It ignores other factors:** The productivity of the labour depends upon several factors such as the quality of raw-materials, nature of capital equipment, efficient management working hours, etc., which are not considered by the theory.

9.5 MODEL QUESTIONS

2 Marks Questions

(a) State the meaning of personal distribution of income.

(b) State the meaning of functional distribution of income.

(c) Give the meaning of marginal productivity.

(d) Give the meaning of average productivity.

(e) What do you mean by rent?

(f) What do you mean by zero-rent land?

(g) What is differential rent?

(h) What is economic rent?

(i) What is transfer earning?

(j) Define wages.

(k) Mention the difference between money wages and real wages.

(l) Give the statement of marginal productivity theory of wages.

5 Marks Questions

(1) Write a note on Quasi-rent.

(2) Discuss briefly the determinants of real wages.

(3) Write a short note on differentials in wages.

(4) Write a note on subsistence theory of wages.

(5) Write a note on wage-fund theory.

10 Marks Questions

(1) Critically examine the 'Marginal Productivity Theory of Distribution'.

(2) Explain the Ricardian Theory of Rent.

(3) Explain the Modern Theory of Rent.

(4) Define wages. Explain differentials in wages.

(5) Critically examine the 'Marginal Productivity Theory of Wages'.

10

Interest and Profits

10.1 INTEREST

The Interest is a reward for capital for its productive service. Interest occupies an important place in economic theory, as well as day-to-day business activity. Importance of the rate of interest is very much important, as it regulates the flow of business and industrial activity in the modern economy, it is one of the strongest weapons used by the central bank to control credits supply of money demand for many thus it regulates entire economic activities.

10.1.1 Meaning and Definitions: In the common language interest is a payment, made by a borrower to the lender, for the use of the capital borrowed. In Economics the word 'Interest' is defined in many ways, Interest is regarded as the payment for the use of service of capital. Thus the interest is the reward paid for the use of capital in production or parting with liquidity.

Many economists have defined the term 'interest' in various ways. The important definitions are:

(i) **Alfred Marshall:** Prof. Marshall defined interest as "Interest is a price paid for the use of capital in any market."

(ii) **J.S. Mill:** J.S. Mill, neo-classical economist, defined interest as "Interest is remuneration for mere abstinence."

(iii) **Prof. Seligman:** Seligman defined interest as "Interest is a return from the fund of capital."

(iv) **Prof. Wicksell:** A great economist Prof. Wicksell has defined Interest as "a payment made by the Borrower of capital, by virtue of productivity as a reward for abstinence".

(v) **Prof. Mayer:** Prof. Mayer defined interest as "Interest is the price made for the use of loanable funds."

(vi) **J.M. Keynes:** J.M. Keynes defined interest as "Interest is the reward for parting with liquidity for a specified time."

Thus, in brief, interest is regarded as the payment for the use of service of capital. It is the reward paid for the use of the capital in production to the capitalist.

10.1.2 Concepts of Interest: The following are the various types or concepts of interest:

(A) **Gross Interest and Net Interest:** The concepts of Interest are classified as 'Gross Interest' and 'Net interest'.

(a) **Gross Interest:** The total amount paid by the debtor to the creditor for the use of capital is known as 'gross interest'. It includes net interest as well as other expenses. Economists have explained the various components of gross interest as under:

(i) **Net Interest or Pure Interest:** It is a payment purely for the services of capital without other expenses such as payment for risk, inconveniences and management.

(ii) **Insurance Against Risk:** The lender is exposed to risks when he lends money. A certain amount must be paid to the lender to cover risk. The greater the risk higher will be the insurance that the lender expects.

(iii) **Wages of Management:** A part of the payment should be for management. The lender has to keep accounts and other records.

(iv) **Reward for Inconveniences:** Moneylender undertakes troubles and inconveniences in providing capital. Therefore a portion of the gross interest is meant for compensating those inconveniences and troubles.

The gross interest can be calculated as:

GI = NI + RE + ME + IE where GI = Gross Interest, NI = Net Interest, RE = Insurance Expenditure against risks, ME = Remuneration to management and IE = reward for inconveniences.

In brief, the gross interest consists of net interest insurance premium against risks, remunerations to management etc.

(b) **Net Interest:** Net interest on the other hand is pure interest or payment for the use of money or capital. In the words of Wicksell "the real rate of interest as that rate, at which the demand for loan capital and the supply of saving exactly agree".

The amount of pure interest may differ from lender to lender, amount of money to amount of money and period to period. The following formula is used to calculate net interest.

Net Interest = Gross Interest – (Payment for risks, inconveniences, Management)

∴ NI = GI – (RE + ME + IE)

(B) Nominal Interest and Real Interest: Economists have also classified the interest as nominal interest and real interest. They are:

(a) **Nominal Interest:** Nominal interest is also known as money interest. It refers to the interest expressed in terms percentage. For ex: Suppose a person borrows ₹ 200 from lender and repays ₹ 230 after one year, the nominal or the money interest ₹ 230–200= ₹ 30 i.e. 15% pa (= 30/200 × 100).

(b) **Real Interest:** Real interest means the rate return on physical capital such as machine, vehicle, tractor, etc. created for the purpose of producing more goods.

10.1.3 Theories of Interest: Economists have developed various theories from time to time to explain the determination of rate of interest. The important theories are as follows:

(A) **Classical Theory of Interest:** The classical theory of interest is also known as real theory of interest. Some economists called it demand and supply theory.

(a) **Statement:** The classical theory of interest states that the equilibrium between demand for and supply of capital determines the rate of interest in capital market. The demand and supply side of the theory is discussed in detail as under.

(b) **Explanation:** According to classical economists, interest is paid because of time preference. Rate of interest arises because people prefer present satisfaction to future satisfaction. If the people prefer to spend more part of their present income for present satisfaction, the size of savings will be low that will affect on rate of interest. Thus, according to classical economists, interest is a price for abstaining from consumption or for waiting. On the other hand, the marginal productivity of capital influences the rate of interest through demand for capital since capital is a productive resource. In brief, the demand for and supply of savings or capital could determine the rate of interest in the capitalist economy.

(i) **Demand for Capital:** Demand for capital comes from all those who require funds for investment purpose. The demand for capital or savings will depend upon the marginal productivity of capital. The shape of demand curve for capital is as follows in diagram 10.1.

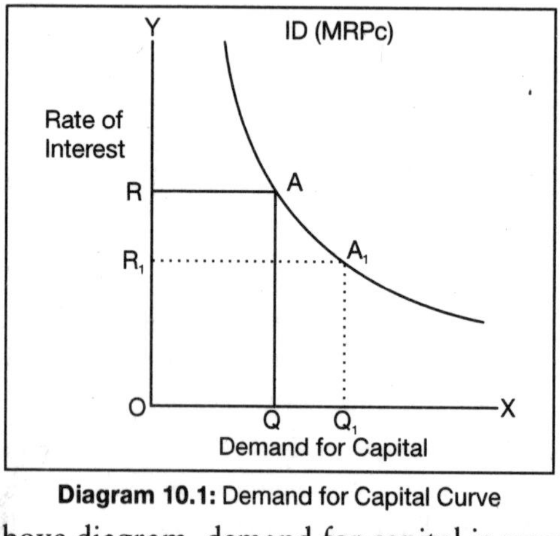

Diagram 10.1: Demand for Capital Curve

In the above diagram, demand for capital is measured along OX axis and rate of interest is measured along OY axis. ID is demand for capital or savings curve which is also called the investment demand curve. It shows the opposite relation between rate of interest and demand for capital. Since demand for capital depends on marginal revenue productivity of capital (MRPC), there is direct relation between the both so MRPC is shown along ID curve which slopes downward from left to the right. The demand for capital is OQ when rate of interest is OR. But as the rate of interest increased to R_1, the marginal revenue productivity of capital move from A to A_1 and so as a result of it the demand for capital increased to OQ_1.

(ii) **Supply of capital:** People, institutions and government save some part of their income and thus it becomes the source to supply of capital or savings. According to classical economists, generally, the supply of savings depends upon rate of interest: higher the rate of interest higher will be the savings and more will be the capital: lower the rate of interest, lower will be the supply of savings or capital. It is illustrated in the following diagram 10.2.

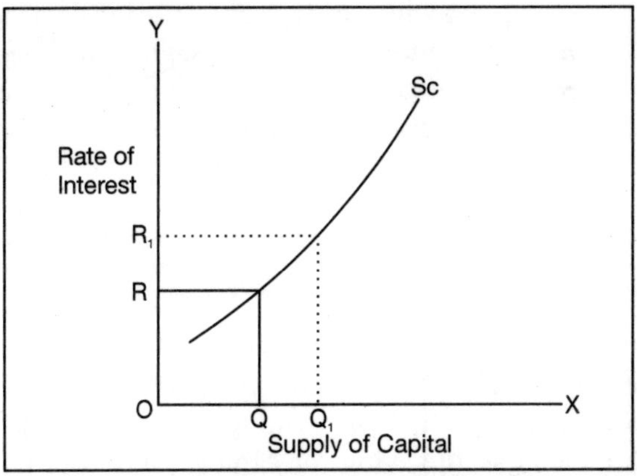

Diagram 10.2: Supply of Capital Curve

In the diagram 10.2, OX axis measures the supply of capital and OY axis measures the rate of interest. The Sc is the supply of savings or capital curve. Sc curve slopes upward from left to the right because there is direct relation between supply of capital and rate of interest. According to classical economists, people save more when the rate of interest is high because they want to get its benefits; on contrary it is *vice versa*. When the rate of interest is OR, the supply of capital will be OQ. As the rate of interest increases to OR_1, the supply of capital increase to OQ_1.

(iii) **Determination of Rate of Interest:** According to classical theory, the rate of interest is determined by the interaction between for demand and supply of capital. The equilibrium between demand for and supply of capital determines the rate of interest.

It is shown in the below diagram 10.3.

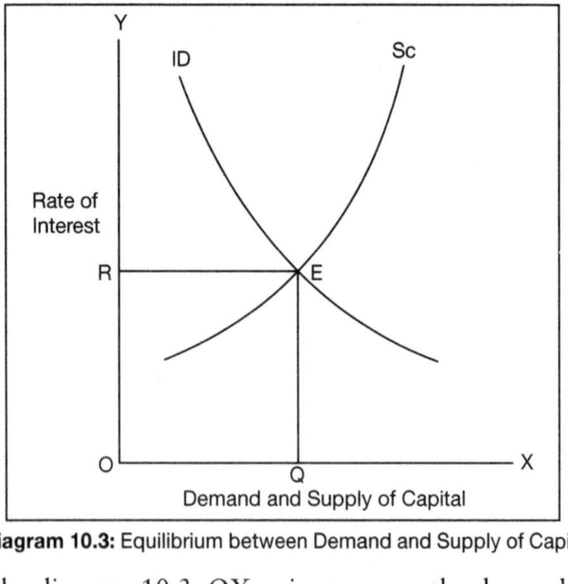

Diagram 10.3: Equilibrium between Demand and Supply of Capital

In the diagram 10.3, OX axis measures the demand for and supply of capital. The OY axis measures the rate of interest. The ID is investment demand or demand for savings or capital curve. The Sc is the supply of savings or capital curve. Both curves are interacted each other at point E, it is the equilibrium point. At the equilibrium point the demand for capital is equal to supply of capital i.e. OQ, so the rate of interest is determined at R. The equilibrium point indicates that savings and investments are equal. Any change in demand or supply of capital or both leads to change in rate of interest.

(c) **Criticisms:** The classical theory of interest has been criticized by modern economists. Prof J.M. Keynes condemned the theory as useless and unrealistic. The important criticisms leveled against classical theory are as follows:

(i) **It is based on unrealistic assumptions:** Like other classical theories, it is also based on the assumptions such as full employment, perfect competition, Static analysis, long-run, etc. According to modern economists these all are unrealistic assumptions in modern context.

(ii) **It ignored the concept of marginal efficiency of capital:** Keynes does not agree with classical economists on the relationship between investment and rate of interest. Investment not only depends on rate of interest but also on marginal efficiency of capital.

(iii) **It neglected the influence of income and expenditure on rate of interest:** According to J.M. Keynes, rate of interest is influenced by income and expenditure. Both savings and investment are depending upon income and expenditure of the people.

(iv) **It ignored the adverse effects of savings:** According to Keynes individual saving is virtue but the saving by the community will definitely reduce effective demand which takes the economy to depression.

(v) **Savings and investment need not be equal:** According to Keynes, savings and investment are equal by definition but they need not be equal by function. The people of saving are different from the people who undertake investment.

However, in spite of criticisms, the classical theory is the base of all other theories on interest.

(B) **Loanable Funds Theory of Interest:** Loanable funds theory of interest is an improvement over classical theory of interest. It is also called neo-classical theory on rate of interest. The neo-classical economists have developed the loanable funds theory of interest. The theory was first formulated by Wicksell but it was well developed by Prof Bertile Ohlin, Gunnar Myrdal, Eric Lindale and Ben Hanson and Prof. D.H. Robertson.

Neo-classicals developed the loanable funds theory to fill the gaps in classical theory of interest. The classical theory explained the phenomena of interest exclusively in terms of real savings and real investment. It allowed no room for monetary factors namely, bank money. But according to Wicksell the total supply of loanable funds does not consists only of real saving, it is also fed by the amount of bank credit.

Alvin H. Hanson defined interest as "the rate of interest is determined by the interaction of demand schedule for loanable funds with supply schedule".

(a) **Statement:** The theory states that the equilibrium between demand for and supply of loanable funds determines the rate of interest in the economy.

(b) **Explanation:** The supply of and demand for the loanable funds determine the rate of interest. The purposes and sources of loanable funds and the statement of the theory are studied as under:

(i) **Demand for Loanable Funds:** There is demand for loanable fund for various purposes. But it depends upon the rate of interest. Higher the rate of interest, lower will be demand for loanable funds; lower the rate of interest, higher will be demand for loanable funds. Thus there is inverse relation between demand for loanable funds and rate of interest. So it is shown by usual demand curve. Following are the main demands for loanable funds.

(1) **Investment Demand (ID):** Businessmen, producers and all types of investors need fund for purposes like purchase of capital goods, machines, buildings, securities, etc. But while undertaking investment they compare between rate of interest and rate of return or profits. If rate of return or marginal revenue productivity is higher than rate of interest, they demand for loanable funds. Thus the demand for loanable funds depends on rate of interest.

(2) **Consumption Demand (CD):** The consumers need money or funds for purchase of durable consumption goods such as house, vehicles, TV, refrigerator, etc. The demand for loanable fund for these purposes depends upon the rate of interest, for instance, demand for house-loan depends upon rate of interest.

(3) **Hoarding Demand (HD):** People prefer to hoard some part of their income and wealth in form of idle cash balance but it also depends upon rate of interest. If rate of interest is low, the demand for hoarding cash balance will be more.

(ii) **Supply of Loanable Funds:** Supply of loanable fund is the other important determinant of rate of interest. Like demand, the supply of loanable fund also depends upon rate of interest. There is direct relation between rate of interest and supply of loanable funds: higher the rate of interest, higher will be the supply of loanable funds; lower the rate if interest, lower will be the supply of loanable funds. So it is shown by usual supply curve.

There are various sources of supply of loanable funds. They are as follows:

(1) **Savings (S):** According to the theory, saving constitute a major source of loanable fund. The savings are household savings, corporate savings and government savings. Household savings is the main source of supply of loanable funds. The supply of savings is influenced by rate of interest. People save more to avail the advantages of high rate of interest; they save less when rate of interest is low.

(2) **Dishoarding (DH):** People hoard money or idle cash balance because they prefer liquidity. They hoard money from their previous income. Dishoarding of the past accumulated money also constitutes the supply of loanable funds. The dishoarding of money also depends upon rate of interest: higher the rate of interest, lower will be dishoarding; on contrary, it will be *vice versa*.

(3) **Disinvestments (DI):** Generally disinvestment means the withdrawal of investments done in establishment of industries, securities, trade, etc. and depreciation reserve funds. Investors

withdraw their funds when they realize that they are suffering losses and rate of interest is higher than the rate of return. So higher rate of interest encourages more disinvestment thereby the supply of loanable funds will increase. Hence, disinvestment is another source of supply of loanable funds.

(4) **Bank Credits (BC):** Banks create credit by giving loans and advances to the investors and consumers. Bank credit is another source of loanable funds. Banks lend more loans and advances when rate of interest is higher; they lend less loans and advances when rate of interest is low. Thus higher the bank credit, higher will be the supply of loanable funds; on contrary, it will be *vice versa*.

(c) **Determination of Rate of Interest:** According to the theory, the equilibrium between demand for and supply of loanable funds determines rate of interest in the economy. It is shown in the following diagram 10.4.

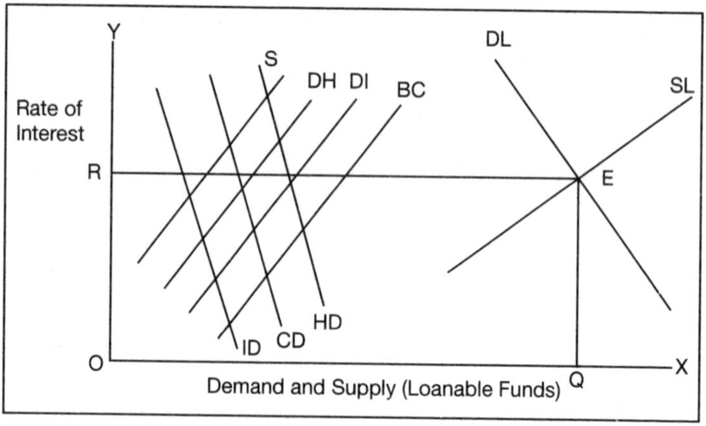

Diagram 10.4: Equilibrium between Demand and

OX axis measures demand for and supply of loanable funds and OY axis measures the rate of interest. ID, CD and HD curves represent investment demand, consumption demand and hoarding demand for loanable funds respectively. DL curve is the total of the demand curves of loanable funds i.e. ID + CD + HD.

S, DH, DI and BC curves represent savings, dishoarding, disinvestment and bank credit respectively which constitute the total supply of loanable funds that is presented by SL curve i.e. S + DH + DI + BC.

SL and DL curves are intersected each other at E, the equilibrium point where demand for and supply of loanable funds are equal i.e. OQ. So the rate of interest is determined at E which is OR or EQ. Any change in demand or supply of loanable funds or both will bring change in rate of interest.

(d) **Criticisms:** The loanable funds theory of interest is superior over the classical theory of interest. However, the theory is criticized by modern economists. Prof. J.M. Keynes and other modern economists criticized the theory as under:

(i) **The concept of hoarding used by the theory is dubious:** It is because, according to Keynes, hoarding simply cannot increase or decrease as long as the amount of money remains the same.

(ii) **The theory neglected that income influences the level of savings:** The rate of interest does not influence the volume of savings because the rich people who save money even though the rate of interest is zero. So it is the income that influences the savings first.

(iii) **It is based on unrealistic assumptions:** Critics pointed out that the theory is also based on the assumptions like income of the community remains constant, full employment, perfect competition, etc. But these are unrealistic assumptions.

(iv) **It fails to explain exactly 'what determines what':** Prof. Hanson says that the theory does not clearly tell us how the rate of interest is determined. Whether the rate of interest determines the demand for and supply of loanable funds or loanable funds' demand and supply determines rate of interest is indeterminate.

(v) **Integration of real and monetary factors is wrong:** The monetary factors have been combined with real factors in the loanable fund theory. But Critics says that factors like savings and investment cannot be combined with monetary factors.

Apart from criticisms the theory holds good because the loanable fund theory of interest contributes more to the theory of interest. It has emphasized on many factors which cause the change in the rate of interest.

(C) **Liquidity Preference Theory of Interest:** Lord J.M. Keynes criticized classical and neoclassical theories on interest on several grounds.

He developed a theory on interest which popularly known as liquidity preference theory.

It is one of the important contributions of Keynes to the world economic thoughts. It is more important theory on interest.

Lord J.M. Keynes in his book *General theory of Employment Interest and Money* developed a new theory of interest. It is known as the liquidity preference theory of interest. Prof. Keynes called it as liquidity preference theory of interest because interest is the price for parting with liquidity. According to him interest is purely a monetary phenomenon.

He defines interest as the premium which has to be offered to induce people to hold they're each in some form or the other. According to Keynes the rate of interest is determined by the demand and supply of money.

Liquidity Preference Theory of Interest is propounded by J.M. Keynes. It is a well recognized theory on rate of interest. He gave new view on interest in his famous book, *The General Theory of Employment, Interest and Money*. According to Keynes, "interest is the reward paid for parting with liquidity for specific period". When a lender lends money means he is parting with liquidity or sacrificing present consumption for future so he must be paid some price for it. Liquidity means readiness of idle cash balance. Therefore there is demand for and supply of idle cash balance in the money market. Liquidity preference means demand for idle cash balance or money to hold.

(a) **Statement:** The theory states that the equilibrium between demand for and supply of money determines the rate of interest in the economy.

(b) **Explanation:** The theory has been explained in a lucid way by discussing its demand and supply side in detail as under:

(i) **Demand for Money:** According to Keynes, people have a strong desire to hold money as it is the most liquid asset available to them. The desire of the people to hold money is called the liquidity preference. People desire to hold money mainly for three motives or purposes. They are:

(1) **Transaction Motive:** People demand money for conducting of their day-to-day transactions. Most people settle their transactions with money and hence they have to carry some money with them. Individuals hold cash in order to bridge the intervals between the receipt of income and its expenditures, it is called income motive. Individuals receive their incomes by the day or week or month or year but their expenditures go on moment by moment or day by day. Similarly business people hold money for their day-to-day expenditures, it is called business motive.

(2) **Precautionary Motive:** Precautionary motive for holding money means holding cash balance for unforeseen contingencies or expenditures. In other words, individuals and business firms will keep additional sums of money on hand to provide protection in the event of emergency.

Keynes regarded transaction and precautionary demand for cash balance or money as function of income. Therefore, it can be written as:

$M_1 = L_1 (Y)$ where, M_1= Cash balance required for transaction and precautionary motives, Y = Money income in the country L_1 = Liquidity Function or Ratio.

Keynes argued that M_1 is income elastic means it increases when income increases and declines with decline in income. But M_1 is interest-inelastic up to a certain point. It is illustrated in the following diagram 10.5.

Rate of interest is measured along OX axis and demand for money is measured along OY axis. TM is 'Transaction Motive Demand for Money' curve and PM is 'Precautionary Motive Demand for Money' curve. Up to interest rate 'r' both are interest-inelastic. If interest rate increases above it, the demand for money for both motives will decline.

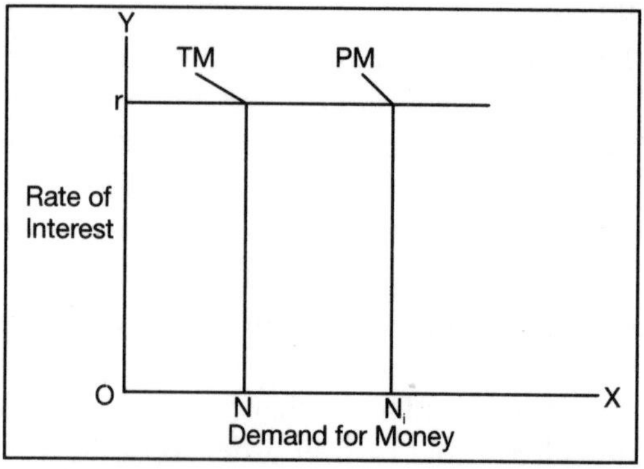

Diagram 10.5: Transaction and Precaution Motive

(3) **Speculative Motive:** Keynes defines speculative motive as the desire of holding money or resources to earn profits by knowing better the movements or changes in the market like rate of interest, price of bonds and securities, etc. in future course of time. The speculative motive demand for money depends upon the rate of interest, so it is interest-elastic. It can be written as:

$M_2 = L_2$ (r) where, M_2 = Speculative Motive Demand for Money or Cash balance, r = rate of interest, L_2 = the function relation.

Thus the total demand for money or cash balance, according to Keynes, is written as:

$$M = M_1 + M_2$$
$$= L_1 (Y) + L_2 (r)$$

In brief, the demand for money can be illustrated in the following diagram 10.6.

Demand for money is measured along OX axis and rate of interest along OY axis. LP curve represents total demand for money i.e. OQ. Total demand for money is known as liquidity preferences (LP). Demand for money is inversely related to rate of interest: higher the rate of interest, lower will be the demand for money and on contrary it is *vice versa*. But when rate of interest declines to r_1 the demand for money will become perfectly interest-elastic (Q_1), it is known as 'absolute liquidity preference' and this portion of LP curve is called 'Liquidity Trap' (LT).

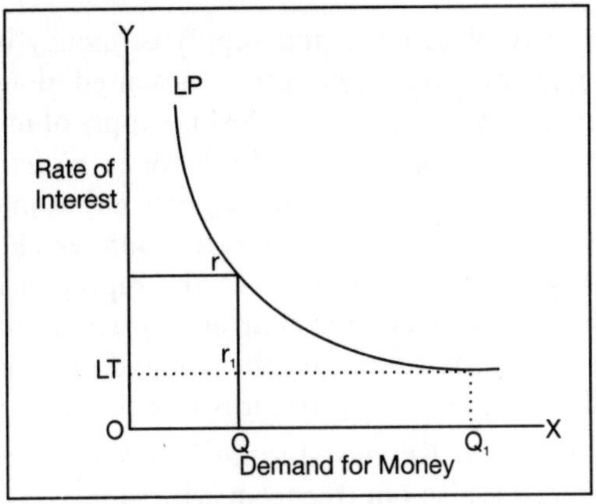

Diagram 10.6: Demand for Money Curve

(ii) **Supply of Money:** According to Keynes, another determinant of rate of interest is 'supply of money'. The total supply of money consists of coins and currencies plus bank-deposits in circulation. The policies of central bank, government and commercial banks determine the supply of money in the economy. Since the supply of money is given at the particular point of time, it is shown by vertical line.

(iii) **Determination of Rate of Interest:** According to Keynes, the equilibrium between the demand for and supply of money determines the rate of interest. It is illustrated in the following diagram 10.7.

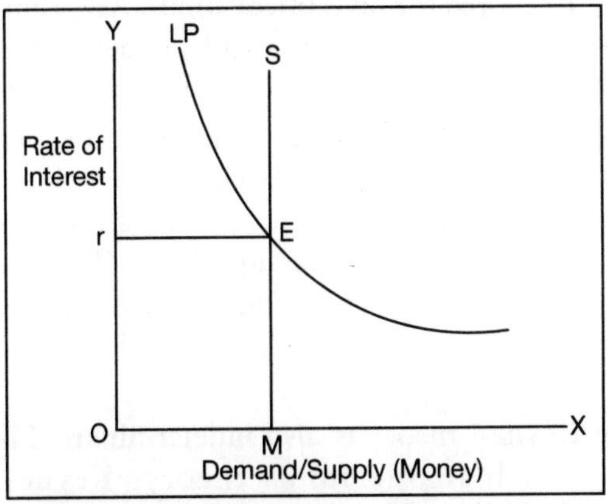

Diagram 10.7: Determination of Rate of Interest

The quantity of demand and supply of money is measured along OX-axis and rate of interest is measured along OY-axis. LP is demand for money curve and SM is supply of money curve. The intersection between LP and SM curve at 'E' determines the rate of interest i.e. EM (= Or). Any change either in demand or supply or both, it leads to change in rate of interest. For instance, if demand for money increases, given the supply of money, the rate of interest will increase. On contrary it is *vice versa*. Similarly if supply of money increases, give the demand for money, rate of interest will decline. On contrary, it is *vice versa*.

(c) **Criticisms:** Keynes' Liquidity preference theory of interest is also not free from criticisms. It is criticized as under:

(i) **Keynes ignored real factors in the determination of interest:** According to critics, liquidity preference is not the only factor to determine the rate of interest but other factors like investment-fund, productivity, savings, etc. will also be considered in determination of interest-rate.

(ii) **Keynes statement suffers from self-contradiction:** It is criticized on the ground that Keynes statement suffers from self-contradiction. The demand for money is largely a demand for idle balance, a non-yielding asset, and it is determined by rate of interest.

(iii) **It ignored the investment-funds:** According to Keynes the rate of interest is independent of demand for investment funds but in reality, this not true.

(iv) **No liquidity without savings:** According to Keynes interest is a reward for parting with liquidity and in no way a reward for saving or waiting. But the critics argued that how the liquidity and its surrender are possible without savings. Hence, Jacob Viner says "Without savings there can be no liquidity to surrender."

(v) **Keynes' theory is also indeterminate:** Like classical and loanable funds theory, Keynes liquidity preference theory is also indeterminate: Keynes' demand for holding money is vague concept because without knowing the income level it is difficult to decide the demand for idle cash for motives such as transactions, speculative, etc.

However the Keynes theory of interest is a milestone in world of the theories of interest.

10.2 PROFITS

10.2.1 Meaning and Definitions: In ordinary language, profit is the surplus income over expenses in production. In economics, profit is a reward of the entrepreneurs. It is a residual income left after the payments for all factors services used in the process of production. In other words, it is a surplus left after the payment for the use of other factors of production like land, labour, capital. Therefore it is a residual income of the organizer.

In brief, the term profit is used to denote the income earned by the entrepreneurs; such income is of residual in character.

Different economists have defined the term profits in different ways asunder:

(i) **Prof. Taussig:** Prof. Taussig has defined profits as "It is a mixed and vexed income." It is a mixed income because the entrepreneur gets his earning from variety of sources. It is a vexed income because many economists do not agree on which of these earnings should be intended within the definition of profits and what determines the evaluation of such profits.

(ii) Prof. Hanson defines profits as "Profit is the residual payment what is left to the producers' income after all other payments have been met."

(iii) Prof. F.H. Knight defined profits as "It is a reward for uncertainty bearing."

Thus Profits means an income which goes to the entrepreneur or a reward for entrepreneurship.

10.2.2 Concepts of Profits: On the basis of nature, economists have classified profits into two types namely gross profits and net profits. These are the two important concepts of profits.

(a) **Gross Profits:** In the common sense profits means the whole of the net income earned by the entrepreneurs or a business entrepreneurs or a business enterprise. Economists have often used the following formula to analyze gross profits.

Gross Profits = Total Revenue – Total Explicit Cost.

$\therefore$ GP = TR – TEC

Gross profits also are described as an Accounting Residual because it is residue that remains after all costs have been accounted for.

Gross profit is a mixture of diverse elements. The gross profits include earnings from anyone or more of the sources or how does it arises? Is mentioned below:

(i) **Price of Factors:** The price paid to the factors supplied by the entrepreneurs himself such as his own capital or land.

(ii) **Wages of Supervision:** Entrepreneurs perform various functions such as manager, accountant, etc. so they must receive income.

(iii) **Maintenance Charges:** Depreciation and repairs and replacements are necessary for maintaining the earning capacity of capital goods so maintenance charges have to be provided.

(iv) **Net Profits:** It should be paid to entrepreneurs mainly for their functions.

(b) **Net Profits:** Net profits, in the economic sense, are obtained by deducting total cost from gross profits. The remunerations attributable to the entrepreneurs' own land, labour and capital are also deducted from gross profits. Net-Profits can be calculated as:

Net Profits = Total revenue – (Total Implicit Costs + Explicit Costs)

$\therefore$ NP = TR – (TIC + TEC)

The implicit cost means the prices of factors supplied by the entrepreneur himself and the wages of his own labour. They are not actual costs because they are usually not shown in books of accounts. Explicit costs, on the other hand, are contractual payments actually made to the owners of factors of production and shown in books of accounts. Net profit is also called 'pure profit' or 'economic profit'. Net profit includes the following incomes:

(i) **Income from risk taking and uncertainty bearing:** There are various risks and uncertainties in production of goods and services or business. The entrepreneur under takes the risk only when the price of the product is expected to be high enough to compensate the possible loss if the product is not sold.

(ii) **Income from innovations:** Innovation means the introduction of new-product, new process, new market, new raw material, etc. The employer who innovates will get extra income.

(iii) **Income from monopoly power:** If the output of any commodity is under the sole control of an entrepreneur, he earns extra income which is a part of his gross profits. Monopoly power arises from licenses, patents and copy rights, etc. Monopolist earns extra income by limiting the supply and creating an artificial scarcity.

(iv) **Income from product differentiation:** Where a product is successfully differentiated from other similar products by advertisements and otherwise, it yields additional income which is a part of the gross profits.

(v) **Wind-fall incomes:** Windfall incomes are unexpected profits due to sudden rise of prices of commodities in short-run. They occur as a result of change of fashions or war or inflation. Such profits are usually temporary.

10.2.3 Difference between Profits and Other Forms of Income. Profit is a reward of the entrepreneur. It is a residual left over after the payment of rewards of other factors of production, namely land, labour and capital.

The other forms of income means money received for the services of land, labour and capital such as rent, wage and interest.

The following are the differences between profits and other forms of income:

(i) Profit is a residual income or non-contractual income. The entrepreneur gets what is left after paying the other factors of production in the form of rent, wages and interest as contractual payments.

(ii) Profit fluctuates more than rent, wages and interest.

(iii) Profit may be negative when entrepreneur incurs losses, but rent, wages and interest can never be negative.

10.2.4 Theories of Profits: There are a large number of theories on profits. According to these theories, the entrepreneur earns profits because he performs certain functions such as risk-bearing, uncertainty-bearing, innovation, etc.

But there are many economists who think that profits cannot be related to entrepreneurs function. Prof. Walker thinks that profit is a form of rent. According to J.B. Cleve profits arises from dynamic changes in the economy. Karl Marx argued that entrepreneurs get profits because the legal system of capitalistic country enables a class of people to appropriate the surplus product of labour. According to Robert Triffin profits are dynamic in origin and institutional in their appropriation.

However, some of the theories are discussed as under:

(A) **Risk Theory of Profits:** The risk theory of profits is explained by an American economist F.B. Hawley. Prof. Alfred Marshall supported this theory. He defined profits, in his book *Enterprises and Productive Process* as "The profit of an undertaking or residue of the product after the claim of land, labour and capital are satisfied, is not the reward of management or coordination but risk and responsibilities that the entrepreneur undertake subjects himself." According to him, profit is the reward for risk taking or risk-bearing in business. He earns profit because he undertakes risks.

According to the theory, there are two types of risks in business, namely (i) insurable-risks and (ii) non-insurable risks. Fire, flood, earth-quake, theft, etc. are insurable-risks so entrepreneurs get protection against them by doing insurance. Marketing of products, price-fluctuations, change in demand and supply conditions, change in fashion, etc. are non-insurable risks so entrepreneurs have to face them at their risk. They are ready to bear such non-insurable risks so they must receive reward as compensation for bearing risks in business. The theory says that higher the risk, higher will be the profit.

The degree of risk varies in different industries and also within the same industry. Different degrees of risk depend upon the ability and inclination of entrepreneurs. The quantum of profits must be high enough to attract the managerial to take risks otherwise supply of business ability and production will fall. Thus profit is a reward for risk taking, which is a part of the normal cost of production.

Criticisms of the Theory

The theory has been criticized on the following grounds:

(i) **Profit is the result of ability of the entrepreneur:** According to Prof. Carver "Profit arises not because risks are borne by the entrepreneurs but because the superior entrepreneurs are able to reduce them. Thus profit is a result of ability of the entrepreneur to reduce their risk."

(ii) **Profit is just chance and good luck:** According to some economist the earnings of an entrepreneur are not entirely due to risk taking but some part is due to superior organizational ability, existence of monopoly power or just chance and good luck.

(iii) **Risk is a subordinate factor:** There are many individuals who prefer salaried post, even if the income is lower, in place of independent business. To such individuals, business risk is a subordinate factor in their choice of occupation. The amount of profits earned is, therefore, not related to the amount of risk undertaken.

(iv) **Risks are avoidable:** It is argued that some risks are not measurable and they can be guard against insurance, for example: Fire and accidents. Some risk can be avoided by the method of grouping the manufacturers. For example: A group can produce several verities of goods setting so that the loss from some verities would be compensated by the gains from the some other verities.

(v) **It is not a complete explanation:** The risk theory of profits, does not furnish a comprehensive explanation of profits. It neglected that profit also arises due to inflation, war, famine, etc.

(B) **Uncertainty Theory of Profits:** Uncertainty Theory of Profits is another important theory on the profit. The American Economist Prof. F.H. Knight was the first economist who propounded this theory. According to him, profit is the reward for uncertainty-bearing. Profit occurs to the entrepreneurs, because he bears uncertainty in business.

According to the theory, the uncertainty about the future occurs due to two types of changes taken place in the business. They are:

(i) **Innovations:** Innovations refer to introduction of new product, new method or technique of production, etc. Such innovations create uncertainty among the rival sellers as well as the entrepreneurs who introduce them. They all are uncertain about the success of such innovations.

(ii) **External Factors:** Change in taste and fashion of the people, government policies regarding tax, labour, trade, etc. business cycles' occurrence, change in income of the people, etc. are the external factor to entrepreneurs. They create uncertainty in business in future.

All these changes create uncertainties in business and may cause negative or positive profits. According to Prof. Knight, these changes or uncertainties create risks in business. He divided risks into two types. They are: (i) Foreseenable risks and (ii) Unforeseen able risk. The foreseeable risks can be foreseen by the entrepreneur and they are insurable. But unforeseenable risks are not foreseen by the entrepreneur so they are non-insurable risks. Prof. Knight says that profit is due to non-insurable risks. The non-insurable risks arise in modern business. They are: (a) competitive risk, (b) technical risk, (c) risk of government intervention and (d) business cycle risk.

Since these risks cannot be foreseen and statistically measured, no insurance company will be prepared to cover against them.

According to Prof. Knight there is a direct relationship between profits and uncertainty-bearing so greater the uncertainty–bearing, higher the volume of profits.

Uncertainty bearing has become so important in business in these days that it has begun to be looked upon as a separate factor of production. Like other factors, it has its supply price.

In other words, the entrepreneur undertakes uncertainty-bearing in the expectation of earning certain level of profits. Thus according to this theory, profit is due to not risk taking but to uncertainty-bearing.

Criticisms

The uncertainty theory of profits has been criticized on the following grounds:

(i) **Uncertainty is not the only duty:** Uncertainty-bearing is only a part of the duties of the entrepreneur he has other duties also like: organization and bargaining.

(ii) **Uncertainty-bearing is a psychological concept:** Uncertainty-bearing is a psychological concept which can be considered as a part of the real cost of production. The supply of a factor of production does not depend on real cost but on opportunity cost. Therefore uncertainty-bearing does not determine the supply price of business ability.

(iii) **It ignored monopoly element:** A part of profits arises from imperfection of competition. Thus if there are obstacles to the entry of new firms into an industry, the existing firms will earn additional income. Such incomes are not due to uncertainty even though they are included profit. Monopoly profit comes under this category.

(iv) **Its explanation is vague:** It has been found that it is possible to measure uncertainty in concrete terms. Therefore the uncertainty theory cannot explain the quantity of profit except in a vague and general way.

Since the theory has above mentioned shortcomings, it does not furnish a comprehensive explanation of profits and, therefore, it is an inadequate theory.

In spite of criticisms, Prof. Knight's theory is still appreciated because the non-insurable risks bring profit to the entrepreneurs.

(C) **The Innovation Theory of Profits:** The important function of enterprise is to undertake innovative. The entrepreneurs have to be rewarded with profit for their innovative functions. The innovation theory of profits has practical significance.

A great scholar Prof. Joseph A. Schumpeter, a German Economist, has propounded the Innovation theory of profits. This theory is appreciated by many economists. He has considered the new changes in the economy. It makes a significant contribution to the doctrine of profit in the economic literature. According to Schumpeter, profit is the reward to the entrepreneur for his innovative functions.

According to the theory, profit arises not on account of uncertainty-bearing but on account of economic innovations. The innovation, according to Schumpeter, refers to the introduction of a new product, new process, opening of a new market, invention of new methods of production, development of a new source of raw material and new method of business organization.

Economic innovation is the sources of profits because the firms which are first in the use of new techniques or new invention would be able to produce more efficiently and enjoy profit till other firms know it. For instance, the automobile firms which are first organized will be able to produce more and more and will also sell them at higher prices and thereby earn large profit. The firms which are organized later may lag behind in respect of efficiency, experience, and making techniques. Therefore, the firms which are more progressive will have superiority over the other firms.

The more able and efficient firms will have better power of anticipation and imagination. By using their imagination, they may open together a new market for their product. They may create a different and a new product. They may discover new and cheaper sources of raw materials. They may attract a large number of army of customers by inventing new market techniques.

Thus all these innovations help the firm in earning profit. No doubt these sources of profit are purely temporary in nature.

Such profit occurs only until these innovations are unknown to other of the firms. In the absence of these innovations the firm may not be able to earn the profit. Therefore Prof. Schumpeter says that "Innovation is the sources of profits."

Criticisms

Prof. Schumpeter's theory has been criticized on many grounds. The following are important criticisms leveled against the theory:

(i) **The theory does not provide a comprehensive explanation of profits:** The theory argues that only innovations cause profit but it is not so because there are several other factors besides innovation which also cause profit. The theory has not taken into consideration such aspects. Therefore it is not nearer to the truth.

(ii) **It ignored risk taking:** The theory does not consider profits as reward for risk-taking. According to Prof. Schumpeter, the entrepreneur is never the risk bearers. The capitalist undertakes risks. But in reality the entrepreneur bears the risks in business and it is his duty.

(iii) **It has narrow view:** The theory has a narrow view regarding function of the entrepreneur. In addition to innovation-function the firm is equally responsible for proper organization of the business.

(iv) **It neglected other causes of profit:** The theory has failed to explain that there are other factors as explained by other theories on profit are causes of profits. Thus it is not so comprehensive theory.

If we compare Schumpeter's theory with other theories of profit, however, it provides a very good explanation about the profits. The contribution made by Prof. Schumpeter is remarkable.

10.3 MODEL QUESTIONS

2 Marks Questions

(a) What do you mean by interest?

(b) Give the difference between real interest and nominal interest.

(c) Give the central idea of classical theory of interest.
(d) Give the statement of loanable fund theory of interest.
(e) Give the central idea of liquidity preference theory of interest.
(f) Define profits.
(g) Give the central idea of risks theory of profits.
(h) Mention non-insurable risks.
(i) Give the central idea of innovation theory of profits.

5 Marks Questions

(a) Write a note on the concepts of interest.
(b) Write short note on demand for loanable funds.
(c) Write short note on supply of loanable funds.
(d) Write a note on the concepts of profits.
(e) Discuss briefly risks theory of profits.

10 Marks Questions

(1) Critically examine the classical theory of interest.
(2) Explain the loanable fund theory of interest.
(3) Discuss the liquidity preference theory of interest.
(4) Critically examine the uncertainty theory of profits.
(5) Discuss the Innovation Theory of Profits.

References

Baumol, William J. 2nd Edition: *Economic Theory and Operation's Analysis*, Prentice-hall of India Ltd., New Delhi.

Chamberlin, E.H. (1948): "Proportionality, Divisibility and Economics of Scale", *Quantitative Journal of Economics.*

Chopra, P.N. 2nd Edition: *Managerial Economics*, Kalyani Publishers, New Delh.

Dewett, K.K. 21st Edition: *Modern Economic Theory*, Shyamlal Charitable Trust, New Delhi.

Douglas, P.H. (1948): "Are there laws if Production?", *American Economic Review.*

Dwivedi, D.N. 2nd Edition: *Micro Economics*, Vikas Publishing House Pvt. Ltd., Delhi.

Ferguson-Kreps: *Principles of Economics*, Oxform and IBH Publishing Company, New Delhi.

Jhingan, M.L. 8th Edition: *Advanced Economic Theory*, Konark Publishers Pvt. Ltd., Haryana.

Koutsoyiannis, A. 2nd Edition: *Modern Micro Economics*. MacMillan Press Ltd., London.

Meyers, A.L. 4th Edition: *Elements of Modern Economics*, Indian Publication. The Word Press Pvt. Ltd.

Mithani, D.M. 8th Edition: *A Course in a Business Economics*. Himalaya Publishing House, Mumbai.

Robinson, Joan, *The Economics of Imperfect Competition*, London, Macmillan and Company Ltd., New York-SI Martin's Press.

Samuelson, P.A. (1947): *Foundation of Economic Analysis*, Cambridge University Press.

Seth, M.L. 13th Edition: *Micro Economics*, Laxmi Narain Agarwal Educational Publishers, Agra.

Stonier, A.W. and D.C. Hague (1972): *A Textbook of Economic Theory*, 4th Edn., John Wiley and Sons, Inc., Chapters 5 and 10.

Sundram, K.P.M. and Vaish, M.C. *Principles of Economics*, Ratan Prakashan Mandir Educational Publishers.

Glossary

Alternative use: Next best use.

Art: An art is the practical application of the principles of science.

Average Product (AP): The output per unit of input.

Blue collar workers: Workers who are engaged.

Cardinal: Number expressing.

Cartel: It is an organization of independent firms producing identical products, which come together to raise prices and reduce output.

***Ceteris peribus*:** Other things being equal.

Classical: Long-established, traditional.

Compensation: Reward or price paid to the service of factor.

Consumer's sovereignty: Consumer's freedom in respect of consumption of goods and services for the satisfaction of his wants.

Consumers' Associations: The associations of consumers formed to protect their own interest. They make efforts to check the unfair trade practices of the sellers.

Consummate: It means 'To satisfy' or 'to fulfill'.

Consumption: destruction utility from goods and services for the satisfaction of wants.

Contractual payments: The payments made by the firm to the owners of factors of production as per the agreement.

Contractual Rent: The gross rent to which the resource owner and the borrower agree. This may include return on different costs incurred to provide that resource. E.g. contractual rent for hiring a piece of land may include a charge for the irrigation facility provided by the owner.

Cost behaviour: Trends in cost related with change in level of output in short-run as well as in long-run.

Cost of production: It refers to the expenditure incurred in producing a commodity or service and making it available to consumers.

Cost: Cost of production or expenditures incurred in production of output of a commodity or service.

Cost-Analysis: Detail study of cost and its elements.

Demand function: Demand is the function of price of commodity. The functional relation between price of commodity and resultant demand.

Demand, Linear: Demand changes in constant proportion to change in price.

Demand, Non-linear: Demand changes in variable proportion to change in price.

Demand: A desire backed by willingness and ability to pay.

Derived demand: Demand in which a good or service is wanted not for its own sake but for its contribution to the production of other goods.

Diseconomies: Disadvantages of expansion of plant or increase in scale of production.

Diseconomies of scale: Cost escalation due to increase in the scale of production.

Economic rent: The surplus earning of a factor of production in excess of its supply price.

Economies: Advantages accrue to the firm due to expansion of plant or increase in scale of production.

Economies of scale: Cost saving resulting from the increase in the scale of production.

Efficiency: Goods or services producing capacity during a given time period.

Elasticity of substitution: It is the extent to which commodity X substituted for commodity Y due to change in the price of Y.

Entrepreneur: A person who sets up commercial business provides the capital, runs the business and takes the risks.

Equilibrium Price: It is the market price at which the supply of an item equals the quantity demanded.

Equilibrium: It is a state of no change. The forces are equally balanced.

Extensive cultivation: It refers to that method of farming, in which additional pieces of land are brought under the plough to increase the output from time to time. This method is practiced mostly in new countries where virgin land is available in plenty.

External Economies: They are also called 'pecuniary economies'. They accrue to the large size firms in the form if discounts and concessions available to all firms in the industry.

Factors of production: Inputs or resources used in production of goods and services firm to another. They are also called basic materials.

Firm: A unit engaged in production of output of identical commodity to get maximum profits

Firm's Equilibrium: A state of balance, or stage or a point where firm neither increases nor decreases its production and gets maximum profits.

Gross profit: Whole of the excess income over expenditures earned by the entrepreneur or a business entrepreneur.

Homogeneous Product: Neither imaginary nor real differences exists between two units of a commodity. These products are identical.

Industry: A group of firms engaged in production of homogeneous goods.

Infrastructure: It is a social and economic overhead capital. It implies communication, power, irrigation, etc.

Innovation: Bringing new and significantly different product to the market, introduction of new production technique or opening up of a new market. The term is associated with Joseph Schumpeter.

Input: Any good or service that goes into production process.

Intellectual Property Rights: Laws related to patents, copyrights, trade secrets, etc. These laws provide the original producer the right to control and he is rewarded for reproduction of his work.

Intensive cultivation: It refers to that method of farming in which more and more doses of capital and labour are applied to the same piece of land to increase the output.

Internal Economies: Cost savings that are internationalized to the firm expanding its scale of production.

Law of Demand: Law explains the relation between demand and price.

Long period: The fixed factors also become variable factors in the long-run. During this period the supply of output is adjusted by changing the size of the plant and machinery.

Marginal land: Land of poor quanlity with regard to agricultural use, and unsuitable for housing and other uses.

Marginal physical product: The physical productivity of additional unit of input. In other words, increase in total output due to a unit change in one of the inputs keeping other inputs unchanged.

Marginal Product (MP): The increase in TP when input is increased by one unit.

Marginal Revenue Product: Marginal revenue product is the addition made to total revenue by employing an additional unit actor, quantity of other factors remaining constant.

Marginalist: Economists who advocate Marginal Revenue and Marginal Cost Analysis to find the firm's equilibrium.

Market period: It is a very short period in which the supply of output is fixed. For example the supply of the perishable commodities like milk, flowers, vegetables, etc. cannot be increased or decreased in the market period.

Minimum wages: The government fixes wage.

Mobility of labour: The movement of labour.

Monopolistic competition: Imperfect competitive market Or many sellers market selling identical or non-identical goods.

Monopoly: Single seller market.

MR and MC Analysis: Marginal Revenue and Marginal Cost approach to study the firm's equilibrium.

National income: Money value of the total value of production of goods and services produced in a country in one year.

Natural rate of interest: This is an equilibrium rate of interest which equates the demand for loans with the supply of loanable funds.

Natural Sciences: Natural Sciences are those which deal with the physical nature of things like matter and energy. Physics, chemistry and biology are known as natural sciences.

Negative slope: It refers to movement of a curve downwards from left to the right.

Neo-classical economists: Profounder of classical economic ideas in reformed way.

Neo-classical school: An alternative name applied to the Cambridge School.

Nominal wage: Wage measured in current.

Non-price competition: After sale services or other activities like gift scheme to particular purchaser, free transport, etc. are undertaken by sellers to promote their sales of output. Given the price of output, it does not of purchasing power over goods and services.

Oligopoly: A type of monopolistic competition.

Optimum firm: It is the firm producing the maximum output at the minimum cost. If the firm expands its output beyond this level the diminishing returns will set in.

Optimum output: It is the output which is produced at the lowest cost per unit or Functional relation between output and input.

Ordinal: Ordinal number like 1st, 2nd, etc.

Output: Any good or service that comes out of production process.

Patent: An exclusive right granted to an innovator to make use or sell a specified invention.

Perfect competition: A market situation where there are a large number of buyers and sellers deal in identical commodities.

Personal discrimination: Charge different prices for different customers on the basis of their ability to pay.

Piece wage: Payments of wage according to the Plant: A production unit.

Price discrimination: The practice of selling the same commodity to different buyers at different prices.

Price Elasticity of Demand: The sensitivity or responsiveness of demand to change in price.

Pricing-theory: The theory of value or theory of pricing of commodity.

Product differentiation: Products are differentiated from the other similar products by advertisements, trade-marks, wrapper, colour, etc.

Production Function: A technological relationship between various inputs and an output.

Production process: The process of physical transformation of one set of goods into another set of goods.

Production: A process by which inputs are transformed (produces or processed) into an output. Creation of utility and addition of value to a commodity.

Production: Creation of utility or making of goods and services.

Productivity: It can be worked out by comparing the output of goods and services to the inputs with which the output is turned out or manufacture.

Profit: It is a reward of the entrepreneur. It is a surplus left after the payment for the use of other factors of production.

Profit maximization: It is the accepted goal of the private sector. Competing firms try their best to utilize the productive resources in the most economical and productive manner.

Profit motive: One of the underline principles of capitalistic free economy is the profit motive. Earning more profit.

Public utility services: These are the services created by the government to protect the consumers from monopoly producers like public transport, supply of cooking gas, water, electricity, etc.

Quasi-rent: The return to a seller of a good or service over and above its average variable cost in the short-run.

Real wages: Wages evaluated with reference to their purchasing power rather than to the money actually paid.

Related goods: Substitutes and complements rent land.

Returns to scale: Responsiveness of the total output when the scale of production or size of change.

Revenue Analysis: Detail study on revenue and its elements.

Short period: The short period is one in which the firms adjust their supply of output to the changing demand without changing their size of plant and machinery. The firm does not alter the fixed factors, as the demand is likely to be short-lived.

Shut down point: At this point the market price is just sufficient to cover the average variable cost. If the market price goes below this point the firm stops the production.

Social Science: Social Sciences deal with the different aspects of human behaviour and consider man as a social animal.

Substitutes: Goods that are used in the place of another or which compete with each other. (e.g. Tea and coffee)

Tax policy: The policy of the government related to imposition of taxes and tax rates.

Technique of production: Method of production.

Total Analyst: Economist who advocates Total.

Total Product (TP): The total quantity produced by using a definite amount of various inputs.

TR and TC Analysis: Total revenue and Total cost approach to firm's equilibrium.

Trade union: An organization of workers in the same skilled occupation or related skilled occupations who act together to secure for all members favorable wages, hours and other working conditions.

Transfer earnings: A factor of production can potentially have several uses. Each use provides the owner a certain return, which he tries to maximize, and the factor remains in that use. Transfer earnings indicate the return from the next best use. It show, what potential earning the factor may have in the next best employment.

Uncertainty: It refers to such changes in business and industry that can be foreseen.

Undistributed profit: A part of the net earnings is so retained and not distributed.

Util: A unit or a yardstick to measure utility. It is used by Alfred Marshall.

Wage: Reward or price paid for the service of where few sellers are existed.

White collar workers: Workers who are not engaged in manual work.

Windfall income: It is an unexpected profit that arises in short-run due to rise in price.